Future of Business and Finance

The Future of Business and Finance book series features professional works aimed at defining, analyzing, and charting the future trends in these fields. The focus is mainly on strategic directions, technological advances, challenges and solutions which may affect the way we do business tomorrow, including the future of sustainability and governance practices. Mainly written by practitioners, consultants and academic thinkers, the books are intended to spark and inform further discussions and developments.

Anna-Sophia Christ
Editor

Corporate Digital Responsibility

Insights, Cases, and Tools for Translating Principles into Practice

Springer

Editor
Anna-Sophia Christ
Business, Innovation, and Transformation Institute (BIT)
University of Bremen
Bremen, Germany

ISSN 2662-2467 ISSN 2662-2475 (electronic)
Future of Business and Finance
ISBN 978-3-032-14792-9 ISBN 978-3-032-14793-6 (eBook)
https://doi.org/10.1007/978-3-032-14793-6

This Springer imprint is published by the registered company Springer Nature Switzerland AG
The registered company address is: Gewerbestrasse 11, 6330 Cham, Switzerland

Foreword

When the Dot-com bubble burst in the early 2000s, it not only took about 80% of the NASDAQ with it. At the time, the early successes of digital business models, broadly speaking, had promised unparalleled growth and market transformation for about a decade. And many investors, managers, politicians, and consumers had literally bought into the rhetoric of endless growth and a rekindled optimism that technology could bring about another economic and social golden age.

But after the burst of the bubble, much of this trust and optimism came under pressure. On the one side, it became clear that not everything that was internet-based was necessarily a great and *economically* sustainable idea. And the survival of only a few internet giants paved the way for the agglomeration of capital and power that would lead to our platform economy today.

As a result, the once shiny veneer of early digital business models started to show its first cracks. In the years since, in which more technological hypes have shaped up to rekindle our economic optimism, more cracks were added. When distributed ledger technologies promised to fundamentally transform how any sort of transaction is done, many were quick to point out that these transformations required a massive amount of energy, all at a time when our understanding of the looming climate catastrophe became more and more pressing. And while many earned a lot of money by speculating on cryptocurrencies, others are likely to pay the price linked to the *ecological* fallout of the underlying mining operations.

A similar trajectory can be observed in the context of artificial intelligence (AI). Again, analysts, visionaries, and evangelists are quick to point out the transformative potential linked to the technology. And while we are all scrambling to find innovative and impactful use cases, we are also beginning to realize that these transformations cost more than we anticipated. Beyond the ecological footprint in terms of computational resources and rare earth elements, we are also increasingly aware of AI's *societal* impacts: From bot-fueled hate speech to the devaluation of human labor, it is clear that AI-based digitalization is far from being a mostly technological problem.

While the list of digitalization hypes that follow a similar trajectory is long, the core challenge remains the same: *Is everything that is technologically feasible also economically, ecologically, and socially desirable and sustainable?*

This is the context in which the concept of Corporate Digital Responsibility (CDR) has risen to popularity. First coined in the industry in the mid- to late-2010s, public policy—especially in central Europe—and academia were quick to pick the idea up. Since then, many groundbreaking initiatives have emerged. For example, the "CDR Building Bloxx" framework under the leadership of the German Association for the Digital Economy (BVDW) or the German federal government's CDR Initiative has synthesized the debate. Similarly, academic publications offer analyses and frameworks. They all provide orientation to organizations that feel that their digitalization efforts need purpose, direction, and guardrails.

And yet, the topic of CDR can still seem overwhelming. This is because it combines at least three key sources of complexity. First, CDR is always linked to an organization's step into the digital age. The centrality of digitalization in this invites a level of *technological and organizational complexity* that challenges many organizations' capabilities and resources. Not only will one need to understand what a technology like AI does and how it works, but one will also need to have a clear understanding of the implications on products and processes that critically co-create such a technology's impact.

Second, responsibly approaching digitalization requires organizations to have a clear understanding of the *norms and values* that guide responsible use of technology. That is, what makes some use of a new technology more responsible than another? And while discussions on digital ethics offer several contemporary points of reference in this debate, social values, legal requirements, and—not least—an organization's own set of norms need to be matched and carefully mapped to digital initiatives. How can traditional company values be translated and made to last when a company shifts toward a digital business model? How can data be handled responsibly and in a legally compliant manner when digitizing a public administration? Without a clear goal in mind, responsibility is often difficult to determine.

Third, an organization's responsibility ambitions need to be translated into action. The best set of norms and the most progressive code of conduct remain without much substance if they fail to translate into organizational routines on the proverbial shopfloor. Especially in recent years, we have seen more attention being paid to this principles-to-practice gap. In response to this challenge, organizations need to build robust *governance* regimes that clearly assign responsibilities, allocate agency, and devise effective safeguards to help their members behave responsibly when, as the management proverb on corporate culture has it, no one is looking.

These three aspects make it clear that starting your own CDR journey can seem daunting, and for good reason. Carefully orchestrating technological and organizational digitalization, developing clear norms and values, and designing an effective governance regime to bring it all together would challenge any organization. But the good news: There are organizations out there that have done it!

At this point in CDR's short but eventful history, we are lucky to have a number of organizations that have brought CDR to life. While not every one of them pulls off CDR as a fully integrated, all-comprehensive project, these early adopters have built many small lighthouses that offer orientation for organizations that are only now embarking on their CDR journeys.

This book, edited by Anna-Sophia Christ, offers a unique synthesis of all of this guidance. The many cases it collects and curates offer inspiration and guidance on many of the aspects that can make CDR a challenge to address. As you are reading through them, I am sure you will find more than one good idea to help you get your CDR project off the ground.

In this, the book also resonates with the work we do at the Business Innovation & Transformation (bit) Institute of the University of Bremen. Here, CDR continues to be one of the central aspects we are investigating when analyzing how digitalization can be led toward sustainable success. Especially in our cooperation with Maastricht University, we continue to build new insights on what CDR is, how it is a unique facet of corporate governance, and how to change organizations effectively.

Embodying this spirit, the book you are reading now will likely become a CDR lighthouse in its own right, shining a light and leading the way toward organizations, economies, and societies in which responsible digitalization is a post-digital reality rather than a noteworthy exception.

Faculty of Business and Economics, Business Innovation & Transformation (BIT) Institute
University of Bremen
Bremen, Germany
August 2025

Benjamin Mueller

Foreword

Digital corporate responsibility means not only using technological developments, but actively, consciously, and purposefully shaping them. In this context, artificial intelligence (AI) competence plays a central role. AI is not an end in itself—it is a tool, an amplifier, and a responsibility all at once.

The European legislator has regulated the (commercial) use of AI systems in the European Union with the EU AI Act, one of the first regulations of that kind worldwide. Its rules are entering into force in a staggered approach, starting on 2 February 2025. Interestingly, one of the first provisions that took effect is the obligation for organizations to ensure AI literacy among their workforce. Art. 4 EU AI Act reads: "Providers and deployers of AI systems shall take measures to ensure, to their best extent, a sufficient level of AI literacy of their staff and other persons dealing with the operation and use of AI systems on their behalf, taking into account their technical knowledge, experience, education and training and the context the AI systems are to be used in, and considering the persons or groups of persons on whom the AI systems are to be used."

In my opinion, this signal makes a lot of sense as AI literacy is the foundation for living up to digital corporate responsibility. "Understanding what you're doing" should be the guiding principle: Companies and their employees must understand how AI works, what it can do—and what it cannot. Because AI is not magic. It does not replace human thinking—especially not the critical, strategic, multidimensional, and creative thinking required in today's complex world.

This is where the difference between blind technology adoption and responsible digital transformation becomes evident. Hence, Corporate Digital Responsibility (CDR) is also a goal in itself as it ensures that commercial activities are carried out in line with the basic values and ethical principles of the European Union, namely human centricity, basic human rights, and freedoms. Concrete examples are the use of AI in a non-discriminatory, non-manipulative, explainable, and transparent way with human oversight at all stages.

The second goal of CDR should be to win and maintain the trust of the customers. A central element is the trustworthy use of AI, especially in a customer-facing context. Concrete examples would be transparency and assurance regarding the mechanisms of autonomous driving, of assessments of creditworthiness, or insurance tariffs that include AI systems and models, almost regularly seen these days. Summed up: A trustworthy offer to customers only emerges when companies use AI with care—transparently, comprehensibly, and in line with ethical principles.

The other side of the coin for trustworthiness is the responsible AI use, which begins internally: with leadership, processes, and the conscious decision to see technology as a means to an end—not as a substitute for sound judgment. This, in turn, is conditioned by AI literacy—and more over—by AI literacy that mirrors the roles and responsibilities of the employee in question. An HR manager needs different knowledge and capabilities than a developer of customer-facing AI systems or a marketing director, and again, another skill set is needed for supervisory bodies and top management.

The importance of systemic and continuous education can hardly be underestimated. All employees, including freelancers, interns, top management, and supervisory board members, should have robust and up-to-date knowledge about the technical, legal, ethical, and practical dimensions of AI and its embedding in the digitized organization.

It is of special importance that humans are aware of the strengths and weaknesses of AI to make use of it in an educated, innovative, value-creating, and legally safe way. This is an effort that needs to be factored in, however. Modern technologies need education, trial and error, leadership, and measurement. It is not the replacement of hard thinking, being self-critical, and aligning activities again and again with the company values and company strategy.

Needless to say, AI can incredibly help to outsource repetitive and housekeeping tasks, to accelerate data analytics, to detect hidden patterns in data lakes, to prestructure decision-making, etc. The clue is that humans need to consciously use AI where AI does not make the digital human mistakes like becoming tired, becoming negligent, or becoming impatient. And NOT to use AI where complex, superintelligent tasks are required, like creative, value-based, critical thinking and decision-making.

Human-digital teams, where humans and machines each contribute their strengths, can be unbeatable. When people bring their experience, values, and creativity, and machines provide data-driven insights, real added value is created. One thing must always remain in focus: the benefit—for the company, for society, and for the people who connect the two. Challenging, but possible—even in times when new technological applications seem to be coming thick and fast, triggering overwhelming and ambiguous reactions.

In these times of complexity and uncertainty, orientation and guidance are essential. This book provides both, bringing together a selection of summarized and translated insights from science, best practice, and experience reports from companies ambitiously paying the way as pioneers, as well as guiding reflections from facilitators who accompany and supervise the implementation of responsible digital transformation.

lawpilots GmbH
Berlin, Germany
August 2025

Cordula Meckenstock

Foreword

Another politician talking about corporate responsibility? You might expect the usual platitudes, but this story is different because it is personal, political, and rooted in transformation. Let me tell you the story of how the structural transformation from coal mining to artificial intelligence (AI) and other future technologies is not only the story of my personal life, but also the future tale of the Ruhr Valley and the Rhenish Mining Area Revier in North Rhine-Westphalia—and how we urgently need corporations to take responsibility for shaping that future.

I grew up in the Saar region, historically an area of coal and steel, and now a hotspot for computer science. Since I was a child, my father told me stories about growing up among coal miners, how it shaped his childhood and adolescence, and the region, even quite literally. In 2008, while I was still in school, a court ruling brought an end to coal mining following significant subsidence damage. The verdict caused rifts between neighbors and friends, between those who lost their jobs and those who feared for their property and safety. Choosing a career path in such an uncertain environment was frightening. Yes, I chose computer science because of my passion for math and technology, but also because it seemed like a safe bet for the future.

Today, I am a computer scientist by training and a scientist at heart. But in recent years, I have become a state legislator for The Greens in North Rhine-Westphalia. Ten years ago, as a university student, I would never have imagined myself in politics. I saw myself researching how to make software systems safer and more secure. Politics felt distant, almost unreachable—and to be honest, I believed that politicians rarely changed our everyday lives. But even back then, I was critical of how we, as computer scientists, underestimated the impact of digitalization on the environment, on people, and especially on women and marginalized communities.

Fast forward to 2025: digitalization has become one of the most significant political fields in Germany, growing well beyond its roots in infrastructure policy. Cyberattacks are an imminent threat. Artificial intelligence is seen as the key to fulfilling our wildest dreams of automation. Social media platforms have become central to how people access information and communicate with one another. In North Rhine-Westphalia, AI is now one of the key future technologies driving structural change in the Ruhr Valley and Rhenish Mining Area, following the official end of all coal mining in 2030. And now more than ever, we need digitalization to be empowering, just, and sustainable—not just technologically advanced, but also socially responsible.

To influence the process of digitalization in this way, I joined The Greens and eventually became a member of the state parliament. My political involvement is built on a fundamental belief: digitalization should be shaped by and for people, rather than solely driven by markets or machines. This is where Corporate Digital Responsibility (CDR) comes into play. Suppose we want digitalization to serve the public good. In that case, we need shared responsibility—and that includes corporations, because one of my most essential realizations in politics is that politics alone cannot transform the world. We need strong partnerships with citizen groups, non-governmental organizations, scientists, and corporations that are based on shared values.

My set of values is pretty straightforward:

- I want digitalization to contribute to a sustainable world, not fuel the climate crisis and destroy habitats through energy consumption and resource mining.
- I want AI to serve the people, to ease routine tasks, to create jobs, not to undermine human connection, harm creativity, or spread misinformation.
- I want science to be an integral part of political decision-making, not a tool for conspiracy theories and misinformation.
- I want digitalization to be inclusive—to break down barriers, not reinforce them.
- I want it to empower queer communities, disabled people, and all those who have been historically excluded from technological progress.
- I want digital tools to reflect the diversity of our society, not erase it.

Currently, there is a lot at stake—democracy is under pressure, especially in many parts of the so-called Western world. Countries that have almost achieved the same rights for all human beings are making giant steps back, and the climate crisis may render our planet uninhabitable for humans. While some tech visionaries imagine escape routes to Mars, the real challenge lies in making Earth a place worth staying for everyone. Our resilience as a human species stems from our diversity. As a species, we can grow food, work, and live in various ecosystems and numerous areas, and we are decades away from recreating such a resilient ecosystem elsewhere. Thus, let us work together to keep our planet habitable for all and make it a welcoming place for everyone.

These values guide my work. However, they require more than just good intentions. They require political will, robust legal frameworks, and effective democratic oversight to become a reality. If we want digitalization to serve the public good truly, we need clear rules, democratic oversight, and courageous political participation. That is where regulation comes in and where I see my role as a state legislator. Democratic oversight is not just a necessity; it is a reassurance that we are on the right path.

While voluntary corporate responsibility is a step in the right direction, it cannot replace clear rules and democratic oversight. As legislators, whether in the European

Parliament, the Bundestag, or state parliaments, we must level the playing field. We need to prevent corporations that embrace our values from having an unfair disadvantage in the market. For example, I want a text-generating AI that is sustainable. One that requires less computing power and energy because it selects words more efficiently—and crucially, one that runs on clean energy rather than relying on polluting power consumption. Such a model should also enable us to compensate artists whose works contributed to its training fairly, and its outputs must be transparent and free from bias or discrimination. Companies and researchers developing such AI should not be overwhelmed or driven out of competition, but instead protected by legislation like the European AI Act and supported through funding within the research and industry we promote.

Enough about values and abstract policies. Let us take a look back at the structural transformation in the Ruhr Valley and the Rhenish Mining Region. Coal mines were once among the largest employers in the area. The low energy prices attracted industries such as steel, glass, and paper manufacturing. The digital and sustainability transformation of these regions relies on two critical factors: first, affordable energy from renewable sources. That is what it takes for these industries to build a sustainable future in North Rhine-Westphalia. At the same time, we avoid dependencies on imports from countries that do not meet our standards for human rights or sustainability. Second, we need companies to invest in and develop future technologies. Since many of these technologies rely directly or indirectly on digitalization, we need companies with a strong sense of CDR. Without it, innovation will not bring prosperity to the people of North Rhine-Westphalia.

Hence, this transformation is about people. The way we design and deploy AI will shape lives, livelihoods, and communities. Automation will change jobs, and people will need new opportunities. At the same time, Germany is facing demographic shifts. Companies must foster inclusive environments where people from around the world want to live and work with their families. Tech companies, in particular, must become more inclusive, especially for women and mothers, disabled people, and other marginalized groups. Lifelong learning, advanced training, and social safety nets for those whose jobs are changing will be essential for a society that truly serves everyone. To combat the climate crisis, digital businesses must significantly reduce their energy consumption and operate in a sustainable manner. That is why CDR matters.

This book, *Corporate Digital Responsibility: Insights, Cases, and Tools for Translating Principles into Practice*, offers a thoughtful and timely introduction to a topic that is close to my heart and central to my political work. The editor gathered many authors who understand the urgency of translating ethical principles into real-world corporate action. For anyone working at the intersection of technology, responsibility, and transformation—whether in business, academia, or politics—this book provides valuable insights and practical tools.

The transformation I witnessed in the Saar region taught me that structural change is never just technical. It is personal, political, and deeply social. So, let us shape a digital future that is just, inclusive, and sustainable together.

Acknowledgments: Generative AI tools—namely, Microsoft Copilot and Grammarly—supported me in refining this foreword. The stories and views expressed are entirely my own. Special thanks to my incredible team for their unwavering support of my political mission.

Green Party in the State Parliament
of North Rhine-Westfalia
Düsseldorf, Germany
September 2025

Julia Eisentraut

Preface

The history of corporate responsibility reads less like a grand design and more like a tale shaped by unintended consequences, where transformation has often followed disasters, not deliberate design. Destructive? The economy had always had its costs—some visible from the outside, others hidden like icebergs beneath the surface, unfolding quietly and unnoticed. However, the backbone of our prosperity today, the fossil fuel-driven economy, never set out to warm our atmosphere or stir the storms we now face. Yet here we are, in another summer marked by weather extremes of heat waves, floods, and fires.

Our uninhibited pursuit of progress has scaled, and with it, so have the environmental and social tolls. Like miners deep in the earth, we have dug relentlessly, extracting resources with no plan for how to restore what we take. And we have done the same in society: driven by the hunger for faster, better, cheaper, we have widened divides, exploited the vulnerable, and accelerated toward physical and mental limits we can no longer ignore. The weather extreme reports are increasingly accompanied by polarization warnings and observations of destabilized democracies, without interpreting causality.

But this is not only a story of loss. In many aspects, we are doing better today than ever before. Flourishing economies fulfill basic needs, provide security, and open pathways to higher education standards, making room for awareness of impacts and intentions. Around the globe, sparks of hope flare. Visionaries, innovators, and communities are reimagining economies that give back more than they take, regenerative systems designed for intergenerational value chains. Even though much of this progress, hard-won as it is, still leans heavily on regulation, it also reflects a changing value system, with regulation coming into place to grant rights and protect what we value.

At the same time, we are in the midst of another revolution: digital transformation. The digital is reshaping value chains at an exponential pace, bringing forth technologies like generative artificial intelligence that can fuel efficiency, spark innovation, and unlock solutions for sustainability. If we wield them wisely. And this is where I see great opportunities to change the narrative of economic growth at the expense of the environment and society toward a more integral approach. Digital technologies create new pressures: to stay competitive, to cut costs, to automate what was once human. We are at a crossroads where technology can either deepen our challenges or help solve them, forcing us to rethink fundamental values guiding our societal systems.

For me, one thing has become clear: digital transformation and emerging corporate responsibilities must no longer be separate paths; they must be unified. By design, not by accident. We are at a point in history where we have both the knowledge and the interconnectedness to act quickly. Technology is never neutral; it is always shaped by values. When creating digital systems to replace human tasks and integrate into daily life, we must intentionally choose our desired outcomes, reject harmful trade-offs, and address potential issues that arise along the way.

Easier said than done. Time and again, in my years of research and consulting, I have encountered the same paradox: the will to act is present, understanding is growing—with valuable frameworks, passionate advocates, and an expanding body of knowledge—yet meaningful change remains elusive. This challenge of bringing digital responsibility principles into corporate practice is not unique to me. It echoes what many working on responsibility and sustainability report; we are rich in knowledge, poor in momentum. And as crises mount, a troubling shift is emerging. The courage and ambition that once fueled sustainability efforts seem to be waning.

Nevertheless, if you look closely, you will find advocates and pioneers of Corporate Digital Responsibility (CDR) appearing: companies daring to lead, researchers bridging the gap between principles and practice, individuals who act not because they must, but because they see what is at stake. CDR is not a formula, a one-size-fits-all solution. It is an evolving mindset, manifested in daily decisions, quiet acts of integrity, and bold innovations that prioritize people and the planet. And in Germany, we are, among others, fortunate to have some of these trailblazers shaping the conversation.

Of them, I have invited some inspiring CDR voices I have met along the way, people doing remarkable work to guide digital transformation responsibly. Their contributions are not a manifesto for a model. It is a collection of ideas and examples meant to steer action, to help CDR grow from principles to practice, not to dictate a single path, but to offer sparks for your own. To show that responsibility is not a constraint, but a compass. That digital transformation does not need to be a threat but a once-in-a-generation opportunity to build an economy that serves people—built by people, for people.

Digital technologies are accelerating. So must our positive impact. As the world grows more complex, the question is no longer whether we transform, but how. Every transformation has its cost. The choice before us is: who pays for it? With intentional, responsible design, we can share those costs fairly. We can build systems that protect, include, and uplift. That is the invitation of this book: to rethink how we transform our businesses, not for short-term gain, but for a future where technology and responsibility walk hand in hand.

Let's take the next step, together.

Hamburg, Germany
September 2025

Anna-Sophia Christ

Acknowledgments

This book is based on my experiences working with companies on digital transformation and corporate responsibility, as well as the insights I gained through academic research. In many ways, it developed as a knowledge transfer project from my dual PhD journey in information systems and management studies at the University of Bremen, Germany, and Maastricht University in the Netherlands. The book aims to translate scientific findings into practical knowledge beyond the German context and to gather insights from practice. I am especially grateful to Prof. Benjamin Mueller and Dr. Lara Lobschat for providing me with the opportunity and resources to dedicate time to this book project as part of my research.

However, this project would not have been possible without the many dedicated collaborators and contributors who generously shared their knowledge, time, and perspectives. More than fifteen researchers brought together their findings and translated them into tangible insights that practitioners can apply. Representatives from six companies documented their real-world experiences, including what worked for them, the challenges they faced, and which strategies and approaches might serve as best practices for others. Fourteen facilitators contributed their learnings from working with diverse companies and experts, while also presenting tools and methods for implementing Corporate Digital Responsibility (CDR). Together, this diversity of perspectives offers a uniquely valuable insight into CDR, particularly from the European and especially the German market, while presenting it in English to make it accessible to a broader international audience.

At this point, my profound thanks also go to Springer Nature for their collaboration in bringing this book to publication. Their guidance throughout the process was invaluable, not only in shaping the book as an editorial volume but also in ensuring that this important topic could be presented in a way that bridges research and practice. The expertise and experience of their team made it possible to create a format that allows knowledge to flow both from research into practice, from practice back into research, and within the rich interplay of the two.

Moreover, a special word of thanks goes to the reviewer team of six CDR experts from both research and practice. Their support in reviewing the chapters, offering constructive feedback, and guiding the refinement process has been essential in ensuring the quality, clarity, and accessibility of this book. Their dedication has helped strengthen the transfer of knowledge between communities and ensured that the contributions remain impactful and relevant.

Reviewer Team

- **Beatriz *Bilfinger*** studied business administration with a focus on sustainability in Germany, Brazil, and the United Kingdom. Since the beginning of her career at the German Federal Working Group for Environmentally Conscious Management (BAUM) e. V., the twin transformation has been the focus of the nachhaltig.digital project. Since 2022, she has been shaping the topics of sustainability, digital responsibility, and new work at the German Association for the Digital Economy (BVDW) e.V.
- **Mag. Karin *Dietl*** is a legal expert specializing in data protection and a Certified Data Privacy Solutions Engineer, who founded the influential CDR Austria initiative. Her consultancy, VALUE DESIGN, bridges legal expertise with strategic thinking in CDR, advising organizations on digital governance and sustainability. As a pioneer in the field, she actively shapes the discourse on responsible digital transformation through academic lectures and professional events like the CDR Congress in Vienna.
- **Dr. Lara *Lobschat*** is a tenured Assistant Professor of Marketing at Maastricht University and a recognized expert in the intersection of digital transformation and digital responsibility. She co-coined the term Corporate Digital Responsibility (CDR) in her seminal Journal of Business Research article, contributing a foundational framework for aligning responsible digital practices with corporate strategy. Her research on CDR bridges academic insight and managerial relevance, offering actionable guidance on how firms can ethically navigate the digital transformation. Through her ongoing academic publications, invited talks, and leadership in CDR-focused initiatives, Dr. Lobschat actively shapes discourse on the responsible use of digital technologies in business.
- **Prof. Dr. Benjamin *Mueller*** is the professor for Digital Business at the University of Bremen, Germany. His work focuses on how advanced information and communication technologies transform organizations. He pays particular attention to mechanisms through which individuals augment their work with technology, the corresponding organizational benefits, and governance to ensure corporate digital responsibility.
- **Prof. Dr. Georg *Müller-Christ*** is a professor of sustainable management with more than twenty years of teaching and research experience at the University of Bremen. Over the course of his career, he has worked extensively with national and international companies, supporting them in rethinking their decision-making processes and value proposition toward more regenerative solutions with mitigated externalities. By applying exploratory constellations, he fosters new epistemic practices that bridge science and practice. Sustainability is emerging as such a complex challenge that conventional models of thought are no longer sufficient. Addressing it requires a fundamental rethinking of the interrelationship between economy and society in order to shape a more sustainable and digitally advanced world.

- **Prof. Dr. Markus *Westner*** is a professor of information systems at OTH Regensburg and the university management's representative for course development. He studied business administration (Dipl.-Kfm.) and computer science (Master of Computing, Unitec/NZ), earned his doctorate (Dr. rer. pol.) in the field of information systems, and gained industry experience at Bain & Company, the Boston Consulting Group, Vodafone New Zealand, and Microsoft Germany, among others. His research and teaching focus on IT strategy, IT governance, and IT sourcing, including cloud, low/no-code, and business-managed IT. He heads the Regensburg Strategic IT Management Laboratory and combines scientific rigor with a strong practical orientation. In 2025, he received a Bavaria-wide award for excellence in digital teaching

Overall, this book is also the result of the inspiring and encouraging words I received from all the remarkable people I have met along the way. Their commitment to advancing CDR and their valuable work deserve to be shared, scaled, and built upon. My intent in curating this volume has been to embody the principle of lifelong learning from each other, collecting not only the know-how but also the know-why of CDR. By bundling diverse perspectives, scaling knowledge, and joining forces, we can move this important field forward together. I hope that this book contributes to that shared journey.

- Prof. Dr. [illegible] is a professor of information systems at OTH Regensburg [illegible] management [illegible] development. He studied business administration (Dipl.-Kfm.) and computer science [illegible]

Contents

About the Editor and Contributors

About the Editor

Anna-Sophia Christ is a doctoral researcher in a dual program with Maastricht University's School of Business and Economics and the University of Bremen's Chair of Digital Business. Her research focuses on the intersection of information systems, corporate responsibility, and ethics, with a particular emphasis on digital responsibility in corporate contexts. She examines what is genuinely new about responsibility in the digital era compared to the broader discourse on corporate responsibility and explores how technologies can be designed and governed to reflect societal values. Central to her work is the question of how the values we want to see embodied in digital systems can go beyond theory to meaningfully guide decision-making and practice. Her academic journey began with a Bachelor of Science in International Business Studies at the University of Paderborn, followed by a Master of Science in International Management, Marketing, and Entrepreneurship at Otto-von-Guericke University Magdeburg. She expanded her studies through international stays at the Universidade de Santiago de Compostela, Universitat de Barcelona, and National United University of Taiwan, experiences that enhanced her global outlook and interest in cross-cultural perspectives on technology and responsibility. Alongside her academic research, Anna-Sophia works as an IOBC-certified coach, consultant, and Infosyon-certified system and organizational constellation facilitator, helping organizations address sustainability challenges and navigate digital transformation. Before entering academia, she spent four years at PwC Germany, advising companies across industries such as automotive, telecommunications, and energy. In this role, she guided organizations at the intersection of regulation, corporate responsibility, and digitalization, helping them ensure legal readiness while also encouraging them to go beyond compliance by aligning digital practices with corporate values. Through her combined academic and professional work, Anna-Sophia offers a holistic and practice-oriented perspective to the evolving conversation on responsible digital transformation.

Contributors

Saskia Becke PwC Germany, Munich, Germany

Marie Blachetta Initiative D21, Berlin, Germany

Alexander Brink CONCERN GmbH, Cologne, Germany

Kübra Çalışkan Department of Management Information Systems, Business School, Sakarya University, Sakarya, Türkiye

K. Valerie Carl Information Systems and Information Management, Goethe University Frankfurt, Frankfurt, Germany

Jean Enno Charton Merck KGaA, Darmstadt, Germany

Anna-Sophia Christ Business, Innovation, and Transformation Institute (BIT), University of Bremen, Bremen, Germany

Lars Diestelrath PwC Germany, Munich, Germany

Saskia Dörr WiseWay, Bonn, Germany

Ismael El-Hadj SKAD, Frankfurt am Main, Germany

Frank Esselmann CONCERN GmbH, Cologne, Germany

Sergio Genovesi SKAD, Frankfurt am Main, Germany

Daniela Hanauer PwC Germany, Munich, Germany

Leonhard Henke CONCERN GmbH, Cologne, Germany

Maria Hinz BARMER, Berlin, Germany

Oliver Hinz Information Systems and Information Management, Goethe University Frankfurt, Frankfurt, Germany

Christopher T. Johnson Chair of Digital Business, University of Bremen, Bremen, Germany

Melanie Kubin-Hardewig Deutsche Telekom, Bonn, Germany

Simon Lucas Merck KGaA, Darmstadt, Germany

Marike Mehlmann-Tripp Deutsche Telekom, Bonn, Germany

Cristina Mihale-Wilson Information Systems and Information Management, Goethe University Frankfurt, Frankfurt, Germany

Katharina Mosor KPMG Austria, Vienna, Austria

Lena-Sophie Müller Initiative D21, Berlin, Germany

Romana Pflieger Weleda AG, Schwäbisch Gmünd, Germany

Alexandra Prinz KPMG Austria, Vienna, Austria

Bartosz Przybylek ifok GmbH, Hamburg, Germany

Moritz Schirmer IHK Digital, Berlin, Germany

Maike Scholz Deutsche Telekom, Bonn, Germany

Felix von Roesgen ifok GmbH, Hamburg, Germany

Anna Wannhoff Munich Business School, Munich, Germany

Jakob Wößner Weleda AG, Schwäbisch Gmünd, Germany

Jan Zibuschka Robert Bosch GmbH, Renningen, Germany

Introduction

Anna-Sophia Christ

Abstract

This introductory chapter provides an overview of the editorial volume "Corporate Digital Responsibility (CDR): Insights, Cases, and Tools for Translating Principles into Practice". It starts by elaborating the evolving nexus between digital transformation and corporate responsibility, leading to the emerging concept of CDR. In an era where digital technologies shape economic, social, and environmental systems, organizations face the dual challenge of harnessing technological innovation while upholding ethical, sustainable, and accountable practices. The editorial provides a comprehensive overview of how CDR extends traditional corporate responsibility into the digital realm, addressing issues such as data governance, algorithmic transparency, fairness, and digital inclusion. The three parts of the editorial volume are briefly introduced, including all the chapters, their focus topic, and the authors, together with their respective affiliations. The first section develops theoretical foundations and conceptual clarity; the second explores real-world applications across industries; and the third reflects on systemic and policy-oriented approaches to embedding responsibility in digital ecosystems. Together, the contributions illustrate how CDR can move from aspirational discourse to operational practice, bridging gaps between normative ideals and organizational realities.

A.-S. Christ (✉)
Business, Innovation, and Transformation Institute (BIT), University of Bremen, Bremen, Germany
e-mail: achrist@uni-bremen.de

A.-S. Christ (ed.), *Corporate Digital Responsibility*, Future of Business and Finance, https://doi.org/10.1007/978-3-032-14793-6_1

In today's world, where digital technologies permeate nearly every aspect of society, the question is no longer whether digital transformation is changing how we live and do business, but how organizations can navigate this change in ways that enable long-term, effective resilience (cf. Carroll et al., 2023; Wessel et al., 2025). Progressively, digital solutions streamline internal operations by automating routine tasks, freeing employees to focus on more complex and value-adding activities. Predictive maintenance powered by sensors and machine learning helps industrial firms avoid costly downtime and extend equipment lifespan. Cloud-based collaboration platforms boost efficiency across distributed teams, enabling faster decision-making and smoother coordination across global operations.

Meanwhile, the dynamics of economic life are shifting: success is no longer solely dependent on financial performance achieved through efficiency and productivity. Increasingly, the right to operate depends on how well organizations govern responsibilities towards society at large, adopting strategies to respect planetary boundaries while contributing to fair and equitable living conditions for all (cf. Rupp et al., 2024; Wickert, 2021). This is not just about responding to stakeholder demands of employees, customers, or value-chain partners. It has become a story of resilience, as environmental change directly disrupts business models, and social movements reshape the legitimacy of corporate operations.

Aligning the two developments—digital transformation and evolving corporate responsibilities—becomes increasingly a necessity, since impacts are not isolated but are part of deeply interwoven dynamics that increasingly shape one another (cf. Ologeanu-Taddei et al., 2024; Zimmer et al., 2023). Their interaction generates synergies that can be leveraged for innovation and value creation, yet also produces externalities that must be mitigated, managed, or altogether prevented. This requires companies to have an opportunity-oriented but risk-mitigated dual transformation approach to account for corporate responsibilities in the digital realm.

Retailers, for example, are rethinking supply chain operations by using real-time data analytics to reduce waste and ensure more sustainable logistics. At the same time, such efficiency-driven models can inadvertently exclude smaller suppliers who cannot meet new digital standards, thereby raising questions of fairness and inclusivity. Similarly, financial providers are redesigning their products by embedding algorithmic decision-making into credit assessments, improving speed and consistency, but also introducing risks of algorithmic bias, opacity, and accountability gaps that can directly affect people's financial safety. In manufacturing, the shift towards connected products, such as smart appliances or mobile platforms that generate ongoing data flows, requires companies to balance innovation with responsibility in data use and consumer trust.

To steer this complex interplay between technological change and corporate responsibility, the concept of Corporate Digital Responsibility (CDR) emerged (cf. Carl & Hinz, 2024; Lobschat et al., 2021). Building on the long-standing tradition of Corporate Social Responsibility (CSR), CDR extends the responsibility discourse into the digital domain, focusing on what is fundamentally new in the challenges and opportunities introduced by digital transformation. CDR calls for accountability not only for environmental impacts (e.g., energy consumption of data centers or extraction of rare earth minerals for digital devices) but also for the social requirements (e.g., strengthening digital literacy, safeguarding autonomy, and ensuring accessibility and fairness) and governance dimensions of digital technologies (e.g., robust data privacy and security measures and transparent and controllable algorithms).

Despite the urgency of these challenges—in times of exponential digital developments and overwhelming sustainability crisis—many normative claims about corporate digital responsibility remain aspirational. They are often articulated as visions, resolutions, or future goals, but fall short of becoming embedded practices (cf. Christ, 2025; Merbecks, 2023; Mueller, 2022). This implementation gap is rooted in several difficulties: the widespread belief that only what can be measured can be managed; the challenge of translating broad ethical ideas into the granular processes of business operations; and the reality that principles themselves often conflict, making responsibility a matter of prioritization and trade-offs rather than simple compliance.

Nevertheless, across industries, pioneering companies are beginning to confront these challenges directly, experimenting with frameworks, tools, and governance models to make responsibility actionable in the digital domain. Researchers too, are contributing by unpacking the underlying mechanisms and facilitatory development approaches that help organizations navigate this transformation. Together, these efforts illustrate that CDR is not only a conceptual framework but a practical agenda, one that requires courage, innovation, and collaboration to align digital transformation.

This editorial book aims to explore the evolving operationalization of CDR as both a theoretical idea and a practical effort. It provides a three-part structure guiding readers through the current state of the field. Part I offers insights from research, establishing conceptual clarity and academic foundations. Part II features case studies from companies, demonstrating how organizations of various sizes and industries tackle CDR in real-world applications. Part III shares experiences and tools from facilitators who assist businesses in applying CDR principles to daily operations. Collectively, these perspectives seek to bridge the gap between theory and practice, highlighting how abstract corporate values can be meaningfully integrated into routines, processes, and decisions that shape digital business. The closing section presents a research experiment examining CDR from the emerging future.

1 Part I: Insights from Research

The first part of the editorial presents insights into the ongoing discourse on CDR through an academic lens, drawing on the perspectives of several scholars in the field. The six chapters in this section establish a theoretical foundation for the CDR concept, presenting key literature and established concepts in a way that is tangible and relevant for practitioners. They offer essential background information, a broader perspective from digital values to impact assessment, and open pathways for bridging theory with practice.

A meta-level exploration of what drives the **CDR corporate governance gap** between normative claims and their operationalization is presented by *Anna-Sophia*

Christ. Tracing the roots of corporate governance back to the shift of the industrial revolutions, she highlights how these historical changes continue to shape economic systems today. She examines how modern organizational decision-making is defined by trade-offs between time and stakeholder impact, and introduces five key differentiators governing digital responsibilities apart from its industrial-era predecessors (Chapter "Beyond Corporate Responsibility Blueprints: Rethinking Corporate Governance Dynamics for Digital Complexity").

The contribution by *Christopher Johnson* on **CDR values** draws on literature from digital ethics and general management to offer a values-based perspective that highlights the novel aspects of CDR in comparison to earlier approaches to corporate responsibility. The perspective offered is grounded in empirical work showing how firms articulate values within their own CDR regimes, thereby shedding light on the practical ways in which abstract concepts are translated into organizational action (Chapter "What Do We Mean by CDR Values and Where Do They Come From?").

Dr. K. Valerie Carl introduces key **CDR frameworks and tools** developed in Europe and the UK. With particular attention to the needs of SMEs and startups that often lack dedicated CDR expertise, she offers practical insights into how organization can assess their maturity, select fitting frameworks, and make CDR more actionable at different stages of their journey (Chapter "A Map of Corporate Digital Responsibility Frameworks, Codes, and Tools").

A study of **synthesis between CDR and corporate responsibility reporting** is contributed by the two researchers, *Anna-Sophia Christ* and *Anna Wannhoff*. The scope of six CDR frameworks from research and practice is compared to the disclosure requirements of the Corporate Sustainability Reporting Directive (CSRD) by the European Union. Convergence, resonances, and divergences are revealed, based on which a pathway is proposed for operationalizing CDR matters while acknowledging the limitations of reporting as a lever for transparency rather than performance (Chapter "Operationalizing Corporate Digital Responsibility (CDR) Through Reporting: A CSRD Assessment of Convergence, Resonance, and Divergence").

Another research project presented by the scholars *Dr. K. Valerie Carl, Dr.-Ing. Jan Zibuschka, Dr. Cristina Mihale-Wilson*, and *Prof. Dr. Oliver Hinz* investigate the **consumer perspective** on CDR. Their analysis of consumer preferences leads to a segmentation strategy, offering organizations guidance to align their CDR activities with consumer expectations. The presented approach not only uncovers opportunities for value creation but also strengthens practical implementation by connecting responsibility with market relevance (Chapter "What Do Consumers Ask for When It Comes to CDR?").

Closing the first book part, a **structured overview of the evolving CDR literature**, tracing its progression from early normative theorizing to more recent efforts at operationalization, is provided. The authors, *Anna-Sophia Christ* and *Kübra Çalışkan*, map how CDR emerged from industrial concerns around digitality and ethics and how CDR grew across multiple disciplines. The collected overview offers definitional work, the identification of core dimensions, and the development of models for organizational integration, offering scholars and practitioners an accessible entry point into this fragmented but rapidly expanding domain (Chapter "Tracing the Evolution of Corporate Digital Responsibility (CDR) Conceptualization: A Literature Overview").

2 Part II: Corporate Cases—Stories from the Field

The second part of the editorial shifts from research to practice, illustrating how various organizations implement CDR. The selected company cases reveal that although the discussion on CDR may be based on common principles, its actual application varies widely depending on a company's business model, industry setting, organizational structure, and available resources. Each chapter offers insights into specific strategies, governance frameworks, and initiatives to share lessons learned and best practices for responsibility in the digital age.

In their contribution, *Simon Lucas* and *Dr. Jean Enno Charton* examine three central challenges of digital responsibility and how **Merck KGaA** addressed them systematically: designing a dynamic ethics framework, embedding it into daily operations to prevent ethics shopping, and applying semi-automated risk assessments to cope with digital complexity. The case demonstrates how a global **science and technology company** can translate abstract ethical principles into practical measures, bridging the gap between high-level aspiration and everyday business practices (Chapter "Three Challenges of Operationalizing Digital Ethics in a Science and Technology Company: The Case of Merck KGaA").

The chapter by *Maike Scholz*, *Melanie Kubin-Hardewig*, and *Marike Mehlmann-Tripp* explores **Deutsche Telekom**'s approach to positioning CDR as a central management principle. The company integrated sustainability, ethics, data protection, and democratic values into its overall strategy, with initiatives ranging from expanding inclusive networks and applying green AI guidelines to advancing media literacy and social cohesion. This case illustrates how a **telecommunications provider** can measure and scale impact while balancing profitability, societal responsibility, and long-term commitments, such as the path to net-zero emissions (Chapter "Deutsche Telekom Connects People: Our Business, Our Responsibility").

From the sector of **statutory health insurance**, *Maria Hinz* presents how CDR can be institutionalized in a highly regulated environment. The case of **BARMER** emphasizes five guiding principles that are put into practice through initiatives such as the DigitCoaches program, the DigiTal learning platform, and transparent e-health services like the electronic patient record. The company's approach shows how CDR can be applied to foster trust, patient autonomy, and social impact, while also contributing to public discourses and policy innovation (Chapter "Digital Responsibility in Practice: How BARMER Anchors Ethics in Healthcare Innovation").

Illustrated as a strategic shift from corporate responsibility to a broader framework of corporate social and digital responsibility, Alexandra *Prinz* and *Katharina Mosor* present the case of **KPMG Austria**. Their approach combines internal governance reform with client-focused tools, making use of the CDR Building Bloxx as a guiding framework. By integrating trustworthy AI, robust cybersecurity measures, and the KITE training program alongside efforts to foster a culture of responsibility, the consultants demonstrate how a large professional **tax, audit, and advisory service provider** can align norms and governance (Chapter "Responsibility in the Digital World: From Corporate Social Responsibility to Corporate Social and Digital Responsibility at KPMG Austria in the Context of Sustainability Management").

Romana Pflieger and *Jakob Wößner* introduce the case of a **natural cosmetics and dietary supplements** company known for its long-standing commitment to sustainability. **Weleda AG** has developed twelve digital ethics principles that are integrated into operations and product development. An illustrative example is the company's AI-powered chatbot WeAsk, which supports employee learning and innovation while adhering to strict standards of ethical AI and data security. A compelling case of how values-driven organizations can innovate responsibly without compromising economic and ethical commitments (Chapter "Tradition Drives Innovation: CDR at Weleda AG").

3 Part III: Meta-Perspectives and Ways Forward

The third part of the editorial zooms out to offer a broader perspective on CDR. Consultants, subject experts, and initiative leaders reflect on their cumulative experiences across corporate environments, networks, and policy arenas. Their chapters combine critical analysis with constructive foresight, highlighting present barriers, such as misaligned incentives, limited digital literacy, and regulatory ambiguity, while pointing toward practical pathways forward. Together, these contributions invite researchers to see CDR not only as a corporate task but as a collaborative and societal learning process.

The **entrepreneur** *Dr. Moritz Schirmer* examines **three blind spots of AI applications** that currently hinder the advancement in Germany's public sector. By unpacking the fundamental challenges behind these issues, he offers stakeholders valuable clarity for shaping the digital future of government institutions. Rather than focusing solely on risk mitigation, he frames responsibility as an opportunity, presenting a perspective that highlights both ethical guidance and innovation potential. In doing so, he shows how public institutions can move beyond incremental improvements to pursue lean, forward-looking innovation that aligns technological progress with societal values (Chapter "AI for AI: Leveraging AI to Enable AI Opportunities in Germany's Public Sector").

In here chapter, *Dr. Saskia Dörr*, an early expert voice in the CDR discourse, reports from experiences in working with SMEs. She presents the prototype project **Ethos Advisor**, a domain-specific AI tool developed by **WiseWay** and used to assist sustainability and responsibility leads in ethical communication, guideline drafting, and capacity building. Evaluations reveal improvements in efficiency, content quality, and user confidence, while trust was enabled through transparency and human-in-the-loop design. Her experiences show how generative AI, if carefully designed, can evolve from an abstract ethical debate into a social technical practice for embedding responsibility in lean organizational settings (Chapter "Making CDR Work: Generative AI as a Catalyst for Responsible Innovation in SMEs").

As part of the **German CDR Initiative**, the experts Prof. *Dr. Alexander Bring*, *Frank Esselmann*, and *Leonhard Henke* propose a **CDR Maturity Model**. Grounded in ethical principles and structured around five key fields of action, the model provides a structured pathway for organizations to advance their digital responsibility across five maturity levels. By combining the logic of capability maturity models with practice tools such as the CDR Quick Check, the framework enables organizations to integrate responsibility into their strategies in a stepwise yet systematic way (Chapter "The CDR Maturity Model: Guiding Digital Responsibility in Turbulent Times").

Addressing the implications of the EU AI Act, the **SKAD consultants** *Dr. Sergio Genovesi* and *Ismael El-Hadj* share experiences from working with companies on **AI governance** and how to structurally address its operationalization. They argue that compliance alone is insufficient and that organizations must embed CDR principles into everyday processes. Further, they highlight the importance of cross-functional collaboration, continuous AI literacy training, and clear role assignments as prerequisites for responsible AI deployment (Chapter "Corporate Digital Responsibility (CDR) and Its Role in AI Governance").

Turning specifically towards challenges and opportunities SMEs face, particularly in light of new legal frameworks such as the European Accessibility Act and the EU AI Act, two **ifok consultant** give insights into their experiences. *Bartosz Przybylek* and *Felix von Roesgen* share their **four-stage framework for SMEs**, allowing them to gradually embed CDR into organizational structures. Complemented with practical examples, the framework reframes CDR as a lever for strengthening resilience, competitiveness, and employer attractiveness while enabling responsible digital transformation (Chapter "CDR Implementation in SMEs: Overcoming Typical Challenges").

Dr. Marie Blachetta and *Lea-Sophie Mueller* from Germany's largest digital initiative, **Initiative D21**, situate CDR in the broader societal and regulatory context in their chapter. They argue that digital technology is not technologically predetermined but shaped by collective decisions and shared responsibilities. The authors trace the roots of CDR in digital ethics, emphasize Europe's role as a regulatory pioneer, and call for an expanded ecosystem of **Organizational Digital Responsibility (ODR)** in which the digital society is not a passive recipient but an active co-creator (Chapter "Shaping the Next Phase of Digital Transformation: CDR and the Digital Society").

The selection concludes with a contribution from the **PwC Germany** consultants *Daniela Hanauer*, *Saskia Becke*, and *Lars Distelrath* introducing a **strategic triad of technology, sustainability, and digital ethics**. They emphasize that by embedding regulatory compliance into strategic planning, fostering ethical technology adoption, and empowering people across organizations, companies can transform compliance burdens into innovation levers. Further, practitioners are encouraged to view resilience as a proactive capability—anchored, interconnected, responsible, and future-oriented business models (Chapter "Digital Ethics, Resilience, and Strategic Corporate Management").

4 How to Use the Book

The editorial volume is a collection of insights and experiences with CDR. It brings together the current state of knowledge from research, practice, and subject-matter expertise, presenting a wide range of perspectives that together form a rich landscape of the field. By placing these diverse contributions side by side, the book not only reflects the plurality of CDR as a concept and practice but also provides multiple entry points into the discourse, allowing readers to engage with the topic from different vantage points. At the same time, the act of bringing these perspectives together serves as a milestone: it bundles competencies, consolidates fragmented knowledge, and helps move beyond the current status quo at a moment when the momentum of CDR development has been slowing down.

Readers from academia are invited to gain a more nuanced understanding of how companies are translating normative ambitions into concrete strategies, processes, and innovations. Practitioners, in turn, are offered the opportunity to learn from the experiences of others, discover best practices, and deepen their understanding through exposure to scholarly insights on the underlying mechanisms of CDR. The contributions from facilitators, consultants, and initiative leaders provide an additional, meta-level perspective, highlighting where the transformation currently stands and what tools and methods are available to support organizations in their efforts. For practitioners, this opens possibilities for inspiration and practical guidance; for researchers and experts, it provides opportunities to leverage existing experiences and scale them across industries and contexts.

Ultimately, the book is both a reflection of where the CDR discourse stands today and a call to action. It demonstrates that progress is possible when normative aspirations are translated into practice, and it encourages continued dialogue, collaboration, and experimentation. All contributors share a common commitment to advancing the field and remain open to further engagement in shaping the future of CDR.

Competing Interests The author has no conflicts of interest to declare that are relevant to the content of this chapter.

References

Carl, K. V., & Hinz, O. (2024). What we already know about corporate digital responsibility in IS research: A review and conceptualization of potential CDR activities. *Electronic Markets, 34*(1), 1–30. https://doi.org/10.1007/s12525-024-00708-0

Carroll, N., Hassan, N. R., Junglas, I., Hess, T., & Morgan, L. (2023). Transform or be transformed: The importance of research on managing and sustaining digital transformations. *European Journal of Information Systems, 32*(3), 347–353. https://doi.org/10.1080/0960085X.2023.2187033

Christ, A.-S. (2025). Corporate governance for digital responsibility: A company study. In *20th International Conference on Wirtschaftsinformatik. Münster, Germany*.

Lobschat, L., Mueller, B., Eggers, F., Brandimarte, L., Diefenbach, S., Kroschke, M., & Wirtz, J. (2021). Corporate digital responsibility. *Journal of Business Research, 122*, 875–888. https://doi.org/10.1016/j.jbusres.2019.10.006

Merbecks, U. (2023). Corporate digital responsibility (CDR) in Germany: Background and first empirical evidence from DAX 30 companies in 2020. *Journal of Business Economics, 1-25*. https://doi.org/10.1007/s11573-023-01148-6

Mueller, B. (2022). Corporate digital responsibility. *Business and Information Systems Engineering, 64*(5), 689–700. https://doi.org/10.1007/s12599-022-00760-0

Ologeanu-Taddei, R., Hönigsberg, S., Weritz, P., Wache, H., Mittermeier, F., Tana, S., Dang, D., Hautala-Kankaanpää, T., & Pekkola, S. (2024). The relationship of digital transformation and corporate sustainability: Synergies and tensions. *Technological Forecasting and Social Change, 210*, 1–18. https://doi.org/10.1016/j.techfore.2024.123809

Rupp, D. E., Aguinis, H., Siegel, D., Glavas, A., & Aguilera, R. V. (2024). Corporate social responsibility research: An ongoing and worthwhile journey. *Academy of Management Collections, 3*(1), 1–16. https://doi.org/10.5465/amc.2022.0006

Wessel, L., Mosconi, E., Indulska, M., & Baiyere, A. (2025). Digital transformation: Quo Vadit? *Information Systems Journal*. https://doi.org/10.1111/isj.12578

Wickert, C. (2021). Corporate social responsibility research in the Journal of Management Studies: A shift from a business-centric to a society-centric focus. *Journal of Management Studies, 58*(8), E1–E17. https://doi.org/10.1111/joms.12775

Zimmer, M., Järveläinen, J., Stahl, B., & Mueller, B. (2023). Responsibility of/in digital transformation. *Journal of Responsible Technology, 16*, 1–5. https://doi.org/10.1016/j.jrt.2023.100068

Anna-Sophia Christ is a doctoral researcher at Maastricht University's School of Business and Economics and the University of Bremen's Business, Innovation, and Transformation Institute (BIT). Her research and teaching focus on systemic aspects of digital responsibility in economic contexts within the field of information systems. In her work as an independent coach, consultant, and system and organizational constellation facilitator, she supports companies in their sustainability and digital transformation.

Insights from Research

Beyond Corporate Responsibility Blueprints: Rethinking Corporate Governance Dynamics for Digital Complexity

Anna-Sophia Christ

Abstract

This chapter explores the fundamental dynamics that make translating principles into practice a persistent systemic challenge in corporate governance. It examines why this challenge becomes particularly complex in the digital age, where technologies, accelerated change, and shifting expectations reshape the landscape. The discussion offers a meta-level perspective on what drives the gap between governance ideals and their realization in practice. It begins by tracing the roots of corporate governance back to the foundational shift introduced by the industrial revolutions – shifts that continue to influence economic systems today. The chapter then examines how decision-making in modern organizations is increasingly defined by trade-offs along two critical dimensions: time and stakeholder impact. Finally, five key differentiators are introduced that distinguish the dynamics of the digital realm from its industrial-era predecessors, highlighting why established governance approaches may no longer be sufficient. The chapter aims to provide a narrative for understanding these complexities and points toward the mindset needed to bridge the gap between principles and effective governance in the digital realm.

A.-S. Christ (✉)
Business, Innovation, and Transformation Institute (BIT), University of Bremen, Bremen, Germany
e-mail: achrist@uni-bremen.de

A.-S. Christ (ed.), *Corporate Digital Responsibility*, Future of Business and Finance, https://doi.org/10.1007/978-3-032-14793-6_2

1 Systemic Transformation: A Perspective on Corporate Governance

Transformation begins in the mind. It begins with shifts in our beliefs, moral standards, and ethical frameworks that direct our decisions, manifesting in guiding principles. These shifts are rooted in fundamental human attitudes, our capacity and willingness to learn and grow (cf. Scharmer, 2016, pp. 75). From the inner change, transformation extends outward, reshaping behaviors, habits, and routines, bringing principles into practice. But when transformation moves beyond the individual and seeks to engage larger social or organizational systems, the path forward is rarely a linear root-cause-effect. Thus, in organizational systems, careful steering of concurrency is required, needing a corporate governance-based transformation and adjustment of steering criteria, measures, and obligations for long-term effective impact.

Following system theorist Meadows (2008, p. 11), "a system is an interconnected set of elements that is coherently organized in a way that achieves something," and they naturally tend to preserve and reproduce their existing patterns. Meaningful transformation, therefore, seldom arises from within. Instead, external levers are often necessary: interventions that disrupt entrenched structures and open new possibilities. These levers, whether they take the form of new information, resources, or external pressure, can influence different aspects of a system: its elements, the connection between them, and even the criteria that define its purpose. Transformations introduced through one of the levers will trigger feedback loops aimed at restoring stability through adjusting patterns according to the new criteria, through the selected measures, to achieve the introduced obligations (cf. Luhmann, 2000; Meadows, 2008).

In the following, it is traced on a high and illustrative level how organizational systems have evolved through successive industrial revolutions, each wave of transformation reshaping the elements of the system, the ways they connect, and the criteria by which decisions are made. Over time, organizational systems have become increasingly complex, with multiple transformations unfolding in parallel. Yet complexity brings its own challenges. When a system faces too many simultaneous feedback loops, it risks becoming overburdened. Conflicting dynamics, competing priorities, and limited resources force difficult choices, requiring trade-offs in which some transformations are prioritized over others (cf. Meadows, 2008).

2 Corporate Governance Principles: Following the Industrial Revolution

During the early industrial revolution, ownership and management were often held by the same individuals. The volume of production depended on the input resource: human labor. A key factor in businesses maintaining their relevance in the market was the principle of functionality. Whatever product or service they offered, it sold because it served its intended purpose. However, as businesses scaled through mechanization, electrification, and automation – leading to capital-intensive infrastructure – ownership gradually shifted toward dispersed shareholders, while control became the responsibility of professional managers. This separation presented a fundamental challenge: how to ensure that managers, entrusted with operational control, act in the best interest of those who own the company (cf. Berle & Means, 1932).

The business output was no longer limited to the input of human labor but could be expanded through advancements from steam power, electric power, and eventually computer power. The idea that a company's main responsibility is to its shareholders gained strength, later famously summarized by economist Milton Friedman's assertion: "The social responsibility of business is to increase its profit" (1970). In practice, this meant maximizing revenue while cutting costs – an approach rooted in the management principle of efficiency. Imagine a growing German factory with engineers focused on perfect functionality, now also required to scale processes to the highest level of efficiency, where greater output equals higher profit. While this approach made sense in theory and under the shareholder-focused mindset, it began to reveal weaknesses as real-world complexity increased.

Financial crises, corporate scandals, and managerial excesses exposed flaws in this simplistic view. They emphasized the so-called principal-agent problem, where managers (agents) might pursue personal objectives at the expense of shareholders (principals), often protected by layers of complexity and information asymmetry. In response, corporate governance structures developed as legal and institutional frameworks to align management actions with ownership interests (cf. Jensen & Meckling, 1976; Shleifer & Vishny, 1997). Governance transitioned from being solely about oversight to becoming a dynamic system embedded in broader cultural, regulatory, and economic contexts that must continually adapt to ensure both performance (achieving goals) and conformance (complying with laws and evolving norms).

As the foundational Cadbury Report succinctly states, corporate governance is "the system by which companies are directed and controlled" (1992). Emphasizing power structures like board and executive incentives, along with accountability and transparency mechanisms, made legality a core principle. Of course, laws existed beforehand, but like most regulations, they tend to solidify when a void or crisis makes them necessary. As businesses became more complex and started trading on public markets, formal legal oversight became essential. Compliance was no longer optional – it was required for managerial legitimacy.

Yet, as the world moved into the second half of the twentieth century and globalization brought prosperity to the more developed societies and the world at large, the divide and its origins did not go unnoticed. It became increasingly clear that companies do not operate in isolation. What emerged was what economists like Klaus Schwab, founder of the World Economic Forum, call today a shift from shareholder capitalism to stakeholder capitalism (2021). This was, and continues to be, a societal-driven transition that opens the doors to boardrooms for business ethics. No longer confined to academia or philosophy departments, where ethics is studied as a scientific discipline exploring moral beliefs, ethical obligations have become an operational principle. Companies are increasingly viewed as corporate citizens, with a duty to consider their societal impact, often driven by a growing, consumer-driven society. In response, some companies have taken the initiative to define their own goals for ethical behavior and have formally committed to them through written codes of conduct.

However, anyone trying to establish guidance for ethical business conduct faces the question: if ethics is seen as the pursuit of moral good, who decides what is "good" and for whom? Such ambiguity complicates the traditional roles of corporate governance, management, and control, which are often clarified through checklists with yes-or-no answers. Therefore, contemporary business ethics is often viewed as navigating the gray area between straightforward managerial decisions with clear right and wrong answers (cf. Donaldson & Dunfee, 1994; Goodpaster, 1991). Today, many ethical uncertainties are attempted to be solved through legal obligations, industry standards, and government guidelines (e.g., GDPR, DIN EN ISO 2600:2021-04 on social responsibility). Strictly speaking, if a company is legally bound to an obligation, it is only an ethical obligation in the sense of good compliance.

Alongside these social awareness shifts, the environmental cost of industrial activity became undeniable. Issues like pollution, deforestation, and declining biodiversity – externalities of our growing industry – nobody intended, but they could no longer be ignored. Activism encouraged companies to move beyond eco-efficiency (which was a primary response, focusing on sustainability through efficient resource use), urging them to rethink their role in conserving natural resources. News reports of Greenpeace's anti-whaling actions and protests against oil companies went viral, bringing images of externalities into living rooms worldwide. Starting with the Brundtland Report by the United Nations (World Commission on Environment and Development, 1987), governments around the world collaboratively addressed environmental degradation, encouraging companies to take responsibility for their negative impacts on shared resources so that future generations could still have a planet that supports their needs.

The principle of regenerative business actions was added to the decision-making criteria portfolio, now recognized worldwide as the 17 Sustainable Development Goals (United Nations, 2015). Since little progress was made in preserving the planet over the following years, governments are increasingly enforcing regulations to meet sustainability obligations through legality, exemplified by the latest EU implementation of the Corporate Sustainability Reporting Directive (CSRD). The core concept of double materiality (inside-out perspective, a company's impact on its environment; outside-in perspective, the environment's impact on the company) aims to elevate sustainability reporting to the same level as financial reporting. However, a reporting directive simply requires companies to disclose their actions; it does not mandate achieving specific sustainability goals.

2.1 Plurality of Business Decision-Making Principles

To this day, ethical and sustainability criteria still struggle to stand as equal priorities alongside other corporate obligations such as output numbers, profit margins, and compliance settings. In the pursuit of a win-win narrative, these criteria are often merged with other business obligations (e.g., eco-efficiency, social responsibility laws) or pushed to the bottom of the list. As a result, they often remain unfulfilled, with the recurring argument that it is impossible to address all obligations simultaneously, and higher forces dictate capital-oriented decision-making (cf. Brower & Dacin, 2020; Lynn, 2021). This challenge of responsible corporate governance calls Mueller-Christ's (Mueller-Christ, 2023, pp. 210) wrangling of the five central decision-making premises (Fig. 1), requiring a more nuanced understanding of corporate governance than building the function between ownership and management of steering and control. Two principles are of desired quality: (1) functionality (does it work?) and (2) efficiency (is it profitable?) While the three other principles are of limiting quality: (3) legality (is it compliant with the law?), (4) ethics (is it morally sound?), and (5) sustainability (does it preserve essential resources?).

The interplay between these principles creates a complex web of considerations. Sometimes, they align; ethical sourcing may enhance brand value and efficiency, but often, they conflict, such as cutting costs that might harm sustainability, or legal compliance might slow down innovation of functionality. This is where corporate governance becomes more of a mindset than a discipline. The systemic approach encourages managers to navigate these tensions holistically, identifying when principles are complementary, neutral, or in conflict (cf. Carmine & De Marchi, 2023; Mueller-Christ, 2023).

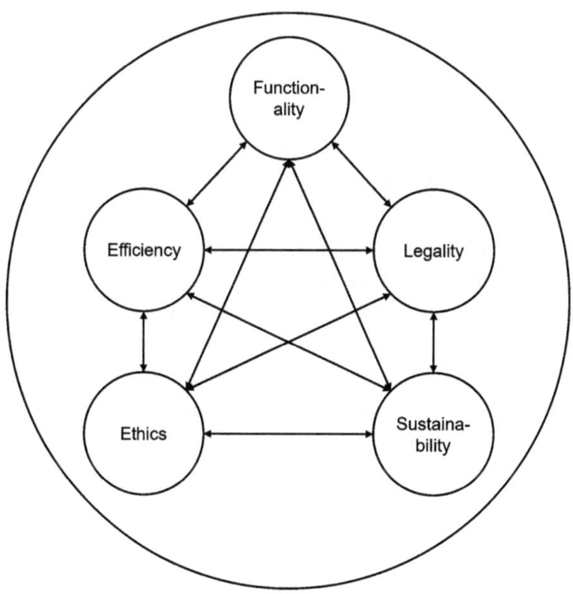

Fig. 1 Principles of business decision-making (based on Mueller-Christ, 2023, pp. 212)

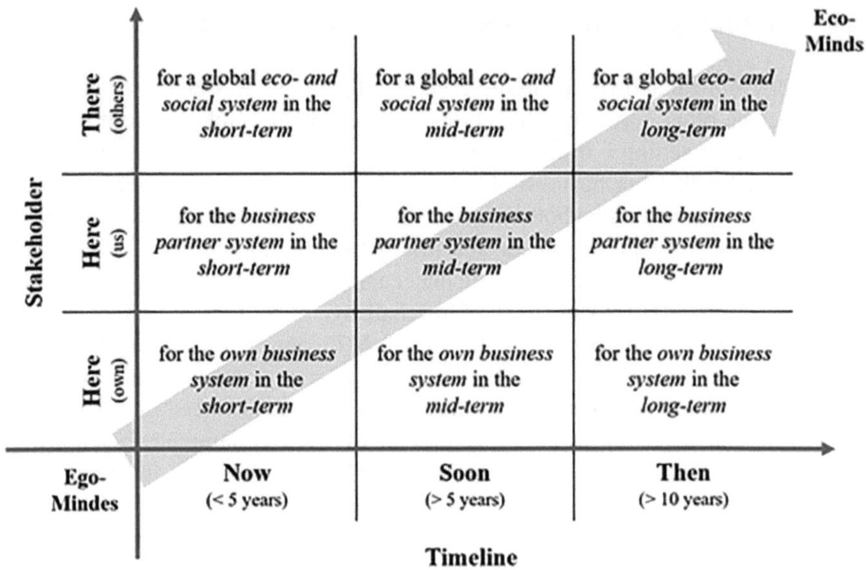

Fig. 2 Trade-off dimensions (Christ, 2025b, p. 10)

2.2 Principles Trade-Offs Along Timeline and Stakeholder Impact

As the above explanation demonstrated, corporate governance must set aside the desire for win-win-win outcomes and evolve beyond its current level of complexity to manage emerging trade-offs. The trade-offs between principles depend on impacted stakeholders and the time scale. As illustrated in Fig. 2, the stakeholder scale ranges from here (for the own business or business partner system) to there (for others, including eco- and social systems). The timeline scale begins at now (short term) and extends to then (long term), emphasizing the regenerative aspect for future generations (cf. Dao et al., 2011; Mueller-Christ, 2023).

The underlying systemic transformation that is required for corporate governance to steer and control a company under these principles is a shift from an ego-mind (shareholder-focused) to an eco-mind (stakeholder-focused) attitude, requiring a simultaneous pursuit in the presence of ambiguity, nonlinearity, and incomprehensibility. Thus, in pursuit of fulfilling multiple principles, trade-offs are a continuous balancing act rather than a one-time decision – like juggling multiple balls (cf. Carmine & De Marchi, 2023; Hahn et al., 2018). A fluid system must be established with sufficient forecast to keep all balls (principles) in the air; if one gets too low, it needs immediate and increased attention, potentially taking away too many resources from the others, bringing the system out of balance.

3 The News Industrial Revolution: The Digital Realm

Alongside a growing transformation in business ethics and corporate sustainability, the industrial revolution unfolded further over the course of the twentieth century, as industries moved beyond the age of mechanical power and mass production into the domain of computing of operation technologies and later information technologies. The transformation can be traced through three interrelated stages (cf. Hess et al., 2016; Verhoef et al., 2021). Starting with digitization, the simple conversion of analog materials into digital formats, like handwritten contracts into digital documents. Extended by digitalization, digital tools were integrated to enhance existing processes, such as online banking or digital calendar applications. Leading to digital transformation, requiring companies to rethink their business models entirely, for instance, after Uber transformed the mobility economy, and Netflix shifted the entertainment industry to a platform economy.

These changes are not just historical milestones; they signal an ongoing recalibration of what it means for a company to be relevant and resilient in a technology and data-driven world (cf. Vial, 2019; Wessel et al., 2025). Businesses are no longer limited to outsourcing physical labor, such as strength and speed, to machines; now, they can also delegate knowledge processing, for instance, AI agents in e-commerce placing and tracking orders, utility-based agents trading at the stock market, or chatbots overtaking customer service. Like the previous industrial revolutions, this digital leap brought a profound shift in corporate expectations, reshaping how organizations govern themselves and deliver value (cf. Vial, 2019).

Companies that wish to maintain legitimacy and relevance are now compelled to undertake digital transformation for good reasons of functionality and efficiency. This is not merely a technological upgrade but a strategic adaptation – rethinking the organization's value proposition and internal operations in light of rapidly evolving tools and expectations (cf. Carroll et al., 2023). For instance, car manufacturers are reorienting to mobility providers, and telecommunication providers are evolving to multimedia companies. As this transformation gains momentum, it also intersects more closely with the profound evolutions in business ethics and sustainability.

It is not only a matter of coinciding timelines – the digital era and the era of broader corporate responsibility consciousness emerged in parallel – but also a deepening awareness of how digital and ethical obligations are entwined. This confluence has given rise to new phenomena that articulate the interplay between technological progress and responsible business conduct. Recently brought forward as a twin transformation or transition, a mutually reinforcing relationship between digital technologies and corporate responsibility goals is highlighted. It is about leveraging digital capability to enable sustainability and ethics, while also using sustainability goals and ethical conduct as a compass to guide the trajectory of digital progress (cf. Christmann et al., 2024; Zimmer et al., 2023).

Digital technologies can certainly advance environmental and social sustainability goals, as seen in solutions like solar photovoltaic systems, online education platforms, and smart infrastructure solutions. But the relationship is not always harmonious if obligations appear as non-neutral or reinforcing. If trade-offs cannot be solved at the managerial decision-making level, potential externalities are passed on, leading to ethical tensions and unintended consequences, for instance, mobile devices for everyone resulting in mounting e-waste that cannot be recycled, inequalities in access and literacy increasing the digital divide, instabilities of democracies intensified by fake news, and the environmental toll of high-energy-consuming AI systems.

In the EU, the Future Industry Strategy (European Commission, 2021) and the Green Deal (European Commission, 2019) are efforts to constructively steer the dynamics of using digital technologies to address environmental challenges, alongside efforts to make digital tools themselves more sustainable – hence the emergence of green IT or sustainable IT. Reflecting the political direction, the six new AI factories across Europe are to be designed to construct low-energy processing – in theory, if it holds in practice, only the future can tell. This is a valuable intent of eco-efficiency, which must be governed consciously to not fall into the trap of rebound effects, where efficiency gains lower costs, only to lead to increasing consumption, effectively negating the environmental savings.

Another example where digital technologies are used to manage the growing complexity of sustainability efforts is automating ESG reporting (cf. Hofmann et al., 2024), but the ethical value of such initiatives deserves scrutiny. While these systems may save human labor and enhance transparency, they do not, in themselves, improve sustainability outcomes directly. They merely help companies assess and communicate what they are doing, not necessarily do better. The driving force behind these tools is often efficiency and legal compliance, not moral commitment or environmental stewardship. In this evolving landscape, it becomes clear that the integration of digital technologies and corporate responsibility is not just about synergy but about intentionality (cf. Zimmer & Minkkinen, 2024). How companies choose to navigate this convergence, whether as an opportunity to truly reshape their impact or as a strategy to optimize existing systems, will determine the real meaning of transformation in the decades ahead.

A close analysis of the arguments presented above invites a legitimate inquiry: why should digital responsibility be treated as a distinct corporate responsibility? On the surface, digitalization appears to amplify existing challenges in corporate responsibility rather than introduce fundamentally new ones (cf. Herden et al., 2021; Wade, 2020). The surge in energy consumption emphasizes the ongoing need to shift from fossil fuels to renewable sources. Similarly, the digital economy exacerbates issues such as resource recycling and the widening digital divide, particularly through the spread of misinformation. From this perspective, digital transformation seems to compound, rather than transform, the familiar dilemmas addressed by modern principle-based corporate governance.

However, this framing underestimated the deeper structural shift introduced by digital technologies; while it may be tempting to translate analog models of responsibility into the digital realm, economic progress reports reveal a troubling gap between ethical commitments and tangible outcomes. Measures to address corporate responsibility are present, yet often fall short in impact and timeliness, especially when set against the backdrop of a rapidly evolving, interconnected global economy driven by an insatiable pursuit of growth. Digital technologies do more than intensify existing issues; they introduce new scales and speeds of change, creating layers of complexity that render traditional approaches insufficient (cf. Lobschat et al., 2021; van der Merwe & Ziad Al, 2022). This realization forms the core rationale for developing Corporate Digital Responsibility (CDR) not as a separate or optional initiative, but as a reimagined framework grounded in new assumptions, better suited to address the transformative effects of the digital age concerning the scope of corporate responsibility (cf. Dörr, 2021; Mueller, 2022).

4 Digital Realm: New Dynamics, New Implementation Challenges

Compared to the preceding industrial revolutions, digital information technologies have introduced new and/or intensified dynamics into the realm of corporate governance. Above all, they drive transformation at an unprecedented speed, propelled by parallel and interdependent waves of innovation that cross organizational boundaries (Fig. 3). This rapid pace brings immense opportunities, but it often outstrips the ability of ethical reflection and debate to keep up. Their ubiquity across all areas of

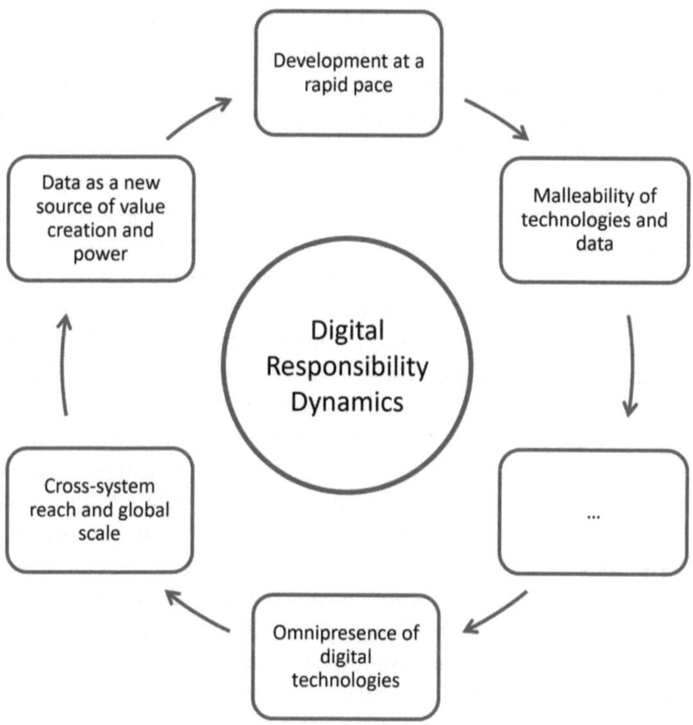

Fig. 3 Dynamics of responsible digital transformation

an organization, combined with their fluid, borderless nature, makes it difficult to ensure that technologies continue to serve their original, intended purposes once released (cf. Lobschat et al., 2021; Mihale-Wilson et al., 2021; van der Merwe & Ziad Al, 2022).

Moreover, by turning data into a new source of value creation, digital technologies are not only revolutionizing entire business models but also reshaping power structures with the new role of data scientist at its heart (cf. van der Aalst, 2016). Furthermore, their deployment across diverse cultural contexts and value systems demands deeper negotiation and collaboration (cf. Asgary & Mitschow, 2002), pushing companies beyond simply operating in parallel toward a more integrated and often more complex engagement across differing moral frameworks. These new dynamics show that the digital – being another progression on the industrial revolution stage – is not just another context but a factor that changes the dynamics of how principles of business contact can be brought into action.

4.1 Dynamic 1: Development at a Rapid Pace

Digital technologies are evolving at breakneck speed, far outpacing the slower, more linear progression of laws, ethical norms, and governance structures (cf. Royakkers et al., 2018). This gap is widening as AI, especially generative AI, drives exponential advancements. When tools like ChatGPT and other general large language models hit the market, their potential became obvious almost overnight. People quickly saw how they could boost productivity: employees used AI to draft emails or reports, students got help with writing assignments, and developers accelerated software creation with AI-generated code.

But while these possibilities capture attention, the deeper, long-term consequences are less understood. Regulators, educators, and companies alike are still grappling with questions we did not see coming fast enough. For example, what kind of personal information is safe to enter into systems like translation tools, and who is responsible if sensitive data is leaked? When students upload copyrighted literature or their own work, who owns the outputs: the AI, the authors, the student, or the software provider? Are our school assignments still testing the skills we intended, or are we just testing who can best prompt? And in software development, if anyone can now generate code in seconds, how do we ensure that security risks, ethical standards, and quality controls are upheld? To put this in perspective: it is as if society is trying to regulate high-speed trains using rules designed for horse-drawn carriages. The tools have changed dramatically, but our systems for overseeing them have not kept up.

For corporate governance, this reality means the old ways of thinking, where we separate "run the business" from "change the business," may no longer work. The pace of technology demands that continuous adaptation becomes the norm (cf. Carroll et al., 2023). Decision-making can no longer be about setting policies that last for years; instead, it must be about making the best possible decisions with today's information, while remaining ready to adjust as circumstances evolve.

To navigate this landscape, organizations must create space for ongoing evaluation and recalibration. This includes facilitating transparency and explainability, not expecting perfection from the start, but committing to progressively improving visibility into how these technologies work and are governed. We will not have all the answers at the outset, but we can aim for a journey where we steadily enhance understanding, oversight, and trust with an ethics-by-design approach from the beginning (e.g., value-based engineering with IEEE 7000-2021).

4.2 Dynamic 2: Malleability of Technologies and Data

Next to speed, another key challenge lies in the malleability of digital technology and data. Unlike a traditional industrial machine, designed and built for a single, specific task, like stamping metal sheets or weaving fabric, digital tools are inherently flexible. They can be endlessly repurposed, recombined, and redirected, often in ways their creators never imagined, but still are a technical construct which is always value-led (cf. Martin, 2022).

Consider social media platforms: tools like Facebook or X were initially built to connect people, foster communities, and encourage the free exchange of ideas. But over time, those same platforms became powerful vehicles for spreading disinformation and misinformation, enabling electoral interference, amplifying conspiracy theories, and fueling psychological manipulation. Today, most of their value propositions focus on the data economy for marketing purposes, but also for political intents. The original intent behind a technology, no matter how positive, does not set permanent boundaries on its future use.

This adaptability creates a moving target for corporate responsibility. A company may have designed a tool for good, but that does not shield it from accountability when the tool evolves or is co-opted for harm. Governance frameworks, therefore, need to address both intended uses and unintended, emergent effects, a challenge that traditional corporate responsibility, built around more predictable industrial risks, is ill-equipped to handle (cf. Lobschat et al., 2021; Mueller, 2022). This gap, the lag between a technology's development and society's full understanding of its impact, reflects a deeper structural issue: we simply cannot foresee the full consequences of digital innovation at the moment of launch. This uncertainty produces a profound governance dilemma.

On the one hand, if companies are held fully accountable for all future uses and misuses of their technologies, they face an overwhelming and arguably impossible burden. This is a tension many nations are grappling with today. Take the EU, for example, its rigorous regulatory environment (e.g., AI Act, Digital Service Act), aiming to prevent harm, has at times slowed digital innovation and contributed to concerns about losing technological sovereignty. On the other hand, if companies are not held accountable at all, we risk allowing technology to evolve unchecked, with potentially devastating social consequences, for example, as the case of Facebook is telling.

4.3 Dynamic 3: Omnipresence of Digital Technologies

Moreover, the omnipresence of digital systems across all sectors and layers of business intensifies the issue. Digital transformation is not an optional trend; it is now a basic precondition for remaining competitive and resilient (cf. Awad & Martín-Rojas, 2024; Copestake et al., 2024). Technologies once confined to back-office efficiency improvements now mediate core business functions and customer interactions. Companies that fail to embrace digital tools risk obsolescence. But with digitalization becoming ubiquitous, the potential for unintended consequences expands proportionally. Everything from hiring decisions to supply chain logistics and product recommendations may now be governed by algorithmic systems – raising questions about bias, fairness, and accountability at every step. As digital systems infiltrate every facet of corporate operations, they simultaneously embed ethical choices – many of which remain opaque to end-users and even to company leadership.

There is hardly any way to duck out and not participate in the digital age. If our family and friends are active on social media and actively share information, our involvement is also affected in the form of passive participation, as images are shared or connections can be established through belonging. The same goes for the development of service robots that are becoming part of everyday life, whether it is waiters in restaurants or, in a broader sense, self-driving cars. It is not just the person using them who is affected, but also the people around them. In this regard, there is a growing need for social discourse and for decisions not to be left solely to companies.

4.4 Dynamic 4: Data as a New Source of Value Creation and Power

Another major shift reshaping the corporate governance landscape is the rise of data as a new engine of value creation and power, a current of profit that earlier corporate responsibility frameworks largely overlooked (cf. Kitchin, 2014; Zhang et al., 2022). In the industrial and postindustrial economies, corporate value was anchored in tangible assets: factories, machines, natural resources, and human labor. Profit came from transforming raw materials into goods or delivering services.

Today, data has become the raw material of the digital economy, an invisible but immensely powerful resource. Companies generate significant profit not just from seeing products or services, but from collecting, analyzing, and monetizing the digital footprints we leave behind. And often, consumers participate in this process without even realizing it. Every click, swipe, purchase, or pause on a video feeds the algorithms that drive modern business models.

This transformation underpins what Shoshana Zuboff calls "surveillance capitalism": a system where companies treat personal data – our behaviors, preferences, relationships, and even emotions – as raw material to fuel predictive algorithms and profit-making engines (Zuboff, 2015). In this new order, consumers are no longer just buyers; they are "prosumers": both producers and consumers at once, co-creating value by simply existing and interacting online. Mostly unknowingly, prosumers generate the data that powers the algorithms shaping their digital experience and generating a return on investment for a third player (cf. Christ et al., 2025).

This shift introduces new ethical frontiers that traditional corporate responsibility never had to confront. In the past, consumers' rights focused on straightforward questions: is this product safe? Is it made responsibly? Today, the question runs deeper: who owns the knowledge about me? Do I have the right to understand or control how I am being profiled? Where is the line between helping me find what I want and manipulating my choices? When personalized recommendations anticipate your desires, is that convenience or subtle coercion?

Regulators have begun to respond. The EU's Data Act (Regulation (EU), 2023/2854) offers a promising example of trying to address these moral questions – but again, through legal actions. But even this regulation is not purely about protecting individual rights. It also aims to stimulate Europe's data economy, encouraging hardware and software owners to turn the vast quantities of data they produce – deliberately or as a by-product – into new streams of profit. The focus remains on efficiency and opportunity, using what is already there. But this raises a tension: profit and efficiency continue to sit at the heart of decision-making, even as we wrestle with the ethical and societal implications of treating personal data as a commodity.

4.5 Dynamic 5: Cross-System Reach and Global Scale

Perhaps most importantly, when trying to find answers to responsible digital governance, the systemic reach and global scale of digital technologies are changing the discourse parameters the most. Unlike earlier corporate practices, which were more easily shaped and contained by national regulations, digital products and services almost always operate across borders, influencing societies far away from the company's legal jurisdiction. A firm headquartered in California can shape political discourse in Myanmar, sway consumer behavior in Brazil, or affect social norms in Germany – all through the design of algorithms and moderation policies.

This global reach makes national frameworks of corporate responsibility increasingly inadequate. Ethical standards that are acceptable in one region may be controversial or even harmful in another region with different moral understandings. For example, the way data privacy is treated in the European Union – where GDPR (Regulation (EU) 2016/679) sets strict rules – is vastly different from practices common in the United States or China. Yet the same digital platform must navigate both landscapes simultaneously. Thus, the question is not what is ethically right but what is ethically adequate for the specific context, and if ethics do not align, what are the necessary consequences? This transnational complexity intensifies the other challenges: ensuring consent, managing unintended consequences, and maintaining ethical oversight become exponentially harder when actions in one jurisdiction can ripple across multiple societies with vastly different norms and legal frameworks.

5 Mindset: The Starting Point for Digital Responsibility

In sum, the digital transformation does not merely add another layer to existing corporate responsibility frameworks – it reshapes the nature of responsibility itself. Traditional models of corporate governance, designed to manage tangible assets and well-understood risks, are not equipped to deal with intangible, malleable, and globally digital networked systems. The emergence of digital responsibility marks a shift from managing known harms to navigating unknowns, from reacting to observable effects to anticipating invisible ones, and from governing within national frameworks to engaging with a transnational ethics of impact (cf. Lobschat et al., 2021; Stahl, 2024).

While debates continue over whether digital responsibility should be treated as a standalone category or integrated into broader corporate responsibility frameworks (cf. Baiyere et al., 2023; Weber-Lewerenz & Traverso, 2025), one thing is clear: the digital age introduces fundamentally new challenges that cannot be fully addressed by inherited models. Companies that wish to be not only legally compliant but also ethically and socially legitimate must adapt their thinking and their governance systems to reflect these new realities. The future of responsible business depends on it. However, translating the principles of CDR into real-world practice is not a straightforward journey. It is shaped by the specific business model, decision-making preferences, and the broader context in which a company operates (cf. Christ, 2025a; Merbecks, 2023). Nonetheless, stakeholders should not interpret the challenges as reasons to delay or avoid action – rather, they should view them as signposts indicating where thoughtful effort, guidance, and shared learning can make the greatest difference, starting with the relevant mindset.

1. **Embrace the volatility and brittleness of the digital landscape**: Digital technologies evolve rapidly. New tools, platforms, and risks emerge faster than governance frameworks can fully adapt. This volatility can make practitioners feel anxious about making the "wrong" choice. Picture a retail company that launched a chatbot to enhance customer service – only to face backlash because the AI system echoed biases embedded in its training data. The recommendation here: build CDR into iterative processes – pilot, learn, and adapt. Accept that perfection is unrealistic; resilience comes from responsiveness.
2. **Navigate nonlinearity and complexity with humility and anticipation**: Digital systems are rarely linear. A technology tailored to solve one problem can create unexpected side effects elsewhere. Imagine a logistics firm that adopts AI-driven route optimization to cut emissions, but discovers that the system's decisions result in unfair workload distribution among drivers. Recognizing this, practitioners should anticipate complexity and design cross-functional impact assessments. Bring together diverse teams – ethics, operations, legal, and tech – to map potential unintended consequences.
3. **Balance transparency ideals with realistic safeguards**: Transparency and explainability are core principles of digital responsibility, but practitioners must accept that full comprehensibility of advanced digital systems (especially

GenAI) may never be entirely achievable. Rather than waiting for perfect explainability, companies can define control mechanisms. For example, a fintech company might not fully decipher every decision its machine learning model makes, but it can ensure human oversight for high-impact decisions and document processes thoroughly for accountability.

4. **Acknowledge and navigate ambiguity in business obligations**: Sometimes, digital responsibility matters will clash with other legitimate business priorities. Consider a startup under investor pressure to scale fast, which faces tough choices about slowing down to ensure better data protection practices. Practitioners need to acknowledge these tensions openly, create space for ethical reflection, and articulate the long-term value of responsible choices, not just for compliance but for brand trust and market resilience.
5. **Shift from "resolving" to "adapting to" uncertainty**: The narrative needs to change. The goal is not to eliminate uncertainty in digital responsibility, which is unattainable. Instead, practitioners should focus on building capabilities for managing uncertainty. This could mean setting up ethics review boards, creating rapid-response protocols for digital harms, or participating in industry consortia to share learnings and approaches.

References

Asgary, N., & Mitschow, M. C. (2002). Toward a model for international business ethics. *Journal of Business Ethics, 36*, 239–246. https://doi.org/10.1023/A:1014057122480

Awad, J. A. R., & Martín-Rojas, R. (2024). Digital transformation influence on organisational resilience through organisational learning and innovation. *Journal of Innovation and Entrepreneurship, 13*(1), 69. https://doi.org/10.1186/s13731-024-00405-4

Baiyere, A., Grover, V., Lyytinen, K., Woerner, S., & Gupta, A. (2023). Digital "x"—Charting a path for digital-themed research. *Information Systems Research, 34*. https://doi.org/10.1287/isre.2022.1186

Berle, A. A., & Means, G. C. (1932). *The modern corporation and private property*. Macmillan.

Brower, J., & Dacin, P. A. (2020). An institutional theory approach to the evolution of the corporate social performance–corporate financial performance relationship. *Journal of Management Studies, 57*(4), 805–836. https://doi.org/10.1111/joms.12550

Cadbury, A. (1992). *Report of the Committee on the Financial Aspects of Corporate Governance*. Gee.

Carmine, S., & De Marchi, V. (2023). Reviewing paradox theory in corporate sustainability toward a systems perspective. *Journal of Business Ethics, 184*(1), 139–158. https://doi.org/10.1007/s10551-022-05112-2

Carroll, N., Hassan, N. R., Junglas, I., Hess, T., & Morgan, L. (2023). Transform or be transformed: The importance of research on managing and sustaining digital transformations. *European Journal of Information Systems, 32*(3), 347–353. https://doi.org/10.1080/0960085X.2023.2187033

Christ, A.-S. (2025a). Corporate governance for digital responsibility: A company study. Proceedings of the 20th International Conference on Wirtschaftsinformatik, Münster, Germany.

Christ, A.-S. (2025b). Responsible digital transformation: A corporate governance perspective. In *Proceedings of the 33rd European Conference on Information Systems, Amman, Jordan.*

Christ, A. S., Carl, K. V., Kurtz, C., Lobschat, L., Mueller, B., & Zimmer, M. (2025). Taking digital responsibility for data: Toward a governance model for user-generated data. *Schmalenbach Journal of Business Research*. https://doi.org/10.1007/s41471-025-00225-6

Christmann, A.-S., Crome, C., Graf-Drasch, V., Oberländer, A. M., & Schmidt, L. (2024). The twin transformation butterfly: Capabilities for an integrated digital and sustainability transformation. *Business & Information Systems Engineering, 66*(4), 1–17. https://doi.org/10.1007/s12599-023-00847-2

Copestake, A., Estefania-Flores, J., & Furceri, D. (2024). Digitalization and resilience. *Research Policy, 53*(3), 104948. https://doi.org/10.1016/j.respol.2023.104948

Dao, V., Langella, I., & Carbo, J. (2011). From green to sustainability: Information Technology and an integrated sustainability framework. *The Journal of Strategic Information Systems, 20*, 63–79. https://doi.org/10.1016/j.jsis.2011.01.002

Donaldson, T., & Dunfee, T. W. (1994). Toward a unified conception of business ethics: Integrative social contracts theory. *Academy of Management Review, 19*(2), 252–284. https://doi.org/10.5465/amr.1994.9410210749

Dörr, S. (2021). *Corporate digital responsibility. Managing corporate responsibility and sustainability in the digital age*. Springer.

European Commission. (2019). *The European Green Deal*. Retrieved July 5, 2025, from https://commission.europa.eu/strategy-and-policy/priorities-2019-2024/european-green-deal_en

European Commission. (2021). *European industry strategy. Accelerating the twin transition*. Retrieved July 5, 2025, from https://single-market-economy.ec.europa.eu/industry/strategy_en#accelerating-the-twin-transitions

Friedman, M. (1970). A Friedman doctrine—The social responsibility of business is to increase its profits. *New York Times*. https://www.nytimes.com/1970/09/13/archives/a-friedman-doctrine-the-social-responsibility-of-business-is-to.html

Goodpaster, K. E. (1991). Business ethics and stakeholder analysis. *Business Ethics Quarterly*, 53–73.

Hahn, T., Figge, F., Pinkse, J., & Preuss, L. (2018). A paradox perspective on corporate sustainability: Descriptive, instrumental, and normative aspects. *Journal of Business Ethics, 148*(2), 235–248.

Herden, Alliu, E., Cakici, A., Cormier, T., Deguelle, C., Gambhir, S., et al. (2021). Corporate digital responsibility. New corporate responsibilities in the digital age. *Nachhaltigkeitsmanagement Forum, 29*, 13–19. https://doi.org/10.1007/s00550-020-00509-x

Hess, T., Matt, C., Benlian, A., & Wiesböck, F. (2016). Options for formulating a digital transformation strategy. *MIS Quarterly Executive, 15*, 123–139.

Hofmann, J., Dangers, M., & Metz, A. (2024). *Erfolgsfaktoren gelingender doppelter Transformation*. Bertelsmann Stiftung. https://doi.org/10.11586/2024156

Jensen, M. C., & Meckling, W. H. (1976). Theory of the firm: Managerial behavior, agency costs and ownership structure. *Journal of Financial Economics, 3*(4), 305–360. https://doi.org/10.1016/0304-405X(76)90026-X

Kitchin, R. (2014). Big data, new epistemologies and paradigm shifts. *Big Data & Society, 1*(1). https://doi.org/10.1177/2053951714528481

Lobschat, L., Mueller, B., Eggers, F., Brandimarte, L., Diefenbach, S., Kroschke, M., & Wirtz, J. (2021). Corporate digital responsibility. *Journal of Business Research, 122*, 875–888. https://doi.org/10.1016/j.jbusres.2019.10.006

Luhmann, H. (2000). *Organisation und Entscheidung*. VS Verlag für Sozialwissenschaften.

Lynn, A. (2021). Why "doing well by doing good" went wrong: Getting beyond "good ethics pays" claims in managerial thinking. *Academy of Management Review, 46*(3), 512–533. https://doi.org/10.5465/amr.2018.0250

Martin, K. (2022). Algorithmic bias and corporate responsibility: How companies hide behind the false veil of the technological imperative. In K. Martin (Ed.), *Ethics of data and analytics* (pp. 36–50). Auerbach Publications.

Meadows, D. (2008). *Thinking in systems*. Earthscan.

Merbecks, U. (2023). Corporate digital responsibility (CDR) in Germany: background and first empirical evidence from DAX 30 companies in 2020. *Journal of Business Economics, 94*(7), 1025–1049.

Mihale-Wilson, C., Zibuschka, J., Carl, K., & Hinz, O. (2021). Corporate digital responsibility – Extended conceptualization and empirical assessment. In *Proceedings of the 29th European Conference on Information Systems, Marrakech, Morocco.*

Mueller, B. (2022). Corporate digital responsibility. *Business and Information Systems Engineering, 64*(5), 689–700. https://doi.org/10.1007/s12599-022-00760-0

Mueller-Christ, G. (2023). *Sustainable management: Coping with the dilemmas of resource-oriented management.* Springer Nature. https://doi.org/10.1007/978-3-031-45791-3

Regulation (EU) 2023/2854 of the European Parliament and of the Council of 13 December 2023 on harmonised rules on fair access to and use of data and amending Regulation (EU) 2017/2394 and Directive (EU) 2020/1828 (Data Act). Official Journal of the European Union, L (2023) 2854, 22 December 2023. https://eur-lex.europa.eu/eli/reg/2023/2854/oj/eng

Royakkers, L., Timmer, J., Kool, L., & Van Est, R. (2018). Societal and ethical issues of digitization. *Ethics and Information Technology, 20*(2), 127–142.

Scharmer, C. O. (2016). *Theory U: Leading from the future as it emerges.* Berrett-Koehler Publishers.

Schwab, K. (2021). *Stakeholder capitalism: A global economy that works for progress, people and planet.* John Wiley & Sons.

Shleifer, A., & Vishny, R. W. (1997). A survey of corporate governance. *The Journal of Finance, 52*(2), 737–783.

Stahl, B. C. (2024). From corporate digital responsibility to responsible digital ecosystems. *Sustainability, 16*(12), 4972.

United Nations. (2015). *Transforming our world: The 2030 agenda for sustainable development (A/RES/70/1).* United Nations. https://sdgs.un.org/2030agenda

Van Der Aalst, W. (2016). Data science in action. In W. van der Aalst (Ed.), *Process mining: Data science in action* (pp. 3–23). Springer.

van der Merwe, J., & Ziad Al, A. (2022). Data responsibility, corporate social responsibility, and corporate digital responsibility. *Data & Policy, 4.* https://doi.org/10.1017/dap.2022.2

Verhoef, P. C., Broekhuizen, T., Bart, Y., Bhattacharya, A., Dong, J. Q., Fabian, N., & Haenlein, M. (2021). Digital transformation: A multidisciplinary reflection and research agenda. *Journal of Business Research, 122*, 889–901. https://doi.org/10.1016/j.jbusres.2019.09.022

Vial, G. (2019). Understanding digital transformation: A review and a research agenda. *The Journal of Strategic Information Systems, 28*(2), 118–144. https://doi.org/10.1016/j.jsis.2019.01.003

Wade, M. (2020). Corporate responsibility in the digital era. *MIT Sloan Business Review.*

Weber-Lewerenz, B., & Traverso, M. (2025). How can corporate digital responsibility (CDR) be measured in line with corporate social responsibility (CSR)? A new theoretical approach in construction 4.0. *Sustainable Development, 33*(1), 287–308. https://doi.org/10.1002/sd.3094

Wessel, L., Mosconi, E., Indulska, M., & Baiyere, A. (2025). Digital transformation: Quo vadit? *Information Systems Journal.* https://doi.org/10.1111/isj.12578

World Commission on Environment and Development. (1987). *Our common future: Report of the World Commission on Environment and Development (UN Document A/42/427).* United Nations.

Zhang, Q., Sun, X., & Zhang, M. (2022). Data matters: A strategic action framework for data governance. *Information & Management, 59*(4). https://doi.org/10.1016/j.im.2022.103642

Zimmer, M., & Minkkinen, M. (2024). Narrative approach to futures: Future-oriented perspective to responsible digital transformation. In *Proceedings of the 32nd European Conference on Information Systems, Paphos, Cyprus.*

Zimmer, M., Järveläinen, J., Stahl, B., & Mueller, B. (2023). Responsibility of/in digital transformation. *Journal of Responsible Technology, 16*, 1–5. https://doi.org/10.1016/j.jrt.2023.100068

Zuboff, S. (2015). Big other: Surveillance capitalism and the prospects of an information civilization. *Journal of Information Technology, 30*(1), 75–89.

Anna-Sophia Christ is a doctoral researcher at Maastricht University's School of Business and Economics and the University of Bremen's Business, Innovation, and Transformation Institute (BIT). Her research and teaching focus on systemic aspects of digital responsibility in economic contexts within the field of information systems. In her work as an independent coach, consultant, and system and organizational constellation facilitator, she supports companies in their sustainability and digital transformation.

What Do We Mean by CDR Values and Where Do They Come From?

Christopher T. Johnson

Abstract

Corporate Digital Responsibility (CDR) governance mechanisms are increasingly visible, yet the underlying values that guide them are often taken for granted. This chapter addresses that gap by asking what CDR values are and where they come from. Drawing on literature from the digital ethics and general management domains, I outline a values-based perspective that illuminates some of the novel aspects of CDR compared to previous approaches to corporate responsibility. I ground this perspective in ongoing empirical work illustrating how firms articulate values within their specific CDR regimes. For researchers, a closer engagement with values represents a potential mode of enquiry into whether CDR represents a fundamentally new phenomenon or rather an extension of existing moral frameworks. This has implications for practitioners depending on whether the most successful instances of CDR resolve ethical dilemmas by relying on established ethical frameworks, by developing novel approaches tailored to the digital context, or through a hybrid solution.

1 Introduction

One does not have to look far to discover the range and diversity of Corporate Digital Responsibility (CDR) governance approaches in practice, with pertinent examples set out in Part II of this book. Yet corporate governance does not operate in a vacuum. Such mechanisms are visible manifestations of the underlying values that guide and scaffold firm behavior, through which organizations ensure their ethical use of digital technology. While other chapters in this book offer a solid

C. T. Johnson (✉)
Chair of Digital Business, University of Bremen, Bremen, Germany
e-mail: cjohnson@uni-bremen.de

A.-S. Christ (ed.), *Corporate Digital Responsibility*, Future of Business and Finance, https://doi.org/10.1007/978-3-032-14793-6_3

description of CDR from the governance perspective, here I examine the foundational values upon which these governance mechanisms draw in order to effectuate responsible behavior.

I use the terms "values," "norms," and "principles" interchangeably, firstly, to reflect their heterogeneous use in business settings and, secondly, for want of terminology that encapsulates the essence of values as "the weight which corporate decision makers attach to alternative goals when making their decisions" (Thomsen, 2004, p. 29). Values, for the purpose of this chapter, are any implicit or explicit statements that genuinely guide, inform, or justify corporate decision-making and action, rather than merely rhetorical or instrumental labels.

CDR regimes generally consist of a set of rules, roles, and responsibilities which, in turn, draw on a set of "values" as a way to align organizational behavior with the normative expectations of stakeholders, including customers, employees, and non-users (Lobschat et al., 2021, p. 875). These values act as a benchmark for firms to differentiate themselves competitively in the eyes of the consumer or to avoid reputational and financial fallout from mismanaging stakeholder expectations. Yet despite the growing interest in CDR, the literature leaves several key questions unanswered. What exactly is this idealized behavior that firms seek to emulate under the banner of CDR? Where do the values that underpin this behavior originate? And through what processes are these values translated into governance mechanisms? These questions point to a gap in our understanding of the relationship between values and responsible digital conduct, thereby justifying the need for a closer examination of CDR from a values-based perspective.

A core tension that frames this inquiry is whether CDR values are corporate-centered, that is, internally selected and shaped largely in isolation by individual firms, or corporate-oriented, emerging in response to external pressures and stakeholder influence. We also lack clarity as to whether values are proactive or reactive. Under the former, employees tackle ethical issues from the bottom up, or there may be top-down self-regulation, while the latter involves value-setting as a reaction to legal compliance or external stakeholder pressure. Bundling the aforementioned gaps in the literature along with this core tension, I frame the research question: *What are CDR values, and where do they come from?*

Answering the above question is important, I argue, because it helps us understand what is truly unique or novel about CDR. The fact that we observe governance functions that look somewhat different from previous approaches to corporate responsibility, such as the triple bottom line or Corporate Social Responsibility (CSR), does not necessarily mean that firms are embracing CDR as a separate construct with its own ethical foundations. Understanding what CDR values are and where they come from provides a further piece of the puzzle in determining whether CDR is a fundamentally new phenomenon or an extension of preexisting moral frameworks where established principles are repurposed in response to digital challenges. This has implications for best practice depending on whether the most successful instances of CDR solve ethical dilemmas with existing moral frameworks, with novel approaches developed uniquely for the digital context, or perhaps using a hybrid approach.

This chapter starts by highlighting why we should take a closer look at values in the first place. I point to an unresolved fracture in the computer and digital ethics literature where scholars are at odds as to the role of values in governing the ethical use of digital technology, specifically. On the one hand, values help us apply existing behavioral expectations to digital contexts, while, on the other hand, they guide the formulation of new rules for situations where pre-digital norms no longer apply (Johnson & Snapper, 1985; Moor, 1985). The point of this exercise is not to argue for one side or the other but to use the values-based perspective as a way to uncover novel aspects of CDR compared to previous approaches to corporate responsibility.

In the second section, I clarify a working definition of values as understood generally in the business and management literature. I then turn to the CDR literature to describe how the concept of values is treated within this domain. Both fields treat values as either a property of the organization or a process of action by valuing certain beliefs, behaviors, or ideal states. Linking these observations back to the computer ethics debate, I posit that the novelty of CDR compared to previous approaches lies not only in the more visible governance structures. Rather, CDR's novelty lies in challenging the path-dependent evolution of the values on which such governance rests, thereby creating the possibility for organizations to orient themselves toward alternative courses of action in both the present and the future.

Empirically, there is scant research on the values-as-action perspective. As such, the final section offers an anonymized preview into ongoing empirical work, allowing us to see how firms actually use values under the remit of CDR. Based on expert interviews with CDR practitioners, the data hints that while firms continue to rely on longstanding corporate values to navigate digital uncertainty, there is also emerging evidence that new or evolving value formulations are used to justify firm behavior in the face of ethical challenges unique to the digital age.

2 Values Created or Transformed Through Digital Technology

According to Moor (1985), a pioneer in computer and AI ethics, technology changes what we value or creates new values entirely. As per his example, the value of property was traditionally tied to physical scarcity. Owning a book denotes exclusive access to a single tangible object. However, with the advent of computer software, which can be copied and distributed infinitely at negligible cost, any model of value based on resource scarcity breaks down in the digital space. The ease of replication afforded by technology challenges conventional values of ownership and authorship.

Furthermore, the mere recombination of existing technology, as opposed to its outright invention, is enough to induce value changes on the societal level. Ride-hailing platforms like Uber or Lyft have revolutionized urban mobility by combining existing infrastructure like GPS, app interfaces, and algorithmic matching. While they did not invent any new technology *per se*, their specific combination of existing infrastructure raises new ethical questions; should gig workers have the same rights and protections as formal employees? Is algorithmic pricing efficient or discriminatory? Who owns the data trails generated by everyday mobility? In grappling with these questions, stakeholders articulate novel values reflected in terms such as platform accountability and algorithmic fairness, while existing concepts like privacy, autonomy, and labor rights are reinterpreted through a digital lens.

The potential ethical horizon is vast if we also factor in Moor's (1985) notion of logical malleability, the idea that digital technologies can be adapted to virtually unlimited use cases based on their computational nature. This is before we consider the potential of quantum computing to process many possibilities at once. Whereas in classical computing, a bit is either 0 or 1, in quantum computing, a qubit can be in a superposition of both 0 and 1 simultaneously, leading to a huge proliferation of potential use cases and, therefore, value configurations. Ultimately, the specific technology configuration, be it quantum computing or otherwise, is irrelevant to the outcome. The challenge practitioners face in terms of shaping their CDR regimes remains the same: how can businesses make a normative commitment while remaining flexible to accommodate variability in values that shift and change through evolving and unpredictable technological use cases?

This challenge is reflected in the current fragmentation of the CDR research landscape regarding the role and function of values. One stream of thought argues that CDR as a concept can be extrapolated from previous thinking on CSR and should focus on achieving broader societal goals related to sustainability in general (Herden et al., 2021; Christ et al., 2024). A second stream, however, posits that CDR ought to be a fully independent concept (Elliott et al., 2021; Lobschat et al., 2021; Mihale-Wilson et al., 2022; Trittin-Ulbrich & Böckel, 2022). The authors in the latter group highlight this necessity because CSR does not consider the centrality of digital technologies and their role in creating or intensifying existing social and economic issues. In this sense, there are issues unique to the emergent structure of a digital world that increase the complexity of moral decision-making and corporate responsibility.

A more nuanced engagement with values offers a promising way to bridge this conceptual divide. This is because CDR values permeate and are inseparable from the arguments on both sides of the conceptual divide regarding whether CDR should be considered an extension of or separate from CSR. For example, Lobschat et al. (2021) build upon Moor's (1985) aforementioned notion of the "malleability" of digital technology, questioning the extent to which traditional moral norms still apply in a digital age as justification for their separate consideration of CDR (Lobschat et al., 2021, p. 876). On the other hand, Herden et al.'s (2021) proposition that CDR is but an extension of CSR, albeit one which takes into account the ethical opportunities and challenges of digitalization, mirrors Johnson and Snapper (1985), who argue that while computers may create new ethical *situations*, they do not necessarily create new ethical *problems*. If we extrapolate their view into the present, then we do not need CDR as a novel framework, just a thoughtful application of existing moral principles already considered by CSR. Yet, which path are firms actually pursuing in practice, and should one be considered more appropriate or effective than the other?

3 A Conceptual Account of (CDR) Values

Taking a closer look at the business and management literature, corporate values are understood as the guiding principles that define what the organization collectively stands for and how it expects people to behave and make decisions. Lee et al. (2005, p. 4) define corporate values as "a corporation's institutional standards of behavior." Serrat (2017, p. 703) describes corporate values as "first-order operating philosophies or principles, to be acted upon, that guide an organization's internal conduct and its relationship with the external world." In effect, these values articulate the ideals that management deems important for how employees interact with one another, with customers, and with wider stakeholders. Taher (2023) suggests corporate values are the "visionary, ethical, and managerial orientations" that organizations publicly declare, promote, and practice as commitments toward stakeholders. While Volk and Zerfass (2018) note that corporate values serve as a compass helping to align a company's communication, culture, behavior, and human resources practices with longer-term company strategy.

The above extracts provide the sense that values are treated either as commitments (to guide firm or employee behavior) or as benchmarks (criteria to measure this behavior). This is in line with work that focuses on corporate responsibility, in which values underpin organizations' efforts by governing judgment and choices in day-to-day business (Treviño et al., 2006). CSR has been one of the most practiced and studied forms of corporate responsibility for some time, and such frameworks typically incorporate economic, environmental, and social values to address stakeholder needs (Carroll, 1991; Matten & Moon, 2008). Recent discussions, however, have shifted toward a more precise focus on organizational responsibility in the digital realm (Floridi et al., 2019). This shift has led to the emergence of CDR, a concept that integrates digital responsibility into organizational values, translating ethical principles into actionable practices that guide corporate activities to ensure ethical and sustainable digital engagement (Lobschat et al., 2021; Wirtz et al., 2023).

In the CDR literature, we see a similar stakeholder-oriented view of values but also a more precise focus on practical implementation. Starting with the stakeholder-oriented view of values, the CDR literature frames implementation in terms of linking ethical principles with the expectations of stakeholders. For example, Lobschat et al. (2021, p. 875) define CDR as "the set of shared values and norms guiding an organization's operations with respect to four main processes related to digital technology and data." Similarly, Mueller (2022, p. 692) notes that CDR is "strongly related to computer/digital ethics as a source of the underlying values or norms." In this view, CDR extends business ethics and CSR into digital contexts, ensuring that technology use aligns with fundamental principles. A complementary stakeholder-oriented perspective holds that firms should uphold broader societal values and go beyond compliance. For instance, Trier et al. (2023, p. 463) argue that digital responsibility involves "stakeholders such as individuals, corporations or public institutions to contribute to a sustainable, more inclusive, fair, and value-based digital society…beyond the legal minimum." This approach centers on values like inclusivity, fairness, and trust, positioning CDR as a voluntary ethical commitment to meet stakeholder and societal expectations. In terms of practical implementation, this strand focuses on integrating values into technological practices and corporate governance. Lobschat et al. (2021) illustrate this translation from principles to practice, showing how an organization's shared values and norms regarding CDR can be translated into actionable guidelines for users. Researchers have also begun mapping CDR issues to concrete domains by aligning them with established Environmental, Social and Governance categories (Merbecks, 2023).

Other research dealing directly with the concept of CDR values includes Elliott et al. (2021), who discuss the black box nature of AI and the need for harmonized ethical principles. Their work links values with societal commitments and for whom CDR is about "…committing to upholding the collective interests of society and the planet via innovative, appropriate, and permissible use of technologies" (Elliott et al., 2021, p. 185). Londoño-Cardozo and Pérez de Paz (2021, p. 11) stress the need to continually review CDR's foundational ethical bases in order "to protect social values from technological risks." For an organization, CDR values "form the basis of the future that it wants to build." Weber-Lewerenz (2021) proposes ethical guidelines for the application of digital transformation and AI in the construction industry to ensure CDR. For the author, CDR is a "way to recognize the values of a society in corporate culture and decision-making processes, empowering human growth, technological development, trust, responsibility, and consciousness" (p. 9).

We also find research demonstrating which values in particular underpin CDR regimes; Van der Merwe and Al Achkar (2022) argue that data responsibility should be a primary corporate objective. Furthermore, they engage with the debate concerning whether "…technology shapes societal norms and values" or, conversely, whether "…societal and cultural norms, developed by individuals and groups go on to shape technologies, control them, and place them at the service of society" (p. 6). Beyond protecting individual user rights, CDR is also seen as a means to generate broader social and environmental value. Dörr (2021) suggests that integrating CDR can help balance economic objectives with societal well-being, while Carl and Hinz (2024, p. 27) conceptualize CDR in such a way that fosters human and social value creation in a way that is "… aligned with ethical norms and values." They argue that the concept of CDR "better reflects reality where responsibilities do not occur isolated but rather in an interconnected way with potential influences on one another" (Carl & Hinz, 2024, p. 27).

From this short description and in combination with the general management understanding of the term, we begin to understand CDR values as the normative foundations that guide corporate conduct in digital contexts in two ways: firstly, as reference points against which corporate actions can be judged and, secondly, as actionable processes of valuing through which organizations prioritize ethical decisions in their design, deployment, and governance of digital technologies.

With this two-pronged definition in hand, we can now visualize the importance of understanding where CDR values come from. Hitherto, approaches to corporate responsibility, such as CSR, reflect a relatively static set of corporate values that mirror the wider expectations of society related to, for example, fairness or sustainability. From here, rules and constraints are developed and embedded into business practices. Yet digital technology changes what counts as fair or sustainable, as new choices for actions are made that did not previously exist (Moor, 1985). In this way, CDR's novelty lies less in the application of established values to a new domain than in its recognition that values themselves evolve or are created anew in response to advances in technology. If we accept this line of thought, and values under CDR are a reinterpretation or renegotiation of what responsibility means, then these values become levers for steering the organization to a desired future. Pending empirical validation, if this does turn out to be the case, then it is important to know whose interests and visions of the future are embedded in CDR, where values may reflect the influence of corporate actors, policymakers, and professional bodies, but may also arise from grassroots employee demands. Other practical implications also emerge. For example, a firm whose CDR regime binds them too tightly to societal expectations through mechanisms of stakeholder dialogue, while useful for risk avoidance, may restrict experimentation with technologies that carry uncertain or controversial outcomes. Firms, therefore, may self-limit by discarding ideas that, while innovative, fall outside current socially acceptable boundaries.

4 Sketching a Picture of CDR Values in Practice

Considering the high level of diversity and variability in the scale, scope, and level of CDR operationalization, it is fair to say that firms are treating CDR as a separate governance domain in practice. However, the perceived novelty of governance processes alone does not imply a shift in the underlying value system. If CDR is grounded in the same values as pre-digital notions of corporate responsibility, it may reflect more of an evolution rather than a revolution. Conversely, the emergence of new values would indicate a more fundamental transformation in how firms conceptualize their responsibilities in digital contexts.

To probe these opposing views, I investigate the origin of CDR values. Values may be reactive, whereby organizations align their values with external expectations, including laws, regulations, or pressure from consumers or, additionally, from "cultural-cognitive conditions" tied to factors such as public opinion, moral and religious codes, or cultural sensitivities (Risi, 2022, p. 306). Conversely, such normative sources may also be proactive, in which employees tackle ethical issues from the bottom up, or firms may self-regulate. In this way, they anticipate and address ethical challenges before they become regulatory requirements or public concerns, for example, privacy-by-design in product development or the formation of ethics advisory panels. Further empirical investigation may also challenge the binary proactive vs. reactive conceptualization of values.

Based on exploratory interviews with winners and nominees of the Corporate Digital Responsibility Award (CDR Award, 2023) in the DACH region, this short research preview shows how some firms construct coherent CDR strategies underpinned by a set of norms and values fit for the digital age. I spoke with representatives directly responsible for the implementation of CDR projects within their respective organizations. The interviews lasted 60 minutes on average and were based around five core topic areas including defining CDR, motivations, impact assessment, CDR governance, and CDR values. Participant names, roles, and organizations remain anonymous as data analysis is still ongoing. The analysis also includes additional documents supplied by the interview partners.

Our discussions show that the basis for CDR often stems from the company's view on the role of business in society, with one participant saying that due to the millions of international customers that use and rely on their services, the company has "…an immense responsibility to society." In a separate document, a member of the board of this large telecommunications company states, "We are convinced that technological development has to be oriented more strongly toward values." Under this remit, they devised a CDR framework to scaffold their digital behavior, ensuring that the company continues to deliver human-centered technology with human values at heart.

In other cases, CDR represents a targeted approach to the ethical issues that arise due to the unique characteristics of their own digital solutions. For example, one company founder and CEO is aware that their products can sometimes alienate individuals, given that their software makes AI-driven matching decisions based on the characteristics of large groups. "In my view, developers of digital solutions are just as responsible for their end effects as the companies who use and employ them." For that reason, as developers themselves, they constructed an internal CDR-Codex to help keep their focus on the individual even when designing big data solutions.

Our interviewees stressed the importance of creating an environment conducive to participation in a digitalizing world. One employee of a quasi-governmental organization, CDR, is closely related to "digital literacy" in the sense that "everyone should have the necessary skills and aptitude to master digital situations in everyday life." The organization works closely with the government of an EU member state to "identify relevant levers for increasing digital literacy in the country." Based on the European Reference Framework for Digital Competences and the European Qualifications Framework, they designed a self-assessment tool to evaluate employee digital competences. From here, they offer several software-as-a-service solutions that can be used by companies in the context of digital literacy to "keep employees fit for the digital age."

An understanding of norms and values can also guide employees in their digital activities, where specific rules or guidelines do not currently exist. In relation to digital grey areas, such as the use of generative AI in the workplace, CDR can provide a set of common-sense ethics to make sure staff reflect company principles through their use of emerging technologies. A compliance officer at a large pharmaceutical company noted that CDR can "fill in the gaps in these grey areas, providing advice to go beyond what is not yet established by law." In terms of their specific CDR approach, the company created a codified CDR framework consisting of a Digital Ethics Charter, as well as providing access to training and guidance for the most common and relevant digital activities to their employee base. There is also a Digital Ethics Steering Committee, which provides strategic input and is available for consultation across teams and levels.

These early findings suggest that CDR values, in some cases, are grounded in the organization's understanding of its societal role and responsibility, while in others they emerge from the ethical risks perceived in specific digital products and services. Public frameworks and supranational policy initiatives provide further normative reference points that organizations then translate into practice. Finally, firms develop internal charters, steering committees, or codes to fill regulatory gaps around emergent technologies.

5 Conclusion

This chapter sheds light on the role of values underpinning CDR governance in practice, an underexplored theme in the wider CDR literature. While existing research focuses on what values are embedded in CDR, such as data privacy, fairness, and sustainability, I extend the conversation by asking where these values come from and how they create new possibilities for action. I first propose that understanding the normative sources of these values is key to assessing whether CDR is a novel ethical construct or merely a digital extension of CSR or other approaches. I then examine how digital technologies reshape or generate new values, thereby showing how ethical expectations evolve in tandem with technological developments. This helps explain the increased complexity of value selection in CDR regimes.

I then present a conceptual account of (CDR) values, showing that they can be understood as criteria for judging behavior or as processes of valuing that influence organizational conduct in digital contexts. Recognizing where such values come from is important, I argue, as their origins reveal whose interests and visions of the digital future are being embedded in corporate practice. Where values come from and how they are operationalized carry practical implications. While alignment with stakeholder expectations may enhance legitimacy or risk avoidance, it may also constrain innovation by narrowing the space of acceptable behavior. This returns us to the ongoing debate regarding whether CDR should be seen as part of CSR or as a separate concept, and I take the position that understanding the origins of CDR values can help bridge this conceptual divide.

In the final section, I present insights from exploratory interviews on the nature of CDR. These cases reveal first insights into the possible range of CDR values and where they come from. Combining our conceptual understanding of CDR from the literature with preliminary empirical results appears to challenge the binary view of CDR as either an extension of CSR or a completely distinct governance paradigm. Instead, I note that organizations also adopt hybrid approaches. Some draw heavily on established CSR traditions, while others formulate entirely new ethical constructs tailored to challenges specifically related to digital technology. This suggests that CDR cannot be fully understood without accounting for both continuity and innovation in digital ethics.

For companies, a deeper engagement with values is important because it may determine the potential their specific regime has to open up new courses of action in the digital space, or whether it remains a rhetorical exercise, a mere poster on the wall with little influence on day-to-day decisions. For academics, tracing the origins of CDR values is a worthy exercise because it helps us contrast the novelty of this emerging business phenomenon with what has come before, thereby opening up an exciting avenue for future research.

Competing Interests The author has no conflicts of interest to declare that are relevant to the content of this chapter.

References

Carl, K. V., & Hinz, O. (2024). What we already know about corporate digital responsibility in IS research: A review and conceptualization of potential CDR activities. *Electronic Markets, 34*(27). https://doi.org/10.1007/s12525-024-00708-0

Carroll, A. B. (1991). The pyramid of corporate social responsibility: Toward the moral management of organizational stakeholders. *Business Horizons, 34*(4), 39–48. https://doi.org/10.1016/0007-6813(91)90005-G

CDR Award. (2023). *Corporate responsibility award. Bayern innovative and BVDW*. Retrieved August 31, 2025, from https://www.cdr-award.digital/

Christ, A. S., Mueller, B., & Lobschat, L. (2024). Corporate digital responsibility (CDR): Achieving synthesized coherence with C (S) R learnings on corporate governance. In *Proceedings of the 45th International Conference on Information Systems, Bangkok, Thailand.*

Dörr, S. (2021). *Corporate digital responsibility. Corporate responsibility and sustainability in the digital age*. Springer.

Elliott, K., Price, R., Shaw, P., Spiliotopoulos, T., Ng, M., Kovila, C., & Aad, v. M. (2021). Towards an equitable digital society: Artificial intelligence (Al) and corporate digital responsibility (CDR). *Society, 58*(3), 179–188. https://doi.org/10.1007/s12115-021-00594-8

Floridi, L., Cath, C., & Taddeo, M. (2019). Digital ethics: Its nature and scope. In C. Öhman & D. Watson (Eds.), *The 2018 yearbook of the digital ethics lab* (pp. 9–17). Springer. https://doi.org/10.1007/978-3-030-17152-0_2

Herden, C. J., Alliu, E., Cakici, A., Cormier, T., Deguelle, C., Gambhir, S., et al. (2021). "Corporate Digital Responsibility". New corporate responsibilities in the digital age. *Sustainability Management Forum, 29*(1), 13–29. https://doi.org/10.1007/s00550-020-00509-x

Johnson, D. G., & Snapper, J. W. (1985). *Ethical issues in the use of computers*. Wadsworth Publ. Co.

Lee, R. V., Fabish, L., & McGaw, N. (2005). The value of corporate values. *Available at SSRN*. https://doi.org/10.2139/ssrn.956170

Lobschat, L., Mueller, B., Eggers, F., Brandimarte, L., Diefenbach, S., Kroschke, M., & Wirtz, J. (2021). Corporate digital responsibility. *Journal of Business Research, 122*, 875–888. https://doi.org/10.1016/j.jbusres.2019.10.006

Londoño-Cardozo, J., & Pérez de Paz, M. (2021). Corporate digital responsibility: Foundations and considerations for its development. *Revista de Administração Mackenzie, 22*(6).

Matten, D., & Moon, J. (2008). "Implicit" and "explicit" CSR: A conceptual framework for a comparative understanding of corporate social responsibility. *Academy of Management Review, 33*(2), 404–424. https://doi.org/10.5465/amr.2008.31193458

Merbecks, U. (2023). Corporate digital responsibility (CDR) in Germany: Background and first empirical evidence from DAX 30 companies in 2020. *Journal of Business Economics, 94*(7), 1025–1049. https://doi.org/10.1007/s11573-023-01148-6

Mihale-Wilson, C., Hinz, O., van der Aalst, W., & Weinhardt, C. (2022). Corporate digital responsibility: Relevance and opportunities for business and information systems engineering. *Business & Information Systems Engineering, 64*(2), 127–132. https://doi.org/10.1007/s12599-022-00746-y

Moor, J. H. (1985). What is computer ethics? *Metaphilosophy, 16*(4), 266–275.

Mueller, B. (2022). Corporate digital responsibility. *Business & Information Systems Engineering, 64*(5), 689–700. https://doi.org/10.1007/s12599-022-00760-0

Risi, D. (2022). Business and society research drawing on institutionalism: Integrating normative and descriptive research on values. *Business & Society, 61*(2), 305–339. https://doi.org/10.1177/0007650320928959

Serrat, O. (2017). A primer on corporate values. In *Knowledge solutions: Tools, methods, and approaches to drive organizational performance* (pp. 701–709). Springer. https://doi.org/10.1007/978-981-10-0983-9_76

Taher, A. (2023). Do corporate values have value? The impact of corporate values on financial performance. *Future Business Journal, 9*(1), 76. https://doi.org/10.1186/s43093-023-00254-9

Thomsen, S. (2004). Corporate values and corporate governance. *Corporate Governance: The International Journal of Business in Society, 4*(4), 29–46. https://doi.org/10.1108/14720700410558862

Treviño, L. K., Weaver, G. R., & Reynolds, S. J. (2006). Behavioral ethics in organizations: A review. *Journal of Management, 32*(6), 951–990. https://doi.org/10.1177/0149206306294258

Trier, M., Kundisch, D., Beverungen, D., Müller, O., Schryen, G., Mirbabaie, M., & Trang, S. (2023). Digital responsibility: A multilevel framework for responsible digitalization. *Business & Information Systems Engineering, 65*(4), 463–474. https://doi.org/10.1007/s12599-023-00822-x

Trittin-Ulbrich, H., & Böckel, A. (2022). Institutional entrepreneurship for responsible digital innovation: The case of corporate digital responsibility. *Creativity and Innovation Management, 31*(3), 447–459. https://doi.org/10.1111/caim.12513

Van der Merwe, J., & Al Achkar, Z. (2022). Data responsibility, corporate social responsibility, and corporate digital responsibility. *Data & Policy, 4*. https://doi.org/10.1017/dap.2022.2

Volk, S. C., & Zerfass, A. (2018). Alignment: Explicating a key concept in strategic communication. *International Journal of Strategic Communication, 12*(4), 433–451. https://doi.org/10.1080/1553118X.2018.1452742

Weber-Lewerenz, B. (2021). Corporate digital responsibility (CDR) in construction engineering—Ethical guidelines for the application of digital transformation and artificial intelligence (AI) in user practice. *SN Applied Sciences, 3*(10), 1–25. https://doi.org/10.1007/s42452-021-04776-1

Wirtz, J., Kunz, W. H., Hartley, N., & Tarbit, J. (2023). Corporate digital responsibility in service firms and their ecosystems. *Journal of Service Research, 26*(2), 173–190. https://doi.org/10.1177/10946705221130467

Christopher T. Johnson is a research associate at the Faculty of Business and Economics at the University of Bremen, where he is also a member of the interdisciplinary Diginomics graduate group. His research focuses on how organizations conceptualize responsibility, in particular, the role of values in guiding corporate behavior in the digital age.

A Map of Corporate Digital Responsibility Frameworks, Codes, and Tools

K. Valerie Carl

Abstract

Corporate Digital Responsibility (CDR) has garnered significant attention in recent years, leading to the emergence of various frameworks, codes, and tools in parallel designed to facilitate its practical application. This chapter aims to illuminate prominent CDR approaches that have developed in Europe and the UK. In this way, this chapter specifically aims to address the challenges SMEs and startups face when initially approaching CDR due to the absence of (internal) dedicated CDR experts. By providing accessible insights into these frameworks and tools, this chapter seeks to support companies in initiating their CDR journey and assessing their current maturity levels. The discussion highlights the commonalities and distinctions among different CDR approaches, emphasizing the importance of selecting a framework that aligns with a company's culture, values, and strategic objectives. For newcomers to CDR, this comparative analysis serves as a guide to choosing the most suitable approach for initial implementation, while for more experienced organizations, it broadens the understanding of CDR and identifies potential areas for further engagement. Further, this chapter contributes to bridging theoretical debates and practical applications of CDR by presenting and comparing actionable tools, thus making the concept more tangible and actionable for organizations seeking to enhance their CDR engagement.

K. V. Carl (✉)
Information Systems and Information Management, Goethe University Frankfurt, Frankfurt, Germany
e-mail: kcarl@wiwi.uni-frankfurt.de

A.-S. Christ (ed.), *Corporate Digital Responsibility*, Future of Business and Finance, https://doi.org/10.1007/978-3-032-14793-6_4

1 Introduction

Corporate Digital Responsibility (CDR) gained increasing attention over the last few years, both in practice and in the scholarly debate. Lately, a group of practitioners, scholars, and actors from governmental organizations and civil society have agreed on one overarching definition of CDR that should incorporate the different viewpoints and aims at further supporting the operationalization of CDR. The agreed-upon definition states that "CDR stands for holistic responsible corporate action with regard to the impact of digital technologies and data" (Carl et al., 2025, p. 1425). Such a definition can support practitioners' initial approach to the concept of CDR. Still, frameworks, codes, and tools are another important building block to translate theoretical debates on CDR to practice by making the concept more tangible and easier to apply. However, the variety of different approaches can be challenging and potentially deterrent. In small and medium-sized companies (SMEs) and startups, oftentimes there is no dedicated CDR expert who solely concentrates on CDR, but someone who additionally takes over the topic of CDR (e.g., data protection officers, marketing, product design). Therefore, easy access to the topic can support more companies in initially pursuing CDR and assessing their current maturity level. This chapter should enlighten on the most discussed CDR frameworks and codes that emerged in Europe and the UK. Besides frameworks and codes, online tools have been developed that should further support transferring knowledge on CDR to actual CDR engagement in practice. Discussing both frameworks and codes, as well as tools in the context of CDR, should help scholars and practitioners navigate the landscape of different approaches to the concept and give an overview of supporting resources.

For CDR newbies, introducing those different approaches to CDR and ultimately comparing them should support practice in choosing the most suitable approach to CDR for the initial implementation. The different approaches share commonalities but differ in regard to their specific foci. Therefore, it is important for companies to adopt the particular approach that best aligns with the company's culture, values, and (strategic) goals. Giving an overview and comparing the different approaches should ease selecting the right one and reduce the necessary time to navigate the landscape of CDR frameworks and tools. Besides, for more proficient CDR companies, the discussion of the different approaches should enable an even broader understanding of the scope of CDR and can point to additional fields of CDR that might be worth pursuing in the future. Besides, several tools can help CDR pros to check whether their CDR engagement can keep up with their expectations and to further develop activities.

2 CDR Frameworks and Codes

This chapter deliberately concentrates on frameworks and codes that emerged in practice rather than including frameworks stemming from scholars (e.g., Carl & Hinz, 2024). Such a focus should follow the idea of translating principles to practice in a manner as relatable as possible, therefore solely concentrating on approaches originally stemming from practitioner initiatives.

2.1 CDR Code

The CDR Initiative was founded in 2018 and has developed the CDR Code (ConPolicy GmbH, 2023) in collaboration with its members and further contributing parties (companies, advisories, a ministry). The CDR Code is intended to provide guidance for other companies and sets out guidelines for assuming corporate responsibility in the digital context (Bundesverband Digitale Wirtschaft e.V., 2023). Nine basic principles are pursued with the CDR Code (ConPolicy GmbH, 2023): (i) core social values, (ii) human-centric technology, (iii) generating benefits, (iv) avoiding harm, (v) autonomy, (vi) fairness, (vii) transparency, (viii) responsibility, and (ix) sustainability. These basic principles form the basis for CDR's five fields of action in accordance with the CDR Code illustrated in Fig. 1 (ConPolicy GmbH, 2023).

The members of the CDR Initiative publish CDR reports in which, based on these basic principles and fields of action, they report on corporate activities related to CDR (ConPolicy GmbH, 2023). This means, every company being a member of the CDR initiative collects and describes all CDR activities conducted in one company-wide CDR report each and publishes this report every two years. These reports can inspire further nonmember companies whose activities might be worth pursuing themselves, serving as beacon projects. Further, it ties the reporting companies to their CDR initiatives and demonstrates accountability for their CDR commitment.

Fig. 1 The five CDR fields of action according to the CDR Code (ConPolicy GmbH, 2023)

2.2 CDR Building Bloxx

The CDR Building Bloxx were developed by the BVDW (Bundesverband Digitale Wirtschaft e.V., 2025), more specifically by their working group on Digital Responsibility, and first published in 2020. The association represents corporate interests in politics, among other things, but also in society as a whole. The Digital Responsibility department has developed the CDR Building Bloxx together with its corporate members. The aim of this framework is to establish a uniform understanding of CDR and to support companies in taking on more responsibility and communicating it. The CDR Building Bloxx represent a structured approach to CDR activities, particularly for Germany and Europe. The framework is designed for business, politics, and society as a whole.

The structured approach to CDR is intended to support both the initial engagement with CDR and the further development of existing CDR strategies. The framework consists of general and specific CDR Building Bloxx. The general CDR Building Bloxx form the basis for all specific Building Bloxx. In contrast, the specific CDR Building Bloxx represent core aspects of assuming corporate responsibility in a digital context (Bundesverband Digitale Wirtschaft e.V., 2025). The Building Bloxx address responsibility toward both employees and consumers. By directly involving companies and their representatives in the development, the approach was designed to be very practical. The CDR Building Bloxx framework is based on the general and specific Building Bloxx illustrated in Fig. 2.

2.3 CDR Manifesto

The CDR Manifesto (Price, 2023) was developed in 2021. Scientists, business practitioners, and other relevant stakeholders worked together to develop a summarized understanding of CDR based on various prevailing definitions and views. The CDR Manifesto follows a highly international approach. Experts from across the world teamed up to provide the manifesto in multiple languages across Europe, Asia and the Middle East, Africa, Australasia, and the Americas. This systematization is a very practical approach and accessible for a multitude of actors across the world, facilitating the understanding of CDR worldwide. Seven principles manifest corporate responsibility in the digital context, summarized in Fig. 3 (Price, 2023).

2.4 Digital Responsibility Goals

Identity Valley Research gGmbH has developed the Digital Responsibility Goals (DRGs) together with digital experts from various fields. These DRGs are intended to contribute to a human- and planet-centric digitalization. The DRGs are based on the understanding that such an approach and the additional assumption of responsibility create trust, which in turn can drive the digital transformation and increase acceptance. The basic understanding behind this is that all parties ultimately benefit when digitalization is implemented responsibly.

Fig. 2 The CDR Building Bloxx (Bundesverband Digitale Wirtschaft e.V., 2025). Translated from top left to lower right in rows: CDR; strategy/guidelines, organization/controls, monitoring, communication; change and transformation; digital well-being; digital empowerment and digital inclusion; responsible innovation; environment and resources; future of work; responsibility for data, privacy, and security; communication; artificial intelligence (AI); values and principles

Visually, as well as in terms of their purpose, the DRGs were developed in line with the United Nations Sustainable Development Goals.[1] The DRGs are aimed at a fundamental social understanding of which dimensions of responsibility are important (goals of the DRGs). In addition, five guiding criteria for companies are provided for each goal, which are intended to support the responsible development and use of digital technologies, products, and services. Finally, derived from this, metrics are also provided for each overarching goal that would allow CDR activities to be measured as part of an index. Figure 4 depicts the seven goals that are at the core of the DRGs (Identity Valley Research gGmbH, 2023).

[1]You can find in-depth information on the United Nations Sustainable Development Goals (SDGs) on the following website: https://sdgs.un.org/goals.

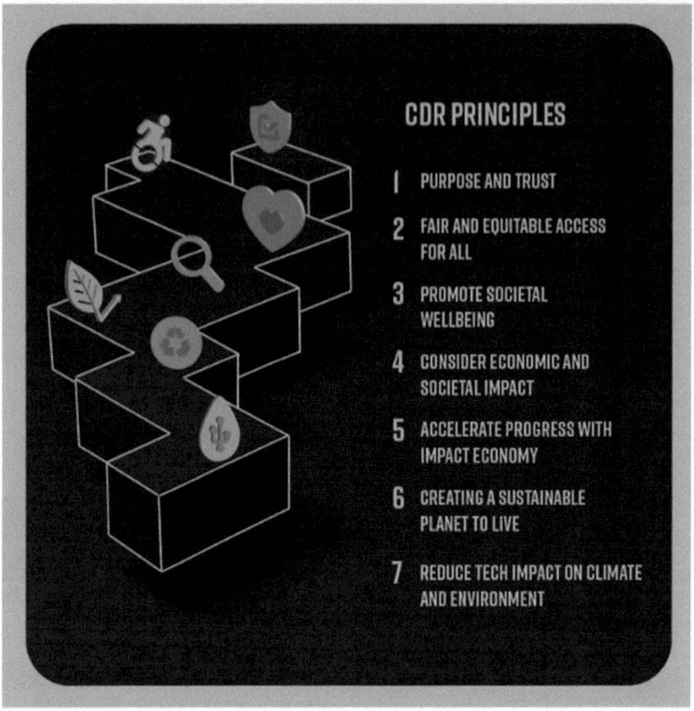

Fig. 3 Seven CDR principles according to the CDR Manifesto (Price, 2023)

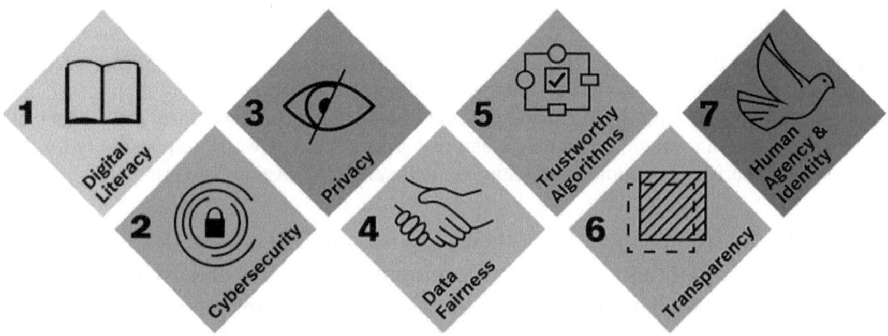

Fig. 4 The DRGs (Identity Valley Research gGmbH, 2023)

2.5 Commonalities and Differences

Those different frameworks and codes share commonalities despite pursuing different foci. Following, companies aiming to approach CDR strategically and to adopt a single framework need to find one that best aligns with their internal focus on digital responsibility (e.g., economic, social, or ecological). For example, the CDR Building Bloxx and the DRGs specifically highlight one technology – Artificial Intelligence (AI), respectively, algorithms in general – when describing CDR. If this technology is highly central to the implementing company, these two frameworks could be particularly suitable, especially to emphasize particularities of assuming responsibility in the context of AI.

Data and its handling, specifically ensuring privacy and security, are central to most CDR frameworks and codes, as also seen for the CDR Code, the CDR Building Bloxx, and the DRGs. Data privacy and security are central consumer concerns in a digital world. In terms of privacy, consumers face the constant trade-off of revealing more (personal) information for more advanced services, and most companies aim to gather an ever-increasing amount of (personal) data. This manifests in the centrality of data handling within the different CDR frameworks.

Environmental sustainability and resource protection play a more central role in the CDR Code, the CDR Building Bloxx, and the CDR Manifesto. Companies with a strong emphasis on environmental sustainability might therefore turn to those CDR frameworks that assign environmental concerns a more central position as a separate dimension, potentially better reflecting the DNA of the implementing company. Similarly, for companies aiming to approach CDR holistically from an internal and an external perspective, the CDR Code and the CDR Building Bloxx might be a suitable backdrop due to their emphasis on internal stakeholders as one specific dimension each.

For companies new to CDR, adopting one specific framework or code can be helpful to strategically guide the development of a CDR strategy and the implementation of the corresponding activities. When choosing a framework, aligning overall strategic goals, values, and the DNA of the company with the focus of one framework can be helpful to kick off initial CDR engagement. Whereas for more advanced CDR companies, considering the foci and differing dimensions of further frameworks can help assume an even more comprehensive approach to and understanding of responsibility, taking into consideration CDR dimensions not originating from the framework already implemented in the company.

3 CDR Tools and Toolboxes

Parallel to different frameworks and codes that were developed, several online tools emerged to further support companies in the context of CDR engagement in a very practical manner.

3.1 CDR Starter Kit

The Swiss Digital Initiative has launched a CDR Starter Kit (Swiss Digital Initiative, 2024), which is available free of charge for businesses. This resource provides a clear and organized introduction to CDR, explaining its significance and outlining steps for effective implementation. Designed to be easily understood by a broad audience, the CDR Starter Kit includes comprehensive informational materials that support newcomers. Additionally, it offers real-world examples from various companies and governance structures that illustrate best practices in CDR. This approach not only helps organizations implement CDR more effectively but also enables them to compare their initiatives against established benchmarks (Fig. 5) (Swiss Digital Initiative, 2024).

3.2 CDR-CAT Tool

The CDR-CAT Tool (Carl et al., 2024a; Project CDR-CAT, 2024), developed through a German research initiative, offers companies an automated and preliminary evaluation of their websites to determine how well they communicate their CDR activities. For organizations, it is crucial not only to implement CDR initiatives but also to effectively convey these efforts to stakeholders, with the website serving as a vital communication channel. The CDR-CAT Tool provides a quick initial assessment, highlighting which CDR activities have been put in place and shared with the public. This tool is especially useful for SMEs, giving them an immediate overview of their CDR status. With the insights gained, companies can identify further actions to take or improve the visibility of their existing initiatives (Fig. 6) (Carl et al., 2024a).

Fig. 5 Overview of the CDR Starter Kit (Swiss Digital Initiative, 2024)

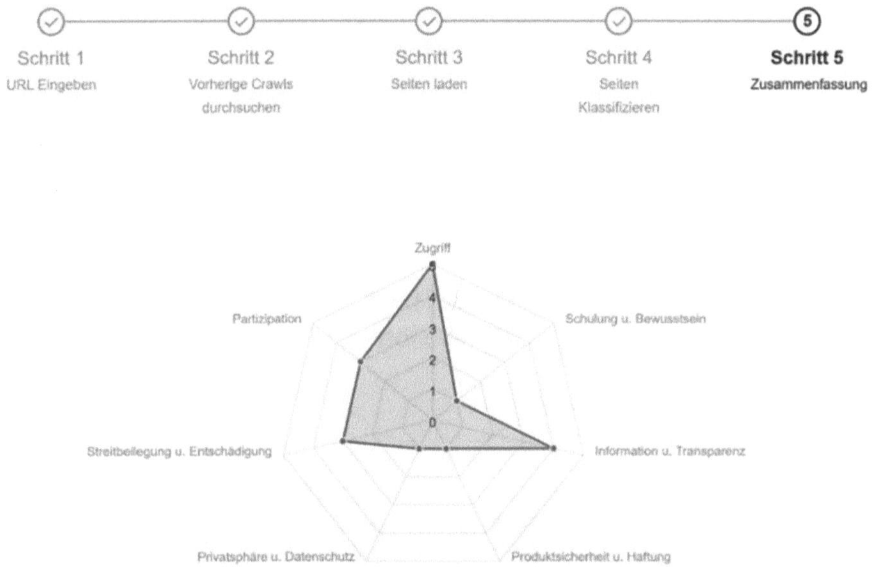

Fig. 6 The CDR-CAT Tool's consolidated evaluation of CDR communication (Project CDR-CAT, 2024). Translated from top left to lower right: Step 1 Enter the URL; Step 2 Search previous crawls; Step 3 Load pages; Step 4 Classify pages; Step 5 Summary; Access; Education and Awareness; Product Safety and Liability; Privacy and Data Protection; Dispute Resolution and Redress; Partizipation

3.3 PwC: Corporate Digital Responsibility and Digital Ethics – Quick Check

Since several years, PwC has offered a so-called Corporate Digital Responsibility and Digital Ethics – Quick Check (PricewaterhouseCoopers, 2025a). This tool should allow companies to get a quick evaluation of their status quo in terms of CDR maturity within five minutes. The evaluation is based on a self-assessment employing five different levels of agreement with statements about CDR engagement. The tool covers several different dimensions of CDR (Fig. 7) (PricewaterhouseCoopers, 2025a).

3.4 Responsabilité Numérique des Entreprises

The Digital Responsibility Questionnaire, created as part of a Swiss research project (Direction générale du développement économique, de la recherche et de l'innovation (DG DERI), 2024), currently exists only in French but can be translated automatically with an external tool. This questionnaire tool allows companies to evaluate their maturity in terms of CDR through a self-assessment format in more depth compared to the tool by PwC. With a structured approach featuring five

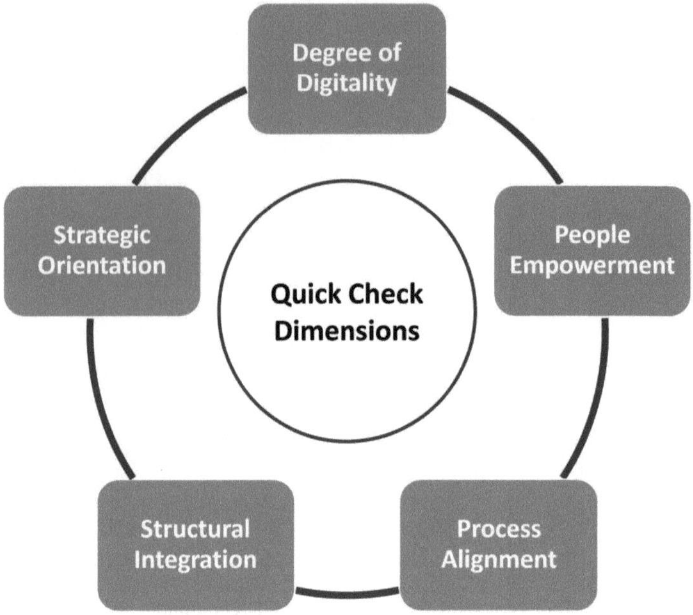

Fig. 7 Excerpt from the Corporate Digital Responsibility and Digital Ethics – Quick Check (based on PricewaterhouseCoopers, 2025b)

response levels, the questionnaire not only helps organizations determine their current CDR maturity but also provides actionable recommendations for improvement based on scientific findings (Thelisson et al., 2019).

Furthermore, it calculates maturity scores overall and within specific areas, offering standardized guidance to enhance CDR engagement. This enables companies to measure their internal efforts, even when those initiatives have not yet been publicly disclosed (Fig. 8) (Direction générale du développement économique, de la recherche et de l'innovation (DG DERI), 2024).

3.5 CDR Now Tool

The CDR Now Tool (Carl et al., 2024b) serves as another digital resource for companies to conduct internal assessments of their CDR engagement. It is designed for organizations at various stages of CDR development, from those beginning to implement a CDR strategy to those already active in CDR who seek to evaluate their progress. The tool presents users with questions that can only be answered with "yes" or "no," facilitating a categorization into different CDR maturity levels while aiming to reduce the risk of overestimating their efforts, as is potentially the case in self-assessments that openly communicate the different

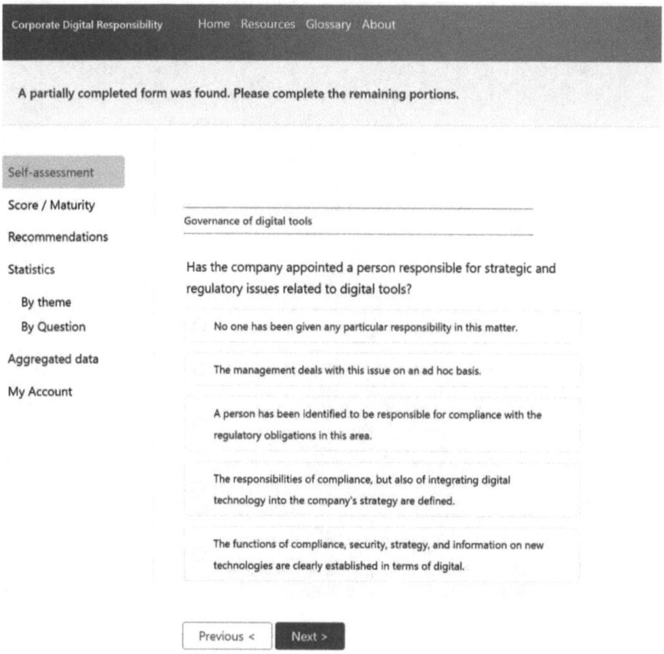

Fig. 8 Excerpt from the self-assessment questionnaire, translated in English (Direction générale du développement économique, de la recherche et de l'innovation (DG DERI), 2024)

levels. It employs a five-level framework for evaluation, resulting in a CDR maturity score that reflects both specific areas of engagement and an overall assessment. This scoring system provides companies with insights into their current CDR status and highlights potential areas for future resource allocation (Fig. 9) (Carl et al., 2024b).

3.6 CDR Maturity Model

Researchers from France proposed a descriptive CDR Maturity Model, suggesting where an organization should develop its capabilities for CDR (Rugeviciute & Courboulay, 2024). This tool builds on five main dimensions with a total of 18 subordinate focus areas, using one-dimensional scales for assessment. Similar to other CDR tools, this approach also employs different levels of CDR maturity – in this case six different levels: (i) nonexistent, (ii) initial awareness, (iii) reactive measures, (iv) proactive and standardized measures, (v) continuous and measured improvement, and (vi) industry leadership and innovation (Rugeviciute & Courboulay, 2024). Figure 10 depicts the dimensions and focus areas of the CDR Maturity Model.

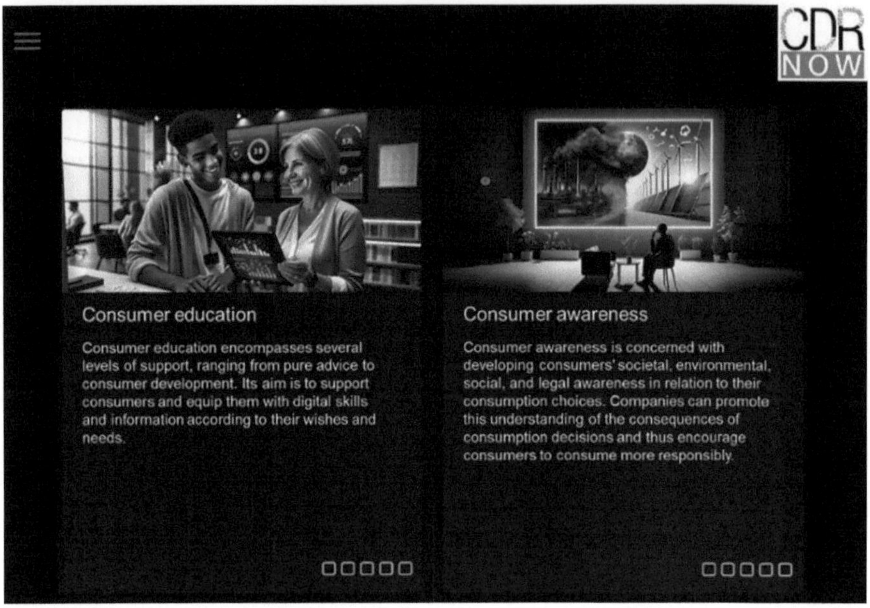

Fig. 9 Excerpt from the CDR Now Tool user interface (Carl et al., 2024b, p. 1581)

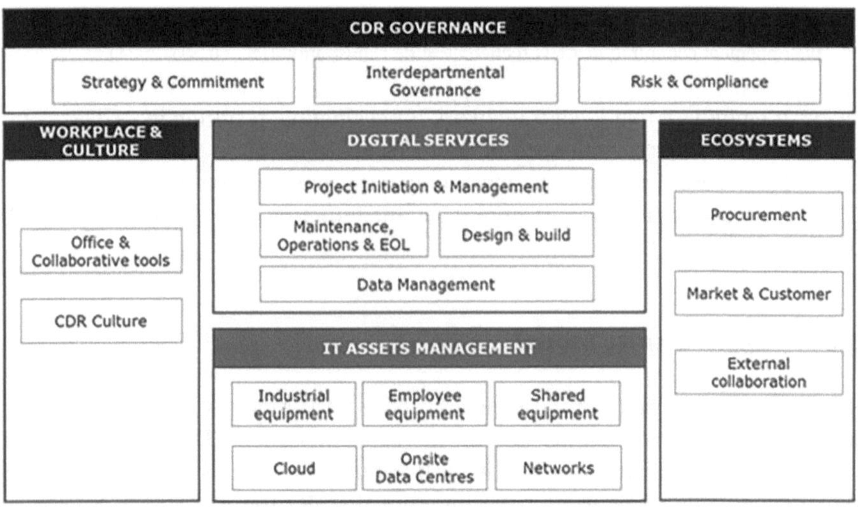

Fig. 10 The CDR Maturity Model (Rugeviciute & Courboulay, 2024, p. 93)

3.7 Ethos Advisor

The Ethos Advisor by WiseWay (Dörr, 2024) is designed to support businesses in integrating sustainable practices into their operations within the digital and tech sectors. Currently, this tool is in a concept prototype stage, testing user acceptance and its relevance in practice. This tool provides a conversational approach to understanding the importance of responsibility and sustainability in the context of technological advancement and outlines (concrete) steps for effective implementation, specifically tailored to the context of the approaching company (if wished).

The Ethos Advisor is a GPT-based service that supports CDR and sustainability experts of different experience levels. It is based on ChatGPT (by OpenAI) and specifically trained with expert knowledge from Dr. Saskia Dörr. Furthermore, the tool allows for the validation of these automated insights through collaboration with WiseWay. This combination of AI-generated recommendations and expert validation aims to assist organizations in developing and refining their sustainability strategies. By facilitating access to both immediate insights and deeper analyses, the Ethos Advisor supports companies in navigating their responsibility and sustainability challenges (Fig. 11) (Dörr, 2024).

3.8 Commonalities and Differences

The presented tools range from facilitating the initial approach to CDR (e.g., the CDR Starter Kit) to supporting more advanced CDR initiatives in companies (e.g., the Ethos Advisor). Some tools even employ a measuring approach to evaluate the status quo of CDR engagement, automatically (e.g., the CDR-CAT Tool) or as a self-assessment (e.g., the CDR Now Tool, the CDR Maturity Model).

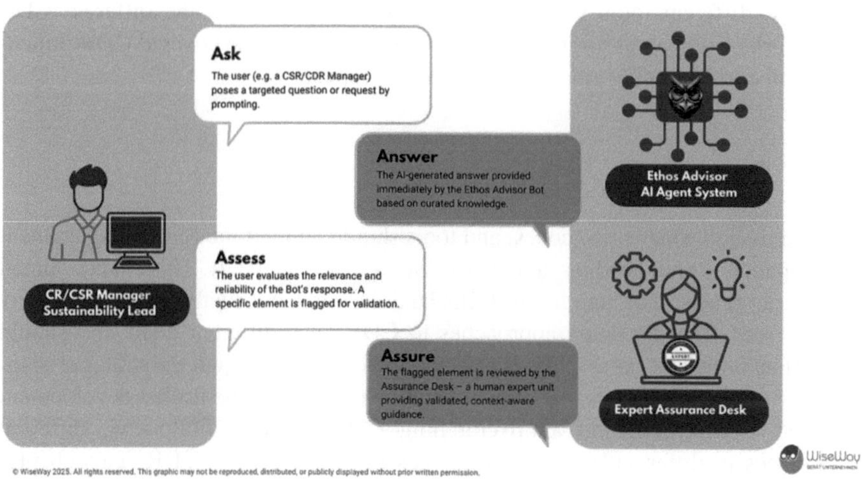

Fig. 11 Ethos Advisor interaction loop (illustration by Saskia Dörr, all rights reserved)

Companies initially approaching the topic of CDR can start with the CDR Starter Kit to develop a first understanding of what CDR actually is, what it can look like, and potentially already imagine how to pursue CDR themselves. This tool is especially supportive for developing basic knowledge needed to enable companies to devise a CDR strategy themselves.

Building on this basic understanding, companies might want to assess their status quo before developing further CDR activities and formalizing a CDR strategy. For a quick evaluation of the status quo, companies can choose an automated approach based on their website data, using the CDR-CAT tool, for example. If an internal perspective is to be analyzed independently of communication, the Corporate Digital Responsibility and Digital Ethics – Quick Check tool helps gain a quick initial insight into the present CDR commitment. It may also be useful to link these two tools in order to check, as a first step, whether the internal perspective and external communication are aligned.

When diving deeper into developing further CDR activities and a potential CDR strategy, a more comprehensive analysis of current CDR engagement and corresponding further development can be helpful. The Responsabilité Numérique des Entreprises tool, the CDR Now Tool, and the CDR Maturity Model can enable a structured approach to a more thorough analysis from the internal perspective. Those three tools follow different systematizations of CDR and therefore emphasize different aspects of responsibility in a digital world. Based on the derived evaluation of the current CDR commitment, companies can develop future CDR activities and foster improvement in specific dimensions of CDR. Especially for the further development of CDR activities, their refinement, and actual implementation, the Ethos Advisor can be a sparring partner, supporting the process and refining ideas.

To sum up, all presented tools can be helpful in different stages of a CDR strategy development and the analysis of the status quo of CDR engagement and developing future activities. Based on the existing expertise on CDR in the applying company, different tools might be most suitable. Similar to the different CDR frameworks, companies might also choose tools based on the covered CDR dimensions and corresponding emphasis on different aspects.

4 Outlook

The discussed frameworks, codes, and tools should support the further engagement of companies – both newbies and pros – with the topic of CDR. This chapter aimed to provide some sort of map for the CDR landscape to navigate the emerging variety of resources. The discussed approaches to CDR have different goals and should support an initial access to CDR, the evaluation of the status quo, the strategic adaptation of internal decisions, the implementation of CDR, or the further development of CDR engagement and an overarching CDR strategy. Following, different approaches fit different purposes and needs in the context of CDR. This chapter should support especially practitioners in discovering the most suitable approach to CDR and identifying helpful resources. Mapping the landscape of CDR should add tools and frameworks to practitioners' toolboxes, thereby enhancing and easing CDR engagement in practice. Further, systematizing different frameworks, codes, and tools should encourage further efforts from research and practice to add to the CDR toolbox and develop complementary tools and frameworks, fostering a further democratization of CDR knowledge. For example, specific frameworks providing step-by-step pathways for enhancing CDR strategies can be helpful, coupled with a better empirical understanding of successful CDR initiatives (e.g., employing case studies and real-world examples that illustrate successful applications). Further, the development of predictive tools, like simulations, can potentially support companies in assessing risks associated with their digital practices and the effects of CDR engagement in the future.

Competing Interests The authors have no conflicts of interest to declare that are relevant to the content of this chapter.

References

Bundesverband Digitale Wirtschaft e.V. (2023). CDR Building Bloxx. Bundesverband Digitale Wirtschaft (BVDW) e.V. Retrieved August 31, 2025, from https://www.cdr-building-bloxx.com/

Bundesverband Digitale Wirtschaft e.V. (2025). *CDR Building Bloxx*. Bundesverband Digitale Wirtschaft (BVDW) e.V. Retrieved August 31, 2025, from https://www.cdr-building-bloxx.com/

Carl, K. V., & Hinz, O. (2024). What we already know about corporate digital responsibility in IS research: A review and conceptualization of potential CDR activities. *Electronic Markets, 34*(27). https://doi.org/10.1007/s12525-024-00708-0

Carl, K. V., Arnold, T., Medzhybovska, N., Gurevych, I., & Hinz, O. (2024a). Wie können Corporate-Digital-Responsibility-Aktivitäten gemessen werden? Ein Ansatz mit Hilfe eines automatisierten Tools. *Transfer – Zeitschrift Für Kommunikation Und Markenmanagement, 70*(2), 46–51.

Carl, K. V., Hauer, M. P., & Arnold, T. (2024b). Are we still on track with our responsibility strategy? Introducing an internal assessment of corporate digital responsibility engagement. In *Proceedings of the INFORMATIK 2024* (pp. 1573–1585). https://doi.org/10.18420/inf2024_137

Carl, K. V., Blachetta, M., Bilfinger, B., Brink, A., Cerulli-Harms, A. K., Christ, A.-S., et al. (2025). Establishing common ground in corporate digital responsibility: Integrating understandings, definitions, and expert perspectives. In *Proceedings of the INFORMATIK 2025*. (pp. 1415–1428). Gesellschaft für Informatik e.V. https://doi.org/10.18420/inf2025_125

ConPolicy GmbH. (2023). *Gemeinsam Verantwortung übernehmen – Die CDR-Initiative*. Corporate Digital Responsibility Initiative. Retrieved August 31, 2025, from https://cdr-initiative.de/initiative

Direction générale du développement économique, de la recherche et de l'innovation (DG DERI). (2024). *Responsabilité Numérique des Entreprises*. Retrieved August 31, 2025, from https://digital-responsibility.info/

Dörr, S. (2024, February 8). *Welcome to Ethos Advisor*. WiseWay BERÄT UNTERNEHMEN. Retrieved August 31, 2025, from https://wiseway.de/ethos-advisor/

Identity Valley Research gGmbH. (2023). *A digital world built on trust and responsibility*. Identity Valley Research gGmbH. Retrieved August 31, 2025, from https://identityvalley.eu/drg

Price, R. (2023). *Corporate digital responsibility manifesto*. Corporate Digital Responsibility. Retrieved August 31, 2025, from https://corporatedigitalresponsibility.net/cdr-manifesto

PricewaterhouseCoopers. (2025a). *Corporate Digital Responsibility (CDR)*. PwC. Retrieved August 31, 2025, from https://www.pwc.de/de/cloud-digital/digital/digitale-transformation/corporate-digital-responsibility-cdr.html

PricewaterhouseCoopers. (2025b). *Digital ethics*. PwC. Retrieved August 31, 2025, from https://www.pwc.de/en/sustainability/digital-ethics.html

Project CDR-CAT. (2024). *CDR-CAT WebApp*. Retrieved August 31, 2025, from https://cdr-cat.ukp.informatik.tu-darmstadt.de/

Rugeviciute, A., & Courboulay, V. (2024). Empowering organizations for sustainable digitalization: A corporate digital responsibility maturity model approach. In *Proceedings of the 10th International Conference on ICT for Sustainability* (pp. 87–98).

Swiss Digital Initiative. (2024). *CDR Starter Kit*. Retrieved August 31, 2025, from https://swiss-digital-initiative.org/corporate-digital-responsibility/

Thelisson, E., Morin, J.-H., & Rochel, J. (2019). AI governance: Digital responsibility as a building block: Towards an index of digital responsibility. *Delphi Interdisciplinary Review of Emerging Technologies, 2*(4), 167–178. https://doi.org/10.21552/delphi/2019/4/6

K. Valerie Carl is a postdoctoral researcher at the chair of information systems and information management at Goethe University Frankfurt. She is interested in research on (corporate) digital responsibility, artificial intelligence (particularly human–AI augmentation), digital resilience, and digital ecosystems.

Operationalizing Corporate Digital Responsibility (CDR) Through Reporting: A CSRD Assessment of Convergence, Resonance, and Divergence

Anna-Sophia Christ and Anna Wannhoff

Abstract

As digital technologies transform how companies create value, Corporate Digital Responsibility (CDR) has emerged as a response to both the risks and opportunities of the digital realm. However, despite the normative importance of, for example, transparent algorithms, green IT, or responsible AI, practical applications remain limited. Additionally, scholars and practitioners continue to debate the boundaries between CDR and corporate social responsibility (CSR) matters, leaving the scope and relevance of CDR unclear for many stakeholders. This chapter addresses these ambiguities. We derived 27 CDR dimensions through a content analysis of six CDR frameworks and synthesized them with the 82 disclosure requirements of the European Union's Corporate Sustainability Reporting Directive (CSRD). Our analysis yielded 13 dimensions showing convergence, 9 dimensions demonstrating resonance, and 11 dimensions indicating divergence, based on which we propose a pathway for operationalizing CDR into reporting structures. Through the synthesis of CDR and CSRD, our chapter advances theoretical understanding of CDR and proposes how established reporting measures can enhance CDR in practice, recognizing that reporting primarily ensures mandatory transparency rather than actual performance achievements.

A.-S. Christ (✉)
Business, Innovation, and Transformation Institute (BIT), University of Bremen, Bremen, Germany
e-mail: achrist@uni-bremen.de

A. Wannhoff
Munich Business School, Munich, Germany
e-mail: anna.wannhoff@munich-business-school.de

A.-S. Christ (ed.), *Corporate Digital Responsibility*, Future of Business and Finance, https://doi.org/10.1007/978-3-032-14793-6_5

1 Introduction

The accelerated digital transformation of the global economy has reshaped organizational structures, business models, and stakeholder interactions, for instance, big data analytics in procurement processes, AI-based decision-making, or service robotics in customer service. While these technologies have unlocked substantial opportunities for innovation and efficiency, they have also brought about complex ethical, social, and environmental impacts (Ngereja et al., 2024; Zimmer et al., 2023). Issues such as algorithmic bias, digital surveillance, and the carbon footprint of digital infrastructures have made it increasingly clear that companies cannot treat digital transformation as a value-neutral process. Instead, business decision-makers must actively govern and scrutinize digital technologies in terms of their broader societal impacts (Christmann et al., 2024; Ologeanu-Taddei et al., 2024).

Against this backdrop, the concept of Corporate Digital Responsibility (CDR) has gained traction as a framework, encompassing principles and practices that guide companies in the ethical and sustainable use of digital technologies (Lobschat et al., 2021; Wirtz et al., 2023). CDR exceeds compliance requirements, like data protection laws, by making proactive commitments to responsible digital practices, including data fairness, responsible AI, and algorithmic transparency (Carl & Hinz, 2024; Mueller, 2022). Scholars emphasize that taking digital responsibility requires a multidimensional approach, spanning internal governance structures, technological design practices, and external stakeholder engagement (Urban & Plattfaut, 2025; Mueller, 2022; Wright & Kreissl, 2014) beyond risk mitigation toward value-led digital business (Martin, 2022).

Through the discourse, several frameworks have emerged to articulate and govern the notion of CDR matters. These include nonprofit codes (e.g., Digital Responsibility Goals by Identity Valley (2025)), initiative manifestos (e.g., CDR Building Bloxx by the BVDW (2025)), and academic models (e.g., Responsibility Clusters by Dörr (2021)) that define thematic dimensions, obligations, and risks and opportunities. However, while some promising pioneering CDR measures emerged in practice (e.g., Principles at Risk Assessment at Merck KGaA; CDR Council of the Weleda AG), companies have not yet reached a broad impact scope (Christ, 2025; Merbecks, 2023), and researchers have not yet progressed sufficiently in transforming normative concepts into (empirical studies on) practical implementation (Carl & Hinz, 2024; Mueller, 2022).

While the concept of CDR has only recently emerged as a distinct field of inquiry, scholars build on related fields, such as corporate social responsibility (CSR). The discourse on interdependencies and overlaps is ongoing (Christ et al., 2024; Dörr, 2021) with publications proposing extensions of the CSR concept to the digital realm (e.g., Herden et al., 2021; Wade, 2020) and others examining specific differences (e.g., Lobschat et al., 2021; Mihale-Wilson et al., 2022). The chapter builds on this interdependence and adds to the theoretical puzzle by further investigating potential synergies between CDR and CSR matters to advance the distinction of CDR principles and their applicability in practice. In our chapter, we pursue this by synthesizing a selection of CDR frameworks with the Corporate Sustainability

Reporting Directive (CSRD) (European Parliament and Council of the EU, 2022). The legal requirement introduced by the European Union in 2023 becomes progressively binding for companies operating within the EU. Accordingly, the CSRD shapes how business decision-makers conceptualize and address their broader corporate responsibility obligations. Following the discourse that the digital domain constitutes a new context for CSR matters (e.g., Dörr, 2021; Lobschat et al., 2021), we pose the following research question: *To what extent does the CSRD encompass CDR dimensions, and where do limitations or gaps remain?*

Through this synthesis of CDR matters and CSR reporting, our chapter makes a twofold contribution: First, we advance the theoretical understanding of CDR by categorizing a list of matters (dimensions) into convergence, resonances, and divergences relative to established corporate responsibility reporting categories. Second, we derive implications and limitations for how CSR reporting can be leveraged to strengthen the long-term effectiveness of CDR obligations. Specifically, we discuss the limitations of corporate reporting as an operationalization measure, since the CSRD merely compels companies to examine their impact and make their performance transparent, but does not directly require them to achieve specific goals or adhere to boundaries.

The remainder of this chapter is structured as follows. The next section provides a conceptual introduction to CDR and the developments in corporate responsibility reporting, followed by our methodological process. Afterward, the results section presents, first, the CDR dimensions we derived and, second, the results of the synthesis analysis on CDR and the CSRD. Closing, we discuss the applicability of a CDR-integrated CSRD and propose a way forward.

2 Corporate Digital Responsibility (CDR) Foundation and Frameworks

As an academic field, CDR has evolved rapidly over the past 5 years, situated at the intersection of business ethics, corporate management, and information and communication technologies (Bednárová & Serpeninova, 2023; Knopf & Pick, 2023). Scholars have proposed several CDR definitions since then (e.g., Lobschat et al., 2021; Merbecks, 2023; Wade, 2020), culminating in a recent consensus-oriented effort by scholars, practitioners, and subject experts: "*CDR stands for holistic responsible corporate action with regard to the impact of digital technologies and data*" (Carl et al., 2025, p. 11). This definition emphasizes the responsibility of companies not only for technologies but also for data, thereby situating CDR within the broader corporate responsibility discourse. So far, researchers have approached the integration of digital concerns into corporate responsibility with varying conceptual alignments. Some scholars argue for embedding CDR matters into existing CSR frameworks (e.g., Orbik & Zozul'aková, 2019; Thelisson et al., 2019), while others advocate for a distinct conceptualization (e.g., Lobschat et al., 2021; Mihale-Wilson et al., 2022). To date, involved stakeholders have not reached a consensus on this relationship, leaving a theoretical puzzle to which the present study contributes to advance the scoping of CDR matters on a principle level and the implementation in practice.

Generally, scholars experience the current research landscape of CDR as fragmented. The majority of researchers focused largely on conceptual contributions, such as identifying relevance (e.g., Wirtz et al., 2023), defining impact categories (e.g., Thorun et al., 2017), or specifying actors and processes (e.g., Lobschat et al., 2021). However, more recently, some scholars brought forward empirical studies, including the *CDR Maturity Model* by Rugeviciute and Courboulay (2024), qualitative company cases (e.g., Christ, 2025; Merbecks, 2023), and performance-oriented analysis (e.g., Oduro et al., 2024; Zhu et al., 2025). These first movers signal a shift from descriptive accounts toward the generation of theory-driven and action-oriented insights grounded in empirical evidence.

Furthermore, early, Mueller (2022) introduced a conceptual distinction that outlines two domains within CDR: the normative level, which addresses the principles guiding responsible behavior in the digital context, and the governance level, which involves how these principles are applied in organizations. This study seeks to integrate both domains. It first examines the normative level by considering what constitutes CDR matters in relation to broader CSR matters and then considers how these findings can be operationalized. Recently, a few scholars already started exploring synergies and gaps between CSR and CDR reporting, in pursuit of transparency and standardization, highlighting the limited disclosure of digital responsibility. Examples include the DAX20 investigation by Merbecks (2023), the examination of DIN ISO 26000 for integration potential by Carl et al. (2022), and the proposed performance indicators aligned with CSR by Weber-Lewerenz and Traverso (2025). However, much of the existing literature still emphasizes the instrumental use of digital technologies to enhance responsibility reporting (e.g., Appiah-Kubi et al., 2025; Pizzi et al., 2024), rather than addressing responsibilities arising directly from digitalization. Our study advances this discussion by focusing explicitly on CDR standardization in relation to the CSRD.

Parallel to academic discourse, practice-driven frameworks have proliferated and shaped both organizational practice and scholarly debate. Among them, four prominent frameworks are the following: the *CDR Code – Fields of Action,* developed by the CDR Initiative (2025). It represents an early government-backed initiative (Federal Ministry of Justice and Consumer Protection), offering normative legitimacy through voluntary commitments across participation, self-determination, fairness, and sustainability. The *CDR Building Bloxx* (BVDW, 2025) provides a modular toolkit with 136 building blocks for operationalizing CDR in corporate processes; however, its industry-driven origin limits policy endorsement. The CDR Manifesto (2021) articulates ten civil society principles for ethical digital conduct that serve as an aspirational compass rather than a procedural guide. The *Digital Responsibility Goals* (Identity Valley, 2025), which adapted the UN SDGs to digitalization, set forward-looking objectives on privacy, literacy, and trustworthy AI.

We understand these practice frameworks as complementary to research propositions such as the CDR Topics by Herden et al. (2021), the Responsibility Clusters by Dörr (2021), or the DR Principles by Trier et al. (2023). Taken together, these scholarly and practice-driven developments illustrate both the conceptual richness and the persistent fragmentation of the CDR discourse. For this study, we will focus on the conceptualization of CDR on the dimension, principle, or category level, scoping areas of digital responsibility topics. Other CDR conceptualization approaches, such as the *CDR Cultural Model* by Lobschat et al. (2021), the *CDR Maturity Model* by Rugeviciute and Courboulay (2024), or the *Ecosystem Model* by Wirtz et al. (2023), focus on the CDR steering level and are thus rather of indirect relevance for the further situating of our study in the CDR discourse.

3 Corporate Social Responsibility (CSR) and Corporate Reporting

CSR has already become a subject of academic inquiry, public discourse, and corporate strategy during the second half of the twentieth century – a period marked by rapid economic growth accompanied by significant social and environmental externalities (Lee, 2008). Growing public awareness led to the release of the influential Brundtland Report (1987), defining sustainable development as "development that meets the needs of the present without compromising the ability of future generations to meet their own needs" (p.41). For scholars and practitioners, this definition has since become a cornerstone in corporate responsibility discourse, extending the scope of stakeholders to be considered to future generations.

Parallel, scholars informed the CSR discourse with key conceptual frameworks from early on: the CSR-Pyramid (Carroll, 1991), categorizing corporate responsibilities into four tiers (economic, legal, ethical, and philanthropic) and the Triple Bottom Line (Elkington, 1998), emphasizing the need for organizations to balance economic, environmental, and social responsibilities and corporate social performance (CPS) as the "configuration of principles of social responsibility, processes of social responsiveness, and policies, programs, and observable outcomes" (Wood, 1991, p. 693). However, the holistic and balanced approach to corporate conduct became neither a prominent voluntary reality for scholars nor for practitioners. Consequently, CSR was increasingly pushed forward through mandatory regulatory levers (Haack et al., 2012; Trittin-Ulbrich, 2023).

In practice, the first translations of corporate responsibility operationalization into corporate management were, for instance, done through the voluntary DIN ISO 14001 (2015), standardizing environmental management systems already in the 1990s and the German Sustainability Code (German Council for Sustainable Development, 2025) introduced in 2001 and continuously developed since. However, legal obligations for nonfinancial reporting began only in 2004 with the implementation of the EU Amendment Directive 2003/51 (Modernization Directive) through the Accounting Law Reform Act (European Union, 2023). Large corporations were compelled to examine their impact and to disclose relevant nonfinancial performance indicators in their management reports, particularly regarding environmental and employee matters.

About 10 years later, developments, particularly in the wake of the euro crisis and growing pressure for corporate transparency, led to an expansion of nonfinancial reporting requirements. Directive 2014/95/EU – the Non-Financial Reporting Directive (NFRD) – introduced a binding obligation for large public-interest entities with over 500 employees to disclose nonfinancial and diversity information, particularly concerning environmental, social, employee, human rights, and anti-corruption matters (European Union, 2014). Meanwhile, at the global level, the 17 Sustainable Development Goals (SDGs), adopted by the United Nations (2015), became emblematic of the shared sustainability agenda. Both governments and corporations aligned their strategies with these goals, setting voluntary responsibility targets in the form of an "Agenda 2030." However, the nonbinding nature of the SDGs allowed entities to set and pursue objectives at their discretion, with no legal consequences for failing to meet compliance.

Consequently, in another attempt to progress corporate responsibility objectives, on the EU level, reporting regulations were further tightened and the scope extended, resulting in the currently assumed most significant advancement in responsibility reporting, the CSRD (European Parliament and Council of the EU, 2022), enacted as of 2023, replacing the NFRD. The reporting scope of the CSRD is defined by the twelve European Sustainability Reporting Standards (ESRS) (Regulation, 2023/2772). Divided into two cross-cutting standards (ESRS 1 and 2), five environmental standards (ESRS E1–E5), four social standards (ESRS S1–S4), and one governance standard (ESRS G1), the overall reporting scope comprises a total of 82 disclosure requirements (DR) and additional reporting conditions on objective, metrics, and impact (Fig. 1). As such, the CSRD scope is closely tied to the ESG concept (Environmental, Social, and Governance) which originates from the finance discipline and has become a decisive set of investment criteria alongside traditional

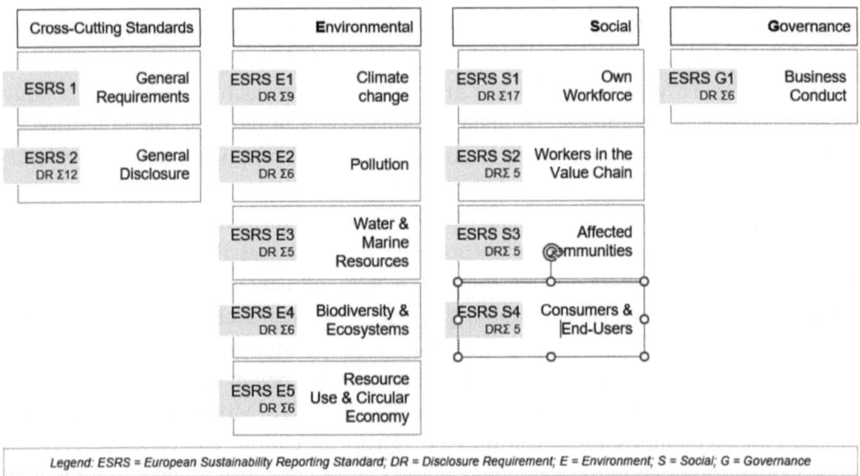

Fig. 1 Overview of European Sustainability Reporting Standards. (Authors' illustration based on Directive 2023/2772)

financial metrics (Friede et al., 2015). This alignment reflects a broader shift toward corporate responsibility, requiring companies to articulate and disclose concrete responsibility objectives that extend across the entire value chain, beyond their own operations and even beyond European borders.

The CSRD signals a clear shift from voluntary initiatives to a strong regulatory framework for most companies, placing the EU's corporate responsibility reporting among the most comprehensive and standardized worldwide. It also responds directly to the ongoing shortfall in meeting established responsibility targets (e.g., SDGs) and that CSR activities are still strongly perceived as greenwashing and nice to have (Brower & Dacin, 2020; Haack et al., 2012). However, it is essential to note that the CSRD and overall reporting focus on mandatory transparency, not mandatory performance. Companies are not required to meet responsibility obligations, but they must report thoroughly and honestly about how sustainable (or not) they are and what actions they are taking. Hence, it can be regarded only as an indirect measure of operationalization. While it obligates companies to examine and disclose their impacts, it does not require them to act upon the findings. Any subsequent measures depend largely on the moral commitment of the companies themselves or on (external) stakeholders who may exert pressure for change.

4 Methodology

In pursuit of building synthesized coherence (Locke & Golden-Biddle, 1997) between CDR dimensions and corporate responsibility reporting, we applied a two-stage research approach. First, we adopted a five-step qualitative document analysis (Bowen, 2009; Mayring, 2015) of six prominent CDR frameworks to derive a consolidated set of CDR dimensions. Using a content analysis approach (Hsieh & Shannon, 2005), we applied a three-level inductive coding structure, moving iteratively from first-order codes to second-order themes and ultimately to aggregate dimensions (Gioia et al., 2013; Thomas, 2006). Our methodological approach combines the open exploration of concepts with theory-informed categorization to ensure both conceptual richness and analytical coherence (Myers & Newman, 2007).

Second, to structure the comparison and surface omissions, we followed the research method of a General Morphological Analysis (GMA) (Ritchey, 2018) to investigate the relationship of convergence, resonance, and divergence between CDR and the CSRD. Our research approach is exploratory in purpose (Stebbins, 2001) and theory-informed in execution, leveraging established concepts to advance the operationalization of CDR within responsibility reporting (Locke & Golden-Biddle, 1997). By intentionally including practice frameworks and official policies, we have a multifaceted impact at the interface of research, practice, and policy (Wickert et al., 2020), tailored to the already transdisciplinary CDR discourse.

4.1 Content Analysis of Six CDR Frameworks

Step 1. Define Sample We defined a "convenience sample" (Etikan et al., 2016) of six CDR frameworks. The approach is applied in exploratory research when targeting information-rich and context-relevant sources. We selected the six frameworks based on their prominence in the European discourse, conceptual level, accessibility, and diversity of institutional origins, thereby ensuring representation from policy, industry, civil society, and academia. This pluralistic selection allowed us to identify redundancies and overlaps, as well as the detection of unique thematic contributions. The selected frameworks are the *CDR Fields of Action* from the CDR Initiative (2025), the *CDR Building Bloxx* proposed by the CDR Committee of the BVDW (2025), the CDR Manifesto (2021) from a community of CDR experts, the *Digital Responsibility Goals* (DRG) developed by Identity Valley (2025), the *CDR Clusters* proposed by Dörr (2021), and the *CDR Topics* compiled by Herden et al. (2021). Hereinafter referred to only by the italicized framework title.

Step 2. Identify Sources We assessed and extracted the relevant source material in June 2025. Each framework included an explicit list of CDR-related dimensions, which were developed either through expert discourse or scientific studies. For the analysis, we considered both the dimension labels and their accompanying descriptions, as a label-only comparison was deemed insufficient due to significant variation in terminology and definitional depth. This method allowed us to concentrate on the core meaning of each dimension instead of superficial wording, enhancing comparability across the framework texts. Through an iterative reassessment, we determined that the source scope provides coherent insights across the sample (Sarker et al., 2013).

Step 3. Code Data For the coding of data, we conducted the following established qualitative research procedure (Gioia et al., 2013; Strauss & Corbin, 1998). The process encompassed three analytical levels. First, we derived first-order concepts through open coding of each framework's content. This step resulted in the identification of 51 concepts for the *CDR Fields of Action*, 134 for the *CDR Building Bloxx*, 75 for the *CDR Manifesto*, 101 for the *DRGs*, 144 for the *CDR Clusters*, and 136 for the *CDR Topics*. Second, we broke down the first-order concepts into second-order themes by framing them in relation to corporate responsibility obligations, with a focus on identifying both similarities and differences across frameworks. Third, we abstracted the themes into 43 aggregate themes, deliberately keeping them broad to facilitate their formulation as overarching principles of corporate responsibility obligations. This process resulted in a final set of 27 aggregate dimensions, as we exemplarily presented in Table 2 (the ID column indicates the framework and respective code line). Through iterative discussion between the coders, the aggregate themes were aligned in pursuit of mutual exclusivity and collective exhaustivity, enabling the building of categories that are distinct but also capture the entire domain (Minto, 2009) (Fig. 2).

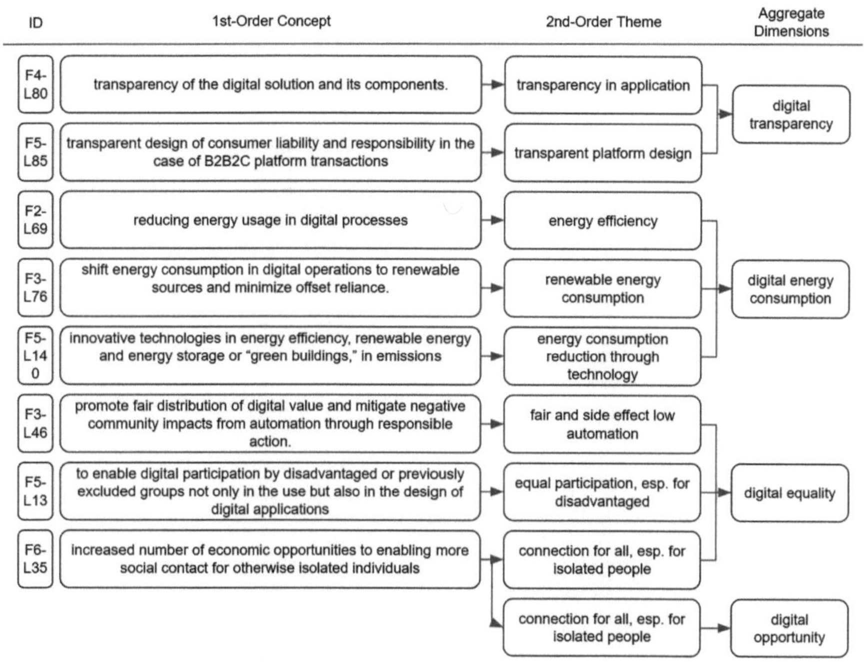

Fig. 2 Exemplary inductive coding results. (Authors' illustration oriented on Gioia et al. (2013))

Step 4. Determine Reliability Two independent coders double-coded all six frameworks, and measured their agreement using Cohen's Kappa (Cohen, 1960), which adjusts for chance agreement (McHugh, 2012). Across the CDR frameworks, results indicated substantial to almost perfect agreement based on the thresholds proposed by Landis and Koch (1977), confirming the robustness and reproducibility of the coding scheme. Our assessed detailed κ-values and observed agreement percentages are presented in Table 1. Disagreements were resolved through discussion, leading to refined category boundaries and clearer coding guidelines.

Step 5. Result Presentation We calculated the relative distribution of each aggregate dimension within and across the frameworks. We chose to do so to present the content analysis results using relative numbers to account for the different totals of coded lines per framework, as shown in step 3, which helps facilitate comparisons among the frameworks.

4.2 Modeling CDR-CSRD Synthesis

In our pursuit of synthesis between CDR, represented by the derived 27 aggregate dimensions, and corporate responsibility reporting categories, scoped by the CSRD, we followed the approach of a GMA (Ritchey, 2018). GMA is a structured research

Table 1 Inter-coder reliability results for the CDR framework analysis (own illustration, adapted from Rau and Shih (2021))

Framework	Total items	Agreements	Disagreements	Observed agreement (PoP_o)	Expected agreement (PeP_e)	Cohen's κ	Interpretation
CDR Fields of Action	51	48	3	0.9412	0.50	0.88	Almost perfect
CDR Building Bloxx	136	127	9	0.9338	0.50	0.87	Almost perfect
CDR Manifesto	81	74	7	0.9136	0.50	0.83	Almost perfect
DRGs	101	95	6	0.9406	0.50	0.88	Almost perfect
Responsibility Clusters	144	130	14	0.9028	0.50	0.81	Substantial – almost perfect
CDR Topics	136	126	10	0.9265	0.50	0.85	Almost perfect

technique for exploring multidimensional problem spaces and identifying gaps or overlaps between conceptual domains. As the inclusion criteria, we set the 82 ESRS disclosure requirements published in the Commission Delegated Regulation (EU) 2023/2772. We obtained the legal text of the ESRS, published in 2023, from the official EUR-Lex portal in June 2025. Since the "ESRS 1 General Requirements" serves more as the regulation's "user manual" on why, what, and how to report responsibility matters, no disclosure requirements are included; thus, we excluded the ESRS from the modeling.

Our modeling process assessed three possibilities for each aggregate dimension of CDR: (1) already addressed by an existing ESRS disclosure requirement (explicit synthesis = x), (2) could be integrated into the current structure (implicit synthesis = (x)), or (3) would necessitate the creation of a new disclosure requirement and/or standard (no synthesis = 0). It was also included if an aggregate dimension was not comprised by a framework (symbolized by /). We did the modeling manually using a structured two-dimensional matrix (Morphospace) in which each aggregate dimension (column) per CDR framework was evaluated for synthesis with the ESRS disclosure requirements (row). For the result presentation, we summarized the Morphospace on the level of the 12 ESRS for illustrative purposes in Table 2 below.

We conducted the analysis primarily at the level of the 27 aggregate dimensions of CDR, which were formulated as high-level and actionable principles. However, to ensure precision in alignment, we consistently referred back to the second-order themes from which the aggregates were derived, thereby preserving the original orientation and intent of each responsibility obligation (Gioia et al., 2013). This ensured that the modeling process remained systematic and consistent across all dimensions (Saldaña, 2021). For example, the aggregate dimension *AD13: Digital Literacy* demonstrated variation across frameworks in terms of stakeholder scope. In some frameworks, it was defined narrowly as an internal responsibility toward employees, aligning with "ESRS S1: Own Workforce" (Regulation, 2023/2772, pp. 191–236). Others adopted a broader scope encompassing external stakeholders, corresponding to "ESRS S3: Affected Communities" (Regulation, 2023/2772, pp. 256–272), while certain frameworks limited the focus to the upstream value chain of service and product users, aligning with "ESRS S4: Consumers and End-Users" (Regulation, 2023/2772, pp. 273–290). Throughout the process, we ensured transparency and traceability by systematically documenting each modeling decision in the Morphospace, including the coding rationale (explicit, implicit, or no synthesis). This allowed us to trace every decision back to the underlying framework codes and ESRS requirements, enabling replication or reanalysis. While qualitative judgment was unavoidable – particularly in assessing implicit connections – we mitigated subjectivity through assessing coding consistency using Cohen's kappa (Cohen, 1960).

Table 2 Distribution of CDR dimensions (authors' illustration)

	Within-framework distribution (%)						Cross-framework coverage	
Aggregate CDR dimensions	CDR fields of action	CDR Building Bloxx	CDR Manifesto	DRGs	CDR Clusters	CDR Topics	Relative share	Framework coverage
Σ codes	51	134	75	101	144	136	100%	n.a.
Σ AD	18	21	21	17	23	23	n.a.	123
AD01: Cybersecurity	5.88%	2.24%	2.67%	15.84%	/	4.41%	4.68%	5
AD02: Data Privacy	/	1.49%	4.00%	10.89%	2.08%	1.47%	3.28%	5
AD03: Data Protection	1.96%	/	1.33%	5.94%	4.86%	11.03%	4.68%	5
AD04: Digital Accessibility	5.88%	/	1.33%	2.97%	2.78%	5.15%	2.81%	5
AD05: Digital Accountability	/	14.93%	10.67%	3.96%	2.08%	8.82%	7.33%	5
AD06: Digital Climate Protection	1.96%	/	5.33%	0.99%	2.08%	/	1.40%	4
AD07: Digital Energy Consumption	1.96%	2.24%	4.00%	/	2.78%	2.94%	2.34%	5
AD08: Digital Ethics by Design	/	8.96%	5.33%	/	6.25%	3.68%	4.68%	4
AD09: Digital Ethics Policies	5.88%	7.46%	5.33%	/	/	2.94%	3.28%	4
AD10: Digital Explainability	/	/	/	2.97%	1.39%	2.21%	1.25%	3
AD11: Digital Fairness	5.88%	0.75%	4.00%	5.94%	4.17%	/	2.96%	5
AD12: Digital Integrity	/	3.73%	5.33%	3.96%	12.50%	2.21%	5.30%	5
AD13: Digital Literacy	11.76%	9.70%	4.00%	4.95%	6.25%	5.88%	6.86%	6
AD14: Digital Opportunity	1.96%	0.75%	6.67%	1.98%	3.47%	3.68%	2.96%	6
AD15: Digital Sovereignty	7.84%	1.49%	/	8.91%	3.47%	3.68%	3.90%	5
AD16: Digital Sustainability	5.88%	2.24%	4.00%	2.97%	/	/	1.87%	4
AD17: Digital Transparency	5.88%	9.70%	8.00%	12.87%	3.47%	5.88%	7.49%	6
AD18: Digital Waste	/	/	1.33%	0.99%	3.47%	7.35%	2.65%	4
AD19: Digital Well-Being	/	4.48%	1.33%	/	2.78%	5.15%	2.81%	4
AD20: Digital Work	3.92%	8.00%	/	/	4.86%	3.68%	3.12%	4
AD21: Ethical Data Economy	1.96%	/	/	/	0.69%	2.94%	0.94%	3

AD22: Ethical Data Handling	13.73%	0.75%	/	7.92%	0.69%	8.09%	4.37%	*5*
AD23: Human-Centered Technology	1.96%	4.48%	4.00%	5.94%	13.19%	1.47%	5.77%	*6*
AD24: Natural Resources for Technologies	/	0.75%	/	/	/	2.21%	0.62%	*2*
AD25: Regenerative Processes	3.92%	2.24%	5.33%	/	6.25%	/	2.81%	*4*
AD26: Responsible AI	/	0.75%	1.33%	/	0.69%	0.74%	0.62%	*4*
AD27: Stakeholder Engagement	11.76%	16.42%	14.67%	/	9.72%	4.41%	9.20%	*5*

5 Results on CDR Dimensions

Table 2 summarizes the results of the content analysis, the distribution of the CDR dimensions across the frameworks. In the left column, the 27 aggregate dimensions (AD) of CDR are listed. The middle section, structured by the six analyzed frameworks, covers the *Within-Framework Distribution*, showing how each CDR dimension is represented within a framework. Additionally, the second row displays the total of codes derived for a framework, and the third row shows the total of ADs within a framework. The right section presents the *Cross-Framework Coverage*, indicating the relative share of each dimension across all frameworks as well as the number of frameworks in which each dimension appears. Taken together, these results capture both the intensity)how strongly a dimension is emphasized within a framework) and the breadth (how widely it is represented across frameworks).

5.1 Within-Framework Distribution

Overall, we derived 27 ADs from the content analysis, of which not all are present in every framework. With a total of 23 ADs, the *CDR Clusters* and the *CDR Topics* frameworks cover the largest proportion. The *CDR Building Bloxx* comprises 21 ADs, while the *CDR Fields of Action* only contains 18 ADs, and the *DRGs* 17 ADs, as our analysis revealed. At the AD level, this corresponds to the total number of coded instances, ranging from 51 in the *CDR Fields of Action* and 75 in the *CDR Manifesto*, to 101 in the *DRGs*, 134 in the *CDR Building Bloxx*, 136 in the *CDR Topics*, and 144 in the *CDR Clusters*. The values in the *"Within-Framework Distribution (%)"* columns indicate the relative share of each AD within its framework. For example, *AD02: Data Privacy* accounts for 1.49% of all codes in the CDR Building Bloxx (2 AD codes / Σ 134 codes = 1.49%), reflecting its comparatively limited emphasis in this model.

Our analysis revealed distinct distributions of ADs within each framework, indicating differences in topic emphasis, but with limited extremes. Most of the ADs do not exceed five percent within a framework, yet together they account for more than half of the total ADs within each framework, except for the CDR Areas of Action, which resulted in a little less. Only up to three ADs within a framework surpass the ten percent threshold, suggesting focal tendencies within specific frameworks. For the *CDR Fields of Action*, the three ADs that stood out highlight a shared focus on stakeholders, their competencies, and data processing: *AD22: Ethical Data Handling* (13.73%), as well as AD13: Digital Literacy (11.76%) and *AD02: Stakeholder Engagement* (11.76%). In the *CDR Building Bloxx*, AD05: *Digital Accountability* (14.93%) and *AD27: Stakeholder Engagement* (16.42%) dominate, again emphasizing stakeholder involvement. The *CDR Manifesto* mirrors this pattern, with D05: *Digital Accountability* (10.67%) and *AD27: Stakeholder Engagement* (14.67%) prevailing. In contrast, the DRGs reveal different emphasis, with *AD01: Cybersecurity* (15.84%), *AD02: Data Privacy* (10.89%), and AD17: Digital Transparency (12.87%), pointing to a stronger security orientation complemented by transparency toward external parties. For the *CDR Clusters*, *AD12: Digital Integrity* (12.50%) and *AD23: Human-Centered Technology* (13.19%) dominate, underscoring ethical principles and human-centered design. While in the CDR Topics, only *AD03: Data Protection* (11.03%) exceeds ten percent, again reflecting a security orientation, but with a more balanced distribution of the remaining ADs.

The examples we highlighted here represent the most salient ADs within each framework. Overall, the comparison demonstrates that although all frameworks cover a broad range of CDR themes, their internal weighting varies considerably, reflecting different normative orientations, such as compliance, governance, participation, or human-centric design. Hence, we conclude that the difference in scope and intention of the frameworks leads to distinct perspectives on CDR dimensions. Thus, our analysis advances a comprehensive CDR understanding, but the applicability still depends on the user's intentions, business model, or industry.

5.2 Cross-Framework Coverage

The *Relative share* column indicates how much weight an AD carries in the overall dataset ($N = 641$ AD codes), and the *Framework coverage* column shows in how many of the six frameworks an AD was retrieved. Together, these measures allow us to distinguish between dimensions that are broadly recognized and those that remain niche.

No single AD exceeds ten percent of the total. The most prominent dimension overall is *AD27: Stakeholder Engagement,* with 9.20%, present in five frameworks. The next most frequent dimensions – all present in at least five frameworks – are *AD17: Digital Transparency* (7.49%), *AD05: Digital Accountability* (7.33%), *AD13: Digital Literacy* (6.86%), *AD23: Human-Centered Technology* (5.77%), and *AD12: Digital Integrity* (5.30%). The remaining 21 ADs each account for less than five percent of the dataset. At the lower end, *AD21: Ethical Data Economy* (0.94%), *AD26: Responsible AI* (0.62%), and *AD24: Natural Resources for Technologies* (0.62%) are the least frequent.

Comparable to their low frequency, they also have low framework coverage: *AD24* appears in only two frameworks, *AD21* in three, and *AD26* in four. By contrast, only four dimensions are present in all six frameworks: *AD13: Digital Literacy*, *AD14: Digital Opportunity*, *AD17: Digital Transparency*, and *AD23: Human-Centered Technology*. These can be seen as the shared "core set" of CDR dimensions. For the rest, 11 ADs are part of five frameworks, which is the biggest proportion, and nine ADs are part of four frameworks. The extensive framework coverage underscores the consistency of shared dimensions across the frameworks, with only a few niche topics unique to individual frameworks. These findings are in line with the selection approach, indicating that the frameworks conceptualize CDR from a comparable perspective but set different focus points, thereby reinforcing the dataset's coherence and enabling suitability for meaningful comparative analysis.

6 Results on CDR-CSRD Modeling

Table 3 provides an overview of the modeling results from the built synthesis on CDR-CSRD, distinguishing three possibilities. The explicitly synthesized ADs (CDR dimensions) are indicated by simply listing the AD (e.g., AD08) and the implicitly synthesized ADs by enclosing them in brackets (e.g., AD08). The third possibility, divergence, is not included in the table since no synthesis was built.

The identified divergence consists of nine CDR dimensions: *AD08: Digital Ethics by Design*, *AD10: Digital Explainability*, *AD11: Digital Fairness*, *AD14: Digital Opportunity*, *AD17: Digital Transparency*, *AD21: Ethical Data Economy*, *AD22: Ethical Data Handling*, *AD23: Human-Centered Technology*, and *AD26: Responsible AI*. The absence of these CDR dimensions in the ESRS disclosure requirements suggests a structural gap in current CSR reporting standards in addressing technology-specific corporate responsibilities. Although certain aspects (e.g., digital fairness, digital explainability) may be partially embeddable under existing disclosures, their explicit treatment remains limited. In the discussion section, we elaborate propositions for handling these divergences beyond the performed modeled synthesis.

6.1 CDR and CSRD Cross-Cutting Requirements Modeling

Since the "ESRS 1 General Requirements" (Regulation, 2023/2772, pp. 3–43) does not comprise any of the 82 disclosure requirements, we excluded it from the further analysis results presentation. Our analysis revealed five CDR dimensions with synthesis to "ESRS 2 General Disclosure" (Regulation, 2023/2772, pp. 44–77). As specified in the standards' name, the disclosure requirements are "cross-cutting" and therefore also part of other ESRS, leading to overlaps. The CSRD reporting format stipulates that these redundancies in application can be resolved through including references between the ESRS; we are taking the same approach in the following modeling.

Through the modeling process, we aligned three CDR dimensions *AD01: Cybersecurity* (included in all frameworks except the *CDR Clusters*), *AD02: Data Privacy* (included in all frameworks except the *CDR Fields of Action*), and *AD03: Data Protection* (included in all frameworks except the *CDR Building Bloxx*) explicitly with the disclosure requirements "GOV-5 Risk management and internal controls over sustainability reporting" (Regulation, 2023/2772, p. 52) and "SBM-3 – Material impacts, risks and opportunities and their interaction with strategy and business model" (Regulation, 2023/2772, p. 56). The topics of cybersecurity, data privacy, and protection are in many countries regulated through hard laws (e.g., GDPR, EU Cybersecurity Act) and soft laws (e.g., ISO/IEC 27001, IEEE Security and Privacy); thus, we discuss the comprehensiveness of the modeling further in the discussion section concerning the adequate relevance of positioning.

Table 3 CDR-CSRD modeling results on ESRS level (authors' illustration)

CDR frameworks CSRD	CDR fields of action		CDR Building Bloxx		CDR Manifesto		DRGs		CDR clusters		CDR topics	
ESRS 1 General Requirements	n.a.		n.a.		n.a.		n.a.		n.a.		n.a.	
ESRS 2 General Disclosures	AD01		AD01		AD01		AD01				AD01	
			AD02		AD02		AD02		AD02		AD02	
	AD03				AD03		AD03		AD03		AD03	
			AD05		AD05				AD05			
	AD27		AD27		AD27				AD27		AD27	
ESRS E1 Climate Change	(AD06) AD07	(AD16)	AD07	/AD16)	(AD06) AD07	(AD16)	(AD06)	(AD16)	(AD06) AD07		AD07	
ESRS E2 Pollution	/		/		/		/		/		/	
ESRS E3 Water and Marine Resources	/		/		/		/		/		/	
ESRS E4 Biodiversity and Ecosystems	(AD25)		(AD24) (AD25)		(AD25)		(AD18)		(AD18) (AD25)		(AD18) (AD24)	
ESRS E5 Resource Use and Circular Economy	(AD25)		(AD24) (AD25)		(AD25)		AD18		AD18 (AD25)		AD18 AD24	
ESRS S1 Own Workforce	AD13 AD20		AD13 AD19 AD20		/	(AD13)	/	(AD13)	AD13 AD19 AD20	(AD13)	AD13 AD20	(AD13)
ESRS S2 Workers in the Value Chain	/		/		/		/		/		/	
ESRS S3 Affected Communities	/		/		/		/		/		/	
ESRS S4 Consumer and End-Users	(AD04) (AD15)		(AD13) (AD15)		(AD04)		(AD04) (AD15)		(AD04) (AD15)		(AD04) (AD15)	
ESRS G1 Business Conduct	AD09		AD05 AD09 (AD12)		AD05 AD09 (AD12)		AD05 (AD12)		AD05 (AD12)		AD05 AD09 (AD12)	

AD05: Digital Accountability, regarding roles and responsibilities, is part of four frameworks (*CDR Building Bloxx*, *CDR Manifesto*, *CDR Clusters*), and we aligned it explicitly with "GOV-1 – The role of the administrative, management and supervisory bodies" (Regulation, 2023/2772, p. 49). However, the frameworks also include cultural aspects, which is why we modeled *AD05* also to "ESRS G1 Business Conduct" (Regulation, 2023/2772, pp. 291–301). Moreover, we aligned *AD27: Stakeholder Engagement*, included in all frameworks except the *DRGs*, explicitly with the disclosure requirement "SBM2– Interests and views of stakeholders" (Regulation, 2023/2772, p. 55). The more nuanced evaluation of the second-order themes goes beyond the scope of the CSRD, and we further address it in the discussion section.

6.2 CDR and CSRD Environmental Requirement Modeling

We modeled six CDR dimensions against the ESRS environmental disclosure requirements. Of the six, we aligned two CDR dimensions with "ESRS E1 Climate Change" (Regulation, 2023/2772, pp. 78–123): *AD06: Digital Climate Protection,* present in four frameworks (*CDR Areas of Action*, *CDR Manifesto*, *DRGs*, *CDR Clusters*), we implicitly modeled to the steering requirements "E1-1 – Transition Plan for Climate Change Mitigation" (Regulation, 2023/2772, p. 82), "E1-2 – Policies Related to Climate Change Mitigation and Adaptation" (Regulation, 2023/2772, p. 84), "E1-3 – Actions and Resources in Relation to Climate Change Policies" (Regulation, 2023/2772, p. 84), and "E1-4 – Targets Related to Climate Change Mitigation and Adaptation" (Regulation, 2023/2772, p. 85). We further aligned *AD07: Digital Energy Consumption*, included in all frameworks except the *DRGs*, explicitly with "E1-5 – Energy Consumption and Mix" (Regulation, 2023/2772, p. 86).

Additionally, we modeled three CDR dimensions to "ESRS E5 – Resource Use and Circular Economy" (Regulation, 2023/2772, pp. 176–190). The first, *AD25: Regenerative Processes for Technology,* is part of four frameworks (*CDR Areas of Action*, *CDR Building Bloxx*, *CDR Manifesto*, *CDR Clusters*). We modeled *AD25* implicitly to all steering requirements, particularly "E5-1 – Policies Related to Resource Use and Circular Economy" (Regulation, 2023/2772, p. 179), "E5-2 – Actions and Resources Related to Resource Use and Circular Economy" (Regulation, 2023/2772, p. 179), "E5-3 – Targets Related to Resource Use and Circular Economy" (Regulation, 2023/2772, p. 180), and "E5-6 – Anticipated Financial Effects from Resource Use and Circular Economy-Related Impacts, Risks and Opportunities" (Regulation, 2023/2772, p. 183).

For the two other ADs, our analysis resulted in more differentiated explicit alignments, next to the same implicit modeling as for *AD25*. We aligned *AD18*: *Digital Waste* (*DRGs*, *CDR Clusters*, *CDR Topics*) explicitly with "E5-5 – Resource Outflows" (Regulation, 2023/2772, p. 182) and *AD24: Natural Resources Use for Technology* (*CDR Building Bloxx*, *CDR Topics*) explicitly with "E5-4 – Resource Inflows" (Regulation, 2023/2772, p. 181). Additionally, we modeled *AD18*, *AD24*, and *AD25* implicitly to “ESRS E4 – Biodiversity and Ecosystems” (Regulation, 2023/2772, pp. 151–175), reflecting the environmental implications of natural resource extraction for digital technologies, which may grow in significance as digitalization intensifies.

AD16: Digital Sustainability reflects an environmental overarching imperative for digital business models to be sustainable, as long-term viable, regenerative, low in negative externalities, and ideally capable of internalizing such externalities – brought forward in four frameworks (*CDR Fields of Actions*, *CDR Building Bloxx*, *CDR Manifesto*, *DRGs*). While we modeled *AD16* implicitly to all ESRS E, we elaborate on the integration and extension potential further in the discussion section.

In our analyses, we identified no CDR correspondence to “ESRS E2 – Pollution” (Regulation, 2023/2772, pp. 124–137) and “ESRS E3 – Water and Marine Resources” (Regulation, 2023/2772, pp. 138–151). This absence does not suggest irrelevance in the digital domain, particularly given the critical role of water in data centers, but might rather reflect perspective gaps in the analyzed CDR frameworks. Addressing this blind spot could be achieved through reverse modeling, evaluating how environmental issues under E2 and E3 manifest in the context of digital responsibility, however not part of our research objective in this study.

6.3 CDR and CSRD Social Requirements Modeling

Further, through our analysis, we revealed five CDR dimensions that align with the ESRS social requirements. As the four ESRS standards on social topics (“S1 – Own Workforce’, “S2 – Workers in the Value Chain,” “S3 – Affected Communities,” and “S4 – Consumers and End-Users,” Regulation, 2023/2772) are differentiated by stakeholder groups, individual CDR dimensions frequently require multiple, parallel allocations. We derived both explicit and implicit modeling for the same CDR dimension, necessitating a more nuanced evaluation in the following.

First, we identified that *AD13: Digital Literacy* is addressed in all six frameworks with the following variation in focused stakeholder group: Four frameworks (*CDR Fields of Action*, *CDR Building Bloxx*, *CDR Clusters*, *CDR Topics*) emphasize the digital upskilling of employees, hence we aligned them explicitly with the disclosure requirement “S1-13 – Training and Skills Development Metrics” in “ESRS S1 – Own Workforce” (Regulation, 2023/2772, p. 206). The framework *CDR Building Bloxx* also includes responsibilities toward educating consumers for the safe and informed use of digital products and services; thus, we concluded implicit applicability to “ESRS S4 – Consumers and End-Users” (Regulation, 2023/2772, pp. 273–290), for instance, through supplementing the impact requirements with preventive measures of literacy. Furthermore, four frameworks (*CDR Manifesto*, *DRGs*, *CDR Clusters*, *CDR Topics*) articulate a broader societal responsibility for public education on responsible technologies and data use, so we determined implicit alignment across all four ESRS social standards (Regulation, 2023/2772, pp. 191–290).

Second, *AD15: Digital Sovereignty*, present in all frameworks except the *DRGs*, we implicitly aligned with "ESRS S4 – Consumers and End-Users" (Regulation, 2023/2772, pp. 273–290), reasoned through the frameworks reflecting the need to ensure autonomy, agency, and self-determination in the interaction with digital technologies and the handling of personal data. However, the consumer category in the ESRS may be too narrow for the dimension's breadth; depending on the interpretation of what stakeholders are when also part of the consumer category, thus, we concluded that *AD15* could also apply to "S1 – Own Workforce," "S2 – Workers in the Value Chain," and "S3 – Affected Communities" (Regulation, 2023/2772, pp. 256–272) and needs further elaborating in the discussion section.

Third, we modeled *AD19: Digital Well-Being,* which appears in four frameworks, to the social ESRS only for two frameworks. The *CDR Building Bloxx* and *CDR Clusters* define *AD19* as an organizational responsibility toward employees; thus, we aligned them explicitly with "ESRS S1-14 – Health and Safety Metrics" (Regulation, 2023/2772, p. 207). The three frameworks, *CDR Manifesto*, *CDR Clusters*, and *CDR Topics*, extend the concept to a general societal responsibility, framing well-being not only as a reactive measure but also as a prerequisite for the design and delivery of digital products and services. This proactive CDR dimension is not reflected in the current ESRS social disclosure requirements setups, and we will further reflect on it in the discussion on divergences.

Fourth, we implicitly modeled *AD04: Digital Accessibility*, part of all frameworks except the *CDR Building Bloxx*, to "ESRS S4 – Consumer & End-Users" (Regulation, 2023/2772, pp. 273–290). While the current disclosure requirements do not provide potential for implementation, *AD04* could be added, but we will further discuss the resulting divergences in the discussion section. *AD11: Digital Fairness*, present in all frameworks except the *CDR Topics*, has a close relation to *AD04*, but the frameworks rather discuss this CDR dimension as a precondition to be considered when developing digital technology, as well as with regard to shared value approaches (*CDR Manifesto*), and thus, our modeling shows divergence with the current CSRD.

Fifth, we aligned *AD20: Digital Work,* part of four frameworks (*CDR Fields of Actions, CDR Building Bloxx, CDR Clusters, CDR Topics*), explicitly with "ESRS S1 – Own Workforce" (Regulation, 2023/2772, pp. 191–236). Depending on the framework we explicitly allocated *AD20* to single requirements: Three frameworks *(CDR Building Bloxx, CDR Clusters, CDR Topics) are modeled to the requirements* "S1-2 – Processes for engaging with own workforce and workers' representatives about impacts" (Regulation, 2023/2772, p. 198), "S1-4 – Taking action on material impacts on own workforce, and approaches to managing material risks and pursuing material opportunities related to own workforce, and effectiveness of those actions" (Regulation, 2023/2772, p. 200), and "S1-5 – Targets related to managing material negative impacts, advancing positive impacts, and managing material risks and opportunities" (Regulation, 2023/2772, p. 201). While three of the frameworks *(CDR Fields of Actions, CDR Building Bloxx, CDR Clusters)* are also modeled to "S1-6 – Characteristics of the undertaking's employees" (Regulation, 2023/2772, p. 202), since they discuss qualifications in the digital realm, and to

"S1-15 – Work-life balance metrics" (Regulation, 2023/2772, p. 208), for requirements on impacts through flexible working conditions.

6.4 CDR and Governance Requirements Modeling

Furthermore, we modeled three CDR dimensions to the one ESRS on governance, "ESRS G1 – Business Conduct" (Regulation, 2023/2772, pp. 291–301). The first, *AD05: Digital Accountability,* is comprised in all frameworks except the *CDR Fields of Actions.* We aligned *AD05* explicitly with "*G1-1 – Business conduct policies and corporate culture*" (Regulation, 2023/2772, p. 293). Before, *AD05* was already modeled to "*ESRS 2* GOV-1," reflecting four frameworks that also define specific CDR roles. We reasoned this additional inclusion through the cultural, attitudinal, and behavioral aspects mentioned in the frameworks.

The second, *AD09: Digital Ethics Policies, is* present in four frameworks (*CDR Fields of Actions*, *CDR Building Bloxx*, *CDR Manifesto*, *CDR Topics*). We also aligned *AD09* explicitly with "ESRS G1-1 – Business Conduct Policies and Corporate Culture," but to the paragraph addressing corporate policies (Regulation, 2023/2772, p. 293). The third, *AD12: Digital Integrity*, is included in all but the *CDR Fields of Actions*. We modeled *AD12* implicitly with "ESRS G1," thus necessitating an additional disclosure requirement. Like *AD05*, *AD12* reflects a responsible attitude to comprehensive business conduct in the frameworks. However, we modeled the CDR dimension only implicitly, since so far, integrity is not a tangible part of responsibility reporting. We will discuss the applicability in the following.

7 Discussion

In our pursuit of building synthesized coherence (Locke & Golden-Biddle, 1997) between CDR matters and corporate responsibility reporting, we identified thirteen dimensions with explicit alignment and nine dimensions with implicit alignment, i.e., indirectly covered through the existing scope of the CSRD. These numbers comprise an overlap of four CDR dimensions (*AD13*, *AD18*, *AD24*, *AD25*). In addition, our analysis did not lead to any alignment for nine CDR dimensions, plus two CDR dimensions that show some implicit alignment, but a gap remains, indicating limitations in the CSRD regarding digital responsibility requirements.

In short, our results show a 48.1% coherence, 33.3% resonance, and 40.7% divergence. This highlights both the integration potential of the CSRD and current limitations in covering CDR dimensions through existing categories of corporate responsibility reporting. With these findings, we firstly contribute to the ongoing discourse on the interdependency between CDR and CSR matters (e.g., Dörr, 2021; Lobschat et al., 2021; Mihale-Wilson et al., 2021) and, secondly, to the research on leveraging CSR reporting structures for CDR (e.g., Carl et al., 2022; Merbecks, 2023; Weber-Lewerenz & Traverso, 2025) as well as to the overall debate on reporting as a measure for operationalizing a broader understanding of corporate responsibility (e.g., Christensen et al., 2021; Sharma, 2025; Wickert, 2021).

7.1 Implications of the CDR-CSR Interdependency and Resulting Limitations

Figure 3 illustrates the modeled synthesis of the derived CDR dimensions against the CDRD, organized into four columns of ESRS: cross-cutting, environment, social, and governance standards (ESRS). The synthesized CDR dimensions showing convergence are listed below the single ESRS; the ones written in italic only show resonance. At the lower right, the CDR dimensions are listed, for which we conclude divergence.

Convergence is most consistently evident in the environmental pillar (ESRS E1–E5), where we largely synthesized CDR and CSR dimensions, such as energy consumption and waste. Social obligations (ESRS S1–S4) also reveal notable convergence, for instance, regarding literacy and well-being. However, divergences remain, as the CSRD structures social matters by stakeholder groups (own workforce, value chain, consumers, and affected communities), a categorization not completely reflected in the analyzed CDR frameworks, which tend to frame social matters more broadly.

In contrast, the governance pillar (ESRS G1) demonstrates the widest divergence. While the CSRD emphasizes compliance, anti-bribery, and anti-corruption, these categories are only marginally addressed within CDR frameworks. Some overlap exists through cross-cutting governance requirements in ESRS 2, which provide entry points for dimensions such as digital accountability, digital ethics policies, and digital integrity. Yet, the majority of these CDR dimensions can be interpreted as governance-related requirements specified on data and digital technology steering – areas that remain largely absent from the CSRD. This indicates that governance remains the most underdeveloped area in both reporting and practice and thus requires priority attention from scholars, policymakers, and practitioners.

Nevertheless, our proposed implications need to be contextualized in relation to our study's methodological and conceptual limitations to derive actionable insights for research and practice. First, we build the derived CDR dimensions on text-based inductive coding, guided by principles of mutual exclusion and collective exhaustion, but inherently limited by the input texts of the selected frameworks. Each framework reflects the perspective and purpose of its creators (e.g., policymakers, industry associations, civil society, or scholars), which results in differences in scope and emphasis. The six frameworks, therefore, do not cover the full conceptual landscape of CDR, and other models – such as the *CDR Culture Model* (Lobschat et al., 2021) or the *CDR Maturity Model* (Rugeviciute & Courboulay, 2024) – could provide complementary perspectives, particularly regarding organizational steering mechanisms and cultural embedding. Thus, Fig. 3 should not be simply interpreted as a comprehensive representation of CDR matters, transferable into a checklist for

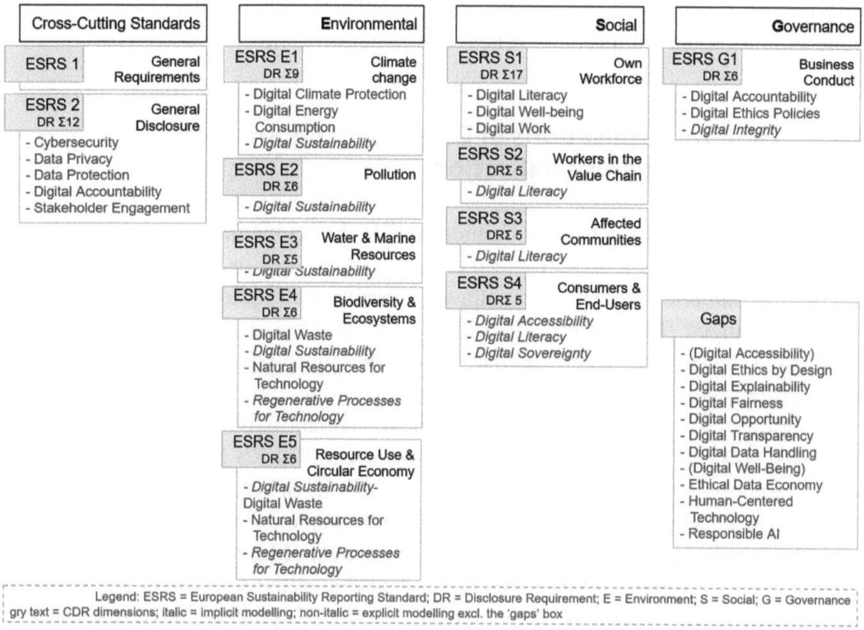

Fig. 3 CDR-CSRD synthesis. (Authors' illustration)

completeness and maturity, without further verifying applicability to industry or business model-specific cases.

Second, our development of CDR dimensions followed an inductive approach, which is inevitably shaped by coder judgment, notwithstanding the intercoder reliability assessment using Cohen's kappa (Cohen, 1960). No deductive validation of comprehensiveness was conducted, which may have led to omissions or overlaps between dimensions. Accordingly, the relationship between CDR and CSR matters requires further systematic validation to achieve conceptual completeness. Future research should apply deductive approaches to test coverage and refine boundaries. Initial evidence suggests that additional CSRD topics, such as ESRS E2 on water resources, which is highly relevant for data center operations, may also pertain to CDR but were not reflected in the frameworks analyzed.

Third, our modeling analysis was conducted at the level of CDR dimensions and ESRS requirements, without fixed metrics or criteria of the respective matters. This limits practical applicability, as companies will need concrete indicators to make CDR obligations assessable on the level of discursive disclosures and quantitative data points, as well as suitable for XBRL tagging (eXtensible Business Reporting Language), required for electronic processing of reporting information. But setting these details for practical reporting application aside, the question of metrics leads us to another conclusion. Derived from the resonances and divergences beyond the simple modeling of synthesis between CDR and the CSRD, implications on reporting as a lever for CDR operationalization can be drawn, which also mitigate some limitations of comprehensiveness and generalizability.

7.2 General Implications of Leveraging Reporting for CDR Operationalization

The CSRD is bound by what can be measured and documented in disclosure form, which is only applicable to some of the CDR matters. For instance, *AD07: Digital Energy Consumption*, for which synthesis is built with requirements of "ESRS E1 Climate Change" (Regulation, 2023/2772, pp. 78–123), can be assessed through established metrics for fossil fuel use, renewable energy consumption, and greenhouse gas emissions. Although data tracking along the entire supply chain remains challenging, this dimension is predominantly quantifiable and documentable. Similarly, *AD13: Digital Literacy*, synthesized with "ESRS S1-13 – Training and Skills Development Metrics" (Regulation, 2023/2772, p. 206), can be quantitatively evaluated via participation rates in training programs and impact assessments, particularly given advances in big data analytics. Moreover, *AD05: Digital Accountability*, synthesized with "GOV-1 – The role of the administrative, management and supervisory bodies" (Regulation, 2023/2772, p. 49), can be documented through the disclosure of roles, advisory bodies, and governance structures. And *AD01: Cybersecurity* can be documented through risk management systems and preventive measures already mandated under instruments such as the EU Cybersecurity Act (Regulation 2019/881).

In contrast, matters such as *AD15: Digital Sovereignty* or *AD12: Digital Integrity* are much harder to measure with metrics. Sovereignty lacks a clear, universal definition in corporate practice, and integrity is challenging for companies to self-assess, as its realization depends on stakeholder perception rather than internal procedures. The difficulty in assessing, measuring, and documenting these stems from the known challenges of intangible business ethics, acknowledged in business conduct. In this context, the *CDR Culture Concept* by Lobschat et al. (2021) suggests that the desired outcomes of CDR develop through shared organizational values, which are translated into norms and sometimes formalized as guiding principles. As a result, what becomes an institutionalized 'norm' can vary across companies, regions, or even generations. This cultural variability increases the complexity of measurement: It is unlikely to find a single, universally applicable set of indicators, especially given the broader challenge of quantifying ethical performance, which calls for new approaches to evaluate ethical business conduct (Gangi et al., 2025; Islam & Greenwood, 2022).

This highlights that the limitations of synthesizing CDR with the CSRD lie not only at the level of thematic coverage but also at the level of application. Several dimensions identified in the resonance or divergence categories may not, despite their conceptual relevance, lend themselves to standardized reporting formats. Reporting itself, therefore, constitutes a limitation for CDR operation, as its structure privileges quantifiable indicators over more normative or value-driven aspects.

Hence, returning to the intention of advancing CDR implementation through reporting measures, it is essential to recognize that reporting primarily functions as a mechanism for mandatory or voluntary transparency, rather than as a tool to compel organizations to achieve specific performance outcomes (e.g., Agenda 2030 of the SDGs). Its influence on behavior is indirect: The expectation is that unfavorable disclosures will trigger stakeholder reactions – whether from consumers, investors, or employees – that translate into reputational costs. While shifts in stakeholder preferences and awareness are evident, their effect on corporate transformation has so far remained limited rather than systemic (Nguyen et al., 2023). Parallel developments, such as ESG-oriented regulatory frameworks (e.g., Sustainable Finance Disclosure Regulation, EU Taxonomy), have tightened external pressures, but they largely shape reporting behavior rather than substantive accountability.

Moreover, when CSR matters become embedded in regulation, they tend to be treated as compliance requirements rather than as catalysts for genuine responsibility in corporate decision-making. Responsible business conduct becomes, then, rather a question of good compliance, which is why CSR scholars keep on highlighting the beyond-regulation aspect (McWilliams & Siegel, 2001). Consequently, disclosure-based mechanisms alone have not yet proven to be strong drivers of improved responsibility performance. In this context, evaluating the expected effects of the CSRD on CDR remains an open and critical task. The reporting directive may enhance transparency and comparability, but its transformative potential will depend on whether stakeholders actively use disclosed information to demand higher standards and whether policymakers complement reporting with enforcement and incentive mechanisms. For CDR matters specifically, this suggests that reporting can provide visibility and benchmarking but must be supplemented by cultural, ethical, and governance instruments to achieve meaningful change.

Recognizing this boundary is crucial, as it prevents the overextension of reporting frameworks while opening the debate on alternative instruments that may complement disclosure-based regulation. To better grasp the direction in which we need to develop governance measures here might lay in the nature of why it is called "taking responsibility" because it is only necessary in a space of freedom where no clear rules and regulations is provided but rather action is required and that becomes responsible if we take the Matten and Moon corporate responsibility definition, they included the sentence "Yet the precise manifestation and direction of the responsibility lie at the discretion of the corporation" (p. 405).

8 Conclusion

This chapter sets out to examine the interrelationship between CDR and CSR matters in the context of corporate responsibility reporting, to assess how existing reporting structures can support the operationalization of CDR. We conducted a content analysis of six CDR frameworks to identify core CDR matters and modeled these against the CSRD. Our findings reveal strong convergence with environmental reporting categories (e.g., energy consumption, waste), partial convergence but mainly resonance with social categories (e.g., literacy, well-being), and substantial divergences in relation to governance requirements for data and digital technologies (e.g., transparency, human-centered).

Taken together, our findings underscore both opportunities to leverage synergies and boundaries of integrating CDR matters into existing reporting regimes. The CSRD provides a valuable platform for enhancing transparency and comparability, yet its effectiveness depends on whether disclosures trigger stakeholder responses and whether policymakers complement reporting with enforcement and incentive mechanisms. Hence, our study also underlines the question of whether the CSRD – limited to mandatory transparency – can adequately cover CDR matters, or whether alternative governance measures are needed to operationalize CDR performance indicators in the long term. For practitioners, this means that while the CSRD offers an entry point to integrate CDR concerns, firms must go beyond compliance and actively develop internal governance and cultural mechanisms. Thus, we conclude that for CDR matters to mature into a meaningful component of corporate responsibility, reporting must be supplemented with cultural and ethical governance instruments capable of addressing the unique risks and responsibilities of the digital age.

Appendix

Cohen's Kappa Calculation: Inter-Coder Agreement on Aggregate Dimensions of CDR

Data Summary

- Agreement of two coders on the aggregate dimensions (total of 27), ESG and ESRS assigned to each 1st-order and 2nd-order concept per CDR framework (1 = agreement, 0 = disagreement).

Cohen's Kappa Formula

$$\kappa = \frac{P_o - P_e}{1 - P_e}$$

$$P_o = \text{observed agreement}$$

$$P_e = \text{expected agreement } by \text{ chance}$$

See Table 4.

CDR Fields of Action

- Total items: 51
- Agreements: 48

Table 4 Cohen's kappa value: level of agreement equivalency

Cohen's kappa statistic κ	Level of agreement
< 0.00	Poor
0.00–0.20	Slight
0.20–0.40	Fair
0.41–0.60	Moderate
0.61–0.80	Substantial
0.81–1.00	Almost perfect

Source: own illustration, adapted from Rau and Shih (2021)

- Disagreements: 3
- $P_o = \frac{48}{51} \approx 0.9412$
- $P_e = 0.5$
- $\kappa = \frac{0.9412 - 0.5}{1 - 0.5} = \frac{0.4412}{0.5} \approx 0.8824$
- Cohen's kappa = 0.88
- This indicates **almost perfect agreement** between the two coders.

CDR Building Bloxx

- Total items: 136
- Agreements: 127
- Disagreements: 9
- $P_o = \frac{127}{136} \approx 0.9338$
- $P_e = 0.5$
- $\kappa = \frac{0.9338 - 0.5}{1 - 0.5} = \frac{0.4338}{0.5} \approx 0.8676$
- Cohen's kappa = 0.87
- This indicates **almost perfect agreement** between the two coders.

CDR Manifesto

- Total items: 81
- Agreements: 74
- Disagreements: 7
- $P_o = \frac{74}{81} \approx 0.9136$
- $P_e = 0.5$

- $\kappa = \frac{0.9136 - 0.5}{1 - 0.5} = \frac{0.4136}{0.5} \approx 0.8272$
- Cohen's kappa = 0.83
- This indicates **almost perfect agreement** between the two coders.

DRGs

- Total items: 101
- Agreements: 95
- Disagreements: 6
- $P_o = \frac{95}{101} \approx 0.9406$
- $P_e = 0.5$
- $\kappa = \frac{0.9406 - 0.5}{1 - 0.5} = \frac{0.4406}{0.5} \approx 0.8812$
- Cohen's kappa = 0.88
- This indicates **almost perfect agreement** between the two coders.

CDR Clusters (Dörr)

- Total items: 144
- Agreements: 130
- Disagreements: 14
- $P_o = \frac{130}{144} \approx 0.9028$
- $P_e = 0.5$
- $\kappa = \frac{0.9028 - 0.5}{1 - 0.5} = \frac{0.4028}{0.5} \approx 0.8056$
- Cohen's kappa = 0.81
- This indicates **substantial to almost perfect agreement** between the two coders.

CDR Topics (Herden et al.)

- Total items: 136
- Agreements: 126
- Disagreements: 10
- $P_o = \frac{126}{136} \approx 0.9265$

- $P_e = 0.5$
- $\kappa = \frac{0.9265 - 0.5}{1 - 0.5} = \frac{0.4265}{0.5} \approx 0.8529$
- Cohen's kappa = 0.85
- This indicates **almost perfect agreement** between the two coders.

References

Appiah-Kubi, E., Dura, C. C., Niță, D., Drigă, I., Preda, A., & Baltador, L. A. (2025). The effect of digitalization on sustainability reporting: The role of sustainability competence, green knowledge integration, and stakeholder pressure. *Business Strategy and the Environment, 34*(1), 1133–1153.

Bednárová, M., & Serpeninova, Y. (2023). Corporate digital responsibility: bibliometric landscape – Chronological literature review. *International Journal of Digital Accounting Research, 23*(29), 1–18. https://doi.org/10.4192/1577-8517-v23_1

Bowen, G. A. (2009). Document analysis as a qualitative research method. *Qualitative Research Journal, 9*(2), 27–40. https://doi.org/10.3316/QRJ0902027

Brower, J., & Dacin, P. A. (2020). An institutional theory approach to the evolution of the corporate social performance–corporate financial performance relationship. *Journal of Management Studies, 57*(4), 805–836. https://doi.org/10.1111/joms.12550

Brundland, G. H. (1987). *Our common future: Report of the World Commission on Environment and Development* (UN Doc. A/42/427). United Nations. https://www.un-documents.net/ocf-ov.htm

BVDW. (2025). *CDR Building Bloxx*. Retrieved August 21, 2025, from https://www.cdr-building-bloxx.com/cdr-building-bloxx-framework/

Carl, K. V., & Hinz, O. (2024). What we already know about corporate digital responsibility in IS research: A review and conceptualization of potential CDR activities. *Electronic Markets, 34*(1), 1–30. https://doi.org/10.1007/s12525-024-00708-0

Carl, K. V., Zilcher, T. M. C., & Hinz, O. (2022). Corporate digital responsibility and the current corporate social responsibility standard: An analysis of applicability. In *Lecture Notes in Informatics (LNI), Proceedings – Series of the Gesellschaft für Informatik (GI).*

Carl, K. V., Blachetta, M., Bilfinger, B., Brink, A., Cerulli-Harms, A. K., Christ, A.-S., et al. (2025). *Establishing common ground in corporate digital responsibility*. IT-Governance und Strategisches Informationsmanagement.

Carroll, A. B. (1991). The pyramid of corporate social responsibility: Toward the moral management of organizational stakeholders. *Business Horizons, 34*(4), 39–48. https://doi.org/10.1016/0007-6813(91)90005-G

CDR Initiative. (2025). *The CDR code. Our fields of action—Making CDR tangible*. Retrieved August 21, 2025, from https://cdr-initiative.de/en/kodex

CDR Manifesto. (2021). *The International CDR Manifesto. Corporate Digital Responsibility*. Retrieved August 21, 2025, from https://corporatedigitalresponsibility.net/cdr-manifesto

Christ, A.-S. (2025). Corporate governance for digital responsibility: A company study. In *Proceedings of the 20th International Conference on Wirtschaftsinformatik, Münster, Germany*.

Christ, A.-S., Mueller, B., & Lobschat, L. (2024). Corporate digital responsibility (CDR): Achieving synthesized coherence with C(S)R learnings on corporate governance. In *Proceedings of the 45th International Conference on Information Systems, Bangkok, Thailand*.

Christensen, H. B., Hail, L., & Leuz, C. (2021). Mandatory CSR and sustainability reporting: Economic analysis and literature review. *Review of Accounting Studies, 26*(3), 1176–1248. https://doi.org/10.1007/s11142-021-09609-5

Christmann, A.-S., Crome, C., Graf-Drasch, V., Oberländer, A. M., & Schmidt, L. (2024). The twin transformation butterfly: Capabilities for an integrated digital and sustainability transformation. *Business & Information Systems Engineering, 66*(4), 1–17. https://doi.org/10.1007/s12599-023-00847-2

Cohen, J. (1960). A coefficient of agreement for nominal scales. *Educational and Psychological Measurement, 20*(1). https://doi.org/10.1177/001316446002000104

DIN. (2015). *DIN EN ISO 14001:2015 Umweltmanagementsysteme – Anforderungen mit Anleitung zur Anwendung* [Environmental management systems – Requirements with guidance for use. Beuth Verlag

Dörr, S. (2021). *Corporate digital responsibility. Managing corporate responsibility and sustainability in the digital age*. Springer Gabler.

Elkington, J. (1998). Partnerships from cannibals with forks: The triple bottom line of 21st-century business. *Environmental Quality Management, 8*(1), 37–51. https://doi.org/10.1002/tqem.3310080106

Etikan, I., Musa, S. A., & Alkassim, R. S. (2016). Comparison of convenience sampling and purposive sampling. *American Journal of Theoretical and Applied Statistics, 5*(1), 1–4. https://doi.org/10.11648/j.ajtas.20160501.11

European Parliament and Council of the European Union. (2022). Directive (EU) 2022/2464 of the European Parliament and of the Council of 14 December 2022 amending Regulation (EU) No 537/2014, Directive 2004/109/EC, Directive 2006/43/EC and Directive 2013/34/EU, as regards corporate sustainability reporting (Text with EEA relevance). *Official Journal of the European Union, L, 322*, 15–59. https://eur-lex.europa.eu/legal-content/EN/TXT/?uri=CELEX%3A32022L2464

European Union. (2014). Directive 2014/95/EU of the European Parliament and of the Council of 22 October 2014 amending Directive 2013/34/EU as regards disclosure of non-financial and diversity information by certain large undertakings and groups. *Official Journal of the European Union, L, 330*, 1–9. https://eur-lex.europa.eu/legal-content/EN/TXT/?uri=CELEX:32014L0095

European Union. (2023). Commission Regulation (EU) 2023/1803 of 13 August 2023 adopting certain international accounting standards in accordance with Regulation (EC) No 1606/2002 of the European Parliament and of the Council.

Friede, G., Busch, T., & Bassen, A. (2015). ESG and financial performance: Aggregated evidence from more than 2000 empirical studies. *Journal of Sustainable Finance & Investment, 5*(4), 210–233. https://doi.org/10.1080/20430795.2015.1118917

Gangi, F., Daniele, L. M., Varrone, N., Coscia, M., & D'Angelo, E. (2025). The impact of business ethics on ESG engagement and the effect on corporate financial performance: Evidence from family firms. *Management Decision, 63*(2), 468–487. https://doi.org/10.1108/MD-10-2023-1931

German Council for Sustainable Development. (2025). *German Sustainability Code (DNK)*. Retrieved August 21, 2025, from https://www.deutscher-nachhaltigkeitskodex.de/en/

Gioia, D. A., Corley, K. G., & Hamilton, A. L. (2013). Seeking qualitative rigor in inductive research: Notes on the Gioia methodology. *Organizational Research Methods, 16*(1), 15–31. https://doi.org/10.1177/1094428112452151

Haack, P., Schoeneborn, D., & Wickert, C. (2012). Talking the talk, moral entrapment, creeping commitment? Exploring narrative dynamics in corporate responsibility standardization. *Organization Studies, 33*(5–6), 815–845. https://doi.org/10.1177/0170840612443630

Herden, Alliu, E., Cakici, A., Cormier, T., Deguelle, C., Gambhir, S., et al. (2021). Corporate digital responsibility. New corporate responsibilities in the digital age. *Nachhaltigkeits Management Forum, 29*, 13–19. https://doi.org/10.1007/s00550-020-00509-x

Hsieh, H.-F., & Shannon, S. E. (2005). Three approaches to qualitative content analysis. *Qualitative Health Research, 15*, 1277–1288. https://doi.org/10.1177/1049732305276687

Identity Valley. (2025). *Digital responsibility goals*. Retrieved August 21, 2025, from https://identityvalley.eu/drg

Islam, G., & Greenwood, M. (2022). The metrics of ethics and the ethics of metrics. *Journal of Business Ethics, 175*(1), 1–5. https://doi.org/10.1007/s10551-021-05004-x

Knopf, T., & Pick, D. (2023). Corporate responsibility for digital innovation: A systematic review of the literature. In *Proceedings of the 18th European Conference on Innovation and Entrepreneurship*.

Landis, J. R., & Koch, G. G. (1977). An application of hierarchical kappa-type statistics in the assessment of majority agreement among multiple observers. *Biometrics*, 363–374. https://doi.org/10.2307/2529786

Lee, P. (2008). A review of the theories of corporate social responsibility: Its evolutionary path and the road ahead. *International Journal of Management Reviews, 10*, 53–73. https://doi.org/10.1111/j.1468-2370.2007.00226.x

Lobschat, L., Mueller, B., Eggers, F., Brandimarte, L., Diefenbach, S., Kroschke, M., & Wirtz, J. (2021). Corporate digital responsibility. *Journal of Business Research, 122*, 875–888. https://doi.org/10.1016/j.jbusres.2019.10.006

Locke, K., & Golden-Biddle, K. (1997). Constructing opportunities for contribution: Structuring intertextual coherence and 'problematizing' in organizational studies. *Academy of Management Journal, 40*(5). https://doi.org/10.2307/256926

Martin, K. (2022). Algorithmic bias and corporate responsibility: How companies hide behind the false veil of the technological imperative. In K. Martin (Ed.), *Ethics of data and analytics* (pp. 36–50). Auerbach Publications.

Mayring, P. (2015). Qualitative content analysis: Theoretical background and procedures. In A. Bikner-Ahsbahs, C. Knipping, & N. Presmeg (Eds.), *Approaches to qualitative research in mathematics education. Advances in mathematics education* (pp. 365–380). Springer.

McHugh, M. L. (2012). Interrater reliability: The kappa statistic. *Biochemia Medica, 22*(3), 276–282. https://doi.org/10.11613/BM.2012.031

McWilliams, A., & Siegel, D. (2001). Corporate social responsibility: A theory of the firm perspective. *Academy of Management Review, 26*(1), 117–127. https://doi.org/10.5465/amr.2001.4011987

Merbecks, U. (2023). Corporate digital responsibility (CDR) in Germany: Background and first empirical evidence from DAX 30 companies in 2020. *Journal of Business Economics*, 1–25. https://doi.org/10.1007/s11573-023-01148-6

Mihale-Wilson, C., Zibuschka, J., Carl, K., & Hinz, O. (2021). Corporate digital responsibility – Extended conceptualization and empirical assessment. In *Proceedings of the 29th European Conference on Information Systems, Marrakech, Marrakech*.

Mihale-Wilson, C., Hinz, O., van der Aalst, W., & Weinhardt, C. (2022). Corporate digital responsibility: Relevance and opportunities for business and information systems engineering. *Business & Information Systems Engineering, 64*(2), 127–132. https://doi.org/10.1007/s12599-022-00746-y

Minto, B. (2009). *The pyramid principle: Logic in writing and thinking*. Pearson Education.

Mueller, B. (2022). Corporate digital responsibility. *Business and Information Systems Engineering, 64*(5). https://doi.org/10.1007/s12599-022-00760-0

Myers, M., & Newman, M. (2007). The qualitative interview in IS research: Examining the craft. *Information and Organization, 17*, 2–26. https://doi.org/10.1016/j.infoandorg.2006.11.001

Ngereja, B. J., Hussein, B., & Wolff, C. (2024). A comparison of soft factors in the implementation and adoption of digitalization projects: A systematic literature review. *International Journal of Information Systems and Project Management, 12*(2), 70–86. https://doi.org/10.12821/ijispm120204

Nguyen, N., Priporas, C.-V., McPherson, M., & Manyiwa, S. (2023). CSR-related consumer scepticism: A review of the literature and future research directions. *Journal of Business Research, 169*, 114294. https://doi.org/10.1016/j.jbusres.2023.114294

Oduro, S., Haylemariam, L. G., & Umar, R. M. (2024). Influence of corporate digital responsibility on financial. *Business Ethics, the Environment & Responsibility, 34*(4), 2259–2273. https://doi.org/10.1111/beer.12766

Ologeanu-Taddei, R., Hönigsberg, S., Weritz, P., Wache, H., Mittermeier, F., Tana, S., Dang, D., Hautala-Kankaanpää, T., & Pekkola, S. (2024). The relationship of digital transformation and corporate sustainability: Synergies and tensions. *Technological Forecasting and Social Change, 210*, 1–18. https://doi.org/10.1016/j.techfore.2024.123809

Orbik, Z., & Zozul'aková, V. (2019). Corporate social and digital responsibility. *Management Systems in Production Engineering, 27*(2), 79–83. https://doi.org/10.1515/mspe-2019-0013

Pizzi, S., Mastroleo, G., Venturelli, A., & Caputo, F. (2024). The digitalization of sustainability reporting processes: A conceptual framework. *Business Strategy and the Environment, 33*(2), 1040–1050.

Rau, G., & Shih, Y.-S. (2021). Evaluation of Cohen's kappa and other measures of inter-rater agreement for genre analysis and other nominal data. *Journal of English for Academic Purposes, 53*(1). https://doi.org/10.1016/j.jeap.2021.101026

Regulation. (2023/2772). Commission Delegated Regulation (EU) 2023/2772 of 31 July 2023 supplementing Directive 2013/34/EU of the European Parliament and of the Council as regards sustainability reporting standards (Text with EEA relevance)Text with EEA relevance. https://eur-lex.europa.eu/eli/reg_del/2023/2772/2023-12-22

Ritchey, T. (2018). General morphological analysis as a basic scientific modelling method. *Technological Forecasting and Social Change, 126*, 81–91. https://doi.org/10.1016/j.techfore.2017.05.027

Rugeviciute, A., & Courboulay, V. (2024). Empowering organizations for sustainable digitalization: A corporate digital responsibility maturity model approach. In *Proceedings of the 10th International Conference on ICT for Sustainability*.

Saldaña, J. (2021). Coding techniques for quantitative and mixed data. In J. A. Onwuegbuzie & R. B. Johnson (Eds.), *The Routledge reviewer's guide to mixed methods analysis* (pp. 151–160). Routledge.

Sarker, S., Xiao, X., & Beaulieu, T. (2013). Guest editorial: Qualitative studies in information systems: A critical review and some guiding principles. *MIS Quarterly, 37*(4). https://doi.org/10.1177/1558689806298224

Sharma, R. (2025). Unveiling the effects of the Corporate Sustainability Reporting Directive (CSRD) on company sustainability reporting practices: A case of German companies. *Sustainability Accounting, Management and Policy Journal*. https://doi.org/10.1108/SAMPJ-01-2025-0091

Stebbins, R. A. (2001). *Exploratory research in the social sciences* (Vol. 48). Sage.

Strauss, A., & Corbin, J. (1998). *Basics of qualitative research techniques*.

Thelisson, E., Morin, J.-H., & Rochel, J. (2019). AI governance: Digital responsibility as a building block: Towards an index of digital responsibility. *Delphi Interdisciplinary Review of Emerging Technologies, 2*(4), 167–178. https://doi.org/10.21552/delphi/2019/4/6

Thomas, D. R. (2006). A general inductive approach for analyzing qualitative evaluation data. *American Journal of Evaluation, 27*(2), 237–246. https://doi.org/10.1177/1098214005283748

Thorun, C., Vetter, M., Reisch, L., & Zimmer, A. K. (2017). Indicators of consumer protection and empowerment in the digital world: Results and recommendations of a feasibility study. In *Consumers international. Coming together for change*.

Trier, M., Kundisch, D., Beverungen, D., Müller, O., Schryen, G., Mirbabaie, M., & Trang, S. (2023). Digital responsibility: A multilevel framework for responsible digitalization. *Business & Information Systems Engineering, 65*(4), 463–474. https://doi.org/10.1007/s12599-023-00822-x

Trittin-Ulbrich, H. (2023). From the substantive to the ceremonial: Exploring interrelations between recognition and aspirational CSR talk. *Business & Society, 62*(5), 917–949.

United Nations. (2015). *Transforming our world: The 2030 agenda for sustainable development* (UN Doc. A/RES/70/1). Retrieved August 21, 2025, from https://sdgs.un.org/2030agenda

Urban, I., & Plattfaut, R. (2025). The interplay of digital responsibility and digital transformation: Empirical insights from a nationwide digital transformation. *Information Systems Frontiers*, 1–32.

Wade, M. (2020). Corporate responsibility in the digital era. *MIT Sloan Business Review*. https://sloanreview.mit.edu/article/corporate-responsibility-in-the-digital-era/

Weber-Lewerenz, B., & Traverso, M. (2025). How can corporate digital responsibility (CDR) be measured in line with corporate social responsibility (CSR)? A new theoretical approach in construction 4.0. *Sustainable Development, 33*(1), 287–308. https://doi.org/10.1002/sd.3094
Wickert, C. (2021). Corporate social responsibility research in the Journal of Management Studies: A shift from a business-centric to a society-centric focus. *Journal of Management Studies, 58*(8), E1–E17. https://doi.org/10.1111/joms.12775
Wickert, C., Post, C., Doh, J. P., Prescott, J. E., & Prencipe, A. (2020). Management research that makes a difference: Broadening the meaning of impact. *Journal of Management Studies, 58*(2), 297–320. https://doi.org/10.1111/joms.12666
Wirtz, J., Kunz, W. H., Hartley, N., & Tarbit, J. (2023). Corporate digital responsibility in service firms and their ecosystems. *Journal of Service Research, 26*(2), 173–190. https://doi.org/10.1177/10946705221130467
Wood, D. J. (1991). Corporate social performance revisited. *Academy of Management Review, 16*(4), 691–718. https://doi.org/10.5465/amr.1991.4279616
Wright, D., & Kreissl, R. (Eds.). (2014). *Surveillance in Europe*. Routledge.
Zhu, S., Lv, K., & Cheng, Y. (2025). The impact of digital technology innovation on firm performance: Based on the corporate digital responsibility perspective. *Business Ethics, the Environment & Responsibility*. https://doi.org/10.1111/beer.12785
Zimmer, M., Järveläinen, J., Stahl, B., & Mueller, B. (2023). Responsibility of/in digital transformation. *Journal of Responsible Technology, 16*, 1–5. https://doi.org/10.1016/j.jrt.2023.100068

Anna-Sophia Christ is a doctoral researcher at Maastricht University's School of Business and Economics and the University of Bremen's Business, Innovation, and Transformation Institute (BIT). Her research and teaching focus on systemic aspects of digital responsibility in economic contexts within the field of information systems. In her work as an independent coach, consultant, and system and organizational constellation facilitator, she supports companies in their sustainability and digital transformation.

Anna Wannhoff holds a Bachelor's degree in Business Psychology from CBS and a Master's degree in Management from ESMT Berlin, graduating summa cum laude. She is currently pursuing a Doctor of Business Administration at Munich Business School and Sheffield Hallam University, with a research focus on Corporate Digital Responsibility (CDR). Since 2022, she has been working at Microsoft as a Cloud Solution Architect, leading AI adoption initiatives for enterprise clients. Her professional experience includes roles in digital strategy, marketing, and innovation across the tech and mobility sectors. She is a recipient of several academic awards and actively contributes to digital leadership and women's empowerment communities.

What Do Consumers Ask for When It Comes to CDR?

K. Valerie Carl, Jan Zibuschka, Cristina Mihale-Wilson, and Oliver Hinz

Abstract

The rapid advancement of digital technologies has led to, for example, enhanced connectivity between various objects and devices and increasingly sophisticated artificial intelligence-based products and services, significantly enhancing value creation opportunities. However, organizations face numerous challenges associated with digitalization, necessitating a comprehensive approach to Corporate Digital Responsibility (CDR). Our empirical evaluation quantitatively investigates consumer perspectives on CDR engagement, aiming to guide organizational activities based on consumer needs. By examining consumer preferences for specific CDR initiatives, we identify critical dimensions and sub-dimensions of CDR that resonate with different segments of the market. The chapter's dual objectives are to elucidate the significance of various CDR aspects for consumers and to propose a segmentation strategy that reveals opportunities for revenue generation through tailored CDR activities. Ultimately, our findings aim to facilitate the practical implementation of CDR, fostering broader acceptance and actionable strategies within organizations striving to enhance their digital responsibility initiatives.

K. V. Carl (✉) · C. Mihale-Wilson · O. Hinz
Information Systems and Information Management, Goethe University Frankfurt, Frankfurt, Germany
e-mail: kcarl@wiwi.uni-frankfurt.de; Mihale-wilson@wiwi.uni-frankfurt.de; ohinz@wiwi.uni-frankfurt.de

J. Zibuschka
Robert Bosch GmbH, Renningen, Germany
e-mail: jan.zibuschka@de.bosch.com

A.-S. Christ (ed.), *Corporate Digital Responsibility*, Future of Business and Finance, https://doi.org/10.1007/978-3-032-14793-6_6

1 Introduction

Continuous advances in digital technology make it possible to connect a wide range of objects or to develop more sophisticated artificial intelligence-based products and services. This development enables more advanced and efficient digital products and services that significantly expand the potential for value creation (e.g., Hess et al., 2016). Nevertheless, managers and companies face a number of challenges and risks that digitalization entails (e.g., Ransbotham et al., 2016; Tarafdar et al., 2013). In this context, the concept of Corporate Digital Responsibility (CDR) has emerged, which aims to seize the opportunities of digitalization while adequately managing the associated risks. The aim of CDR is to create a holistic approach to responsibility in the digital context that goes beyond isolated topics such as data protection (Carl & Hinz, 2024; Mihale-Wilson et al., 2022). However, the practical implementation of these concepts depends heavily on the individual understanding of responsibility within companies and the people involved. Further, most CDR engagement is driven by extrinsic motivators (e.g., consumer needs, enhancing the company's USP) (Carl et al., 2023). Especially in the case of such extrinsic motivators, it can be rewarding for companies to align the external perception with internal activities. Limited budget and personnel resources normally restrict potential CDR activities and necessitate a prioritization of activities. Therefore, aligning CDR activities with consumer needs allows for seizing the chances of CDR engagement despite a limited budget and consequently a restricted multitude of CDR activities.

To this end, we take an empirical approach to quantitatively assessing CDR engagement from the consumers' perspective. This chapter aims to support operationalizing CDR in practice and to consider the different needs and expectations of consumers, aligning the internal view and external perspective on prioritizing CDR activities. We examine consumer preferences for CDR activities to assess the relevance of particular measures for companies as well as to customize their digital offerings. By analyzing the heterogeneous attitudes of consumers, this work has two central objectives: First, to explore the importance of different CDR dimensions for consumers and sequence them and, second, to develop a segmentation approach that highlights the potential for additional revenue from customized CDR activities. These insights should not only contribute to the broad acceptance of CDR in practice but also provide concrete recommendations for the implementation of CDR activities.

2 Corporate Digital Responsibility: Definition and Scope

2.1 Defining CDR

CDR has emerged as a central concept in understanding the ethical obligations of organizations in the digital landscape (e.g., Lobschat et al., 2021). At its core, CDR addresses the ethical challenges posed by the adoption and integration of digital technologies within business practices. This includes considerations related to privacy, security, autonomy, justice, and human dignity (following Royakkers et al., 2018). Following, "CDR stands for holistic responsible corporate action with regard to the impact of digital technologies and data" (Carl et al., 2025, p. 1425). The theoretical foundation of CDR emphasizes the need for organizations to navigate these complexities with a focus on ethical decision-making. CDR specifically targets the unique ethical dilemmas arising from digitalization. As organizations increasingly rely on technologies such as artificial intelligence, data analytics, and digital platforms, the potential for ethical breaches also deepens. The theoretical rationale for CDR is grounded in the recognition that digital technologies significantly impact both business operations and societal dynamics. As technological development accelerates, it becomes clear that an expanded conceptualization of responsibility is necessary to address the unique risks and opportunities related to digital technologies (Lobschat et al., 2021). The "exponential growth in technological development, malleability of technologies and data in use, and pervasiveness of technology and data" (Lobschat et al., 2021, p. 876) underscores the urgency for organizations to adopt dedicated responsible practices addressing the impact of digital technologies.

Both benefits and risks that emerge through more sophisticated digital products, services, and technologies apply to consumers. While they benefit, for example, from more personalized or more ubiquitous support in everyday lives, challenges and threats also affect consumers. For instance, (discriminating) artificial intelligence-based systems in loan or court decisions can have a significant impact on consumers' lives. Even consumers not directly interacting with such technologies can be affected when, for example, their data is used for training. Due to consumers being one of the centrally affected groups from the upside as well as the downside of enhanced digitalization, taking them, their needs, and their preferences into consideration and protecting them is crucial nowadays, thus pursuing a consumer-centric approach to CDR. Moreover, the rise of digital platforms and technologies has led to increased scrutiny from consumers, policymakers, and advocacy groups, who demand greater transparency and ethical conduct from organizations. As such, CDR emerges not only as a response to these societal expectations but also as a proactive commitment to ethical business practices that prioritize consumer welfare and societal good.

2.2 The CDR Dimensions Under Investigation

To facilitate the practical application of CDR and for the empirical assessment, we employed eight dimensions derived from an established framework adaptable to CDR (Thorun et al., 2017) that reflects a comprehensive understanding of responsible digital practices. Several frameworks (e.g., the Building Bloxx, CDR Manifesto) emerged over the last years. Despite their differing nomenclature and foci, they share important cornerstones of CDR and a comparable understanding (see chap. 4; Mihale-Wilson et al., 2022). We therefore opted for one of the earliest frameworks that is adaptable to CDR and covers the mutually agreed-upon aspects and facets of CDR. Further, this framework specifically focuses on activities directed at consumers and does not include an internal perspective, unlike other frameworks (e.g., the Building Bloxx). To analyze consumers' perceptions of CDR activities, such a focus on the external perspective is suitable. To sum up, we opted for the framework by Thorun and colleagues due to their wide coverage of CDR-related topics and their focus on consumers in particular. The following eight dimensions are used for structuring and evaluating CDR in our study:

1. **Access**: Access involves ensuring that all consumers can physically and mentally engage with digital technologies, products, and services. Organizations can strive to eliminate barriers related to affordability, usability, and required prior knowledge (related research, e.g., Díaz Andrade & Techatassanasoontorn, 2021; Hsieh et al., 2008; Lameijer et al., 2017; Venkatesh & Brown, 2001).
2. **Education and Awareness**: Empowering consumers through education and awareness is vital for informed decision-making in the digital realm. Organizations can provide clear information regarding online purchasing processes, data privacy rights, and the implications of digital technologies. By equipping consumers with the tools to understand their rights and the potential consequences of their digital behavior, companies can foster a culture of digital empowerment (related research, e.g., Hsieh et al., 2008; Thorun et al., 2017; United Nations, 2018; Venkatesh & Sykes, 2013).
3. **Information and Transparency**: Transparency is essential for building consumer trust. Organizations can commit to providing comprehensive information about their products and services, including pricing, certifications, further provenance, and data handling practices. By being transparent about the capabilities and limitations of their offerings, companies can meet the growing consumer demand for accountability and ethical practices (related research, e.g., Awad & Krishnan, 2006; Carl & Mihale-Wilson, 2020; Granados et al., 2010; Granados & Gupta, 2013).
4. **Economic Interests**: Recognizing and addressing the economic interests of consumers is a crucial aspect of CDR. Businesses can adopt fair competition policies and consider the economic impacts of their practices on consumers. Engaging with issues such as net neutrality and unbiased recommendation or automated systems can enhance consumer trust and loyalty (related research, e.g., Berente et al., 2021; Bourreau et al., 2015; Lewis, 2013; Truby, 2018; United Nations, 2018; Weisstein et al., 2013; Xiao & Benbasat, 2011).
5. **Product Safety and Liability**: Ensuring product safety in the digital context poses unique challenges due to the interconnected nature of digital products and services. Organizations can proactively address safety concerns and establish clear liability frameworks. By prioritizing accountability and reliability, companies can mitigate risks associated with digital goods and services, safeguarding consumers against potential harms (related research, e.g., Daughety & Reinganum, 1995; Gross et al., 2016; Smith, 2017).

6. **Data Privacy and Security**: Data privacy and security are paramount in the digital age. Organizations must not only comply with legal regulations such as the GDPR but can strive to exceed these minimum standards. By implementing robust data handling and storage practices, businesses can enhance consumer perceptions of trustworthiness and commitment to ethical standards (related research, e.g., Bélanger & Crossler, 2011; Goel & Shawky, 2009; Hann et al., 2007; Heimbach & Hinz, 2018; Mason, 1986).
7. **Dispute Resolution and Awareness**: Establishing effective dispute resolution mechanisms is crucial for addressing consumer concerns. Organizations can promote awareness of available dispute resolution options and ensure that consumers feel supported in navigating challenges that may arise from the use of digital products and services (related research, e.g., Ang & Buttle, 2012; Turel et al., 2008).
8. **Governance and Participation**: Lastly, it is important to highlight the need for governments to consistently adjust regulatory requirements in order to "steer the digitalization process in the right direction" (Thorun et al., 2017, p. 91). Effective governance and participatory mechanisms at the state level, including efficient lawmaking, robust regulatory frameworks, and effective enforcement, in a digital context, are crucial. In this regard, the responsibility for governance and engagement in participatory processes rests primarily with policymakers and nongovernmental regulatory organizations (Thorun et al., 2017), positioning these as exogenous influences within a company's CDR framework. Consequently, we exclude the dimension of governance and participation from further analysis, as this study focuses on the operationalization of CDR within companies rather than the external forces impacting them.

3 Evaluation of Consumer Preferences

As we stated before in the introduction, the overall aim of our consumer studies is to provide guidance on concrete CDR activities in practice based on consumers' perceived importance of these activities. However, the relevant CDR dimensions are comprised of a wide range of possible sub-dimensions, each featuring several concrete activities firms can perform. As we cannot cover all of these potential dimensions and activities in a single consumer study, we chose a multistage approach, first conducting expert discussions, which then informed a set of pre-studies to determine the CDR dimensions consumers perceive as the most relevant (see Mihale-Wilson et al., 2021). Those pre-studies in turn informed the final study, where we could determine consumers' valuation of the CDR dimensions most relevant to them (see Carl et al., 2024). Figure 1 gives an overview of our approach.

The expert discussions were qualitative in nature and validated the high-level dimensions of CDR we derive from literature (Thorun et al., 2017). They also informed our selection of sub-dimensions for each CDR dimension.

The pre-studies are where we started to do large-scale consumer studies. We employed two best-worst scaling (BWS) experiments (Mihale-Wilson et al., 2021).

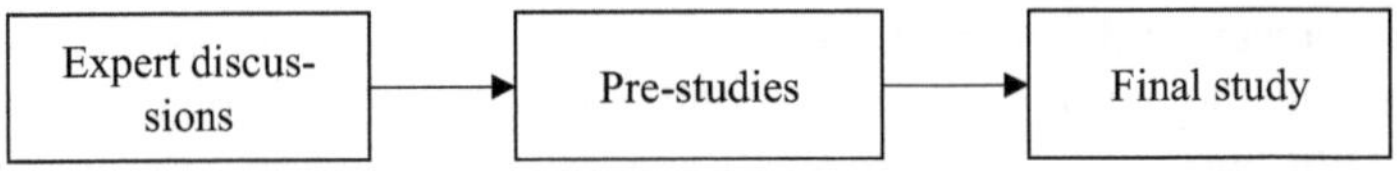

Fig. 1 Overview of our multistage approach (authors' illustration)

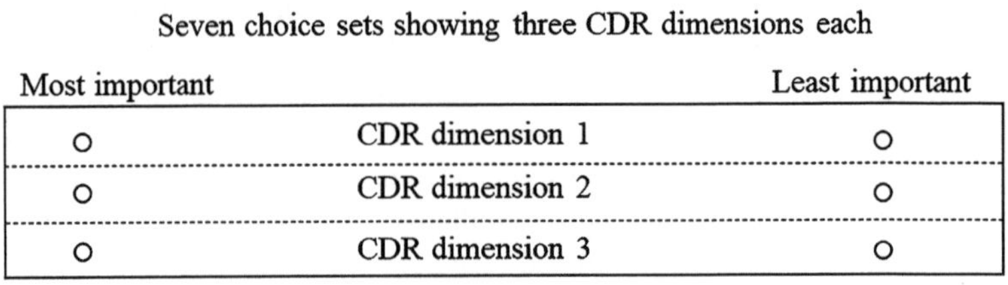

Fig. 2 Exemplary choice set in the pre-studies (authors' illustration)

In BWS experiments, consumers are asked to rank items, in our case, aspects of CDR, by their importance. We chose this approach since rankings are frequently employed in practice and research, therefore ensuring accessible results for a wide audience. To make the consumer feedback manageable in the context of an online survey, the items are grouped in choice sets with three options each, where consumers are asked to point out the most and least important items. Figure 2 illustrates such a choice set. Several choice sets are presented so we can rank more than three items.

The first BWS experiment evaluated consumers' perception of the main CDR dimensions discussed above. We then explored these insights more in depth by sequencing several sub-dimensions of the most important CDR dimension in the second BWS experiment. So, all in all, the aim of the BWS pre-studies was to order the proposed CDR dimensions by relevance to consumers, and similarly also order the sub-dimensions of the top-ranked CDR dimension (Mihale-Wilson et al., 2021). For more details on the methodology, please refer to our full paper (Mihale-Wilson et al., 2021). These results from the BWS experiments then informed the design of our final studies, allowing us to focus on the most relevant aspects of CDR from a consumer perspective. This is necessary as established methods can only deal with a limited number of attributes (Carl et al., 2024). But, due to our multistage approach, only the dimensions least relevant to consumers will be omitted.

For the final study, we use a dual-response (DURE) choice-based conjoint (CBC) approach. Characteristically, CBC repeatedly lets participants trade between multi-attributed product versions in context with a price, which can then be used to determine price contributions of individual attributes. Especially for managers and researchers aiming to understand specific consumer preferences for actual implementation in practice, such an approach can be helpful. First, it allows comparing different variations of a product characteristic (e.g., different communication channels for customer support) against each other. In this case, it is possible to answer the question of which CDR activities should be carried out for certain consumer groups according to their preferences. Second, this method allows for measuring

12 choice sets showing three alternatives each

Please indicate which of the following smart home environments you prefer.

	IoT solution 1	IoT solution 2	IoT solution 3
Information regarding data collection	Tabular form	Detailed	One pager
Access and correction of personal data	Information and correction	Information	Information, correction, and deletion
Notification of incidents	Affected users only	Public broadcast	On request
Price per month	5€	2.50€	5€
	☐	☑	☐

Would you actually subscribe to the smart home environment you prefer?

☑ Yes
☐ No

Fig. 3 Exemplary choice set in the final study (authors' illustration)

varying willingness to pay (WTP) for different combinations of CDR engagement. In this way, managers can evaluate whether some variation of CDR and according costs can keep up with the additional WTP and appreciation by consumers. Thus, the derived results can be a starting point for cost-benefit analysis common for companies evaluating future CDR engagement.

Each choice set in a DURE experiment consists of two trade-offs. Firstly, consumers have to choose one out of several alternative products that they like most. Secondly, they have to decide whether they would buy this preferred product or not. Once again, we present a restricted number of product versions (3 versions per choice), but let the consumer make several choices (see Fig. 3). We also split the study into 2 sub-studies, DURE 1 and 2, with DURE 1 covering data privacy and security (i.e., the most important CDR dimension from the consumers' views) and DURE 2 covering the other dimensions of CDR. Once again, this is because the instrument can only deal with a limited number of attributes (consumers would be overwhelmed if we present them with a large number of choice sets in an online survey). As we need to present realistic products, observing various aspects of CDR (or not), we chose an Internet of Things (IoT) use case. The overall design of the questionnaire is illustrated in Fig. 3. For more details on the methodology, please refer to our full paper (Carl et al., 2024).

4 Ranking of CDR Dimensions

We now present the results of our study. As already described, our first pre-study ranked the perceived importance of the main CDR dimensions. Figure 4 presents the results of this study. It ranks the averaged BW scores of the assessed CDR dimensions, leading to a presentation in decreasing order of importance as perceived by consumers. BW scores reflect the relative importance range from –3 to 3

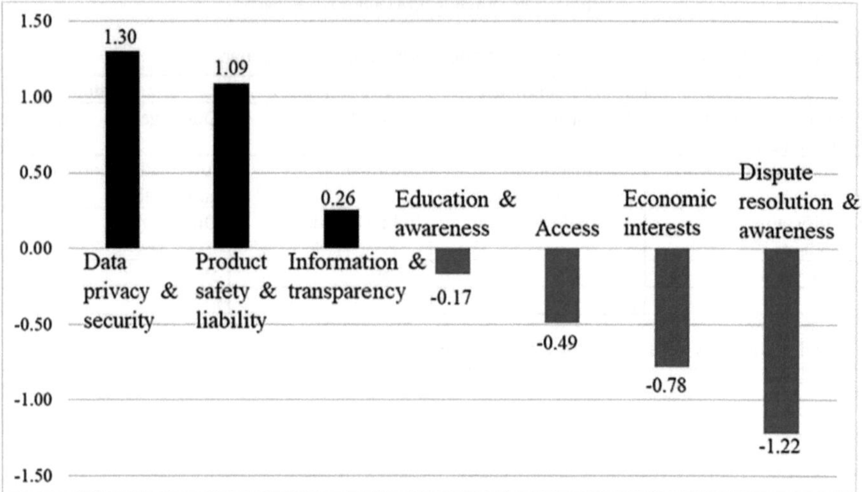

Fig. 4 Averaged ratings of CDR dimensions across participants

according to the counting method[1]. As can be seen from the diagram, consumers saw data privacy and security, product safety and liability, and information and transparency as the most important CDR dimensions, while they appreciated corporate activities related to access, economic interests, and dispute resolution less.

We could not identify concrete product safety and liability activities for empirical assessment. Safety issues are very heterogeneous across product types, and legislation is nationally fragmented. In addition, product safety and liability are strongly regulated fields. Companies have relatively few degrees of freedom when it comes to those aspects of their products. We therefore decided to exclude the product safety dimension from our further studies.

4.1 The Most Prevalent CDR Dimension in Detail

Expanding on these results and consumer preferences regarding the CDR dimensions, we conducted another BWS experiment to assess consumers' perception of possible sub-dimensions within the highest-ranked CDR dimension – data privacy and security.

The OECD Privacy Framework (OECD, 2013) names eight main privacy principles, which we base our BWS study on: (1) collection limitation, (2) data quality, (3) purpose specification, (4) use limitation, (5) security safeguards, (6) openness, (7) individual participation, and (8) accountability principle. The BWS experiment

[1] Each dimension appeared three times to the participants in different choice sets. When choosing the respective dimension as the most important one, we counted +1 for the BW score. When choosing the respective dimension as the least important one, we counted -1 for the BW score to reflect the relative importance for consumers.

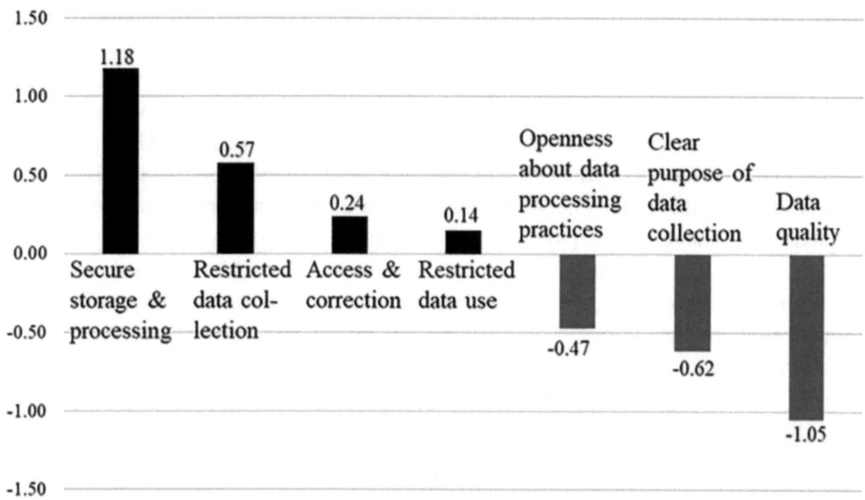

Fig. 5 Averaged ratings of privacy and security sub-dimensions across participants

examined seven of the eight sub-dimensions within the OECD Privacy Framework, excluding the principle of accountability. We were not able to operationalize accountability as an activity, and it is therefore excluded. Still, we do acknowledge it is an important framework condition for compliance with other principles.

Figure 5 indicates the average BW scores of the data privacy and security sub-dimensions. The results underlined the importance of secure storage and processing, restricted data collection, and data access and correction for consumers, while consumers seemed to appreciate openness about data processing practices, high data quality, or a clear purpose of data collection less.

5 One Size Does Not Fit All? Customization of CDR Activities

5.1 Steer CDR Activities in the Most Prevalent CDR Dimension

As described in the section detailing our surveys, we then performed two DURE experiments. Those surveys have three main results: (i) We can identify market segments – consumers who have similar preferences and demographics, but are different from the other segments. (ii) We can determine a WTP associated with each product property, i.e., with each CDR activity we give as an option in the survey. And, lastly, (iii) based on the WTP, we can determine preferred products, in our case preferred CDR activities, for each market segment and the entire sample, along with a WTP for these products.

Our first DURE survey (DURE 1) was concerned with activities related to the data privacy and security sub-dimensions investigated in the second BWS study. We chose information regarding data collection (detailed, one-pager, or tabular), access and correction of personal data (only access, access and correction, or access, correction, and deletion), and notification of incidents (on demand, affected users, or public broadcast), representing restricted data collection, access and correction, and secure storage, respectively. For those activities, we performed a DURE experiment.

We first conducted a market segmentation, statistically identifying consumer groups with similar preferences. We labeled the clusters according to their demographics and the derived psychographic components to distinguish them (see Table 1). Note that the clusters were statistically determined based on their preferences and then labeled according to their psychographics and demographics, and not the other way around.

Segment 1, the *distrustful brave*, exhibits the comparatively lowest average score for trust and the highest for braveness across the various segments. Similarly, we label the other segments *young performer*, *retired traditionalists*, and *technology-affine conservatives*. Table 2 presents the resulting preferred product variations as well as their associated latent value (WTP).

It shows the three most preferred product variations per consumer segment and for the entire sample, alongside their associated monthly WTP. For example, for the distrustful brave, the most preferred product variation features detailed information regarding data collection, information, correction, and deletion access to personal data and the notification of incidents for affected users only, with an associated WTP of 3.17€ per month.

The evaluation of consumer preferences unanimously advises companies to commit to easy access to the information on, correction, and deletion of personal data. We found no interest in other access approaches. Except for this attribute, consumer preferences are quite heterogeneous (see Table 2). This points toward an approach where products can be tailored toward specific market segments, and one product will not fit all consumers.

Table 1 Consumer segments: DURE 1

Cluster analysis	Distrustful brave $N = 32$	Young performer $N = 37$	Retired traditionalists $N = 26$	Technology-affine conservatives $N = 34$	Entire sample $N = 129$
Psychographics					
Braveness	0.60	0.58	−0.27	−0.99	0.00
Trusting nature	−0.87	0.47	−0.10	0.39	0.00
Technology affinity	0.00	−0.21	−0.22	0.40	0.00
Demographics					
Age (average)	47	37	59	46	46
Education (% university degree)	12.51%	83.78%	23.07%	20.59%	37.21%
Employment (% employed)	96.88%	97.30%	0.00%	94.12%	76.74%

Table 2 WTP and preferred products: DURE 1

		Information regarding data collection			Access and correction of personal data			Notification of incidents			Price
	Ranking	Detailed	One pager	Tabular form	Information	Information and correction	Information, correction, and deletion	On request	Affected users only	Public broadcast	WTP (per month)
Distrustful brave	1st	x					x		x		3.17€
	2nd	x					x			x	1.87€
	3rd		x				x		x		1.69€
Young performer	1st	x					x		x		6.52€
	2nd	x					x			x	6.29€
	3rd		x				x		x		5.50€
Retired traditionalists	1st			x			x	x			−0.88€
	2nd			x			x		x		−1.76€
	3rd	x					x	x			−2.55€
Technology affine conservatives	1st		x				x		x		5.62€
	2nd	x					x		x		5.46€
	3rd		x				x			x	5.30€
Entire sample	1st	x					x		x		3.40€
	2nd	x					x			x	2.65€
	3rd		x				x		x		2.50€

5.2 Diversify CDR Activities in Further CDR Dimensions

In our second DURE study, we focused on the other CDR dimensions not covered by DURE 1. DURE 2 covers user support (call center, online, or robo advisor), dispute resolution (manufacturer-specific, manufacturer network, or independent agency), transparency (detailed, one-pager, or tabular), and interoperability (no, semi-, or seamless interoperability). Once again, we performed a market segmentation; the results are given in Table 3.

Like for DURE 1, we labeled the clusters according to their demographics and psychographics to distinguish them. Accordingly, segment 2, the *young achievers*, exhibits the lowest average score for age and the highest for education across the various segments. Similarly, we label the other segments *young expeditives* and *elderly traditionalists*. Table 4 presents the resulting preferred product variations and their associated latent value (WTP).

It shows the three most preferred product variations per consumer segment and for the entire sample, alongside their associated monthly WTP. For example, for the young expeditives, the most preferred product variation features call center support, an independent agency for dispute resolution, a detailed data protection declaration, and seamless interoperability, with an associated WTP of 1.75€ per month. Once again, we can only give a high-level overview of our methods and results. For full details, see Carl et al. (2024).

6 Concluding Remarks

This work contributes to the practical implementation of CDR by empirically assessing its operationalization at the measure level, drawing from pre-studies that ranked various CDR dimensions and sub-dimensions. The primary objective is to provide actionable guidance for implementing CDR activities and establishing effective consumer segmentation strategies. The findings suggest that market segmentation is promising to address the diverse preferences of different consumer

Table 3 Consumer segments: DURE 2

Cluster analysis	Young expeditives $N = 42$	Young achievers $N = 56$	Elderly traditionalists $N = 39$	Entire sample $N = 137$
Psychographics				
In love with the new	1.02	−0.41	−0.51	0.00
Trusting nature	0.10	0.16	−0.34	0.00
Demographics				
Age (average)	40	40	60	46
Education (% university degree)	28.57%	48.22%	23.08%	35.04%
Employment (% employed)	90.48%	100.00%	30.77%	77.37%

Table 4 WTP and preferred products: DURE 2

		User support			Dispute resolution			Transparency regarding data protection			Interoperability			Price
	Ranking	Call center support	Online	Robo-advisor	Manufacturer-specific	Manufacturer network	Independent agency	Detailed	One pager	Tabular form	No intero-perability	Semi-interoperability	Seamless interoperability	WTP (per month)
Young expeditives	1st	x					x	x					x	1.75€
	2nd	x			x			x					x	1.65€
	3rd	x					x			x			x	1.40€
Young achievers	1st	x					x	x					x	0.72€
	2nd	x					x			x			x	0.50€
	3rd			x			x	x					x	0.50€
Elderly tradition-alists	1st	x					x	x					x	0.84€
	2nd	x					x			x			x	0.62€
	3rd	x					x		x				x	0.51€
Entire sample	1st	x					x	x					x	1.07€
	2nd	x					x			x			x	0.81€
	3rd	x			x			x					x	0.69€

segments effectively. However, it is essential to recognize that the understanding and operationalization of CDR are influenced by the unique perceptions of organizations, their employees, and stakeholders. Therefore, it is imperative for organizations to assess the applicability of the empirical findings rather than viewing them as prescriptive directives for CDR implementation.

For organizations prioritizing data privacy and security – the most valued dimension – investing in state-of-the-art solutions is essential, especially for those operating within the EU, where exceeding GDPR requirements can foster consumer trust. However, consumer preferences concerning this dimension are heterogeneous, necessitating targeted psycho-demographic strategies that utilize tailored communication methods. Proactive communication regarding data breaches is generally preferred, indicating an opportunity for companies to exceed legal minimums and enhance consumer satisfaction. While integrating advanced data privacy and security practices, organizations should also consider the associated costs and the likelihood of these investments aligning with consumer appreciation. It is important to note that the work does not conduct a cost-benefit analysis of CDR activities, but it lays a foundational basis for future inquiry on this critical aspect of management by assessing consumers' WTP for particular CDR activities.

Furthermore, once organizations establish a robust foundation for data privacy and security, they should explore additional CDR dimensions, such as information transparency and economic interests, particularly interoperability, in the interest of differentiation. Engaging in industry-wide initiatives that facilitate seamless interoperability can significantly enhance consumer value and expand market opportunities. Again, such initiatives might be costly and not keep up with consumers' monetary valuation. The diverse preferences among consumers further underscore the importance of segmentation, particularly in areas related to information and transparency.

Overall, the results mostly align with the actual societal debate on the need for protecting privacy and enhanced transparency. The societal debate might influence which aspects of CDR consumers perceive as most important or most prevalent. Thus, for organizations, listening to the articulated concerns and adapting CDR engagement accordingly can be beneficial. Especially in an evolving field such as CDR, closely monitoring recent debates and new or intensified needs is vital. In essence, based on the empirical findings in our study, we propose that practitioners:

- *Prioritize activities* related to *data privacy and security* that exceed requirements posed by, for example, the GDPR.
- Particularly *ease the access to and correction of stored data.*
- Continue to offer *human support via telephone* apart from further communication channels.
- *Collaborate* on the development of industry-wide standards or adopt established ones to ensure a high degree of *interoperability.*
- If economically feasible, provide *dispute resolution* involving *independent agencies.*

- Overall, *tailor communication strategies* according to different customer segments, using particularly suiting communication channels to spread adapted communication content (e.g., related to incidents, privacy policies, and data collection practices).

In conclusion, the results indicate that a one-size-fits-all approach might not be fully suitable for CDR. Designing digital products and services that can adapt to the varying needs of different consumer segments is essential. Market segmentation, a standard practice in the digital realm, should extend to CDR dimensions, allowing organizations to tailor their communication strategies and CDR activities to effectively reach and engage their target audiences. The role of pricing remains significant, suggesting that offering streamlined versions of CDR activities may be beneficial for more price-sensitive consumers.

Competing Interests This chapter is based on our publications Mihale-Wilson et al. (2021) and Carl et al. (2024).

References

Ang, L., & Buttle, F. (2012). Complaints-handling processes and organisational benefits: An ISO 10002-based investigation. *Journal of Marketing Management, 28*(9–10), 1021–1042. https://doi.org/10.1080/0267257X.2011.615335

Awad, N. F., & Krishnan, M. S. (2006). The personalization privacy paradox: An empirical evaluation of information transparency and the willingness to be profiled online for personalization. *MIS Quarterly, 30*(1), 13–28. https://doi.org/10.2307/25148715

Bélanger, F., & Crossler, R. E. (2011). Privacy in the digital age: A review of information privacy research in information systems. *MIS Quarterly, 35*(4), 1017–1041. https://doi.org/10.2307/41409971

Berente, N., Gu, B., Recker, J., & Santhanam, R. (2021). Managing artificial intelligence. *MIS Quarterly, 45*(3), 1433–1450. https://doi.org/10.25300/MISQ/2021/16274

Bourreau, M., Kourandi, F., & Valletti, T. (2015). Net neutrality with competing internet platforms. *The Journal of Industrial Economics, 63*(1), 30–73. https://doi.org/10.1111/joie.12068

Carl, K. V., & Hinz, O. (2024). What we already know about corporate digital responsibility in IS research: A review and conceptualization of potential CDR activities. *Electronic Markets, 34*(27). https://doi.org/10.1007/s12525-024-00708-0

Carl, K. V., & Mihale-Wilson, C. (2020). Consumer privacy concerns and preferences for certification and accreditation of intelligent assistants in the internet of things. In H. Roßnagel, C. H. Schunck, S. Mödersheim, & D. Hühnlein (Eds.), *Proceedings of the Open Identity Summit 2020 (OID)* (pp. 157–162). Gesellschaft für Informatik e.V. https://doi.org/10.18420/ois2020_13

Carl, K. V., Kubach, M., & Mihale-Wilson, C. (2023). The motivation of companies to implement corporate digital responsibility activities voluntarily: An empirical assessment. In *Proceedings of the 18th International Conference on Wirtschaftsinformatik.*

Carl, K. V., Mihale-Wilson, C., Zibuschka, J., & Hinz, O. (2024). A consumer perspective on corporate digital responsibility: An empirical evaluation of consumer preferences. *Journal of Business Economics, 94*, 979–1024. https://doi.org/10.1007/s11573-023-01142-y

Carl, K. V., Blachetta, M., Bilfinger, B., Brink, A., Cerulli-Harms, A. K., Christ, A.-S., Dietl, K., Dörr, S., Hauer, M. P., Hinz, M., Jänig, J.-R., Keilhofer, K., Kurtz, C., Mihale-Wilson, C., Mueller, B., Przybylek, B. A., Schaufler, N., Schlegel, I. K., Scholz, M., et al. (2025). Establishing common ground in corporate digital responsibility: Integrating understandings, definitions, and expert perspectives. In *Proceedings of the INFORMATIK 2025* (pp. 1415–1428). Gesellschaft für Informatik e.V. https://doi.org/10.18420/inf2025_125

Daughety, A. F., & Reinganum, J. F. (1995). Product safety: Liability, R&D, and signaling. *The American Economic Review, 85*(5), 1187–1206.

Díaz Andrade, A., & Techatassanasoontorn, A. A. (2021). Digital enforcement: Rethinking the pursuit of a digitally-enabled society. *Information Systems Journal, 31*(1), 184–197. https://doi.org/10.1111/isj.12306

Goel, S., & Shawky, H. A. (2009). Estimating the market impact of security breach announcements on firm values. *Information & Management, 46*(7), 404–410. https://doi.org/10.1016/j.im.2009.06.005

Granados, N., & Gupta, A. (2013). Transparency strategy: Competing with information in a digital world. *MIS Quarterly, 37*(2), 637–641.

Granados, N., Gupta, A., & Kauffman, R. J. (2010). Research commentary—Information transparency in business-to-consumer markets: Concepts, framework, and research agenda. *Information Systems Research, 21*(2), 2. https://doi.org/10.1287/isre.1090.0249

Gross, M. L., Canetti, D., & Vashdi, D. R. (2016). The psychological effects of cyber terrorism. *Bulletin of the Atomic Scientists, 72*(5), 284–291. https://doi.org/10.1080/00963402.2016.1216502

Hann, I.-H., Hui, K.-L., Lee, S.-Y. T., & Png, I. P. L. (2007). Overcoming online information privacy concerns: An information-processing theory approach. *Journal of Management Information Systems, 24*(2), 2. https://doi.org/10.2753/MIS0742-1222240202

Heimbach, I., & Hinz, O. (2018). The Impact of sharing mechanism design on content sharing in online social networks. *Information Systems Research, 29*(3), 592–611. https://doi.org/10.1287/isre.2017.0738

Hess, T., Matt, C., Benlian, A., & Wiesböck, F. (2016). Options for formulating a digital transformation strategy. *MIS Quarterly Executive, 15*(2), 123–139.

Hsieh, J. J. P.-A., Rai, A., & Keil, M. (2008). Understanding digital inequality: Comparing continued use behavioral models of the socio-economically advantaged and disadvantaged. *MIS Quarterly, 32*(1), 97–126. https://doi.org/10.2307/25148830

Lameijer, C., Mueller, B., & Hage, E. (2017). Towards rethinking the digital divide – Recognizing shades of grey in older adults' digital inclusion. In Y. J. Kim, R. Agarwal, & J. K. Lee (Eds.), *Proceedings of the 38th International Conference on Information Systems, Seoul, South Korea.*

Lewis, G. A. (2013). Role of standards in cloud-computing interoperability. In *Proceedings of the 46th Hawaii International Conference on System Sciences (HICSS)* (pp. 1652–1661). https://doi.org/10.1109/HICSS.2013.470

Lobschat, L., Mueller, B., Eggers, F., Brandimarte, L., Diefenbach, S., Kroschke, M., & Wirtz, J. (2021). Corporate digital responsibility. *Journal of Business Research, 122*, 875–888. https://doi.org/10.1016/j.jbusres.2019.10.006

Mason, R. O. (1986). Four ethical issues of the information age. *MIS Quarterly, 10*(1), 5–12. https://doi.org/10.2307/248873

Mihale-Wilson, C., Zibuschka, J., Carl, K. V., & Hinz, O. (2021). Corporate digital responsibility – Extended conceptualization and a guide to implementation. In F. Rowe, R. El Amrani, M. Limayem, S. Matook, C. Rosenkranz, E. A. Whitley, & A. El Quammah (Eds.), *Proceedings of the 29th European Conference on Information Systems (ECIS).*

Mihale-Wilson, C., Hinz, O., van der Aalst, W., & Weinhardt, C. (2022). Corporate digital responsibility: Relevance and opportunities for business and information systems engineering. *Business & Information Systems Engineering, 64*(2), 127–132. https://doi.org/10.1007/s12599-022-00746-y

OECD. (2013). *The OECD privacy framework.* http://www.oecd.org/sti/ieconomy/oecd_privacy_framework.pdf

Ransbotham, S., Fichman, R. G., Gopal, R., & Gupta, A. (2016). Special section introduction—Ubiquitous IT and digital vulnerabilities. *Information Systems Research, 27*(4), 834–847. https://doi.org/10.1287/isre.2016.0683

Royakkers, L., Timmer, J., Kool, L., & van Est, R. (2018). Societal and ethical issues of digitization. *Ethics and Information Technology, 20*(2), 127–142. https://doi.org/10.1007/s10676-018-9452-x

Smith, B. W. (2017). Automated driving and product liability. *Michigan State Law Review, 2017*(1), 1–74. https://doi.org/10.17613/3bj8-z207

Tarafdar, M., Gupta, A., & Turel, O. (2013). The dark side of information technology use. *Information Systems Journal, 23*(3). https://doi.org/10.1111/isj.12015

Thorun, C., Vetter, M., Reisch, L., & Zimmer, A. K. (2017). *Indicators of consumer protection and empowerment in the digital world: Results and recommendations of a feasibility study*. https://www.conpolicy.de/data/user_upload/Studien/ConPolicy_Indicator_study.pdf

Truby, J. (2018). Decarbonizing bitcoin: Law and policy choices for reducing the energy consumption of blockchain technologies and digital currencies. *Energy Research & Social Science, 44*, 399–410. https://doi.org/10.1016/j.erss.2018.06.009

Turel, O., Yuan, Y., & Connelly, C. E. (2008). In justice we trust: Predicting user acceptance of e-customer services. *Journal of Management Information Systems, 24*(4), 123–151. https://doi.org/10.2753/MIS0742-1222240405

United Nations. (2018). *Manual on consumer protection*. https://unctad.org/en/PublicationsLibrary/ditccplp2017d1_en.pdf

Venkatesh, V., & Brown, S. A. (2001). A longitudinal investigation of personal computers in homes: Adoption determinants and emerging challenges. *MIS Quarterly, 25*(1), 71–102. https://doi.org/10.2307/3250959

Venkatesh, V., & Sykes, T. A. (2013). Digital divide initiative success in developing countries: A longitudinal field study in a village in India. *Information Systems Research, 24*(2), 239–260. https://doi.org/10.1287/isre.1110.0409

Weisstein, F. L., Monroe, K. B., & Kukar-Kinney, M. (2013). Effects of price framing on consumers' perceptions of online dynamic pricing practices. *Journal of the Academy of Marketing Science, 41*(5), 501–514. https://doi.org/10.1007/s11747-013-0330-0

Xiao, B., & Benbasat, I. (2011). Product-related deception in e-commerce: A theoretical perspective. *MIS Quarterly, 35*(1), 169–196. https://doi.org/10.2307/23043494

K. Valerie Carl is a postdoctoral researcher at the chair of information systems and information management at Goethe University Frankfurt. She is interested in research on (corporate) digital responsibility, artificial intelligence (particularly human–AI augmentation), digital resilience, and digital ecosystems.

Jan Zibuschka is a security manager with Robert Bosch GmbH, working on sensors and driver assistance systems. When he made the main contribution to this research, he was with the central research department, working on security, privacy, and the Internet of Things.

Cristina Mihale-Wilson is a researcher and entrepreneur working at the intersection of artificial intelligence, digital ecosystems, and societal responsibility.

Oliver Hinz is a professor of information systems and information management at Goethe University Frankfurt. He is interested in research at the intersection of technology and markets.

Tracing the Evolution of Corporate Digital Responsibility (CDR) Conceptualization: A Literature Overview

Anna-Sophia Christ and Kübra Çalışkan

Abstract

This chapter provides a structured overview of the evolving literature on Corporate Digital Responsibility (CDR), tracing its developments from early normative theorizing to contemporary efforts at practical operationalization. It explores how CDR initially emerged from pressing industrial concerns about digitality and ethics, before gaining traction across multiple academic disciplines. While still a relatively young field, CDR is rooted in established research, particularly in computer ethics and corporate responsibility, to which this chapter maps relevant interrelations. Key scholarly contributions are highlighted, including definitional work, the identification of core dimensions, and the development of models for organizational integration. In doing so, the chapter offers both scholars and practitioners an accessible entry point into the fragmented but rapidly expanding field of CDR.

A.-S. Christ
Business, Innovation, and Transformation Institute (BIT), University of Bremen, Bremen, Germany
e-mail: achrist@uni-bremen.de

K. Çalışkan (✉)
Department of Management Information Systems, Business School, Sakarya University, Sakarya, Türkiye
e-mail: kubrac@sakarya.edu.tr

A.-S. Christ (ed.), *Corporate Digital Responsibility*, Future of Business and Finance, https://doi.org/10.1007/978-3-032-14793-6_7

1 The Earliest Echoes of CDR

The origins of corporate digital responsibility (CDR) are not easily traced to a single moment or publication. Rather, like many emerging ethical frameworks, CDR evolved from a confluence of professional practices, academic reflection, political engagement, and societal needs. Its roots extend across boardrooms, consultancies, news blogs, research institutions, and government initiatives, each offering a different piece of the puzzle that is still being assembled today.

1.1 Practitioners Leading the Way

The first thoughts of what would become CDR came not from universities but from the world of business. In 2017, leaders from DHL, Investec, and Fujitsu (Driesens et al., 2017) jointly reflected on digital responsibility in a widely reused (for that time) blog article. Their discussion is practical, anchored in the realities of running organizations amid increasing digitalization. The business decision-makers raise questions about the drivers of CDR, what defines it, and why it matters now more than ever.

Around the same time, two more foundational practitioner voices emerged. In 2018, Joynson articulated a set of CDR principles, spanning digital accessibility, inclusion, convenience, sustainability, fairness in artificial intelligence (AI), data ownership, and digital well-being. And in the same year, Price (2018) published a companion piece emphasizing how CDR could shape a more human digital future. These two efforts helped catalyze what would later become a collective endeavor: the CDR Manifesto (2021), initiated by a diverse group of practitioners, researchers, and leaders from across sectors.

In the chronology of available publications, even before these contributions, Accenture consultants had laid the groundwork for early practitioners. In 2015, they proposed five foundational principles: digital stewardship, transparency, empowerment, equality, and inclusion (Cooper et al., 2015). Corporate concerns about data privacy, ethical governance, and digital transformation shape their insights. While they only briefly touch on deeper ethical roots, their work hints at two long-standing disciplines that CDR later builds on: the field of corporate (social) responsibility (CSR) (e.g., Dörr, 2021; Orbik & Zozul'aková, 2019) and the broader domain of computer ethics (e.g., Cheng & Zhang, 2023; Mueller, 2022).

By 2018, the conversation was picking up momentum in political circles as well (Schymura, 2018). The German Federal Ministry of Justice and Consumer Protection (BMJV) launched the CDR Initiative (2025), gathering companies to formalize digital responsibility commitments. Engaged CDR experts (e.g., Thorun et al., 2017, 2018) began framing CDR through the lens of consumer protection, leveraging the eight dimensions of the United Nations Guideline of Consumer Protection (UNGCP). This expanded the dialogue beyond the corporate sector and toward civil society, picked up by multiple scholars in the following (e.g., Carl et al., 2024; Mihale-Wilson et al., 2021).

Meanwhile, professional networks like the German Association for Digital Economy (BVDW, 2025) established a committee on Digital Responsibility, and the Initiative D21 (n.d.) – Germany's largest nonprofit network for the digital society – formed the working group AG Digitale Ethik. These platforms gave practitioners, policymakers, and researchers a space to collaborate, exchange insights, and elevate the visibility of CDR at the national level.

1.2 Initial Scholarly Research Propositions

While practice laid the early foundations, academia soon followed. The first chronological scholarly mention of CDR came from Esselmann and Brink (2016), discussing CDR in the context of digital transformation in a German university publication. This marked a quiet but crucial turning point – CDR was no longer just an industry concern; it was now a topic for academic inquiry. A more detailed consideration would show that organically, with other disciplines progressing into the digital realm, concerns of digital responsibility arise, simply using different terminologies.

It is no coincidence that Germany played a central role in the early development of CDR. Ethical concerns surrounding digital technologies have long been part of the German discourse, rooted in both philosophical traditions and regulatory foresight. Early academic and hybrid contributions reflect this trend (e.g., Esselmann & Brink, 2020; Grunwald, 2019; Werning & Middeke, 2022).

Among the early research, use cases began to be investigated: how could a media company enact CDR (Altmeppen & Filipović, 2019)? What principles should guide digitalization within government or policy think tanks (e.g., a discussion publication by the Bertelsmann Stiftung and Wittenberg-Zentrum (2020)), collecting voices from experts, or elaborated in the discussion paper by the Federal Ministry for Economic Affairs and Energy (Willrich, 2018). But also, more comprehensive work soon followed: Dörr's (2021) influential book, which dissects the unintended side effects of digitalization and proposes a strategic CDR model comprising 15 clusters and 14 guiding questions for corporate leaders.

However, the impactful academic momentum began only in 2021. A pivotal publication is the conceptual framework introduced by Lobschat et al. (2021), a multidisciplinary collaboration that firmly introduces the concept of CDR to the scholarly community. In the same year, trailblazing research was published, focusing on the sustainability link (Herden et al., 2021) and AI ethics (Elliott et al., 2021), laying the groundwork for future research.

1.3 Cross-Disciplinary and Multicultural

From this point on, CDR scholarship proliferated across disciplines, geographies, and methods. Studies emerged from business, management, and computer science (Bednárová & Serpeninova, 2023; Knopf & Pick, 2023), as well as fields such as psychology, environmental science, economics, and even medicine and engineering (Yadav & Mishra, 2022). Germany continued to lead the discourse, but contributions soon came also, for instance, from Italy (Bernini et al., 2025), France (Arciniega Gil & Ratnane, 2023), Poland (Suchacka, 2019), China (Jin & Yu, 2025), and beyond. With the field expanding, the scope of research has diversified.

Scholars began analyzing CDR through function-specific lenses, such as HR, marketing, construction, and banking (Merbecks, 2023; Mihale-Wilson et al., 2022; Weber-Lewerenz & Traverso, 2025). Other industry-specific contexts examined are hospitality (e.g., Lee et al., 2025), retail (e.g., Scarpi & Pantano, 2024), media (e.g., Nagano, 2024), and service platforms (Wirtz et al., 2023). Moreover, cross-company and supply chain perspectives emerged (e.g., Girrbach, 2021; Nagano, 2023), along with analyses of CDR in small and medium-sized enterprises (e.g., Arciniega Gil & Ratnane, 2023), industry 4.0 (e.g., Londoño-Cardozo & De Paz, 2021), or focusing on innovation (e.g., Zhu et al., 2025) and digital transformation (e.g., Paul et al., 2024), as well as increasingly discussing the implications of AI (e.g., Jin & Yu, 2025; Kunz & Wirtz, 2024; Tóth & Blut, 2024).

In parallel, stakeholder perspectives became another crucial lens, discussing CDR from the needs of the impacted parties. While early research and still a significant part mainly focuses on consumers (e.g., Carl et al., 2024; Mihale-Wilson et al., 2021; Shin et al., 2025; Thorun et al., 2017; Yang et al., 2025), employees (e.g., Clausen et al., 2023; Lee et al., 2025), board of directors (Napoli, 2023), or individual digital actors (e.g., Girrbach, 2021; Londoño-Cardozo & De Paz, 2021), as well as societal stakeholders and institutions (Dörr & Lautermann, 2024) have lately received more attention. However, the company, as the crucial player, has so far gotten little attention, a perspective, critical for translating concepts into practice.

2 Foundational-Related Disciplines

The evolution of CDR reflects a story of convergence. Originating in practice, shaped by politics, and further developed through academic inquiry, it continues to advance through interdisciplinary and cross-sectional collaboration. The chronological elaboration, simply based on publication dates, might not reflect the developments completely, since the time from conceptualization to publication in academia usually takes more time than for practitioner work.

What sets CDR apart is its grounding in lived experience, emerging not from abstract theorizing but from the tangible challenges faced by companies, consumers, and society in an increasingly digital world. Yet, much of what is now framed as CDR drew on longstanding ideas or is phrased under different terminologies. Before examining the current conceptual landscape of CDR, it is interesting to take a brief detour into the two foundational disciplines that have significantly shaped its development: corporate responsibility and computer ethics.

2.1 Building on Longstanding Computer Ethics Insights

Suppose we understand the idea of cybernetics as developed by Wiener in the 1940s as the origin of ethics and the impact areas of responsibilities in computer technology. In that case, the discussion goes almost back as far as technology itself (cf. Bynum, 2000), studied in information systems already in the midtwentieth century (Mueller, 2022; Pick & Knopf, 2023). In the years to come, the pioneers Parker, Weizenbaum, and Maner developed the conceptual understanding of ethics in computer science further, scoping computer ethics in the 1970s officially for the first time (Bynum, 2001). Fundamental work on computer ethics is still defining the research field today, followed by the scholars Johnson (1994) and Bynum (2001), and was supplemented by research in more precise technology areas of the digital realm.

Around that time, Moor (1985) defined computer ethics as "*the analysis of the nature and social impact of computer technology and the corresponding formulation and justification of policies for the ethical use of such technology*" (p. 266). With this, he points out the impact area and the need to have guidelines to steer technologies. Thus, the ethical research and the consideration of responsibility have already made extensive and far-reaching contributions that CDR can build upon (e.g., Carl, 2023; Cheng & Zhang, 2023; Mueller, 2022). And some already do, extending privacy and security research with questions of corporate responsibility (e.g., Agafonova et al., 2021; Carl, 2023) as well as digital trust (e.g., Jelovac et al., 2022; Kluiters et al., 2022), just to name a few.

The effects of digital technologies often go beyond the area of application or encompass various areas of impact (cf. Elliott et al., 2021; Thelisson et al., 2019), a perspective that is missing, as literature reviews show so far (cf. Carl, 2023). Moreover, the corporate and economic aspects have so far been disregarded or neglected in computer ethics research (cf. Christ et al., 2024; Mueller, 2022). Research on CDR that already addresses this gap of holism and interconnection includes, for instance, the work of Trittin-Ulbrich and Böckel (2022) focusing on product and business innovation or the analyses of the correlation between corporate responsibility and digital innovation (e.g., Aitken et al., 2021; Seidl, 2022).

In summary, it can be said that CDR can and is already building on prior research on ethics in digital technologies, including information systems. The concept of CDR goes beyond computer ethics, information ethics, robot ethics, digital ethics, and ethics of emerging ICT and proves to be more suitable for organizational governing (cf. Cheng & Zhang, 2023).

2.2 C(S)R and CDR: Between Convergence and Independence

According to the European Commission's (2011) definition, corporate (social) responsibility (CSR) refers to "*the responsibility of companies for their impact on society*" (p. 7). However, what constitutes "impact on society" is not fixed. It shifts according to the socio-economic and cultural context in which companies operate – contexts that are themselves in constant flux, just like the digital transformation.

The origins of CSR trace back to the work of Bowen (1953), who first articulated the "social responsibilities of business executives" (p. 6). This early thinking eventually crystallized in Carroll's influential CSR Pyramid (Carroll, 1991), comprising four tiers: economic responsibility, legal responsibility, ethical responsibility, and philanthropic responsibility. Over the decades, this model was reinterpreted, challenged, and expanded. One particularly enduring framework is Elkington's Triple Bottom Line (Elkington, 1998), which introduces the now widely recognized triad of corporate responsibilities of economic, environmental, and social – today articulated as ESG (environmental, social, governance), initiated by the finance sector, extending investment categories beyond financial obligations (cf. Friede et al., 2015).

Additionally, the Stakeholder Theory by Freeman (2010) broadens the responsibility of a company beyond shareholders to include all parties affected by corporate actions, moving CSR from a just moral duty to a strategic imperative. Similarly, the more recent concept by Porter and Kramer (2011) on shared value emphasizes how societal and business interests can align, proposing the win-win narrative of companies enhancing profitability by addressing social problems. Overall, common ground has gradually emerged, scoping five core elements of C(S)R: environmental, social, and economic responsibility, stakeholder orientation, and the principle of voluntariness – going beyond compliance (cf. Dahlsrud, 2008; Raworth, 2017). Now, within that, how is the digital to be placed and brought into relation?

The discourse is ongoing among CDR scholars and beyond. Some scholars advocate for a convergence model. In early publications, CDR is often treated as a variation of CSR. For instance, a view expressed by Thelisson et al. (2019), who talk about a "digital corporate social responsibility" (p.168), or Wade (2020), who explicitly labels CDR as a "subset of CSR" (p.1). While other scholars frame it as a synthesis of digital transformation and sustainability, coining terms like "digital CSR" (Orbik & Zozul'aková, 2019), mapping the CDR Pyramid to the digital context (Herden et al., 2021), or positioning digital responsibility as a fourth category alongside economic, environmental, and social responsibility (e.g., Kempkes et al., 2022).

Supporters of this integrated perspective point to the usefulness of established CSR frameworks, which can provide structure and legitimacy to CDR (e.g., Knopf & Pick, 2023; Wynn & Jones, 2023). They also argue that the interconnected nature of sustainability challenges makes a separate consideration of digital responsibility artificial or even counterproductive (e.g., Seidl, 2022).

In contrast, a growing number of scholars argue for a clear distinction. A landmark publication by Lobschat et al. (2021) sets out three core arguments for why CDR warrants its own domain: the exponential pace of technological change, the malleability of data and algorithms, the dual-use nature of digital technologies, and the deep, systemic pervasiveness of data and algorithms in every aspect of business and life. Mihale-Wilson et al. (2022) build on this, describing digitalization as introducing new levels of complexity, consequences, and opportunity into the corporate responsibility landscape. While van der Merwe and Ziad Al (2022) further emphasize the unique power dynamics and global scale enabled by digital technologies, features that fundamentally differentiate CDR from CSR.

This divergence in perspectives opens onto a profound and unresolved question: to what extent will the future of business be shaped by the digital and how far will corporate responsibility itself be redefined by digital technologies (cf. Knopf & Pick, 2023; Mihale-Wilson et al., 2022). The early body of scholarship often highlighted overlap and integration, suggesting a natural extension of established notions of responsibility into the digital domain. In contrast, more recent contributions lean toward differentiation, hinting at the gradual emergence of digital responsibility as a field in its own right. What remains most relevant for this chapter is the absence of a settled consensus, and thus, the conceptual as well as the practical relationship between CDR and CSR continues to be marked by fluidity and negotiation.

Yet what is becoming increasingly clear is that digitalization is neither an end in itself nor an inherently positive force. It is a technological process, one that can either advance or hinder progress toward sustainability, depending on how it is guided. Thus, before one can claim to practice or even define CDR, one must confront its underlying assumptions and recognize that the digital age demands not only new tools but also new forms of ethical reflection and organizational accountability (cf. Stahl, 2024).

This duality of CDR becomes evident when the momentum of digital and responsibility is discussed as a twin transformation (e.g., Burinskiene & Nalivaikė, 2024; Christmann et al., 2024), twin transition (e.g., Fouquet & Hippe, 2022; Hofmann et al., 2023; Ortega-Gras et al., 2021), or responsible digital transformation (Christ, 2025b; Zimmer & Minkkinen, 2024). This additional perspective on CDR is valuable as it puts into focus risks and opportunities, as well as the transformational aspect of shaping qualities towards new system dynamics and barriers that potentially need to be taken into account for future research avenues.

3 Conceptualizing CDR in Research

As is typical with emerging phenomena, early research on CDR has focused on establishing clear definitions to differentiate the phenomenon from related constructs and to demonstrate its theoretical and practical importance. This foundational work also aims to identify the core components of CDR and to build conceptual models that explain its nature, mechanisms, and implications. The following section offers a brief overview of key definitions, proposed scopes of CDR, and commonly used conceptual frameworks, providing an initial glimpse into the current research landscape.

3.1 Scoping CDR Understandings

CDR definitions varying in scope, components, and foci are being proposed, derived from different methodological approaches. Table 1 presents an overview of frequently used and conceptually distinct definitions.

The most frequently applied definition is probably the one by Lobschat et al. (2021). However, foundational, this interpretation leaves critical questions open, particularly around the intended beneficiaries of such norms and the integration of digital responsibility and social equality (cf. Bednárová & Serpeninova, 2023; Knopf & Pick, 2023). Building on experiences and insight in the years that past since, a recent milestone in this conceptual development of a CDR understanding is provided by Carl et al. (2025). The concise yet comprehensive definition brought

Table 1 CDR definitions (author's illustration)

Publications	Definitions
Carl et al. (2022, p. 2)	*"CDR puts, inter alia, privacy and data security attempts in a broader context to provide a more holistic approach to corporate responsibilities and to strengthen consumer trust in corporate activities in a digitized world"*
Dörr (2021, p. 5)	*"CDR refers, on the one hand, to the consideration of digital sustainability and, on the other hand, to the consideration of the social, economic, and ecological effects of digital corporate action in the world"*
Elliott et al. (2021, p. 184)	*"CDR is a voluntary commitment by organisations fulfilling the corporate rationalisers' role in representing community interests to inform "good" digital corporate actions and digital sustainability (i.e. data and algorithms) via collaborative guidance on addressing social, economic, and ecological impacts on digital society"*
Herden et al. (2021, p. 14)	*"CDR is an extension of a firm's responsibilities which takes into account the ethical opportunities and challenges of digitalization"*
Lobschat et al. (2021, p. 876)	*"CDR is the set of shared values and norms guiding an organization's operations with respect to the creation and operation of digital technology and data"*
Merbecks (2023, p. 5)	*"CDR is a management concept that comprises all activities to address the challenges of digitalisation towards all stakeholder groups"*
Suchacka (2019, p. 13)	*"CDR means the awareness of duties binding the organisations active in the field of technological development and using technologies to provide services"*
Thelisson et al. (2019, p. 168)	*"In the company-focused literature, digital responsibility is often understood as 'corporate digital responsibility', meaning a kind of digital Corporate Social Responsibility (CSR)"*
Trittin-Ulbrich and Böckel (2022, p. 448)	*"CDR emphasizes the voluntary, self-regulatory character of corporate commitment to responsible digital innovation"*
van der Merwe and Ziad Al (2022, p. 5)	*"CDR as the set practices, policies, and governance structures of corporations as they relate to the digital transformation"*
Wade (2020)	*"CDR is a set of practices and behaviors that help an organization use data and digital technologies in a way that is socially, economically, technologically, and environmentally responsible"*

forward is a result of a collective effort by leading CDR experts from both academia and industry. It aims to offer a shared understanding that can serve as a common foundation for further dialogue, research, and implementation. The experts framed their understanding as follows (Carl et al., 2025, p. 9):

> CDR stands for holistic responsible corporate action with regard to the impact of digital technologies and data.

The definition may seem broad, but it offers potential for applying it in many cases, while allowing for the specification of certain aspects. For example, what is meant by holistic could be: "*the productive and effective pursuit of the value proposition (economic responsibility) while respecting planetary boundaries (environmental responsibility) and promoting equitable living conditions for all (social responsibility) in transparent accordance with regulations and beyond*" (Christ, 2025b, p. 9). Including data alongside technology highlights the new qualities that the data economy introduces to business conduct, especially by opening a new area for corporate responsibility. Thus, the definition by Carl et al. (2025) offers a holistic but integrated approach, anchoring digital responsibility within the broader framework of corporate responsibility. By adopting this definition, we avoid the spread of fragmented interpretations that have often made the field hard to navigate.

However, an additional relevant distinction is brought forward by Mueller (2022), after analyzing multiple CDR definitions. He highlights a two-domain perspective on CDR governance in companies, which can be summarized as a normative and a practice part of CDR, leading to the guiding questions for effective CDR of (Christ, 2025a):

- *Principles: How do we want to behave in the digital realm?*
- *Practice: How do we achieve and sustain our moral ambitions in our actions?*

The former pertains to values and ethics, topics traditionally explored in fields such as computer ethics (e.g., Cheng & Zhang, 2023). Principles serve not only as an ethical benchmark but also as foundations for behavioral expectations within a company's operational and cultural systems. The latter relates to governance structures, accountability mechanisms, and operational practices (cf. Merbecks, 2023; Mueller, 2022). This perspective reflects both the alignment of digital behavior with ethical values and normative expectations and the proactive disclosure and transparent reporting of actions (Çalışkan, 2025).

3.2 Proposed CDR Dimensions

Drawing on established research across various disciplines, scholars have proposed multiple dimensions, levels, and elements of principles – the terminology differs – that constitute CDR. Building upon existing knowledge provides a foundational approach for differentiating mutually exclusive characteristics and identifying the threshold at which collective principles are exhausted. However, these diverse interpretation approaches stress again the challenge of consistently capturing what determines "holistic" in the Carl et al. (2025) definition. The primary conceptualization of CDR principles is derived from the two previously introduced related fields: corporate responsibility and computer ethics. Additionally, principles from consumer studies and legal discourses have informed CDR's development.

Within the context of corporate responsibility, one widely cited framework is by Herden et al. (2021), which outlines the high-level principles categories of *environmental CDR*, *social CDR*, and *economic CDR* with 20 subtopics. Similarly, Wade (2020) also proposes the three categories of principles but adds a fourth, *technological CDR*, to the cross-dimension differentiation. Other scholars have integrated the "digital" as a fourth principle next to the traditional corporate responsibility triad (e.g., Hildebrandt & Landhäußer, 2017; Kempkes et al., 2022; Weißenberger & Marrocco, 2022), reflecting ongoing discussions about positioning CDR within the established CSR and ESG frameworks as elaborated above.

Building rather on the domain of computer ethics, alternative principles have been proposed. Joynson (2018), for instance, identifies in his blog article the key principles: *digital accessibility*, *digital inclusion*, *digital convergence*, *sustainable automation*, *beneficial AI*, *digital influence*, *data ownership*, and *data well-being*. Trier et al. (2023) introduced eight principles of digital responsibility*: sustainability participation*, *functionality*, *data privacy*, *transparency*, *fairness*, *norms/values*, and *accountability*. Additionally, the CDR Cluster Model by Dörr (2021) offers a combination of both, comprising fifteen responsibility clusters to evaluate the current state of CDR within a company: *digital maturity*, *digital diversity*, *revitalizing respectability*, *open up and share*, *taming the AI*, *digital sustainability*, *transformation of workplaces*, *individual protection in the digital world*, *data empowerment*, *design for greater humanity*, *eco startups and social impact*, *technology deployment for SDG*, *ethical marketing*, *zero waste*, and *ecological footprint of bits and bytes*.

Coming from a consumer perspective, Thorun et al. (2017) propose in their practice-oriented publication eight principles derived from the United Nations Guidelines for Consumer Protection (UNGCP): *access*, *economic interests*, *product safety and liability*, *privacy and data security*, *information and transparency*, *education and awareness*, *dispute resolution and redress*, and *governance and participation*. These dimensions have since been elaborated by other scholars (e.g., Carl et al., 2022). Additionally, Yang et al. (2025), coming from the same perspective, introduce a consumer-centric CDR scale encompassing: *digital transparency*, *privacy*, *equality*, *remedy*, *accessibility*, and *inclusiveness*.

Furthermore, the legal perspective has gained prominence in CDR discourse, particularly due to its intersections with regulatory frameworks, such as "General Data Protection Regulation (GDPR)," "Corporate Sustainability Reporting Directive (CSRD)," "Global Digital Compact," "EU AI Act," "EU Cybersecurity Act," "EU Data Act," or the "Digital Services Act" and "Digital Market Act." Thus, scholars also drive the discourse from this perspective (e.g., Möslein, 2023; Ruff, 2024; Seidl, 2022); however, their interpretation often overlaps with ethical and responsibility discourses.

Additionally, it shall be acknowledged that the influence of public and political initiatives, which have introduced their own CDR frameworks. While these are primarily based on expert consultations rather than empirically validated methodologies, they contribute to the ongoing discourse. Notable examples include the CDR Manifesto (2021), which outlines seven dimensions aligned closely with computer ethics; the CDR Code (CDR Initiative, 2025), consisting of nine principles; the CDR Building Bloxx, which includes three general blocks and eight topic-specific blocks; the Ethos' (2020) seven principles on digital responsibility; the seven digital responsibility goals developed by Identity Valley (2025); and the Dansk Design Center (n.d.), which has also contributed with its Ethics Compass, featuring three thematic areas and a set of guiding questions. Moreover, multiple companies developed their own principles based on organizational values and moral standards (e.g., Merck's Code of Digital Ethics, Deutsche Telekom's House of Digital Responsibility, DATEV's Datenethik Leitlinie).

Building on an examination of both academic and practical CDR frameworks, Çalışkan (2025) proposed a comprehensive model that defines the scope and dimensions of CDR, comprising six core components and eighteen dimensions: *(1) sustainable digital ecosystem* (responsible innovation, adequate digital infrastructure, digital sustainability, and digital well- being), *(2) digital trustworthiness* (digital transparency, accountability, and corporate governance), *(3) digital equity and fairness* (digital accessibility, digital inclusion and diversity, and dispute resolution and redress), *(4) digital empowerment* (digital education and literacy, digital awareness, and digital maturity), *(5) data ethics and human rights* (data ownership, digital privacy, digital security, and autonomy), and *(6) AI ethics* (ethical AI/algorithms).

Thus, the posed normative question above – *How do we want to behave in the digital realm?* – becomes increasingly difficult to answer, given the wide range of interpretations regarding the principles that constitute CDR. Principles can be understood as formalized expressions of normative commitments, which are themselves shaped by underlying values that may vary across organizations. Consequently, a single universally "correct" answer is unlike to exist. The plurality of proposed principles frameworks, while reflecting diverse perspectives, can hinder consistent application across contexts, but offer an opportunity for context-specific solutions.

3.3 Modelling CDR Concepts

As one of the initiating research publications in the field, Lobschat et al. (2021) introduced a **cultural model of CDR** (Fig. 1). In their framework, the scholars present culture as the foundational element shaping how companies perceive and practice CDR. They define culture through shared values and norms, expressed in organizational artifacts and behaviors. Moreover, these elements are understood as interconnected and shaped by social and organizational dynamics. At the same time, CDR is seen as influencing a wide range of stakeholders, categorized as outcomes of CDR. At the broader systems level, Stahl (2024) advocates for an ecosystemic

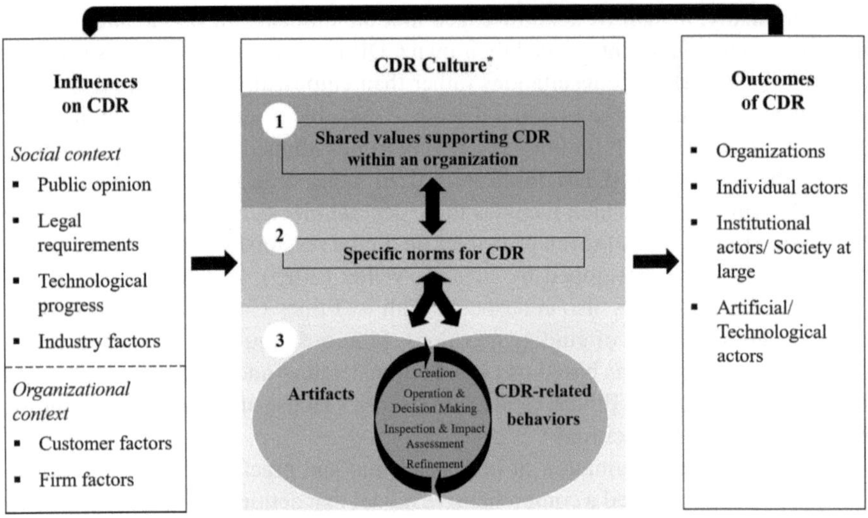

Fig. 1 CDR Culture model (Lobschat et al., 2021, p. 882)

approach, emphasizing how interdependent stakeholders, infrastructures, and regulatory environments shape CDR obligations.

Expanding the conceptual foundation, scholars from the marketing and service platform domain propose the **CDR Calculus** (Wirtz et al., 2023). This model aims to quantify the value of effective CDR. The scholars analyze the root causes of poor digital responsibility practices, identify the trade-offs involved, and reframe these challenges as opportunities to create value through robust CDR engagement. The conceptual landscape is further enriched by inquiries into Corporate Digital Irresponsibility (CDiR) by Shin et al. (2025). The scholars examine how organizational discourses differ when articulating digital responsibility versus irresponsibility, revealing critical nuances in corporate communication and accountability.

Further refining applied perspectives, Tóth and Blut (2024) present a **CDR Roadmap** for implementation (Fig. 2), focusing specifically on AI ethics in financial services. The findings address sector-specific ethical challenges and offer policy and practice guidance on CDR best practices. Their case study provides a structured approach to integrating AI ethics into the broader CDR discourse. A similar approach has been proposed by the Swiss Digital Initiative (2025), called the CDR Starter Kit, comprising seven steps as guidance for companies, developed mainly by experts from practice.

Complementing these models, Rugeviciute and Courboulay (2024) proposed a **CDR Maturity Model** (Fig. 3) based on empirical research with companies in the French market. Their model identifies eighteen focus areas for organizational capability development across five key dimensions on CDR. Building on these findings and existing CDR literature (e.g., the assessment benchmark proposed by Dörr (2021)), the scholars define six levels of maturity: (0) nonexistence, (1) initial awareness, (2) reactive measures, (3) proactive and standardized measures, (4) continuous and measured improvement, and (5) industry leadership and innovation.

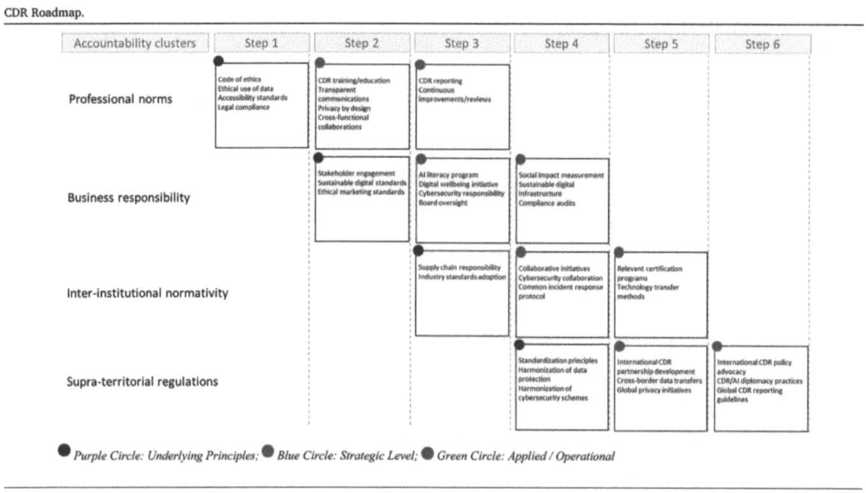

Fig. 2 CDR Roadmap (Tóth & Blut, 2024, p. 7)

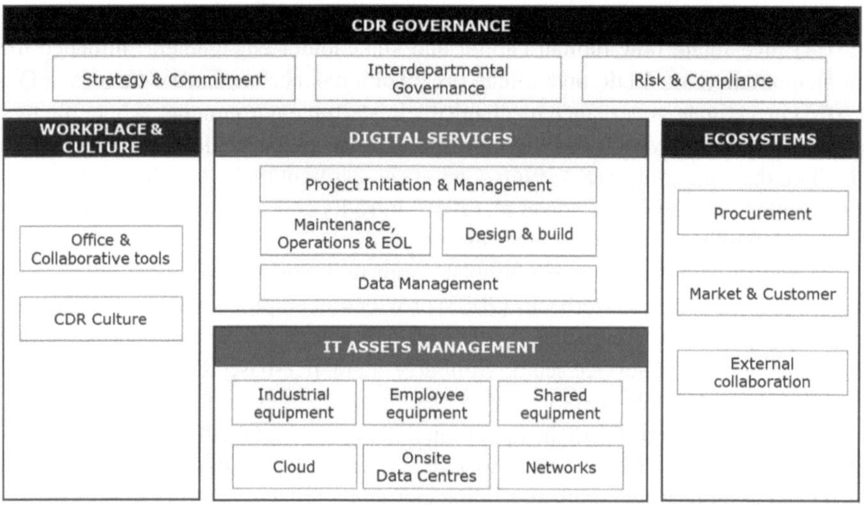

Fig. 3 CDR Maturity model (Rugeviciute & Courboulay, 2024, p. 93)

These frameworks illustrate that CDR models are developed from both theoretical conceptualization (e.g., Stahl, 2024; Wirtz et al., 2023; Lobschat et al., 2021) and empirical research (e.g., Tóth & Blut, 2024; Rugeviciute & Courboulay, 2024), of which more will be presented in the following. However, so far, the theory-building research has only sporadically been supplemented with theory-testing studies, evaluating the applicability of the models on a broader scale as well as validating whether the models prove to represent the phenomena CDR, respectively.

3.4 Empirical Studies

Moving beyond the foundational and strategic models, a body of literature exploring more granular and empirical aspects of CDR emerges. Several empirical studies are dedicated to understanding the impact of CDR on organizational performance. Zhu et al. (2025) examine how responsible digital practices affect performance outcomes across industries, while Oduro et al. (2024) explore how CDR influences access to financial resources via corporate reputation. Lee et al. (2025) focus on the role of CDR practices on employees' emotional (employee satisfaction and organizational pride) and behavioral responses (employee well-being and advocacy behavior). Han (2025) examines the impact of CDR on responsible entrepreneurship via organizational sensemaking from the perspective of technological ethics. Shin et al. (2025) investigate the impacts of both CDiR (ethics, fairness, and privacy) and CDR communication on consumers' brand perceptions. Shin and Jang (2025) explore how perceived barriers to CDR (lack of awareness, economic constraints, technological complexity, and lack of organizational focus) influence their compliance intentions and attitudinal ambivalence toward CDR initiatives.

In addition, recent research has also examined the drivers of CDR. Vo Thai et al. (2024) investigate how human capital and stakeholder engagement influence the implementation of CDR and affect organizational performance. Zhao and Qiu (2025) investigate governance mechanisms in startup environments, where the tensions between innovation and digital responsibility are particularly pronounced. In parallel, there are efforts to develop concrete assessment tools. The digital responsibility index radar by Thelisson et al. (2019) introduces a set of evaluative questions and applicability rankings for services and products.

Moreover, scholars have begun examining real-world applications of CDR in organizational settings. Merbecks (2023) provides an empirical study on CDR practices within DAX30 companies, while Pick and Knopf (2023) assess progress and relevance within the service sector. Similarly, a practice-based case study by Elliott and Copilah-Ali (2024) explores how specific companies implement CDR frameworks, offering insights into the operationalization of digital ethics and responsibility. Christ (2025a, 2025b) brings together a status quo assessment of CDR best practices in pioneering companies in the German market.

Collectively, this diverse body of literature reflects the rapid evolution and increasing maturity of CDR research, spanning conceptual models, empirical investigations, sector-specific applications, and practical frameworks for implementation. Due to the fact that CDR research has only been conducted for a few years, there is still a distinct need for longitudinal and broad-based studies on CDR. In the meantime, synthesis research with related disciplines can advance insights (e.g., Christ et al., 2024) as well as help specify the most relevant focal points for (empirical) studies.

4 Future CDR Research Directions

In summary, the literature on CDR is continuously expanding, drawing from diverse fields of research, insights from practitioners, and policy-driven initiatives. As a result, CDR has developed into a fragmented research landscape in which multiple understandings and conceptualizations coexist, each attempting to capture what CDR means at different levels (cf. Carl & Hinz, 2024; Christ et al., 2024; Mueller, 2022). This plurality poses challenges for building a common and consistent understanding and hinders progress on operationalization due to a lack of clear direction on the "right" way to CDR. The fundamental aspiration for a central guiding "one-size-fits-all" framework, intended to facilitate communication, enhance transparency, and enable comparability, is plausible. It reduces complexity.

However, approaches that are tailored to specific industries, business models, and varying degrees of responsibility are likely to prove more effective. At the same time, it enriches the field by offering a variety of perspectives and tailored approaches that highlight the multifaceted nature of CDR (cf. Christ, 2025a; Merbecks, 2023). For instance, taking into account the plurality of normative theorization due to differences in cultural values, as well as regional variation in regulation, which leads to nuances in boundaries between legislation and ethics, thus determining the degree of voluntariness, as well as the scope of stakeholders determining different answers to the fundamental question, *responsibility to whom* (cf. Stahl, 2024)?

Nevertheless, the CDR literature landscape will most likely further progress toward a set of fundamental agreements on relevance, scope, dimensions, and measures, providing useful baselines, but absolute consensus on a single overarching conceptualization is neither realistic nor necessary. Thus, the progress on CDR should therefore not be evaluated by the extent to which the field converges on one universal concept. Rather, it should be understood in terms of the richness and diversity of a growing body of research that generates insights for a broad range of stakeholders. While the purpose of this chapter has been to provide a tangible overview of the current state of CDR research, far more detailed academic reviews can provide more differentiated insights, also on the meta-level (e.g., Bednárová & Serpeninova, 2023; Carl & Hinz, 2024; Knopf & Pick, 2023; Yadav & Mishra, 2022).

Now, setting aside the more obvious next steps in research development, such as expanding empirical, theory-building studies, conducting longitudinal assessments, or undertaking meta validations to challenge conceptualizations, a more fundamental shift is needed. CDR research needs to progress from primarily retrospective analysis toward experimental, future-oriented inquiry. While learning from the past and extrapolating those insights into the future remains an essential scholarly contribution, it is insufficient for capturing truly novel phenomena. Current developments from digitalization to the sweeping digital transformation of business models driven by emerging technologies such as generative AI, autonomous systems, and quantum computing, suggest that the changes ahead will be radical in scope and will outpace our established timelines of evolution and social impact.

We therefore propose an expansion of mentality regarding how CDR research is tailored and how its obligations are defined. This requires adopting what the system theorist Otto Scharmer describes as an orientation toward learning from the emerging future. Two complementary paths may guide such an approach. The first is to identify and study the context in which elements of the future are already unfolding, reflecting William Gibson's famous attitude reflected in his books; the future is already there; it is just not evenly distributed. The second is to deliberately explore the unknown, moving beyond the scaling of fragmented insights toward the development of new patterns and frameworks that can account for what has not yet been fully conceptualized.

Competing Interests The authors have no conflicts of interest to declare that are relevant to the content of this chapter.

References

Agafonova, A. N., Yakhneeva, I. V., & Mukhametshina, G. R. (2021). Human-centric marketing in the digital era. In S. I. Ashmarina, J. Horák, J. Vrbka, & P. Šuler (Eds.), *Economic systems in the new era: Stable systems in an unstable world* (pp. 10–17). Springer.

Aitken, M., Ng, M., Horsfall, D., Coopamootoo, K. P. L., Moorsel, A. v., & Elliott, K. (2021). In pursuit of socially-minded data-intensive innovation in banking: A focus group study of public expectations of digital innovation in banking. *Technology in Society, 66*.

Altmeppen, K. D., & Filipović, A. (2019). Corporate digital responsibility. Zur verantwortung von medienunternehmen in digitalen zeiten. *Communicatio Socialis (ComSoc), 52*(2), 202–214.

Arciniega Gil, L. R., & Ratnane, M. (2023). The digital transformation of companies: Between responsibility and value creation (an approach to corporate digital responsibility in France). In M. J. Sanzo Pérez, E. Estrada Alonso, C. González Mieres, & L. I. Álvarez González (Eds.), *Transitando hacia una producción y consumo responsables* (pp. 107–131). KRK Ediciones.

Bednárová, M., & Serpeninova, Y. (2023). Corporate digital responsibility: Bibliometric landscape – Chronological literature review. *International Journal of Digital Accounting Research, 23*(29), 1–18.

Bernini, F., Ferretti, P., Gonnella, C., & Fabio La, R. (2025). Measuring machinewashing under the corporate digital responsibility theory: A proposal for a methodological path. *Business Ethics, the Environment & Responsibility, 34*(2), 328–346.

Bertelsmann Stiftung & Wittenberg-Zentrum. (2020). Unternehmensverantwortung im digitalen Wandel. *Ein Debattenbeitrag zu Corporate Digital Responsibility*

Bowen, H. R. (1953). *Social responsibilities of the businessman*. University of Iowa Press.

Burinskiene, A., & Nalivaikė, J. (2024). Digital and sustainable (twin) transformations: A case of SMEs in the European Union. *Sustainability, 16*, 1–25.

BVDW. (2025). *Digital responsibility—Is the contact for responsible digitalization*. Retrieved August 23, 2025, from https://www.bvdw.org/en/committees/digital-responsibility/

Bynum, T. W. (2000). The foundation of computer ethics. *SIGCAS Computers and Society, 30*(2), 6–13.

Bynum, T. W. (2001). Computer ethics: Its birth and its future. *Ethics and Information Technology, 3*, 109–112.

Çalışkan, K. (2025). *A framework for corporate digital responsibility: Conceptualization and operationalization*. Doctoral dissertation, Sakarya University.

Carl, V. (2023). Data privacy and security in the context of corporate digital responsibility: A scoping review. In *Lecture Notes in Informatics (LNI), Proceedings—Series of the Gesellschaft für Informatik*.

Carl, K. V., & Hinz, O. (2024). What we already know about corporate digital responsibility in IS research: A review and conceptualization of potential CDR activities. *Electronic Markets, 34*(1), 1–30.
Carl, K. V., Zilcher, T. M. C., & Hinz, O. (2022). Corporate digital responsibility and the current corporate social responsibility standard: An analysis of applicability. In *Lecture Notes in Informatics (LNI), Proceedings—Series of the Gesellschaft für Informatik.*
Carl, K. V., Mihale-Wilson, C., Zibuschka, J., & Hinz, O. (2024). A consumer perspective on corporate digital responsibility: An empirical evaluation of consumer preferences. *Journal of Business Economics, 94*(7), 979–1024.
Carl, K. V., Blachetta, M., Bilfinger, B., Brink, A., Cerulli-Harms, A. K., Christ, et al. (2025). *Establishing common ground in corporate digital responsibility.* IT-Governance und Strategisches Informationsmanagement.
Carroll, A. B. (1991). The pyramid of corporate social responsibility: Toward the moral management of organizational stakeholders. *Business Horizons, 34*(4), 39–48.
CDR Initiative. (2025). *Digitalization calls for responsibility.* Retrieved August 23, 2025, from https://cdr-initiative.de/en/
CDR Manifesto. (2021). *The International CDR Manifesto.* Corporate Digital Responsibility. Retrieved March 30, 2024, from https://corporatedigitalresponsibility.net/cdr-manifesto
Cheng, C., & Zhang, M. (2023). Conceptualizing corporate digital responsibility: A digital technology development perspective. *Sustainability, 15*(3).
Christ, A.-S. (2025a). Corporate governance for digital responsibility. A company study. In *Proceedings of the 20th International Conference on Wirtschaftsinformatik, Münster, Germany.*
Christ, A.-S. (2025b). Responsible digital transformation: A corporate governance perspective. In *Proceedings of the 33rd European Conference on Information Systems, Amman, Jordan.*
Christ, A.-S., Mueller, B., & Lobschat, L. (2024). Corporate digital responsibility (CDR): Achieving synthesized coherence with C (S) R learnings on corporate governance. In *Proceedings of the 45th International Conference on Information Systems, Bangkok, Thailand.*
Christmann, A.-S., Crome, C., Graf-Drasch, V., Oberländer, A. M., & Schmidt, L. (2024). The twin transformation butterfly: Capabilities for an integrated digital and sustainability transformation. *Business & Information Systems Engineering, 66*(4).
Clausen, S., Braun, L. M., & Stieglitz, S. (2023). Towards more digital wellbeing in knowledge work—A signaling theory perspective. In *Proceedings of the Annual Hawaii International Conference on System Sciences.*
Cooper, T., Siu, J., & Wei, K. (2015). Corporate digital responsibility: Doing well by doing good. *Outlook. The Online Journal of High-Performance Business.* Retrieved July 18, 2025, from https://www.criticaleye.com/inspiring/insights-servfile.cfm?id=4431
Dahlsrud, A. (2008). How corporate social responsibility is defined: An analysis of 37 definitions. *Corporate Social Responsibility and Environmental Management, 15*(1), 1–13.
Dansk Design Center. (n.d.). *The digital ethics compass. Helping companies navigate the ethics jungle.* Retrieved August 23, 2025 from https://ddc.dk/cases/digital-ethics-compass/
Dörr, S. (2021). *Corporate digital responsibility. Managing corporate responsibility and sustainability in the digital age.* Springer.
Dörr, S., & Lautermann, C. (2024). Beyond direct stakeholders: The extensive scope of societal corporate digital responsibility (CDR). *Organizational Dynamics, 53*(2), 101057.
Driesens, T., Oakeley, M., & Schneevoigt, V. (2017). *The rise of corporate digital responsibility.* Retrieved July 18, 2025, from https://web.archive.org/web/20220226064734/www.i-cio.com/management/best-practice/item/the-rise-of-corporate-digital-responsibility
Elkington, J. (1998). Partnerships from cannibals with forks: The triple bottom line of 21st-century business. *Environmental Quality Management, 8*(1), 37–51.
Elliott, K., & Copilah-Ali, J. (2024). Implementing corporate digital responsibility (CDR): Tackling wicked problems for the digital era: Pilot study insights. *Organizational Dynamics, 53*(2).
Elliott, K., Price, R., Shaw, P., Spiliotopoulos, T., Ng, M., Kovila, C., & Aad, v. M. (2021). Towards an equitable digital society: Artificial intelligence (AI) and corporate digital responsibility (CDR). *Society, 58*(3), 179–188.

Esselmann, F., & Brink, A. (2016). Corporate digital responsibility. Den digitalen wandel von unternehmen und gesellschaft erfolgreich gestalten. *Spektrum. Das Wissenschaftsmagazin der Universität Bayreuth, 12(1)*, 38–41.
Esselmann, F., & Brink, A. (2020). Digitalverantwortung als chance. *Ökologisches Wirtschaften-Fachzeitschrift, 2*, 11–13.
ethos. (2020). *Digital corproate responsibility: 7 expectations of ethos*. Retrieved August 23, 2025, from https://www.ethosfund.ch/en/digital-corporate-responsibility-7-expectations-of-ethos
European Commission. (2011). *A renewed EU strategy 2011-14 for corporate social responsibility* (COM (2011) 681 final). Publications Office of the European Union. Retrieved August 23, 2025, from https://eur-lex.europa.eu/legal-content/EN/TXT/?uri=CELEX%3A52011DC0681
Fouquet, R., & Hippe, R. (2022). Twin transitions of decarbonisation and digitalisation: A historical perspective on energy and information in European economies. *Energy Research & Social Science, 91*.
Freeman, R. E. (2010). *Strategic management: A stakeholder approach*. Cambridge University Press.
Friede, G., Busch, T., & Bassen, A. (2015). ESG and financial performance: Aggregated evidence from more than 2000 empirical studies. *Journal of Sustainable Finance & Investment, 5*(4), 210–233.
Girrbach, P. (2021). Corporate responsibility in the context of digitalization. *Tehnicki Glasnik, 15*(3), 422–428.
Grunwald, A. (2019). Digitalisierung als prozess. Ethische herausforderungen inmitten allmählicher verschiebungen zwischen mensch. *Technik und Gesellschaft. zfwu Zeitschrift für Wirtschafts-und Unternehmensethik, 20*(2), 121–145.
Han, K. (2025). Validating the impact of technical application ethics on enterprise transformation based on structural equation model: The moderating effect of digital transformation. *Journal of Computational Methods in Sciences and Engineering, 25*(3), 2240–2252.
Herden, A. E., Cakici, A., Cormier, T., Deguelle, C., Gambhir, S., et al. (2021). Corporate digital responsibility. New corporate responsibilities in the digital age. *Nachhaltigkeits Management Forum, 29*, 13–19.
Hildebrandt, A., & Landhäußer, W. (2017). *CSR und Digitalisierung*. Springer.
Hofmann, J., Ricci, C., Kleinewefers, C., & Laurenzano, A. (2023). Doppelte Transformation. Metastudie – Synopse des aktuellen Forschungsstandes. In *Fraunhofer Institut für Arbeitswirtschaft und Organisation IAO*. Bertelsmann Stiftung.
Identity Valley. (2025). *Digital responsibility goals*. Retrieved 21.08.2025 from https://identityvalley.eu/drg
Initiative D21. (n.d.) *AG Digitale Ethik*. Retrieved August 23, 2025, from https://initiatived21.de/arbeitsgruppen-initiativen/ag-digitale-ethik
Jelovac, D., Ljubojević, Č., & Ljubojević, L. (2022). HPC in business: The impact of corporate digital responsibility on building digital trust and responsible corporate digital governance. *Digital Policy, Regulation and Governance, 24*(6), 485–497.
Jin, C.-X., & Yu, J.-Q. (2025). Does the popularization of artificial intelligence increase the risk of corporate digital responsibility? *Finance Research Letters, 80*.
Johnson, D. G. (1994). *Computer ethics* (2nd ed.). Prentice-Hall, Inc.
Joynson, C. (2018). *Corporate digital responsibility: Principles to guide progress*. Retrieved July 18, 2025, from https://www.linkedin.com/pulse/corporate-digital-responsibility-principles-guide-progress-joynson/
Kempkes, E., Kempkes, J. A., Suprano, F., & Wömpener, A. (2022). Corporate digital responsibility. *Controlling: Zeitschrift für erfolgsorientierte Unternehmenssteuerung, 18*(44), 29–35.
Kluiters, L., Srivastava, M., & Tyll, L. (2022). The impact of digital trust on firm value and governance: An empirical investigation of US firms. *Society and Business Review, 18*(1), 71–103.
Knopf, T., & Pick, D. (2023). Corporate responsibility for digital innovation: A systematic review of the literature. In *Proceedings of the European Conference on Innovation and Entrepreneurship, ECIE 2023*.
Kunz, W. H., & Wirtz, J. (2024). Corporate digital responsibility (CDR) in the age of AI: Implications for interactive marketing. *Journal of Research in Interactive Marketing, 18*(1), 31–37.

Lee, S. A., Shin, H. H., Lee, M., & Jeong, M. (2025). Feelings matter in the digital age: The role of corporate digital responsibility on employee well-being and advocacy behavior. *International Journal of Contemporary Hospitality Management, 37*(7), 2327–2348.

Lobschat, L., Mueller, B., Eggers, F., Brandimarte, L., Diefenbach, S., Kroschke, M., & Wirtz, J. (2021). Corporate digital responsibility. *Journal of Business Research, 122*, 875–888.

Londoño-Cardozo, J., & De Paz, M. P. (2021). Corporate digital responsibility: Foundations and considerations for its development. *Revista de Administracao Mackenzie, 22*(6), 1–31.

Merbecks, U. (2023). Corporate digital responsibility (CDR) in Germany: Background and first empirical evidence from DAX 30 companies in 2020. *Journal of Business Economics*.

Mihale-Wilson, C., Zibuschka, J., Carl, K., & Hinz, O. (2021). *Corporate digital responsibility – Extended conceptualization and empirical assessment*. In *Proceedings of the 29th European Conference on Information Systems, Marrakech, Morocco*.

Mihale-Wilson, C., Hinz, O., van der Aalst, W., & Weinhardt, C. (2022). Corporate digital responsibility: Relevance and opportunities for business and information systems engineering. *Business & Information Systems Engineering, 64*(2), 127–132.

Moor, J. (1985). What is computer ethics? *Metaphilosophy, 16*, 266–275.

Möslein, F. (2023). Towards corporate digital responsibility. In *Research handbook on corporate liability* (pp. 409–433). Edward Elgar Publishing.

Mueller, B. (2022). Corporate digital responsibility. *Business and Information Systems Engineering, 64*(5), 689–700.

Nagano, A. (2023). Institutional values and CDR for green ITC: Transforming e-waste to ethical gems. In *Proceedings of the 10th International Conference on Wireless Networks and Mobile Communications, WINCOM 2023*.

Nagano, A. (2024, December). *Analysing media coverage for responsible AI principles from the CDR*. The International Society for Professional Innovation Management (ISPIM), Manchester.

Napoli, F. (2023). Corporate digital responsibility: A board of directors may encourage the environmentally responsible use of digital technology and data: Empirical evidence from Italian publicly listed companies. *Sustainability, 15*(3), 2539.

Oduro, S., Haylemariam, L. G., & Umar, R. M. (2024). Influence of corporate digital responsibility on financial performance: The mediating role of firm reputation. *Business Ethics, the Environment & Responsibility*.

Orbik, Z., & Zozul'aková, V. (2019). Corporate social and digital responsibility. *Management Systems in Production Engineering, 27*(2), 79–83.

Ortega-Gras, J.-J., Bueno-Delgado, M.-V., Cañavate-Cruzado, G., & Garrido-Ľova, J. (2021). Twin transition through the implementation of industry 4.0 technologies: Desk-research analysis and practical use cases in Europe. *Sustainability, 13*(24).

Paul, J., Ueno, A., Dennis, C., Alamanos, E., Curtis, L., Foroudi, P., et al. (2024). Digital transformation: A multidisciplinary perspective and future research agenda. *International Journal of Consumer Studies, 48*(2).

Pick, D., & Knopf, T. (2023). Corporate digital responsibility–Begriff, Motive und Maßnahmen von Handelsunternehmen. In M. Bruhn & K. Hadwich (Eds.), *Gestaltung des Wandels im Dienstleistungsmanagement: Band 1: Innovationsperspektive–Digitalisierungsperspektive–Nachhaltigkeitsperspektive* (pp. 671–697). Springer Fachmedien Wiesbaden.

Porter, M., & Kramer, M. (2011). Creating shared value: How to reinvent capitalism—And unleash a wave of innovation and growth. *Harvard Business Review, 89*, 62–77.

Price, R. (2018). *Closing the digital divide through corporate digital responsibility*. Atos SE. Retrieved July 17, 2025, from https://www.linkedin.com/pulse/closing-digital-divide-through-corporate-rob-price/

Raworth, K. (2017). *Doughnut economics: Seven ways to think like a 21st-century economist*. Chelsea Green Publishing.

Ruff, D. (2024). Corporate digital responsibility im Kontext eines entstehenden Datenrechts. In *Daten, Plattformen, Smart Contracts* (pp. 167–214). Nomos Verlagsgesellschaft mbH & Co. KG.

Rugeviciute, A., & Courboulay, V. (2024). Empowering organizations for sustainable digitalization: A corporate digital responsibility maturity model approach. In *Proceedings of the 10th International Conference on ICT for Sustainability* (pp. 87–98). IEEE.

Scarpi, D., & Pantano, E. (2024). "With great power comes great responsibility": Exploring the role of corporate digital responsibility (CDR) for artificial intelligence responsibility in retail service automation (AIRRSA). *Organizational Dynamics, 53*(2).

Schymura, J. (2018). *Corporate Digital Responsibility: Vertrauen schaffen, doch was heißt das eigentlich? Politik-digital.* https://www.politik-digital.de/news/corporate-digital-responsibility-154798/

Seidl, M. (2022). Corporate digital responsibility: Stimulating human-centric innovation and building trust in the digital world. In K. Jacob, D. Schindler, R. Strathausen, & B. Waltl (Eds.), *Liquid legal–humanization and the law* (pp. 55–81). Springer.

Shin, H. W., & Jang, H. (2025). Overcoming barriers of corporate digital responsibility in the hospitality and tourism industry: A social identity perspective. *International Journal of Contemporary Hospitality Management.*

Shin, H. H., Lee, M., Lee, S. A., & Jeong, M. (2025). The impacts of corporate digital irresponsibility (CDiR) and corporate digital responsibility (CDR) communications on consumers' brand perceptions. *International Journal of Hospitality Management, 129.*

Stahl, B. C. (2024). From corporate digital responsibility to responsible digital ecosystems. *Sustainability, 16*(12).

Suchacka, M. (2019). Corporate digital responsibility: New challenges to the social sciences. *International Journal of Research in E-Learning, 5*(1), 5–20.

Swiss Digital Initiative. (2025). *Getting started in corporate digital responsibility*. Retrieved August 23, 2025, from https://swiss-digital-initiative.org/corporate-digital-responsibility/

Thelisson, E., Morin, J.-H., & Rochel, J. (2019). AI governance: Digital responsibility as a building block: Towards an index of digital responsibility. *Delphi Interdisciplinary Review of Emerging Technologies, 2*(*4*), 167–178.

Thorun, C., Vetter, M., Reisch, L., & Zimmer, A. K. (2017). Indicators of consumer protection and empowerment in the digital world: Results and recommendations of a feasibility study. In *Consumers international. Coming together for change.*

Thorun, C., Kettner, S. E., & Merck, J. (2018). *Ethik in der Digitalisierung: Der Bedarf für eine Corporate Digital Responsibility*. WISO DIREKT.

Tóth, Z., & Blut, M. (2024). Ethical compass: The need for corporate digital responsibility in the use of artificial intelligence in financial services. *Organizational Dynamics, 20*(2).

Trier, M., Kundisch, D., Beverungen, D., Müller, O., Schryen, G., Mirbabaie, M., & Trang, S. (2023). Digital responsibility: A multilevel framework for responsible digitalization. *Business & Information Systems Engineering, 65*(4), 463–474. https://doi.org/10.1007/s12599-023-00822-x

Trittin-Ulbrich, H., & Böckel, A. (2022). Institutional entrepreneurship for responsible digital innovation: The case of corporate digital responsibility. *Creativity and Innovation Management, 31*(3), 447–459.

van der Merwe, J., & Ziad Al, A. (2022). Data responsibility, corporate social responsibility, and corporate digital responsibility. *Data & Policy, 4.*

Vo Thai, H. C., Hue, T. H. H., Chen, P. F., & Tran, M. L. (2024). Unraveling the influence of human capital and stakeholder engagement on corporate digital responsibility: Implications for firm performance in Southeast Asia enterprises. *Corporate Social Responsibility and Environmental Management, 31*(3), 1934–1958.

Wade, M. (2020). Corporate responsibility in the digital era. *MIT Sloan Business Review*. https://sloanreview.mit.edu/article/corporate-responsibility-in-the-digital-era/

Weber-Lewerenz, B., & Traverso, M. (2025). How can corporate digital responsibility (CDR) be measured in line with corporate social responsibility (CSR)? A new theoretical approach in construction 4.0. *Sustainable Development, 33*(1), 287–308. https://doi.org/10.1002/sd.3094

Weißenberger, B. E., & Marrocco, A. (2022). Corporate Digital Responsibility und ihre Integration in die Unternehmensführung. In S. Roth & H. Corsten (Eds.), *Handbuch Digitalisierung* (pp. 41–58). Vahlen.

Werning, E., & Middeke, L. (2022). Corporate digital responsibility. Digitalisierung im Spannungsfeld von Verantwortung und Obliegenheit. In *Wirtschaftsschutz in der Praxis: Herausforderungen an die Sicherheit im Zeitalter von Digitalisierung und Krise* (pp. 207–223). Springer.

Willrich, S. (2018). Corporate digital responsibility. *Fachgruppe Wirtschaftliche Potenziale & gesellschaftliche Akzeptanz*. Smart-Data-Begleitforschung FZI Forschungszentrum Informatik.

Wirtz, J., Kunz, W. H., Hartley, N., & Tarbit, J. (2023). Corporate digital responsibility in service firms and their ecosystems. *Journal of Service Research, 26*(2), 173–190.

Wynn, M., & Jones, P. (2023). Corporate responsibility in the digital era. *Information, 14*(6).

Yadav, S. S. K., & Mishra, G. (2022). Corporate digital responsibility: Perspectives till date and the way ahead. In *Proceedings of the 5th International Conference on Contemporary Computing and Informatics*.

Yang, P., Ji, C., Prentice, C., Sthapit, E., & Peng, Z. (2025). Scale development and validation of corporate digital responsibility – A consumer perspective. *International Journal of Consumer Studies, 49*(1).

Zhao, Y., & Qiu, J. (2025). Decentralized governance in action: A governance framework of digital responsibility in startups. *Journal of Responsible Technology, 21*.

Zhu, S., Lv, K., & Cheng, Y. (2025). The impact of digital technology innovation on firm performance: Based on the corporate digital responsibility perspective. *Business Ethics, the Environment & Responsibility*.

Zimmer, M., & Minkkinen, M. (2024). Narrative approach to futures: Future-oriented perspective to responsible digital transformation. In *Proceedings of the 32nd European Conference on Information Systems, Paphos, Cyprus*.

Anna-Sophia Christ is a doctoral researcher at Maastricht University's School of Business and Economics and the University of Bremen's Business Innovation and Transformation Institute (BIT). Her research and teaching focus on systemic aspects of digital responsibility in economic contexts within the field of information systems. In her work as an independent coach, consultant, and system and organizational constellation facilitator, she supports companies in their sustainability and digital transformation.

Kübra Çalışkan is a research assistant in the Department of Management Information Systems, Faculty of Business, Sakarya University, Türkiye. She holds a PhD in Management Information Systems. Her research interests include digital transformation, corporate digital responsibility, responsible digital governance, digital ethics, emerging technologies, and human–technology interaction.

Cases from Practice

Three Challenges of Operationalizing Digital Ethics in a Science and Technology Company: The Case of Merck KGaA

Simon Lucas and Jean Enno Charton

Abstract

Technology developers in corporate settings hold responsibility as technologies transition from concept to market. This responsibility is especially urgent for digital solutions, given the rapid and dynamic nature of their transformation and deployment. In this article, we outline three key challenges of this shift and explain how Merck KGaA, Darmstadt, Germany, has addressed them systematically: (1) establishing a tailored ethics framework that keeps pace with novel, constantly evolving digital projects; (2) conceptually linking day-to-day practices with this overarching framework to prevent distractive practices such as "ethics shopping," the selective or retrofitted application of ethical principles to justify existing behaviors; and (3) implementing semiautomated risk assessments to manage the complexity of large-scale data analytics projects, frequent project pivots, and limited in-house ethics expertise. By detailing these challenges and the corresponding solutions, we demonstrate a practical approach that helps bridge ethical theory and corporate practice, offering a model for organizations to integrate ethics throughout digital development.

1 One Cannot Not Engage with Digital Ethics

The appropriate ends and means of commercial enterprises in their technological engagements, and the broader realm of business ethics, remain subjects of profound philosophical contention. This discourse, unfolding at the intersection of philosophical inquiry and pragmatic business leadership, grapples with the fundamental question of corporate responsibility in shaping societal progress. One school of thought

S. Lucas · J. E. Charton (✉)
Merck KGaA, Darmstadt, Germany
e-mail: simon.lucas@merckgroup.com

A.-S. Christ (ed.), *Corporate Digital Responsibility*, Future of Business and Finance, https://doi.org/10.1007/978-3-032-14793-6_8

posits that technological artifacts should be imbued with the explicit purpose of catalyzing positive social change and, by extension, moral progress. Proponents of this perspective advocate for a form of "ethical capitalism" that transcends the mere provision of material goods, embracing moral progress as its primary concern and supporting humanity's perennial quest for meaning – the search for the purpose of life (e.g., Gabriel, 2024). This ambitious vision reimagines the corporate entity as a vehicle for societal betterment, extending its mandate beyond profit maximization to encompass a broader moral imperative.

However, this perspective is not without significant challenges and potential pitfalls. The notion of corporations steering moral progress reflects a problematic faith in linear ethical advancement and technocratic optimism. It presupposes that moral norms can be refined and directed straightforwardly, rather than acknowledging the complex nature of moral evolution and its intricate interplay with historical precedents and established moral traditions. Centralized efforts to guide moral progress, particularly when originating from commercial entities, risk devolving into paternalistic impositions of values if not firmly grounded in civil society institutions. The implementation of such ambitious ethical policies within commercial enterprises is arguably perilous, given the potential conflicts of interest, the possibility of unforeseen consequences, and the complex collective action problems that arise when diverse stakeholders' interests collide. While the principle of corporate ethics engagement is undoubtedly praiseworthy, these tensions demand careful consideration in policy formulation and execution. A particularly insidious risk emerges in what scholars have termed the "managerialization" of ethics – and by extension, the law (Edelman et al., 2001). This phenomenon describes a distortion wherein managerial values and methodologies infiltrate and reshape moral and legal concepts, potentially subordinating ethical considerations to corporate imperatives. While the managerial uptake of ethics may appear to offer a promising avenue for extending moral ideals beyond legal requirements, it requires heightened scrutiny. The intrusion of business entities into civic processes risks usurping genuine political and societal mechanisms, substituting profit-driven agendas for authentic ethical deliberation.

However, technology developers, including those working with digital technologies in commercial settings, are confronted with a peculiar conundrum: they cannot not engage with ethics. This arises from the understanding that technologies are not inherently value-neutral (e.g., Boaz, 2021; Heyndels, 2023); rather, they are conceived as value-laden artifacts, necessitating ethical deliberation not only during the deployment phase but throughout their conception and design. Floridi maintains that technological artifacts should be viewed as "value double-charged" (Floridi, 2023), meaning they are inherently imbued with both positive and negative values. He exemplifies this with the case of a knife: "the blunt, small, and blunt knife given to a child to spread butter can hardly be used to kill someone, whereas a bayonet is the sort of knife with which one may struggle to spread Nutella but is meant to be sharp and long enough to reach a human heart and kill" (Floridi, 2023). The bayonet is, therefore, designed with a value vector that intentionally encourages the user to perceive the blade as a weapon, an inclination largely absent from the butter knife's design. In this light, technologies do not merely reflect moral values; they actively embody them, with some carrying explicit ethical implications, while others are imbued with values through their design process, revealing broader moral implications in social or political contexts.

Engaging with the value vectors of technology demands a nuanced approach that can be systematic, arbitrary, or organically evolving throughout the development process. The least desirable scenario is akin to an ethical "Russian roulette," where well-intentioned but haphazard considerations may lead to unforeseen moral risks. While technology developers and entrepreneurs are predominantly driven by a genuine desire to create meaningful products that enhance their customers' lives, this initial moral impetus alone is insufficient to safeguard against the development of technologies that may later prove ethically problematic. Social media platforms serve as a poignant example: conceived with the positive vectors of efficient communication, community networking, idea dissemination, and global social movement empowerment, they simultaneously harbor clearly delineated negative vectors. These risks include the exacerbation of societal polarization, the fostering of addictive behaviors, the excessive gamification of communication, and potential compromises to user privacy (Nemat & Charton, 2024). Consequently, we argue that a systematic approach to managing the ethical implications of technology, encompassing digital technologies and AI, is important to mitigate potentially harmful societal outcomes. This assertion does not claim to preempt moral developments better addressed through civic processes or regulatory frameworks. Rather, it emphasizes the necessity of a structured ethical framework within the technological development process itself, serving as a complement to broader societal and regulatory mechanisms in shaping the moral trajectory of technological innovation.

In addressing this challenge, we recognize that managing the moral dimensions of technology within a corporate context presents unique complexities. This arises from the deployment of diverse technologies and applications within intricate project infrastructures of large organizations, compounded by the frequent absence of ethical expertise within technology-centric teams. Moreover, the prevailing managerial paradigm, often risk-oriented and compliance-driven, fails to fully appreciate the multifaceted nature of ethics. This limited perspective overlooks the fact that ethics is not merely a prohibitive framework but a facilitator of positive outcomes, a "tool" not only for assessing and mitigating risks but also for identifying and capitalizing on opportunities, thereby enabling the realization of positive value vectors embedded in technology. Our experience suggests that ethics, when properly integrated, can be leveraged within the corporate context to enhance the positive contributions of technology to human flourishing. However, this necessitates a systematic approach. We argue that, despite the best of intentions, the alternative – an organic unfolding of value vectors focusing solely on the use phase – is tantamount to an ethical "Russian roulette." A systematic approach must encompass the entire life cycle of technological development, from conception to deployment and beyond. It requires the integration of ethical considerations at every stage of the process, fostering a culture where ethical reflection is not an afterthought but an integral part of technological innovation. By doing so, organizations can more effectively navigate the complex interplay between technological advancement and societal well-being, ensuring that their innovations contribute positively to human flourishing while mitigating potential harms.

In what follows, we will examine three key challenges that technology corporations can encounter when attempting to operationalize ethics in this context: (1) the design of theoretical frameworks specifically tailored to address the unique challenges of data and AI ethics, (2) the establishment of structures that mitigate the risk of arbitrariness in ethical decision-making, and (3) the complexities of operationalizing ethics within independent organizational units.

2 Three Challenges of Operationalizing Digital Ethics

2.1 Challenge 1: Transitioning from Bioethics to Digital Ethics

Merck KGaA, Darmstadt, Germany (henceforth Merck), is a leading enterprise in healthcare, life sciences, and electronics, with a longstanding tradition of systematically integrating ethical considerations into its business practices. Historically focused on bioethics, this engagement spans a broad spectrum, from clinical trials and artificial reproduction to stem cell technologies and genome editing. To navigate ethical challenges, Merck has established a framework that combines an internal ethics team with external advisory bodies, ensuring independent expertise on ethically complex issues. The insights derived from these efforts have played important roles in shaping and refining corporate principles and policies (e.g., Sugarman et al., 2018).

In recent years, however, Merck has undergone notable digital transformations, reshaping both its internal operations and research activities, as well as the way it develops and conducts business. These changes have introduced ethical challenges that the company's established bioethical framework has not always been equipped to fully address. The first of these challenges, which provided the decisive impetus for a more systematic approach to digital ethics, emerged in 2019 with the founding of Syntropy, a partnership between Merck and Palantir Technologies, Inc. This initiative, aimed at integrating health data from diverse sources and providing scientists and research institutions with a collaborative technology platform for cancer research, confronted the company with new ethical questions.

Principles and approaches commonly applied in bioethics often take on new significance in the context of data and algorithms. Consider, for instance, the issue of data protection: within AI applications and digital data use, privacy concerns often seem to emerge as collective action problems. The use of personal data not only generates opportunities and risks for individuals but also for broader groups, sometimes impacting entire populations (e.g., Véliz, 2020). Similarly, transparency, traditionally regarded in bioethics as a key safeguard of individual autonomy, requires distinct reconsideration in the realm of data and AI ethics. While, for instance, mitigating certain issues related to the information asymmetry in the doctor-patient relationship is central to ensuring autonomy in medical ethics, this framework proves inadequate for addressing the complexities of transparency in large-scale data ecosystems and algorithmic systems. These technologies often remain opaque and largely incomprehensible to most individuals while exerting far-reaching influence over their lives (Becker et al., 2023).

Following the academic engagement with the unique ethical challenges posed by data, as well as the broader issues arising from data expansion and algorithmic advancements, data ethics has increasingly emerged as a distinct discipline (Floridi & Taddeo, 2016). In response, Merck has established a digital ethics mandate to systematically address these new considerations within a corporate context. This mandate establishes digital ethics as an advisory entity within the company, analogous to Merck's established bioethics structures. Its objective is to harness the commercial and scientific opportunities presented by technological advancements in a responsible manner. Here, ethics is conceived as extending beyond what legal frameworks can capture, providing insights that surpass regulatory requirements and addressing moral nuances not yet codified in law. It is supposed to foster responsible conduct and cultivate a culture of accountability, guided by societal values and technological developments, ensuring its continued relevance in a dynamic environment. In this capacity, the mandate was developed independently of existing corporate responsibility initiatives. However, it constitutes an important pillar of Merck's CDR efforts, providing the normative framework that must be implemented across various levels of the organization.

This structured approach to addressing ethical challenges follows a dual-track strategy. First, building on Merck's established collaboration with external, independent ethics advisors, a parallel structure was established in the digital domain with the creation of the Digital Ethics Advisory Panel (DEAP). Composed of experts in digital ethics, law, big data, digital health, data governance, and patient advocacy, the DEAP mirrors the role of Merck's bioethics advisory body in providing independent ethical guidance. The DEAP's core responsibilities include (1) advising on specific ethical questions related to data and algorithmic systems within Merck; (2) evaluating proposals from business units for mitigating ethical risks, incorporating panel recommendations, and providing feedback on implementation; (3) serving as a platform for discussing and assessing new corporate policies with ethical implications, as well as reviewing Merck's existing ethical principles and policy frameworks; and (4) offering proactive counsel on relevant developments and emerging debates in digital ethics (Nemat & Charton, 2024).

In a second track, we recognized the potential for numerous use cases stemming from data analytics and automated data-driven approaches. To guide ethical decision-making across the company, we aimed to create a principle-based framework adaptable to various contexts at scale. This internal guideline should serve as a foundation for developing appropriate strategies and automated procedures for different business sectors and employees, helping them navigate regulatory uncertainties. Furthermore, it is intended to establish a clear structure for evaluating ethical questions by the new DEAP and other decision-makers, ultimately building trust with customers and business partners. To achieve this objective, we adopted an approach that synthesizes an analysis of relevant data and AI ethics guidelines with the extraction of key principles tailored to Merck, subsequently translating these into foundational directives.

Hence, a primary initiative of the new DEAP was the formulation of a comprehensive Code of Digital Ethics (CoDE), constructed around a framework of 20 guiding principles (Becker et al., 2023). This endeavor involved a synthesis of scholarly literature on digital ethics, complemented by an examination of existing ethical guidelines in the public sector. Initially, relevant literature was selected according to predefined criteria. First, all documents included had to address the ethical handling of data or AI. Second, each document was required to contain normative statements concerning data or algorithmic systems. Third, a clear focus on European guidelines was expected to provide the best match for the perspective and requirements of an internationally operating, EU-based science and technology company such as Merck. Applying these criteria yielded a total of 42 guideline documents. The ethical principles embedded within these documents were then identified and consolidated using a reconstructive social science research methodology. In the first step, documents were examined for explicitly named principles, with all corresponding text passages recorded. Recurring topics that were not explicitly labeled as principles but were closely related and frequently mentioned were also included. In the second step, preliminary definitions of these topics were formulated, guided by the scope of the recorded passages. In the third step, these definitions were applied in a second review of the documents to identify and extract passages containing implicit references to the corresponding topics. Implicit mentions were discussed by the team and recorded as referring to the previously agreed-upon topics if consensus was reached unanimously (Fig. 1). In this process, a set of 15 principles was determined, prominently featured in both policy and academic discourse. These, along with 14 additional topics, were subsequently organized into five preamble themes and 20 final principles, which were grouped under five overarching core principles.

The selection aimed to reflect existing principles commonly applied in related fields, particularly bioethics, while also emphasizing issues uniquely relevant to digital contexts. The objective was to develop a framework capable of operationalization. Principles and themes were prioritized based on their frequency of appearance in relevant guidelines – for example, transparency was the most frequently cited principle, appearing in 39 guidelines. Initial assignment of principles to categories was conducted independently by two team members, resulting in a high level of concordance. Remaining discrepancies were then deliberated by the full team and resolved through consensus voting. All principles were then translated into operational guidelines, constituting the actionable core of the CoDE. Each of these guidelines is aligned with a CoDE principle and comprises a central statement outlining Merck's intended actions to uphold the core tenet of the respective principle. This is followed by an elaboration of the statement's content, the reference levels addressed, and an explanation of which subsidiary guidelines – derived from specific principles – support the organization in implementing the core guideline (for details see Becker et al., 2023). Ultimately, the CoDE is anchored in five core principles: justice, autonomy, beneficence, nonmaleficence, and transparency. These

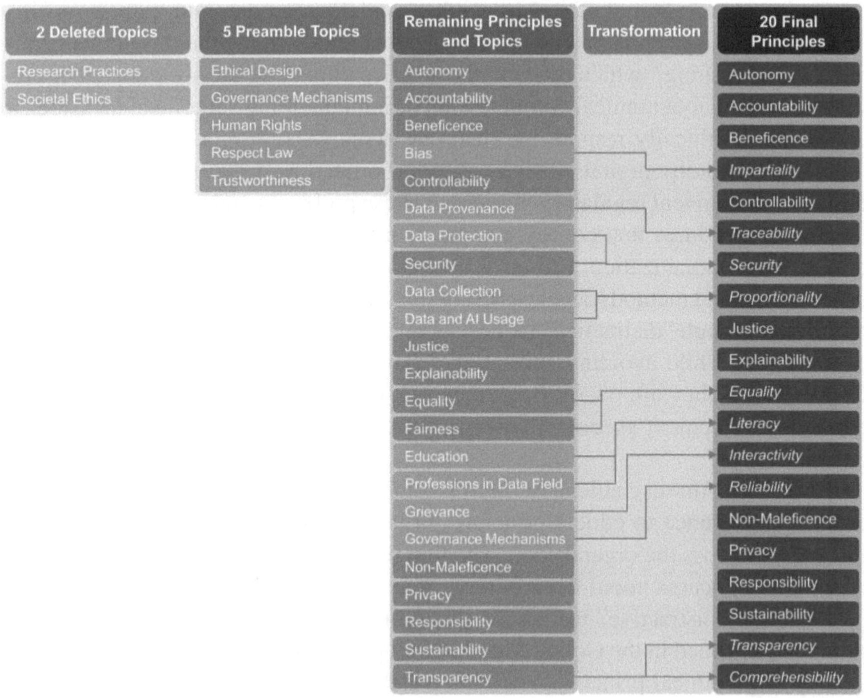

Fig. 1 The process of transforming the initially identified principles and topics into 5 preamble topics and 20 final principles (Becker et al., 2023)

principles, together with their associated guidelines, are designed to facilitate operationalization across diverse contexts, specifically addressing the ethical questions that may arise from the utilization of data and AI. Additionally, the CoDE provides a structured framework for the analysis and evaluation of ethical conundrums, thereby guiding both business units and individual employees in navigating complex scenarios where legal or regulatory guidance may be absent.

2.2 Challenge 2: Avoiding Arbitrary Decision-Making and "Ethics Shopping"

When translating ethics into practice, challenges emerge not only at the level of practical implementation but also in genuinely ethical terms. Floridi (2019) categorizes these challenges into two distinct types: "distractive" and "destructive" problems. The latter encompasses practices that actively circumvent commitments to ethical principles, such as the importation of outcomes from ethically dubious research. However, it is particularly the former – distractive problems – that pose a fundamental obstacle to the initial steps of implementing digital ethics. Distractive problems encompass practices such as "ethics shopping" – the selective adoption, adaptation, or revision of ethical principles, guidelines, codes, and frameworks in a manner that retrofits preexisting behaviors rather than shaping them. Another example is "bluewashing," which refers to the practice of making unsubstantiated or misleading claims about ethical commitments or implementing superficial measures to appear more ethically responsible than one actually is. A related issue is "ethics lobbying," whereby digital ethics is misappropriated as a rhetorical tool to delay, dilute, or circumvent regulatory measures. These problems underscore the necessity for clear procedures that convey a sense of justifiable expectation from all stakeholders of an organization. Effective operationalization must strike a delicate balance: if tools and methods are excessively flexible or vague, they become susceptible to misuse through "distractive" tactics – strategies that create the illusion of ethical commitment while avoiding substantive change as delineated by Floridi (2019). Conversely, if they are overly rigid, they risk being ill-suited to the dynamic complexities and context-specific challenges inherent in digital ethics (Morley et al., 2021a, 2021b).

To address these challenges, Merck's DEAP assumed a dual responsibility: ensuring adherence to ethical principles in its own activities and overseeing their integration across the organization. The first responsibility is particularly critical in countering concerns about the arbitrary selection and application of ethical principles or other "distractive" tactics. To streamline DEAP meetings and prioritize the principles outlined in the CoDE, Merck developed a set of mechanisms that systematically align ethical principles with the panel's work. A central innovation in this effort is the creation of a standardized risk assessment tool, the "Principle-at-Risk Analysis" (PaRA), which positions the ethics panel as both a recipient and a driving force behind the operationalization of digital ethics (Nemat et al., 2023).

The PaRA tool commences with a questionnaire designed to elicit detailed information about the technology, business model, future developments, customers, and so forth, ensuring that the problem is framed in a specific and actionable manner. The process is designed to guarantee that the ethical issue is well-defined and prepared for further analysis. The tool then assesses which CoDE principles may be affected by the specific use case. For each of the 15 subsidiary principles outlined in the CoDE, the PaRA poses three fundamental questions to determine whether the principle is at risk (see Fig. 2 for an illustrative example of the principle "Privacy"). These questions were directly derived from the CoDE text and reformulated as straightforward, easily answerable questions. This close linguistic and substantive alignment with the moral aspirations set out in the CoDE is intended to ensure that the PaRA tool both reflects these aspirations and identifies potential risks to the underlying principles. A principle is deemed affected if at least two questions are answered affirmatively. To address potential gaps in the analysis, the PaRA offers users the option to request a more detailed review if they believe a principle may be at risk, even if it does not meet the threshold. This flexibility ensures that all ethical concerns are considered, regardless of whether they strictly meet the predetermined criteria.

Subsequently, a more in-depth analysis takes place, wherein each affected principle undergoes further scrutiny with three or four additional questions derived from

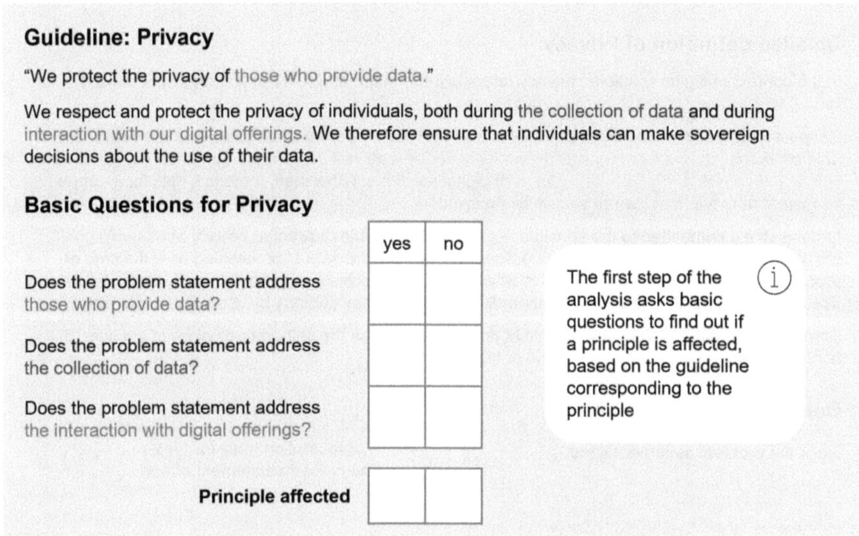

Fig. 2 First stage of the PaRA: Is a principle affected? (Nemat et al., 2023)

the more specific definitions underlying each guideline in the CoDE (see Fig. 3 for an illustrative example of the principle "Privacy"). Again, these questions are formulated based on the foundational text of the CoDE and serve to probe potential conflicts with its core tenets. As in the preceding step, both language and content are closely aligned with the underlying CoDE document to ensure consistency and relevance to the moral aspirations articulated in the CoDE (see color highlighting in Figs. 2 and 3). A principle is considered at risk if at least one of these detailed questions is answered affirmatively. If this threshold is met, the tool prompts users to provide an explanation for why the principle is at risk, offering additional clarification. This phase enables a comprehensive evaluation of the ethical risks associated with the use case, ensuring that all potential issues are thoroughly considered and addressed.

The PaRA tool generates an automated report that summarizes the entire process. This report includes the case summary and problem statement from the initial phase, a graphical overview of the affected and at-risk principles, and detailed explanations for each principle marked as at risk. Additionally, the report ensures transparency by including an appendix with the complete set of questions and answers specific to the PaRA. This report forms the foundation for the DEAP's discussions, providing the panel with a clear, structured overview of the ethical issues at hand. By linking the identified ethical risks directly to the principles of the CoDE, the PaRA tool ensures that discussions within the DEAP are grounded in a consistent and transparent framework. This structured approach aims to prevent arbitrary decisions, guiding the panel to identify responsible parties and potential measures to mitigate risks. Furthermore, the PaRA process strives to ensure that all

Detailed definition of Privacy

In the context of digital solutions, privacy refers to information about, for example, an individual's family, friends, health and financial circumstances.

Respect for privacy means that each user is able to determine what information is shared with others. This concerns information originally provided by the user as well as information generated about the user in the course of his/her interaction with digital solutions. Otherwise, there is a risk, for example, that users may feel that their privacy is being invaded.

Organisations committed to the principle of privacy respect and guarantee privacy at every stage of the data chain: whether at the beginning when determining the type of processing or at the time of processing within the data chain. This is where measures such as anonymization of personal data, the use of synthetic data or software dashboards to control privacy settings by users come into play.

Since the promotion of the sub-principle of privacy recognises the self-determination of the user, it contributes to preserving the core value of autonomy.

Detail Questions for Privacy

Does the problem statement affect…	yes	no	Explanation (only for "yes") The problem statement affects…
…personalized information about, for example, an individual's family, friends, health or financial circumstances?			
…information originally provided by the user?			
…information generated about the user during his interaction with digital solutions?			
…the need for the protection of personalized user data at any stage of the data chain?			
Principle at risk			

Fig. 3 Second stage of the PaRA: Is a principle at risk? (Nemat et al., 2023)

parties involved have clear responsibilities, with the digital ethics team facilitating communication and documentation throughout.

The PaRA tool's design, developed iteratively with feedback from stakeholders, thereby establishes both its usability and effectiveness. Through this process, Merck has created a clear workflow for integrating digital ethics into its operational decision-making, which can be adapted by other organizations to suit their own specific needs. The tool's standardized approach to ethical risk assessment not only facilitates the operationalization of digital ethics – by focusing on the commitments set out in the CoDE and using structured questionnaires to collect background information on each use case and assess how the CoDE's principles and guidelines are affected – but also fosters a culture of accountability, ensuring that ethical considerations are systematically addressed and documented at each stage of the decision-making process.

2.3 Challenge 3: Bootstrapping the Operationalization Gap

The systematic operationalization of digital ethics presents organizations with a triad of novel challenges, each demanding innovative approaches that transcend traditional ethical frameworks. These challenges, particularly acute in environments characterized by high-volume data processing and AI applications, necessitate a paradigmatic shift in how ethical considerations are integrated into organizational processes.

The first challenge emerges from the overwhelming proliferation of use cases, especially within the realm of data analysis, where organizations frequently grapple with thousands of concurrent projects. This sheer volume renders conventional ethical evaluation methodologies, typically executed by dedicated ethics departments or external advisory committees, increasingly untenable. The magnitude of this challenge underscores the imperative for developing scalable, efficient approaches to ethical assessment. Risk-based categorization methods, as elucidated by Mökander et al. (2023), offer a promising avenue for the resource-efficient and reliable classification of use cases. Such methodologies could potentially enable organizations to systematically embed ethical considerations into their operational fabric, ensuring comprehensive coverage without overwhelming existing ethical review mechanisms. This approach represents an important step towards reconciling the demands of rapid technological advancement with the imperative of maintaining ethical integrity.

The second challenge arises from the inherently dynamic nature of project management in data-driven environments. Characterized by incremental and iterative processes, projects in these domains frequently undergo changes in strategy, objectives, and methodologies. This fluidity engenders a propensity for "scope creep," wherein AI systems find deployment in contexts that deviate significantly from their original intended purview. Consequently, static ethical assessments often prove inadequate, necessitating the development of comprehensive and continuous evaluation frameworks. These frameworks must possess the plasticity to adapt to evolving project parameters, ensuring that ethical considerations remain both relevant and efficacious throughout the project's life cycle. This challenge calls for a fundamental reconceptualization of ethical review processes, transitioning from discrete, point-in-time evaluations to dynamic, ongoing assessments that can keep pace with the rapid evolution of technological landscapes and shifting project scopes.

The third challenge stems from the often-subjective nature of ethical deliberations within technical project teams, compounded by the complexities of organizational structures. In these contexts, ethical assessments are invariably colored by personal sensibilities and conflicting interests, such as the tension between project owners' focus on progression and the imperative of ethical oversight. In multinational entities, geographically dispersed teams must navigate a variety of local norms and regulations, leading to ambiguities in delineating ethical issues from legal considerations such as data protection. The distributed nature of data analytics further obfuscates the identification of ethical issues and the attribution of accountability, risking what Floridi and Sanders (2004) describe as a diffusion of responsibility where "everybody's problem becomes nobody's responsibility." Addressing this challenge necessitates the cultivation of a robust ethical infrastructure, or "infraethics" (Floridi, 2012). Such an infrastructure would serve to empower non-ethicists in engaging with moral inquiries while clearly delineating roles and responsibilities within the organizational hierarchy. This approach promises not only to enhance the clarity and consistency of ethics decision-making but also to facilitate ongoing capacity building, fostering a sustained collective consciousness about ethical practices that transcends the limitations of episodic training interventions.

These challenges underscore the imperative for methodologies such as risk-based categorization of use cases to be executed by the responsible project teams, balancing resource efficiency with ethical rigor. However, this approach exacerbates the aforementioned challenges due to the evident paucity of expertise in data and AI ethics within these teams. Consequently, an efficacious operationalization of digital ethics must address not only the immediate ethical considerations but also the broader issues of competency development and accountability that transcend episodic training interventions. Merck's response to these challenges, particularly in contexts necessitating the implementation of ethics at scale, is exemplified by the development and deployment of the "Merck Digital Ethics Check" (MDEC). This instrument was specifically conceived to address the complexities inherent in the field of data analysis and other AI use cases characterized by a high volume of applications. The MDEC represents a semiautomated integration of digital ethics into data analysis processes, offering a structured framework for ethical deliberation within the constraints of corporate technological development (Charton et al., 2025).

The instrument was initially developed for Merck's "Life Sciences Analytics Center of Excellence" (ACE), serving as a pragmatic paradigm for organizations seeking to embed ethical considerations into their digital processes. Subsequently, it has been adapted, with requisite modifications, to other departments and domains of application, spanning from human resources management to digital health. The ACE department fundamentally drives the global data and analytics strategy of the life sciences division, functioning as a service unit. Its primary focus lies in the company-wide monitoring and provision of secure, high-quality, and timely data and applications that facilitate data-driven decision-making. ACE's portfolio currently encompasses over 1000 use cases, which are in a state of continuous evolution and are managed centrally through a data integration platform. The use cases under ACE's purview are diverse, addressing a spectrum of topics including process optimization, quality enhancement, and cost reduction. This breadth and complexity of applications underscore the critical need for a systematic approach to ethical considerations in data-driven initiatives. In the context of ACE, moral issues of considerable complexity can arise, necessitating careful deliberation. These include, but are not limited to, the sensitivity of captured customer information, the imperative for transparency towards customers regarding the handling of data-driven tools, and potential biases that could engender unfair treatment of certain customer segments.

The MDEC has been incorporated into the data integration platform as an inherent component of use case pages, ensuring its integration into daily workflows without impeding employee productivity. This implementation, co-developed with project managers to ensure user-friendliness and facilitate smooth adoption, aims to minimize operational burden and bureaucratic overhead while enabling integration into existing processes. The framework is designed to ensure that (1) risks are identified resource-efficiently, reducing unnecessary effort for employees, (2) risks are continuously assessed throughout the project lifecycle, and (3) it can be effectively utilized by personnel untrained in professional ethics, while simultaneously contributing to the development of their competence in this field. In essence, the MDEC is integrated into the project platform and unfolds in two distinct phases. Initially, the use case undergoes semiautomatic categorization, resulting in the calculation of an overall risk score. Predicated on this score, the project team is subsequently prompted to engage in a tool-driven reflection process to identify and address potential ethical risks. To account for the specific dynamics of the project, each use case is evaluated at two different project stages – one early in the process, and another check closer to industrialization and deployment – using the MDEC.

The core of the semiautomated classification process is based on a questionnaire that encompasses four critical domains: business characteristics, stakeholders, data, and analysis. This questionnaire delves into a spectrum of ethical considerations intrinsic to each use case, establishing the foundation for the MDEC's internal architecture and ensuring a thorough ethical risk assessment. The questionnaire's design is anchored in ethically relevant indicators that integrate data analytics inquiries with the ethical principles enshrined in the CoDE. The underlying logic and corresponding processes have been explicated in detail elsewhere (Charton et al., 2025). In essence, the principles of CoDE have been transmuted into "ethics markers" within the MDEC framework, tailored to address the ethical challenges encountered by ACE in the context of data analysis. These markers have been calibrated to enhance ethics evaluation while simultaneously advancing the strategic objectives of ACE within the data analytics domain. The underpinning assessment architecture, as illustrated in Fig. 4, exemplifies a formal structure wherein these ethics markers are operationalized into quantifiable "observables." These observables are intentionally conceived to be readily measurable by product owners, thereby facilitating the efficient input of pertinent data into the MDEC questionnaire. Each phase of this process contributes to the cultivation of a shared understanding of the ethical implications of each use case, underpinned by the principles of the CoDE and facilitated by the framework of the MDEC.

The principle of "traceability" (Becker et al., 2023) serves as an exemplary illustration of the MDEC's operationalization. Within ACE's data analysis projects, traceability assumes a position of high importance, inextricably intertwined with the concept of data integrity. To instantiate this principle in praxis, the provenance of data and the machine learning methodologies employed are scrutinized and quantified through the ethics markers "machine learning approach" and "data source." The selection of machine learning methodology is particularly salient, as the complexity of traceability exhibits significant variance contingent upon the

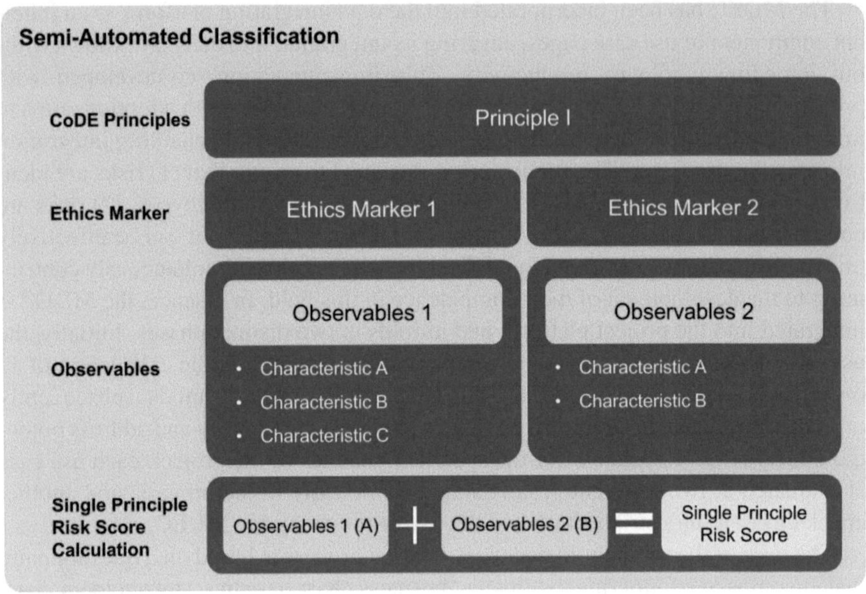

Fig. 4 The semiautomated classification function and its underlying "Principle-Marker-Observable" architecture (Charton et al., 2025)

method employed. Thus, the chosen machine learning approach functions as a critical indicator of the relevance of the traceability principle, with these models serving as quantifiable "observables" within the MDEC questionnaire. The notion of traceability is further nuanced by the origin of data, with externally sourced information generally considered more ethically fraught, thereby intensifying the ethical considerations attendant to its utilization. Consequently, the MDEC employs a differentiation between "externally produced data" and "internally produced data" as observables to adequately assess the degree of traceability. Based on these observables, the MDEC calculates a risk score for each principle enshrined in the CoDE, thereby quantifying the ethical risk and classifying the use case within a tripartite schema of low, medium, or high risk, with classification based on empirically determined and tested thresholds (for details see Charton et al., 2025).

The MDEC subsequently aggregates individual risk scores associated with each use case to generate an overall risk score, calibrated through use case testing and user feedback (Fig. 5). In the overarching MDEC process, use cases are categorized within one of three risk strata: low, medium, or high. The key determinant in this classification is the establishment of thresholds, which serve as evaluative benchmarks for ascertaining the risk level of each use case and the requisite follow-up measures contingent upon the ethical use case criticality.

The second phase of the MDEC shifts focus to the implementation of effective risk mitigation measures, where applicable (i.e., in cases of medium or high risk). The MDEC generates a report based on the results of the initial phase, elucidating the methodology applied, the results achieved, and the corresponding

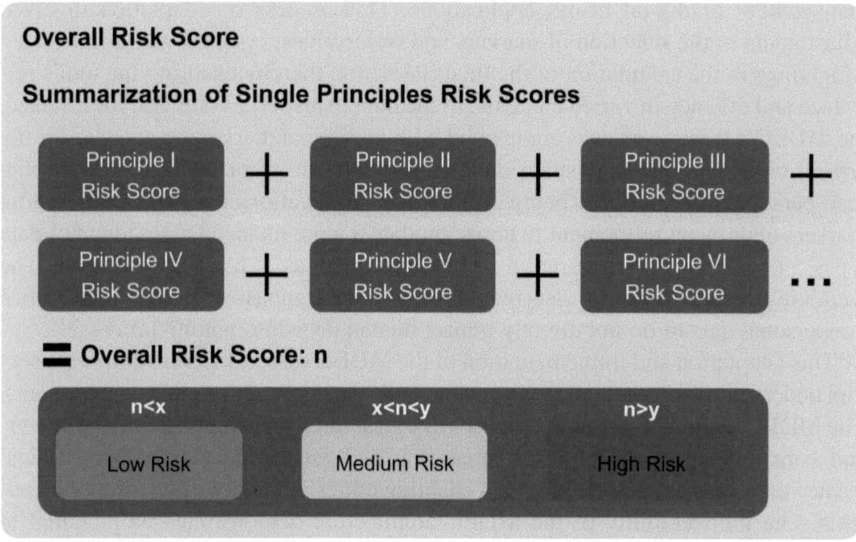

Fig. 5 The calculation of the overall risk score (Charton et al., 2025)

recommendations. In instances of medium or high risk, this phase necessitates a proactive risk analysis through a moderated self-reflection workshop conducted with predetermined inquiries. For medium-risk cases, the internal ACE steering committee is engaged, while high-risk scenarios warrant the involvement of representatives from the ethics department to develop and oversee the implementation of solutions. The CoDE principles form the foundational framework of the self-assessment, designed to catalyze profound ethical reflection within project teams. Supplementary guidelines support teams in the practical implementation of ethical considerations. For example, under the traceability principle, the team is prompted to consider whether data sources are "qualified and verified," reflecting Merck's commitment to using only high-quality, traceable data as set out in the underlying CoDE principle. Additional guidance drawn from both the principle descriptions and supplementary literature is provided to support use case teams during self-assessment. This guidance offers practical advice, such as examining data transformation processes or simplifying technical complexities, thereby enhancing traceability. As such, the MDEC encourages judicious risk-taking and mitigation measures while instituting grassroots ethics initiatives that aspire to cultivate robust ethical capacities within technical teams. This approach holds the potential to influence decision-making processes, ensure accountability, and ultimately anchor an ethical mindset within the data analytics workforce, thereby fostering a culture of ethical responsibility.

The architecture of the MDEC has demonstrated its versatility as a valuable blueprint for facilitating semi-automated ethics assessments across diverse corporate departments. Its adaptability has enabled its transfer, with requisite modifications, to other units within Merck, such as those dealing with human resources management or digital health applications. This process of adaptation involved adjustments to the selection of markers and observables, coupled with recalibrated weightings in the calculation of the final risk score, thereby ensuring the tool's relevance and efficacy in varied contexts. In the human resources domain, for instance, the MDEC's framework was augmented with additional markers to account for the critical consideration of whether data subjects are aware or are made aware that their personal information is being utilized in AI applications. Furthermore, existing markers underwent refinement to accommodate a more nuanced assessment of data types, including the incorporation of biometric data as a distinct observable. The weighting mechanism was also recalibrated to de-emphasize projects that utilize nonpersonal data or do not directly impact human decision-making processes.

This adaptation and implementation of the MDEC across different corporate sectors underscores its potential as a versatile and scalable tool for ethics assessments. The MDEC, and, more broadly, MDEC-like structures represent useful instruments and constitute blueprints for the expansion and further development of ethical frameworks capable of detecting and enabling ethics at scale within corporate contexts. The transferability of the MDEC architecture demonstrates its potential to serve as a model for the systematic integration of ethical considerations across diverse organizational functions. This adaptability is particularly important in the contemporary business landscape, where the ethical implications of data usage and AI applications permeate virtually every aspect of corporate operations.

By providing a flexible yet structured approach to ethical assessment, the MDEC and similar frameworks contribute to the cultivation of a pervasive ethical mindset within organizations. They facilitate the operationalization of abstract ethical principles into concrete, measurable criteria, thereby enabling a more consistent approach to ethical decision-making across various corporate domains. Moreover, the scalability of such frameworks addresses the need for efficient ethical oversight in environments characterized by high volumes of data-driven projects and rapid technological advancement. By enabling the systematic identification and mitigation of ethical risks across diverse organizational contexts, these tools can play important roles in fostering corporate cultures that prioritize ethical considerations as a component of their operational ethos. In essence, the MDEC and its adaptations represent advancements in the practical application of ethical principles within corporate settings, offering a promising avenue for the ongoing development and refinement of ethical assessment methodologies in the face of evolving technological and organizational challenges.

3 Conclusion

We have elucidated three challenges in the operationalization of digital ethics within a corporate milieu. While this enumeration is by no means exhaustive, these challenges exemplify central conundrums that corporations must navigate in their ethical deliberations. Firstly, we confront the genuinely novel ethical quandaries engendered by the digital realm – a proposition that, despite its potential to be perceived as a hackneyed cliché, remains profoundly relevant. These include collective issues pertaining to privacy, questions of transparency, and unprecedented practical challenges, such as the sheer scale of projects necessitating ethical assessment. This novelty underscores the imperative for frameworks of principles that are tailored to the nuances of digital ethics and their specific operationalization. We have addressed this challenge by issuing our Code of Digital Ethics as a binding framework of principles.

The second significant challenge lies in the abundance of ethical frameworks – a veritable cornucopia from which corporations may select ad libitum. This profusion of choice risks engendering what Floridi (2019) terms "distractive" problems, encompassing practices such as "ethics shopping" – the selective adoption, adaptation, or revision of ethical principles, guidelines, codes, and frameworks in a manner that retrofits preexisting behaviors rather than shaping them. To preempt such practices, we have established binding tools such as the PaRA, which conceptually links practical deliberations with our underlying framework of principles, ensuring adherence to the principles we have committed to in our decision-making processes.

Finally, the most significant hurdle proved to be the implementation of ethics at the grassroots level, within individual departments where technically oriented employees deploy AI and data analytics projects at scale. These units face significant challenges in ethics consultations, stemming from the sheer volume of projects – often numbering in the thousands – the dynamic nature of project management characterized by multiple pivots across the project life cycle and the dearth of ethics expertise within these teams. We have showcased our approach in implementing semiautomated ethics assessments such as the MDEC to address these multifaceted issues, enabling ethical considerations to function at scale in dynamic environments while simultaneously building ethics capacity and fostering grassroots ethical ecosystems.

In our view, this approach to operationalizing digital ethics – predicated on the recognition that digital technologies are inherently value-laden and inseparable from ethical considerations – represents a noteworthy advancement in the practical application of moral principles within corporate settings. By addressing the novelty of digital ethics challenges, mitigating the risks of arbitrary ethical framework selection, and enabling ethical decision-making at scale, we have developed a robust methodology for integrating ethical considerations into the fabric of corporate operations. Our approach not only facilitates the systematic identification and mitigation of ethical risks across diverse organizational contexts but also contributes to the cultivation of a pervasive ethical mindset within the corporate sphere. By providing structured yet flexible frameworks for ethical assessment, we enable a more consistent and rigorous approach to ethical decision-making and judicious risk-taking, thereby fostering corporate cultures that prioritize ethical considerations as an integral component of their operational ethos.

In essence, the challenges we have addressed and the solutions we have implemented represent a notable step forward in the ongoing dialogue between ethical theory and corporate praxis. As we continue to navigate the ever-evolving landscape of digital ethics, these methodologies offer a promising foundation for the further development and refinement of ethics assessment frameworks, ensuring that corporate entities can meet the ethical challenges of the digital age with rigor, consistency, and genuine commitment to moral principles.

Competing Interests The authors have no conflicts of interest to declare that are relevant to the content of this chapter.

References

Becker, S. J., Nemat, A. T., Lucas, S., Heinitz, R. M., Klevesath, M., & Charton, J. E. (2023). A code of digital ethics: Laying the foundation for digital ethics in a science and technology company. *AI & Society, 38*, 2629–2639. https://doi.org/10.1007/s00146-021-01376-w

Boaz, M. (2021). Is technology value-neutral? *Science, Technology, and Human Values, 46*(1), 53–80. https://doi.org/10.1177/0162243919900965

Charton, J. E., Lucas, S., Vogd, W., Halter, W., & Becker, S. J. (2025). Operationalising digital ethics: Establishment of an ethics evaluation tool for data analytics. *AI & Society*. in press. https://doi.org/10.1007/s00146-025-02621-2

Edelman, L. B., Fuller, S. G., & Mara-Drita, I. (2001). Diversity rhetoric and the managerialization of law. *American Journal of Sociology, 106*(6). https://doi.org/10.1086/321303

Floridi, L. (2012). Distributed morality in an information society. *Science and Engineering Ethics, 19*, 727–743. https://doi.org/10.1007/s11948-012-9413-4

Floridi, L., & Taddeo M. (2016). What is data ethics? *Philosophical Transactions of the Royal Society A: Mathematical, Physical and Engineering Sciences, 374*(2083), 1–5. https://doi.org/10.1098/rsta.2016.0112

Floridi, L. (2019). Translating principles into practices of digital ethics: Five risks of being unethical. *Philosophy & Technology, 32*, 185–193. https://doi.org/10.1007/s13347-019-00354-x

Floridi, L. (2023). On good and evil, the mistaken idea that technology is ever neutral, and the importance of the double-charge thesis. *Philosophy & Technology, 36*(3). https://doi.org/10.1007/s13347-023-00661-4

Floridi, L., & Sanders, J. W. (2004). On the morality of artificial agents. *Minds and Machines, 14*(3), 349–379. https://doi.org/10.1023/B:MIND.0000035461.63578.9d

Gabriel, M. (2024). *Gutes tun - Wie der ethische Kapitalismus die Demokratie retten kann*. Ullstein.

Heyndels, S. (2023). Technology and neutrality. *Philosophy & Technology, 36*(4). https://doi.org/10.1007/s13347-023-00672-1

Mökander, J., Sheth, M., Watson, D. S., & Floridi, L. (2023). The switch, the ladder, and the matrix: Models for classifying AI systems. *Minds & Machines, 33*, 221–248. https://doi.org/10.48550/arXiv.2407.05341

Morley, J., Elhalal, A., Garcia, F., Kinsey, L., Mökander, J., & Floridi, L. (2021a). Ethics as a service: A pragmatic operationalisation of AI ethics. *Minds & Machines, 31*, 239–256. https://doi.org/10.1007/s11023-021-09563-w

Morley, J., Kinsey, L., Elhalal, A., Garcia, F., Ziosi, M., & Floridi, L. (2021b). Operationalising AI ethics: Barriers, enablers and next steps. *AI & Society, 38*(1). https://doi.org/10.1007/s00146-021-01308-8

Nemat, A. T., & Charton, J. E. (2024). Ethics versus technological advancements: Partners in crime. In N. Siragusa & A. T. Nemat (Eds.), *Bioconvergence revolution*. Springer.

Nemat, A. T., Becker, S. J., Lucas, S., Thomas, S., Gadea, I., & Charton, J. (2023). The principle-at-risk analysis (PaRA): Operationalising digital ethics by bridging principles and operations of a digital ethics advisory panel. *Minds & Machines, 33*, 737–760. https://doi.org/10.1007/s11023-023-09654-w

Sugarman, J., Shivakumar, S., Rook, M., Loring, J. F., Rehmann-Sutter, C., Taupitz, J., Rheinhard-Rupp, J., & Hildemann, S. (2018). Ethical considerations in the manufacture, sale, and distribution of genome editing technologies. *The American Journal of Bioethics, 18*(8), 3–6. https://doi.org/10.1126/science.1164441

Véliz, C. (2020). *Privacy is power*. Penguin (Bantam Press).

Simon Lucas is Lead Expert for Bioethics & Digital Ethics at Merck KGaA, where he translates ethical reasoning into actionable corporate practices. He brings over 15 years of experience in corporate ethics, strategy development, and R&D. Simon holds a PhD in natural sciences and an MA in bioethics.

Jean Enno Charton is Director of Digital Ethics & Bioethics at Merck KGaA, overseeing ethical matters across all divisions. He joined Merck in 2014, initially serving in R&D roles before transitioning into his current leadership position. Jean Enno holds a PhD in immuno-oncology and an MSc in biochemistry.

Deutsche Telekom Connects People: Our Business, Our Responsibility

Maike Scholz, Melanie Kubin-Hardewig, and Marike Mehlmann-Tripp

Abstract

Deutsche Telekom sees Corporate Digital Responsibility (CDR) as a strategic management principle for sustainable business in the digital age. CDR is integrated into the group's corporate strategy and includes key areas of action such as sustainability, digital ethics, data protection and cybersecurity, dialogue, and the promotion of democratic values. The most important measures include the expansion of accessible network infrastructures, the development of sustainable products and services, the implementation of our self-binding ethical and green AI guidelines, and initiatives to strengthen media literacy and social cohesion. The impact of CDR measures is systematically recorded through certified impact measurement processes and ESG key figures. In 2024, 34 million people benefited from digital inclusion measures, and more than 40% of sales were generated by sustainable products. Challenges lie in coping with disruptive technologies and ensuring data sovereignty. Deutsche Telekom is pursuing the goal of achieving net-zero emissions by 2040 and further expanding its pioneering role as a sustainable, digital company.

1 Introduction

For Deutsche Telekom, connecting people is not only a business model but also a fundamental social task. Our purpose forms the basis for our actions in an increasingly digitalized world. Today, "connection" encompasses more than voice or text communication. It means access to education, participation, opportunities, and

M. Scholz (✉) · M. Kubin-Hardewig · M. Mehlmann-Tripp
Deutsche Telekom, Bonn, Germany
e-mail: maike.scholz01@telekom.de

A.-S. Christ (ed.), *Corporate Digital Responsibility*, Future of Business and Finance, https://doi.org/10.1007/978-3-032-14793-6_9

social interaction. Responsibility is inextricably linked to this approach – a responsibility that we actively assume.

For more than three decades, we have been shaping the digital transformation as a technological pioneer. What began with the goal of connecting people via audio has developed into a comprehensive digital infrastructure mission. We are aware that digitization is not an end in itself. It must be designed with an ethical orientation and social objectives. Our aim is therefore not only to accompany technological developments, but also to help shape them actively and responsibly.

At the heart of this claim is our understanding of Corporate Digital Responsibility (CDR). At Deutsche Telekom, CDR is not an isolated measure, but an integral part of our corporate identity. It reflects our values, our corporate culture, and our enduring commitment to acting responsibly. Our digital responsibility is reflected in concrete measures – for example, in the secure design of our networks, in the protection of personal data, in strengthening digital inclusion, and in our social commitment against online hate.

One example of this is the "Open your eyes" campaign (Telekom, 2025), which is part of our company-wide "No Hate Speech" initiative. The aim is to strengthen democratic spaces for discourse in the digital space and to stand up for respect, inclusion, and human dignity – values that we believe are fundamental to a successful digital society.

At the same time, we are facing global challenges such as climate change, demographic shifts, and increasing social polarization. In this context, technology must be used as a tool to strengthen equal opportunities and social cohesion – not as a driver for exclusion or fragmentation. Deutsche Telekom is therefore committed to technology-supported progress based on the principle of sustainability.

Our understanding of responsibility permeates all levels of the company: from the implementation of digital ethics in AI governance structures to data protection and cybersecurity to the integration of social and environmental aspects into our supply chains and the circular economy with a view to digital technologies. Digital responsibility is not a buzzword for us. We are convinced that customers will only use technologies – and recommend them to others – if our products and services are sustainable and trustworthy.

Accordingly, CDR is firmly **anchored in our corporate responsibility strategy** (Fig. 1). Within our ESG framework, digital responsibility plays a key role in the **governance pillar** and has a unifying effect on key issues such as information security, data protection, risk and compliance management, sustainable supply chains, and HR and financial processes.

This integrated approach ensures that digital responsibility is not only proclaimed but operationalized. Our digital innovations are created in line with our values. For us, technological progress is only sustainable if it is supported by integrity and responsibility.

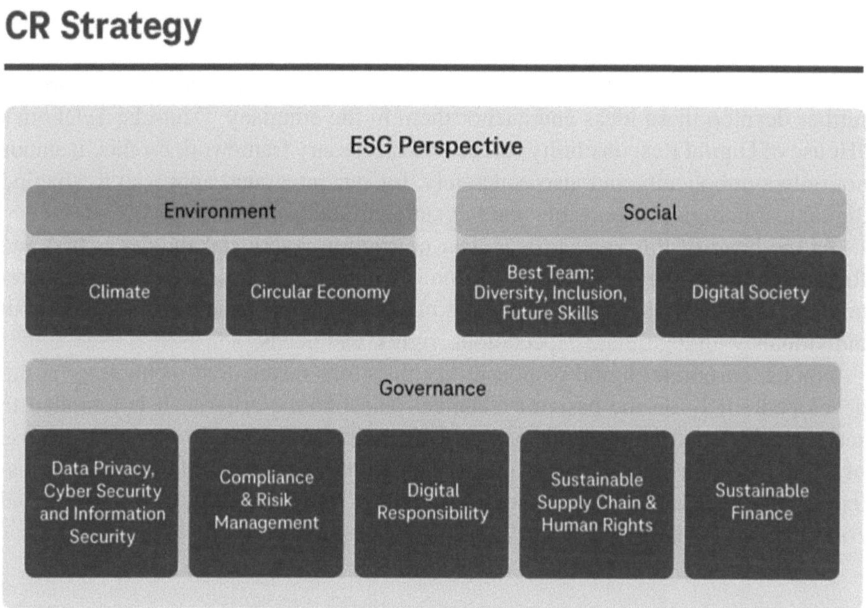

Fig. 1 Corporate responsibility strategy (Deutsche Telekom, 2025d)

1.1 People Are at the Center of Everything We Do

Behind the measures mentioned is the clear tone from the top of the Board of Management of Deutsche Telekom, representative of which is the statement of Timotheus Höttges, CEO of Deutsche Telekom AG:

> *The transformation of our world has accelerated rapidly. Climate and demographic change, social inequality, and technological progress – these changes affect us all, positively and negatively. We as a society face the challenge of shaping and mastering these changes - only if we are successful can we continue to develop further. At Deutsche Telekom, we all follow the goal: getting everyone connected. That is our contribution. Being able to take part in the digital world is such a central need that it affects everyone. We are committed to this and obligate our business partners and suppliers to do the same.*
>
> *Responsible digitalization represents the extension of our practiced corporate responsibility into an increasingly digitalized world. Based on this conviction, we design our internal processes, business activities, and business relationships; we adapt our product portfolio and service offerings; we stand up for community and campaign against the division of society. With this document, we are demonstrating the spectrum of our digital responsibility. We are creating transparency as to how we at Deutsche Telekom are helping to get society more connected in the long term – every person in all of their individuality. People are at the heart of everything we do.* (Deutsche Telekom, 2025c)

2 The House of Digital Responsibility

Digital responsibility begins with ideas – and at the same time needs structures to further develop these ideas and anchor them in the company. Deutsche Telekom's "House of Digital Responsibility" creates the necessary framework for this. It stands not only symbolically, but also concretely, for our integrated approach to shaping digital technologies responsibly and human-centrically.

At the heart of this concept is a clear conviction: every stakeholder is first and foremost a human being – whether customers, employees, business partners, shareholders, or society as a whole. They are not anonymous elements of a system, but individuals with legitimate expectations, rights, and needs.

For us, corporate digital responsibility therefore means that technology is not developed solely on the basis of technical or economic criteria. It is intended to serve, support, and empower the people who use it. This is exactly where the "House of Digital Responsibility" comes in – as a structural expression of our claim to systematically integrate ethical and social guidelines into technology development and corporate governance (Fig. 2 and Table 1).

2.1 The House of Digital Responsibility: Structure and Impact

The "House of Digital Responsibility" initiative forms the conceptual framework for the implementation of digital responsibility at Deutsche Telekom. It is not based on physical structures, but on clear values, principles, and lived measures. The architecture of this building is symbolic but effective: it stands on an ethical

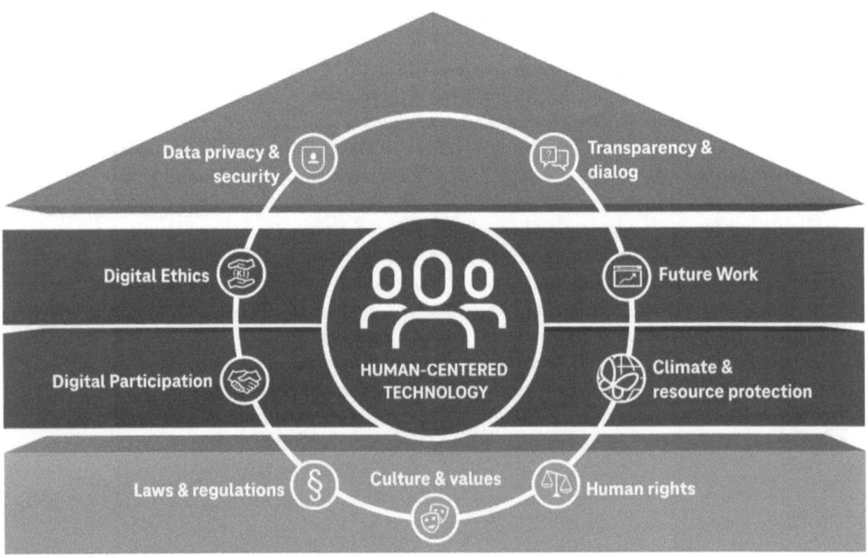

Fig. 2 The house of digital responsibility (Deutsche Telekom, 2025b)

Table 1 The house of digital responsibility (Deutsche Telekom, 2025b)

Our foundation for digital responsibility	
Laws and regulations	We act in compliance with applicable laws and regulations and adopt digital rights in our daily activities accordingly
Human rights	We are expressly committed to the United Nations Guiding Principles on Business and Human Rights and stand for digital sovereignty, freedom from discrimination, and freedom of expression
Culture and values	As a global company, we appreciate cultural differences while promoting a common understanding of values
Our principles of digital responsibility	
Data privacy and security	We stand for security and the responsible handling of data
Transparency and dialog	We shape the dialogue about the opportunities and risks of digitalization and make our actions transparent
Actions we take for digital responsibility	
Digital ethics	Ensuring sovereignty and supporting people are our focus. We design digital technologies responsibly
Digital inclusion	Deutsche Telekom wants everyone to take part in the digital society. Everyone should have access to the many opportunities afforded by digitalization
Future of work	Digital responsibility at Deutsche Telekom means thinking about future work as part of its dynamic transformation process and ensuring that, despite all the changes, people remain the focus of all decisions
Climate and resource protection	Protecting the climate together and using resources responsibly – with and through digitalization

foundation, is open to a wide range of perspectives, and offers orientation for responsible action in the digital age.

The house acts as a living orientation framework that serves as a reference point for ethically sound decisions on digital products and services throughout the company – from product design to compliance work. Every project that is aligned with ethical principles and every decision that is made in a human-centered way strengthens this construct. The initiative is supported and further developed by employees, which gives it a high level of acceptance and credibility within the company (Table 1).

It provides guidance on how to deal with regulatory requirements and helps to integrate ethical aspects into technical and organizational implementation processes. In addition, it bridges the broader corporate responsibility frameworks for a company like Deutsche Telekom AG to the specific aspects of the digital world. It is thus a practical tool for a value-based operationalization of compliance and technological progress.

The feedback from the company has been consistently positive. Employees thus understand the interaction of the individual reference areas. The metaphor of the house has proven to be helpful in this regard – it makes abstract values tangible and supports internal and external discussions about ethics, responsibility, and digitalization. The house has the people in its center – human-centered technology – and brings its values and culture into new, digital contexts.

2.2 Putting People First: Our Approach to Human-Centered Technology

At the heart of every technological development is a decisive factor: people. At Deutsche Telekom, this focus is not just an aspiration, but a central guiding principle of our actions. Regardless of technological maturity, sustainable success can only be achieved if people have confidence in the respective technology. This trust is not based on innovation alone, but on a clear purpose and ethical orientation. Digital technologies must serve people – not the other way around. They must be designed responsibly, carefully, and value-oriented in order to avoid negative side effects and undesirable social effects. This aspiration forms the basis of our understanding of **digital responsibility** – a humanistic approach based on clear ethical guidelines.

In terms of implementation, this means that people are involved in technological development processes at an early stage, sensibly and actively. Human-centered technology cannot be prescribed top-down. It must be shaped together with those who use it and apply it in their everyday lives. Against this background, we actively promote a committed community of employees who are committed to this principle.

Deutsche Telekom's goal is to **give everyone access to the digital society**. Participation must not be dependent on place of residence, income, or individual abilities. Inclusion and participation are, therefore, central components of our CDR approach. Under the strategic motto "**Access, Affordability and Ability**" (Deutsche Telekom, n.d.-b), we are pursuing concrete measures to promote digital inclusion:

Access Access to modern information technologies is an important key to participation in the information and knowledge society. That is why we are continuously investing in the expansion of our network infrastructure in order to provide access that is as comprehensive as possible. In addition, we cooperate with partners, especially in structurally weak or remote regions, to ensure connectivity there as well.

Affordability The Internet has become an indispensable part of everyday society. Despite the numerous benefits that digitalization brings, there are still people who face challenges in order to fully participate in the digital world. We are committed to ensuring that all people have the opportunity to participate in the digital world. We also offer different tariffs for every budget, a social tariff, and reduced basic fees, for example, for schools. With our 5G smartphones, T-Phone 2 and T-Phone 2 Pro, we also give consumers access to the latest technologies at an affordable price. In this way, we are trying to make digital access financially possible for everyone.

Ability Digital inclusion also requires skills. That is why we teach people the skills to stay safe and reflect on trends in the digital spaces. One focus is on democratic discourse and defending human rights online. The "No Hate Speech" initiative, which has been running since 2020, raises awareness of the dangers of digital violence and strengthens a respectful, inclusive communication culture in the digital space (Deutsche Telekom, 2025e).

2.3 Human-Centered Technology as a Lived Practice: Digital Ethics and Bottom-Up Initiatives at Deutsche Telekom

The "Digital Ethics" initiative was formed within Deutsche Telekom back in 2017 with the aim of systematically and sustainably anchoring the ethical use of new technologies such as artificial intelligence (AI) in the company.

A special milestone in this development was the year 2022: Within the Legal and Integrity department, the topic of digital ethics was anchored in the organization, within the framework of a squad structure consisting of an interdisciplinary team (Compliance, Legal, Data Protection, Security, T-Labs, Service, Business, etc.), with a defined project structure and hierarchical control at board level (Deutsche Telekom, 2025f). AI governance in the group is thus implemented in a co-creation approach by a controlling, technical, and regulatory authority. These interdisciplinary structures enabled a rapid response to developments in the field of AI.

Over the years, other interdisciplinary, bottom-up communities have developed from this impulse – including the "Human-Centered Technology Community" (Bilfinger et al., 2024) with a focus on human-centered technology design and the AI community, which is more focused on technical implementation.

The Human-Centered Technology Community brings together employees from different departments, hierarchical levels, and international locations. Together, they are committed to shaping technological developments in an empathetic, responsible, and purpose-oriented manner. Participation is voluntary, driven by personal motivation and a shared ethical self-image. The network is open to everyone – regardless of whether they contribute technical expertise or have a strong value orientation.

Collaboration in the community is collaborative and iterative: regular virtual meetings, short check-ins, and formats such as barcamps or hackathons promote the continuous exchange of knowledge and ideas. The results are made visible via an internal platform – not only as a repository, but as a dynamic space for transparency, collaboration, and innovation. Numerous projects have emerged from this, such as an app to promote reflective social media use, a checklist for ethical product design, or approaches for environmentally friendly IT solutions. The community shows how company-wide changes beyond classic structures can be made possible – supported by managers but without central control.

The community now has over 400 active members, and the trend is rising. Her self-image goes beyond the reflection of digital responsibility: she lives this responsibility in everyday life. This example of bottom-up innovation in action stands for an inclusive, organically grown, and impact-oriented form of technology design.

The activities on the topic of digital ethics are embedded in a larger transformation strategy. Through training formats, communication campaigns, and everyday dialogues, employees carry the content of digital ethics into many areas of the company. A complementary instrument is the digital@work program, which supports employees in building up digital skills. With the help of around 25 modular tools, participants put together their personal digital toolbox with the aim of shaping their digital working day confidently and responsibly (Deutsche Telekom, n.d.-a).

The commitment to digital ethics does not end at the company's borders. Our experts actively monitor legislative developments at the EU and national levels. Deutsche Telekom is involved in leading industry associations such as BDI (n.d.), Bitkom (n.d.), BVDW (2025), Initiative D21 (2025), the GSMA (2025), and CEN CENELEC (2025) at the standardization level.

We also underscore our commitment to the responsible use of AI through voluntary commitments: On September 25, 2024, we joined the EU Commission's AI Pact (European Commission, 2025).

2.4 Human-Centered Responsibility as a Strategic Attitude

Deutsche Telekom's human-centered approach is not an abstract concept but has a concrete impact on our business activities – both in the digital and physical space. It forms the basis for the design of our products, processes, and principles. Our understanding of CDR is also derived from this attitude: for us, legal compliance and digital responsibility are **not separate areas**, but closely linked.

Legal requirements form the indispensable basis, but responsible action goes beyond that. Deutsche Telekom voluntarily commits to more far-reaching standards, especially where social impact and long-term trust are crucial. Our mission statement is based on values, not just duties – because integrity comes from attitude, not just by following the rules.

As a founding member of the **CDR Initiative** (2025) – a platform developed under the auspices of the German Federal Ministry for the Environment, Nature Conservation, Nuclear Safety and Consumer Protection (BMUV) – Deutsche Telekom has been actively involved in the formulation of a **common CDR Code**. This code defines fundamental principles for a responsible digital society, which we continue to follow.

2.5 Cultural Anchoring of Responsibility

A value-oriented corporate culture plays a central role in this. As an internationally active company, Deutsche Telekom sees cultural diversity not as a challenge, but as a strategic advantage. Our company culture is based on shared values that apply regardless of location, function, or time zone. They connect employees worldwide and provide orientation in everyday life.

These values are not just formulated principles, but lived reality – anchored, among other things, in the **company-wide Code of Conduct** (Deutsche Telekom, 2025a), which defines clear expectations of the behavior of all employees. At Deutsche Telekom, leadership does not only mean setting direction, but also actively taking responsibility. That is why we make targeted investments in **leadership development programs** tailored to different levels of experience.

Leadership at Deutsche Telekom means **building trust, promoting transparency, and being a role model for democratic values**. These values do not fade when the conversation becomes digital – on the contrary, they gain in importance. For us, digital ethics is not an afterthought, but a consistent **continuation of our moral compass**, which also guides the actions of all those involved in the digital space.

2.6 Human Rights, Data Protection, and Digital Responsibility

In an increasingly interconnected world, human rights are taking on new digital dimensions. Deutsche Telekom expressly acknowledges its responsibility in this context and is committed to the **Guiding Principles on Business and Human Rights (United Nations,** 2025). The focus is on the promotion of digital sovereignty, the protection of freedom of expression, and the fight against any form of digital discrimination.

Today, technology has a significant impact on how we live, work and communicate. Deutsche Telekom is responding to this reality with the necessary sense of responsibility. For example, through targeted initiatives such as the **"A Message from Ella" video campaign** (2023), the company raises awareness of the importance of informed consent and the potential risks of thoughtlessly sharing personal information of third parties in the digital space. The company understands that in the digital age**, every interaction carries ethical weight** – and takes seriously the associated public expectation of responsible leadership.

A central component of this self-image is the responsible handling of data. At Deutsche Telekom, **data protection and data security** are not only understood as technical or regulatory obligations, but as a prerequisite for trust. To this end, the company has implemented comprehensive structures that ensure compliant data processing at all levels – from local processes to global IT systems.

In addition, the commitment is not limited to the security of the data, but also includes **transparency about its use** (Telekom, n.d.-b). Here, Deutsche Telekom discloses what data is collected, for what purpose it is used, how long it is stored, and under what conditions it is passed on. This openness is part of an overarching objective: to reflect on the opportunities and risks of digitization in social dialogue.

In this dialogue, Deutsche Telekom is in contact with **regulatory authorities, customers, and the interested public** to ensure that ethical issues are systematically included in technological decision-making processes. The basic principles of **data protection and security**, as well as **transparency and dialogue** – together with legal requirements, the corporate culture, and the commitment to human rights – form the **binding framework for action** in the so-called House of Digital Responsibility.

For Deutsche Telekom, digital ethics is thus much more than a programmatic concept – it acts as a **compass that provides orientation**. Every decision in the context of digital technologies is examined against the background of whether it strengthens the **dignity, freedom, and self-determination** of people. Where this question cannot be answered unambiguously, the company sees a need for further action. This critical questioning is not an obstacle, but the prerequisite for **sustainable, value-based innovation**. This ensures that technological advances serve people – and do not work to their detriment.

3 Digital Inclusion and New Working Environments as Components of Digital Responsibility

As already described above, the conviction that digital ethics is a central component of corporate responsibility leads to the consistent promotion of **digital inclusion**. Deutsche Telekom is aware of the fact that in a digital society, **access to technology is a prerequisite** for equal participation in society. Based on this understanding, the company is committed to ensuring that all people – regardless of age, disability, income, or level of education – can benefit from the digital transformation.

Digital inclusion is understood as a component of social inclusion. It is not just about providing connectivity, but about **access to opportunities, self-determination, and social participation**. This includes accessible and affordable offerings as well as the development of tools and platforms that meet people's needs. In addition, the aim is to strengthen the necessary **digital skills and confidence in the safe use of technology**.

Another central field of action for digital responsibility is the **future of work**. Deutsche Telekom understands that responsible digital transformation includes the workplace itself. The focus is not only on technological systems and software solutions, but also on leadership **understanding, trust, cooperation, and cultural change**.

More than 10 years ago, the company initiated the change towards a **more flexible, human-centered work culture**. This transformation process is continuously being developed and is based on a mission statement developed together with employees: the **"New Way of Working" manifesto**. It reflects the conviction that meaningful work does not have to be tied to a location, but is based on **mutual respect**, the availability of suitable tools, and openness to new forms of cooperation.

The corporate culture is understood as a **dynamic system** that develops, learns, and grows with the people in the company. The design of the world of work thus becomes part of a comprehensive understanding of digital responsibility – with the aim of reconciling technological progress with social sustainability.

4 Digital Responsibility with a View to Environmental and Social Sustainability

An integral part of digital responsibility is the contribution to ecological and social sustainability. Deutsche Telekom pursues this goal with the two labels **#GreenMagenta** and **#GoodMagenta** (Deutsche Telekom, n.d.-c), among other things, which make concrete measures visible and provide orientation for sustainable decisions.

#GreenMagenta identifies environmentally friendly products, processes, and initiatives. The aim is to systematically integrate climate and resource protection into business models and innovation processes. **#GoodMagenta** stands for social commitment and initiatives aimed at fairness, security, and participation – especially in the digital space.

Both labels are seen as a visible expression of a strategic orientation towards how Deutsche Telekom lives up to its responsibility towards the environment and society in concrete products and services. They complement established sustainability seals such as the Blue Angel or TÜV Green Product with company-specific, easy-to-understand labelling. Through the transparent labelling of sustainable offers, customers and employees are sensitized to responsible decisions and at the same time informed in a simple way.

4.1 Assessment of Digital Ethics: Structures, Governance, and Green AI

As part of the company-wide **Digital Ethics Initiative**, Deutsche Telekom takes a proactive approach to ensuring that the development and implementation of new technologies is consistent with ethical principles. This principle is operationalized under the guiding principle of "**Ethics by Design**" – i.e., the systematic anchoring of ethical guidelines in all phases of the technology development process.

A central instrument is the **Digital Ethics Assessment**, which is closely linked to the established **Privacy and Security Assessment (PSA)**. This assessment procedure serves to identify ethical requirements – especially in connection with the use of artificial intelligence – at an early stage and to implement them in a structured manner. It ensures that the company's internal ethical AI guidelines and the new EU AI Act (Regulation (EU) 2024/1689) are consistently applied to all products and services with AI components. The aim is to promote value-based technology development from the conception phase onwards.

The **Digital Ethics Assessment** also fulfills a practice-oriented function: it provides employees with a clear framework for integrating ethical issues into their daily work. At the same time, it helps to reduce personal liability risks, avoid delays in product development, and create a common understanding of responsible digitalization. In this way, the assessment contributes to strengthening trust with stakeholders, improving the customer experience, and promoting technological solutions that are powerful and at the same time user-oriented and ethically justifiable.

This approach is additionally flanked by the principle of "**Privacy by Design**." To this end, Deutsche Telekom has established a **Privacy and Security Assessment** that ensures that privacy-related issues are addressed at an early stage of development. No system or service with personal data goes into operation without explicit permission. Data protection is thus understood as an integral part of the product life cycle – not as a downstream obligation.

For systematic implementation, Deutsche Telekom has defined clear **data protection guidelines for data-driven business models**. These include six central basic rules for handling personal data and involving data subjects in order to promote acceptance and trust in data-driven innovations. In addition, practical handouts, methods, and best practices have been developed that facilitate implementation in day-to-day operations – including in the company-wide **supplier code** (Deutsche Telekom, 2024a).

The activities deliberately go beyond compliance with regulatory requirements. With the aim **of actively shaping the future of data protection, a Data Protection Advisory Board** was established. In addition, a group-wide **data protection audit** is carried out every 2 years, combining qualitative and quantitative survey methods. This is based on online surveys of a representative sample as well as supplementary on-site audits by internal and external inspection bodies. This combination enables continuous improvement and agile adaptation to changing regulatory, technological, and societal requirements.

To promote feasibility, all guidelines have been enriched with concrete application examples and implementation tips. In addition to **legal compliance, the focus is on the practice-oriented design of data security, transparency, and clear responsibilities for AI systems**.

Finally, Deutsche Telekom pursues a claim that goes beyond pure compliance: cooperation with data protection experts, the further development of technical standards, and the commitment to **maximum transparency** are central elements of this understanding. Trust is built not only through technology, but also through responsible action, traceability, and **ethical foresight** – as the basis for a sustainable digital transformation.

4.2 Principles for Green Artificial Intelligence (Green AI)

In view of the considerable energy and resource consumption associated with AI applications, Deutsche Telekom has formulated clear guidelines for sustainable development and the use of AI, along with the self-binding, ethical AI guidelines. They pursue the goal of integrating environmental sustainability into the life cycle of AI technologies from the very beginning.

To this end, Deutsche Telekom has defined nine principles for green AI that provide guidance on how ecological risks – in particular a rising energy demand and connected CO_2 footprint – can be identified and minimized at an early stage. These principles apply to all phases of the value chain and address aspects such as the use of renewable energies, the multiple use of hardware, software, and data, and the dynamic scaling of IT resources to avoid oversizing them.

Other key elements are the selection of optimized AI models and efficient algorithms ("green coding"), the avoidance of duplication of work by reusing software components, and the consistent monitoring of the CO_2 footprint across the entire product chain. In doing so, Deutsche Telekom is not only taking responsibility for its own AI systems, but is also providing impetus for companies, politics, and science to establish sustainable standards for AI technologies.

The implementation of these principles is an essential part of the House of Digital Responsibility. There, ecological sustainability and climate protection complement the ethical, social, and legal dimensions of corporate digital responsibility. In this way, Deutsche Telekom ensures that innovations in the field of AI are not only innovative and powerful but also environmentally friendly and future-proof.

5 Responsible Partner for Education and Social Inclusion

Deutsche Telekom sees itself as an active partner in a responsible digital society. In this context, the company has been supporting education and participation projects for many years in order to make digitization equitable and secure – especially for young people, educational institutions, and older generations.

5.1 Contribution to the Digitalization of the Education Sector

In the field of education, Deutsche Telekom is committed to systematically supporting schools in Germany in their digital transformation. In doing so, the company pursues two central objectives:

Making technological know-how accessible: The provision of modern digital solutions is intended to help create optimal learning environments. A well-educated generation is crucial for innovation, economic development, and societal resilience.

Playing its role as a digitalization partner: With a powerful network, a broad portfolio of solutions, and strong partner structures, Deutsche Telekom is in a position to support schools nationwide and sustainably.

5.2 Commitment to the Protection of Minors and Families in the Digital Space

Beyond the school environment, Deutsche Telekom is committed to the protection of children and young people – often beyond the minimum legal requirements.

This commitment is operationalized by the Teachtoday initiative, among other things. **Teachtoday** (Deutsche Telekom, n.d.-d) addresses concrete challenges in the digital everyday life of children, parents, and educational professionals. The initiative is available in several languages, is based on international best practices, and provides practical materials and recommendations for action. In addition, the **AwareNessi** (Deutsche Telekom, 2024) – the Cyber Activity Book program offers children aged 8–12 a playful introduction to digital security literacy. Through stories, creative activities, and age-appropriate approaches, topics such as phishing, fake news, and cost traps are conveyed in a low-threshold manner.

Our employees also share this commitment. Around 500 Deutsche Telekom volunteers have joined forces to form a community through our DIGITAL@School initiative (Deutsche Telekom, n.d.-a) to empower children as active, self-determined creators in the digital world. It is under the label **#GoodMagenta** and combines technical know-how with social commitment.

The focus is on the playful and age-appropriate teaching of STEM skills (mathematics, computer science, natural sciences, technology). Programming is presented in a practical way in order to arouse interest and create a sense of achievement. In addition, DIGITAL@School promotes media literacy for the responsible use of digital media in order to take advantage of opportunities and counter risks such as data protection and cyberbullying.

Deutsche Telekom employees volunteer in schools and at events to actively support digital education. In addition, the Deutsche Telekom Foundation was established in 2003 with a capital of 150 million euros – one of the largest corporate foundations in Germany. Its focus is on promoting STEM education (science, technology, engineering and mathematics) for young people aged 10–16. In addition to technical skills, cross-sectional skills such as critical thinking, creativity, communication skills, and teamwork are specifically promoted.

5.3 Digital Inclusion for Older Generations

Digital inclusion does not end when people reach retirement age. Deutsche Telekom is therefore developing specific products and services that are tailored to the **needs of elderly people** – training courses such as “Connected in old age” (Telekom, n.d.-a) but also end devices with a simplified user interface (Telekom, n.d.-c), emergency call functions, and clearly structured user interfaces.

In addition, the company is involved in various cooperation projects, such as with the BAGSO (Federal Association of Senior Citizens’ Organisations, n.d.) and the Digital Compass project. The aim of these activities is to enable senior citizens to use digital technologies safely, curiously, and in a self-determined manner.

6 Conclusion: Corporate Digital Responsibility at Deutsche Telekom

Deutsche Telekom’s Corporate Digital Responsibility is firmly anchored in the concept of the House of Digital Responsibility, whose central guiding principle is human-centered technology. This attitude is the protective umbrella for the entire company and reflects the conviction that behind all stakeholder groups – customers, employees, partners, shareholders, and society – there are people with individual rights and needs.

The house rests on a stable foundation of law and order, a commitment to the UN Guiding Principles on Business and Human Rights, and a value-based, culturally sensitive understanding. Privacy, security, transparency, and dialogue are integral principles that permeate action.

Accordingly, technological developments and their application are consistently aligned with four fields of action: the responsible design of digital ethics, the promotion of digital participation, the human-centered transformation of the world of work, and climate and resource protection. In this way, Deutsche Telekom ensures that progress is always in the service of people and society – as an expression of holistic, sustainable digital responsibility.

References

BDI. (n.d.). *Climatecongress*. Retrieved July 6, 2025, from https://english.bdi.eu/

Bilfinger, B., Scholz, M., Cramer, A., Pfender, J., Leffler-Krebs, S., & Wößner, J. (2024). CDR aus Sicht der Building Bloxx. In A. Brink (Ed.), *Corporate digital responsibility. Menschenzentrierte Digitalisierung* (pp. 113–130). Nomos.

Bitkom. (n.d.). *Germany's digital association*. Retrieved July 6, 2025, from https://www.bitkom.org/EN

BSGSO. (n.d.). *Digital-Kompass - Gemeinsam digitale Barrieren überwinden*. Retrieve July 6, 2025, from https://www.bagso.de/projekte/digital-kompass/

BVDW. (2025). *Gremium digital responsibility*. Retrieved July 6, 2025, from https://www.bvdw.org/en/committees/digital-responsibility/

CDR Initiative. (2025). *Corporate Digital Responsibility Initiative*. Retrieved July 6, 2025, from https://cdr-initiative.de/

CEN CENELEC. (2025). *CEN CENELEC*. Retrieved July 6, 2025, from https://www.cencenelec.eu/

Deutsche Telekom. (2024, June 13). *Digital@School. AwareNessi: Ein innovatives Erlebnis in der digitalen Bildung*. https://www.digitalatschool.de/aktuelles/artikel/awarenessi-ein-innovatives-erlebnis-in-der-digitalen-bildung-1

Deutsche Telekom. (2024a). *Verhaltenskodex für Lieferanten*. Retrieved July 6, 2025, from https://www.telekom.com/resource/blob/498828/f670c8ac99c787528d105daaaf14287d/dl-240320-lieferantenkodex-data.pdf

Deutsche Telekom. (2025a). *Code of conduct. The way we work*. Retrieved July 6, 2025, from https://www.telekom.com/en/company/compliance/code-of-conduct

Deutsche Telekom. (2025b). *Corporate digital responsibility*. Retrieved July 6, 2025, from https://www.telekom.com/en/company/digital-responsibility/cdr

Deutsche Telekom. (2025c). *Corporate digital responsibility – Our perspective*. Retrieved July 6, 2025, from https://www.telekom.com/en/company/digital-responsibility/details/corporate-digital-responsibility-our-perspective-1008402

Deutsche Telekom. (2025d). *Corporate responsibility. Our approach*. Retrieved July 6, 2025, from https://www.telekom.com/en/corporate-responsibility/governance/details/our-approach-353746

Deutsche Telekom. (2025e). *No hate speech*. Retrieved July 6, 2025, from https://www.telekom.com/en/company/topic-specials/no-hate-speech

Deutsche Telekom. (2025f). *The EU AI Act at Deutsche Telekom*. Retrieved July 6, 2025, from https://www.telekom.com/en/company/digital-responsibility/details/the-eu-ai-act-at-deutsche-telekom%2D%2D1090710

Deutsche Telekom. (n.d.-a). *Digital@School. Digital Voraus. Mit Herz & Verstand*. Retrieved July 6, 2025, from https://www.digitalatschool.de/

Deutsche Telekom. (n.d.-b). *ESRS S4-1 – Policies related to consumers and end users*. Retrieved July 6, 2025, from https://report.telekom.com/annual-report-2024/sustainability-statement/social/esrs-s4-consumers-and-end-users.html?tabc=2e1

Deutsche Telekom. (n.d.-c). *Green and Good Magenta*. Retrieved July 6, 2025, from https://green-magenta.com/en/green-und-good-magenta/

Deutsche Telekom. (n.d.-d). *Techtoday*. Retrieved July 6, 2025, from https://www.teachtoday.de/

European Commission. (2025). *AI Pact. Shaping Europe's digital future*. Retrieved September 26, 2025, from https://digital-strategy.ec.europa.eu/en/policies/ai-pact

GSMA. (2025). *GSMA open gateway*. Retrieved July 6, 2025, from https://www.gsma.com/

Initiative D21. (2025). *AG Digitale Ethik*. Retrieved July 6, 2025, from https://initiatived21.de/arbeitsgruppen-initiativen/ag-digitale-ethik

Regulation (EU) 2024/1689 of the European Parliament and of the Council of 13 June 2024 laying down harmonised rules on artificial intelligence (Artificial Intelligence Act). European Union. https://eur-lex.europa.eu/eli/reg/2024/1689/oj/eng

Telekom. (2023). *Message from Ella. Without consent*. Retrieved July 6, 2025 https://www.telekom.com/de/medien/medieninformationen/detail/nachricht-von-ella-without-consent-1048362

Telekom. (2025). *'Open your eyes'—Telekom and partners position themselves with a new campaign against hate on the Internet*. Retrieved July 6, 2025, from https://www.telekom.com/en/company/details/no-hate-speech-open-your-eyes-1092966

Telekom. (n.d.-a). *Angebote für Senioren. Vernetzt im Alter: Digitalisierung für alle*. Retrieved July 6, 2025, from https://www.telekom.de/telekom-akademie/angebote-fuer-senioren

Telekom. (n.d.-b). *Ihre Daten bei der Telekom*. Retrieved July 6, 2025, from https://www.telekom.de/ueber-das-unternehmen/datenschutz/datentransparenz

Telekom. (n.d.-c). *Seniorenhandys. Endecken Sie unsere Auswahl an Seniorenhandy*. Retrieved July 6, 2025, from https://www.telekom.de/unterwegs/seniorenhandys

United Nations. (2025). *UN guiding principles*. Retrieved July 6, 2025, from https://www.business-humanrights.org/en/big-issues/governing-business-human-rights/un-guiding-principles/

Maike Scholz is Squad Lead for Digital Ethics at Deutsche Telekom and a senior expert in compliance, AI governance, and corporate digital responsibility. She has successfully led international projects at the intersection of AI ethics and governance and crisis management across the Group over the years. Maike is also a board member of the CDR division at BVDW, where she contributes her expertise to advancing responsible digital innovation. Maike holds a degree in Business Administration and a Master's degree in Compliance and Integrity Management.

Melanie Kubin-Hardewig is Vice President, Group Corporate Responsibility at Deutsche Telekom. She is responsible for the group-wide design and execution of Deutsche Telekom's Corporate Responsibility Strategy. This covers a wide range from environmental to social aspects, including sustainable supply chains and finance, as well as the development of DT's targets and KPIs. She also leads DT's top sustainability initiatives. Melanie has previously held various management roles at different entities of Deutsche Telekom. She is a trained lawyer and holds an MBA.

Marike Mehlmann-Tripp, Cluster Lead Social Engagement, Deutsche Telekom AG, has a degree in Psychology and an MBA in General Management. Since 2011, she has been working for Deutsche Telekom in various functions in the human resources as well as in the corporate strategy area. In her current role as Cluster Lead Social Engagement, she is part of Corporate Responsibility and is responsible for the global social engagement strategy for Telekom Group.

Digital Responsibility in Practice: How BARMER Anchors Ethics in Healthcare Innovation

Maria Hinz

Abstract

Corporate Digital Responsibility (CDR) is increasingly recognized as a pivotal governance framework for organizations navigating digital transformation. This chapter explores the BARMER case, a leading German statutory health insurance, which operationalizes CDR through an ethically anchored digital strategy. Within highly regulated healthcare environments and evolving data ethics standards, BARMER integrates CDR across five core domains: data governance, digital ethics, employee empowerment, climate impact, and inclusive access. By implementing a values-based approach including transparency, patient centricity, and autonomy, BARMER advances responsible digital innovation while fostering trust, sovereignty, and social impact. Key initiatives such as the DigiCoaches program, the digital learning platform "DigiTal," and transparency-enhancing services like the ePA (electronic patient record) exemplify how ethical digitalization can be embedded in practice. Furthermore, the case reflects BARMER's active role in shaping public discourse through its commitment to the CDR-Initiative and collaboration on cross-sectoral policy innovation. This contribution provides actionable insights for practitioners and policymakers, demonstrating how digital responsibility can be institutionalized within complex health systems to enhance societal resilience and organizational legitimacy.

M. Hinz (✉)
BARMER, Berlin, Germany
e-mail: maria.hinz@barmer.de

A.-S. Christ (ed.), *Corporate Digital Responsibility*, Future of Business and Finance, https://doi.org/10.1007/978-3-032-14793-6_10

1 Introduction: Digital Responsibility in a Regulated Sector

Digital transformation is a double-edged sword for health insurance providers. On the one hand, digitalization offers tools for improving efficiency, enhancing user experience, and reducing administrative burdens. On the other hand, it introduces complex ethical challenges and regulatory ambiguities, especially when applied in highly sensitive domains like healthcare. This duality provides statutory health insurers with open ethical questions and therefore increases pressure to act not only as administrators of services but also as ethical pioneers in digital governance.

The BARMER health insurance, Germany's second-largest statutory health insurance, has embraced this challenge by anchoring Corporate Digital Responsibility (CDR) at the core of its digital strategy. While CDR as a concept has matured in academic and policy discussions, practical application remains fragmented and uneven across sectors. Particularly in the healthcare sector, where regulations often lag behind technological innovation, a pragmatic approach is needed to navigate the dynamic landscape. BARMER defines CDR as a proactive, value-driven commitment to shaping digital transformation responsibly. By adhering to the CDR Code of the CDR Initiative and implementing an internal ethical framework, BARMER ensures that digital innovation consistently aligns with the public interest and patient welfare, beyond regulatory compliance. Thus, BARMER took the leap into becoming the first health insurance actively driving the strategic implementation of CDR (BARMER, 2022b). This article examines how BARMER operationalizes digital responsibility by translating abstract ethical values into concrete governance mechanisms and digital solutions. It displays how a value-based framework, organizational alignment, and participatory implementation strategies can collectively foster a responsible digital transformation, even in a highly regulated environment.

The case of BARMER contributes to the broader discourse on CDR by offering empirical insights into the alignment of principles and practice. It also demonstrates how CDR can serve not just as a compliance tool but also as a strategic lever for trust, risk prevention, innovation, and legitimacy in the digital era.

2 Strategic Framing: Anchoring CDR in Leadership and Values

At BARMER, the commitment begins at the highest organizational level. In 2021 the digital ethics compass was put into action by a joint task force of high-level managers who were confronted with different ethical questions throughout the first years of the digital transformation process (BARMER, 2021). By officially implementing the ethics compass, the health insurance anchored CDR at the board level at the same time, with the Deputy Chairman of the Board and the Chief Digital Officer (CDO) jointly responsible for its strategic advancement. The Innovation

Unit (BARMER.i), with a dedicated Digital Coordinator, led the translation of values into practice and coordinated the operational implementation.

In late 2024, the responsibility for CDR was structurally embedded within a newly established interdisciplinary team on healthy work, diversity, sustainability, and CDR, reflecting the recognition that these areas share ethical foundations and mutually reinforce one another in digital transformation efforts.

2.1 The Digital Ethics Values

Central to BARMER's digital transformation is its digital ethics compass, a set of eight core values that guide all digital decisions: people-centeredness, security, autonomy, solidarity, transparency, responsibility, cost-efficiency, and usefulness (BARMER, 2021, pp. 12–17). These values have been developed in a participatory and scientifically grounded process and are guiding all departments (Fig. 1).

More than a declarative framework, they function as a practical decision-making foundation for all digital initiatives, including product development, communication, and service innovation, whenever there are open ethical questions.

These values do not stand in isolation. They form the conceptual and operational basis for BARMER's Digital Agenda, which aligns projects, priorities, and success metrics with the overarching goal of ethical digital transformation. Digital projects at BARMER, which include high risks or open ethical questions, undergo a "CDR check" to assess their conformity with the digital ethics compass before proceeding to implementation. This alignment ensures that innovation does not come at the expense of trust, fairness, or data protection. It also helps to answer questions and find ways to mitigate ethical risks (Table 1).

BARMER's engagement with the German CDR-Initiative and its signing of the CDR-Code in 2020 further embeds the organization within a broader framework of corporate accountability (BARMER, 2025c). The CDR-Initiative (2025) is a public-private partnership led by the German Federal Ministry for the Environment, Nature Conservation, Nuclear Safety and Consumer Protection (BMUV) to promote ethical digital transformation in business. It provides a voluntary framework (the CDR Code) that guides companies in integrating digital responsibility into their practices beyond legal requirements. The code defines principles such as autonomy,

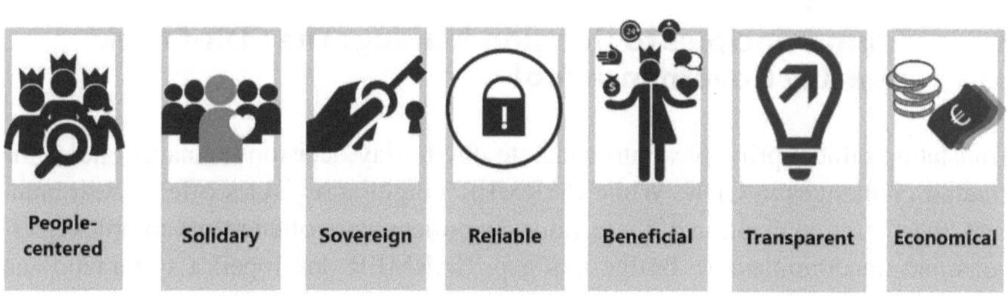

Fig. 1 BARMER digital ethics values (©BARMER)

Table 1 BARMER digital ethics values and explanations (©BARMER)

BARMER digital ethics values	Explanation
People-centered/ patient-oriented	BARMER places individuals at the core of digital health technologies. This means always asking: What does this mean for the insured person/ employee? Solutions must enhance lives and actively involve users through feedback and participation
Secure/protected	The highest standards are applied to the protection of social and health data. Security includes both technical safeguarding and promoting digital literacy for informed data use
Sovereign/ self-determined	BARMER supports people in actively managing their own health by enabling access to data (e.g., via digital patient records) and providing tools for transparent health decisions
Solidarity/ cooperative	As a solidarity-based institution, BARMER encourages responsible data sharing for research that benefits all, supporting digital progress without commercial exploitation
Transparent/ enlightening	Transparency is key. BARMER explains decisions, clarifies digital products, and promotes awareness about the opportunities and risks of digitalization (e.g., disinformation, cyberbullying)
Responsible/ reliable	Responsibility must be clearly defined, particularly for digital applications. Technologies must be fair, inclusive, evidence-based, and understandable, ensuring accountability and trust
Economical/ focused	BARMER is committed to using members' contributions efficiently. Digital projects are assessed for economic viability and implemented in a financially responsible manner
Beneficial/ supportive	Digitalization is pursued not because it is possible, but because it serves people. Solutions are designed to provide clear added value to the users

transparency, fairness, and sustainability: principles that resonate strongly with BARMER's own values. By publicly committing to the code and submitting annual transparency reports, BARMER demonstrates its willingness to be held accountable, learn from peers, and contribute actively to shaping digital responsibility in the healthcare sector (CDR-Initiative, 2021).

This dual anchoring, in internal value systems and external frameworks, positions BARMER as a role model for embedding CDR holistically in corporate governance. It also ensures coherence between strategic ambitions, operational decisions, and societal expectations.

3 From Principles to Decision-Making: The CDR-Check as a Key Governance Tool

Translating ethical principles into concrete day-to-day decisions remains one of the greatest challenges in CDR. While BARMER's eight core values offer a clear compass, the operationalization of these values in project work often raises complex questions and uncertainties. To bridge this gap, BARMER developed a systematic and participatory decision-support tool: the CDR-Check. The CDR-Check enables project teams to assess the ethical viability of planned initiatives by reflecting on each of the eight CDR values (BARMER, 2020). The central question posed in this structured workshop format is: "What must happen in this project to do justice to our values?"

Rather than offering predefined answers, the CDR-Check facilitates a dialogical and interdisciplinary reflection process. Project stakeholders, often from product development to marketing, collaboratively consider how people-centeredness, transparency, or digital sovereignty might be compromised or reinforced in their context. This reflection frequently leads to insights and questions that would not have arisen in routine development discussions. The results of the CDR-Check are documented and include specific action recommendations. These recommendations clarify under what conditions a project may proceed or must be revised. In doing so, the CDR-Check creates both a procedural and ethical basis for decision-making, supporting consistency with the organization's overarching Digital Agenda.

Beyond its immediate evaluative function, the CDR-Check has also proven to be a capacity-building instrument: it fosters ethical awareness, strengthens interdisciplinary collaboration, and cultivates a shared language for digital responsibility across the organization. This internalization of values is further supported by a network of Digital Coordinators and more than 600 DigiCoaches (BARMER, 2025a). The Digital Coordinators are embedded within the various departments and are responsible for identifying and addressing digital questions arising in their respective fields. They serve as key contact persons for raising potential ethical concerns and clarifying them in dialogue with the central Digital Coordinator of the BARMER.i, ensuring that ethical questions are made visible, contextually assessed, and appropriately discussed.

The DigiCoaches, on the other hand, bring digital awareness and competence to all 15,000 employees. As peer facilitators, they promote understanding and engagement with CDR principles throughout the organization, making the values accessible and actionable at every level. While the Digital Coordinators act as navigators across functional boundaries, identifying sensitive issues early on, the DigiCoaches bring CDR principles know-how to everyday operations, serving as multipliers, and sparring partners within their teams.

By embedding such tools into its innovation and governance structures, BARMER demonstrates that value-based digital transformation is not only a matter of commitment but of concrete, repeatable practice.

4 Ethical Challenges and Decision Ambiguities

Despite BARMER's comprehensive value framework and governance structures, implementing CDR in practice remains a complex and iterative process. Ethical dilemmas in digital transformation are often characterized by competing priorities, legal uncertainty, and evolving expectations from society, users, stakeholders in the healthcare system, and regulators.

Digital tools in healthcare promise enhanced efficiency and personalization, but they also raise critical questions: What level of data transparency is necessary without compromising privacy? How much automation is appropriate in decision-making processes that affect patients' lives, and who holds responsibility when technologies fail?

Ambiguity further arises from regulatory gaps and lagging legal frameworks. Many digital developments, especially those involving artificial intelligence, predictive analytics, or new data-sharing models, outpace current legislation. In this vacuum, companies like BARMER must proactively define their own norms and thresholds. This self-regulation, however, requires a careful balance between risk-taking and accountability.

Bringing up ethical questions and discussing them strategically has proven to be particularly valuable in this context. The dialogical structure of the CDR-Check, for example, allows ethical tensions to be addressed before they escalate into public concerns or internal friction. Yet the tool also surfaces new complexities: engaging with values can make projects more demanding, not less. Questions often emerge that were not initially visible, about power dynamics in data access, unintended exclusions in algorithmic models, or the trade-off between usability and informed consent.

This process of questioning and self-reflection is intentionally productive. It reveals ethical blind spots and fosters organizational learning. As new technologies continue to evolve, BARMER's approach acknowledges that CDR is not a one-time compliance task but a continuous process of interpretation, negotiation, and adaptation. It requires leadership commitment, structural support, and cultural openness to uncertainty.

By confronting these ambiguities directly and transparently, BARMER positions itself not as a company that claims to have all the answers, but as one willing to ask the right questions and evolve responsibly in the process.

5 CDR Implementation in Practice: BARMER's Measures by CDR Fields of Action

CDR at BARMER is operationalized through a comprehensive set of measures structured along the action fields defined by the German CDR-Initiative's Code. This alignment ensures that ethical considerations are systematically embedded in strategic and operational processes, thereby strengthening BARMER's contribution to responsible digital transformation. BARMER published a wide variety of their CDR activities (including the following) in their CDR report (BARMER, 2022a).

5.1 Handling of Data

As a statutory health insurance, BARMER handles particularly sensitive personal data. Accordingly, the ethical and secure management of data is paramount. Profiling practices are used strictly within the bounds of regulatory frameworks and are transparently communicated to users. For instance, the development of personalized

Fig. 2 BARMER data security (©BARMER)

services such as pregnancy newsletters and chronic disease management programs (DMPs) relies on explicitly consented data, with clear opt-out mechanisms.

Bias mitigation is addressed through internal awareness and cross-departmental collaboration. It started in the "KIDS" (KI/Data Science) community, which was the first place to discuss such issues. The Digital Coordinator/CDR Lead then sets up leadership workshops and knowledge formats such as "Lunch & Learn" sessions to foster data ethics literacy among staff, particularly regarding AI-supported decisions. BARMER is currently working on in-depth AI knowledge programs and has included the most important topics in its mandatory yearly compliance training (Fig. 2).

In terms of user autonomy and data, tools such as the digital compass in the BARMER-App provide real-time tracking of benefit applications. This increases transparency and reduces perceived bureaucratic opacity. The digital cost overview allows users to see what the BARMER pays for their care, while the eCare electronic health record enables secure, user-controlled data sharing with healthcare professionals. The app-based digital vaccination planner, digital pregnancy companion, and secure messaging tools all contribute to a transparent, people-centered digital ecosystem.

From a technical perspective, BARMER has implemented a security-by-design approach in the eCare platform, developed in collaboration with IBM. A unified secure user account system provides access to all digital services under a high-security standard, meeting or exceeding the legal requirements for data protection and authentication (BARMER, 2025c).

5.2 Education

BARMER supports broad internal and external education initiatives to strengthen digital and ethical (health) literacy. The DigiCoaches program is central: over 600 trained employees act as multipliers for digital transformation within their respective units while following their original occupation, such as customer support. They are allowed to dedicate time to this role, underlining institutional commitment. These coaches not only introduce new tools but also contextualize their use from a values-based perspective, enabling practical conversations around privacy, accessibility, and transparency (Fig. 3).

To further support competence-building, BARMER developed "DigiTal," an interactive learning environment that uses gamification and inclusive design principles. The platform explains technical terms in simple language and offers peer-created tutorials and service walkthroughs. It is integrated into daily workflows and supports learning on demand. BARMER has developed the "DigiTal" in a user-centric design thinking process, including several colleagues from all departments.

Complementing these initiatives is a 50-min e-learning module that introduces the organization's view on digital transformation and discusses implications for daily work. It places a special emphasis on ethical questions and the relevance of digital values in healthcare. In addition, cultural education formats such as the cultural trip ("Kulturreise") and internal Think Tank formats deepen the strategic understanding of change and strengthen ethical resilience in decision-making.

Externally, BARMER collaborates with educational institutions and initiatives to promote digital health literacy, especially among vulnerable groups. For example, a former cooperation with www.krisenchat.de has supported youth facing cyberbullying, and dedicated web content explains misinformation and digital health risks in plain language. Another flagship project is the annually conducted Sinus Youth Survey, a cooperation between BARMER, the D21 Initiative, and the Sinus Institute. The 2023/2024 edition included new focal areas such as artificial intelligence, climate anxiety, and cyberbullying. Surveying over 2000 adolescents aged between 14 and 17, the study revealed nuanced insights into young people's attitudes toward digital transformation. For example, 79% of respondents expressed optimism about their future, while AI was seen both as a professional opportunity and a source of

Fig. 3 Digital literacy platform BARMER DigiTal (©BARMER)

uncertainty. The results help the BARMER to better understand generational concerns and tailor its communication and education offerings to the real-world contexts of young users (BARMER & SINUS-Institut, 2024).

5.3 Climate and Resource Protection

BARMER has set itself the ambitious target of becoming climate-neutral by 2030 and views digital transformation as a core lever toward this goal. A major initiative has been the digitization of correspondence and forms, significantly reducing the organization's reliance on printed communication. This includes the rollout of secure online applications, the introduction of digital claim tracking, and the implementation of app-based administrative services (Fig. 4).

The organization also partners with sustainable infrastructure providers, such as Deutsche Telekom, which hosts BARMER's customer portals in emission-reduced data centers powered by 100% renewable energy. Internally, BARMER has modernized its print infrastructure, reduced its paper consumption by over 30% between 2020 and 2021, and introduced digital signature processes in procurement and management workflows.

Additionally, BARMER promotes climate-conscious employee behavior. A CO_2 audit of digital services and infrastructure was conducted to identify further potential for energy savings. Through campaigns and challenges, such as the "Data Cleanup Day," employees are encouraged to delete unnecessary data and archives, freeing up digital resources while promoting digital mindfulness and increasing digital competency.

Fig. 4 BARMER Data Cleanup Day encourages employees to free up digital resources (©BARMER)

5.4 Inclusion

Digital inclusion is both a value and a design principle for BARMER's digital products. The "Pflegecoach" is a digital service tailored to support caregiving relatives by offering accessible information and advice. (BARMER, 2025d) Likewise, the memoreBox project introduced gamified therapy solutions in elderly care settings, now integrated into regular service provision. Barmer developed both services with a focus on simplicity, user empowerment, and therapeutic benefit.

To avoid digital exclusion, BARMER maintains hybrid service models combining digital, phone-based, and in-person support. This includes user-centric hotlines, accessibility-compliant websites and apps, and barrier-free design for key services such as the BARMER-App and the eCare platform. Specific use cases, such as viewing personal contributions, managing medication plans, or accessing cost breakdowns, are made intuitively accessible through easy-to-use interfaces.

Furthermore, BARMER provides educational content for people with disabilities and their caregivers, supports accessible formats such as easy language, and invests in digital health literacy through participatory design. Pilot projects in collaboration with social and care institutions test how to improve digital participation among underrepresented and digitally marginalized populations. The goal is to ensure that digital transformation does not reinforce inequality but actively contributes to overcoming it (Fig. 5).

An additional step toward inclusion is collaborations with partners such as the EiS-App, which supports children with language development delays by promoting basic communication skills. Through a BARMER partnership, affected children and their families received access to the app, which serves as a pocket-sized dictionary

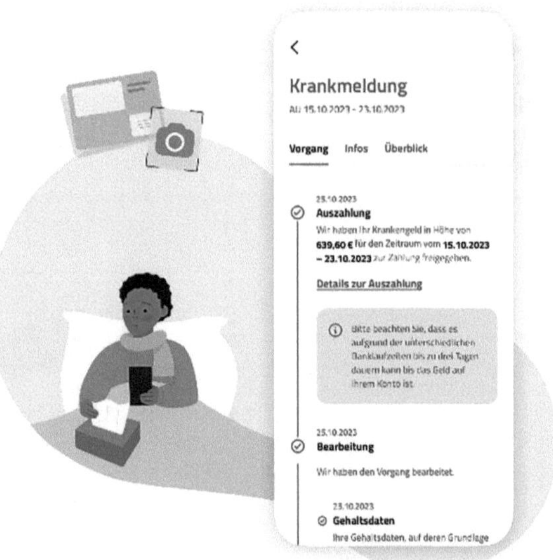

Fig. 5 BARMER-App offers transparent information for everyone (©BARMER)

for learning fundamental signs from German Sign Language (DGS). The app combines four sensory inputs, symbol, word, audio, and video, to support comprehension and usage. It enables children, adolescents, and even adults to express themselves regardless of their ability to speak, hear, read, or write. For families and educators, the app provides time-saving support. Particularly for children with developmental disorders, repeated exposure is critical, and the EiS-App facilitates consistent, engaging repetition. It lays a foundation for everyday communication and fosters broader participation and inclusion. BARMER had offered limited memberships of the EiS-App to its insured families in need (BARMER, 2025b).

5.5 Employee Participation

BARMER sees employee involvement not as a side activity but as a core pillar of its responsible digital transformation. The commitment to CDR is reflected not only in strategic leadership but also in the participatory and empowering structures available to employees. This is crucial in a working environment that has not always been digital. Employees originally chose BARMER for their working life in order to help patients stay or become healthy with no digital transformation in mind. Combined with very low fluctuation rates, the health insurance aims to be a partner throughout the working life of its employees.

A central component of this effort is the culture trip ("Kulturreise"), a multiphase reflection and engagement format in which the staff explores the impact of digital transformation on collaboration, service, and workplace culture. These dialogues, which include participation from board members, foster open conversations about values, expectations, and cultural change.

Beyond dialogue, practical involvement is emphasized. During the first 3 years of the newly implemented innovation department BARMER.i, employees across all units had the possibility to join temporary rotation programs, where they engaged in agile innovation processes and applied user-centered methods to real-world digital challenges. This hands-on approach has equipped them with tools like Design Thinking, Scrum, and prototyping, while also anchoring CDR principles in product development.

Feedback formats such as internal surveys, learning platforms, and co-creation workshops ensure that digital tools and ethics frameworks are grounded in the day-to-day experiences of employees. The DigiCoaches play an essential role here: Not only do they train teams in new technologies, but they also act as ethical ambassadors who connect local practice to the broader CDR framework.

This structured inclusion empowers employees to critically engage with digitalization and contributes to a shared responsibility culture. Ultimately, the integration of employee voices and capacities strengthens the legitimacy, effectiveness, and sustainability of BARMER's digital ethics agenda.

6 BARMER in the National CDR-Initiative

BARMER's commitment to CDR extends beyond internal strategy. Since joining the CDR-Initiative led by the German Federal Ministry for the Environment (BMUV), BARMER has contributed as a key actor in the national discourse on digital ethics.

As the first statutory health insurance to sign the CDR-Code, BARMER has actively helped to translate the initiative's nine principles into practice. The organization participates in working groups and contributes to collective publications, such as whitepapers on tackling hate speech and disinformation. These efforts demonstrate BARMER's willingness to shape sector-wide standards, not only follow them (CDR-Initiative, 2025).

The cooperation with the CDR-Initiative exemplifies a public-private partnership at its best: BARMER brings in the regulatory perspective of a highly governed sector while learning from cross-sectoral innovation. This exchange helps ensure that ethical governance frameworks reflect real-world constraints and sector-specific needs.

Moreover, BARMER's visible role in the CDR network has created new reputational opportunities. The organization was invited to present the complex question of handling health data responsibly, but also user-friendly with patient sovereignty in mind, at the German Federal Government's Digital Summit and the first national CDR conference in Austria. Media coverage, requests for academic collaboration, and recognition by the CDR-Award jury illustrate the resonance of this work.

Through its proactive attitude, BARMER contributes to institutionalizing digital responsibility as a shared societal task. The organization's participation demonstrates that CDR is not a competitive differentiator alone, but a platform for shared learning, accountability, and progress.

6.1 Deep Dive: Collaborative Impact – The Diversity Impact Assessment

One of the key outcomes of BARMER's collaborative engagement in the CDR-Initiative is the co-development of the Diversity Impact Assessment (DIA) – a practical tool designed to help organizations reflect on diversity impacts in the design and implementation of digital technologies. Published jointly by several members of the CDR-Initiative, the tool guides project teams through a series of structured questions to identify blind spots and mitigate unintentional exclusion or bias.

BARMER contributed health sector expertise to the development of the tool and is the first statutory health insurance to apply it in practice. The DIA invites teams to consider aspects such as accessibility, age, language, education level, culture, or gender identity. Typical questions include: Who may be disadvantaged by our service? Whose needs are overlooked? Are visuals and language inclusive? Was the user testing group sufficiently diverse?

Internally, BARMER has started using the DIA in a pilot project regarding the "DigiTal." The structured reflection process has helped uncover the need for further participation formats and more inclusive design elements. The tool fosters internal dialogue, anchors CDR in usability discussions, and supports BARMER's ambition to develop digital services that meet the needs of all insured persons.

The DIA shows how organizations can collaboratively raise ethical standards and ensure diversity-sensitive digital transformation. The tool is freely available via the CDR-Initiative (CDR-Initiative, 2024a).

6.2 Deep Dive: Digital Data Cleanup as a Multi-Value Intervention

One of the most successful internal initiatives under BARMER's CDR program has been the "Digital Data Cleanup." This organization-wide project invited all departments to review, evaluate, and delete outdated or unnecessary data. Surprisingly, the impact of this initiative was multidimensional:

Digital and Data Literacy: The campaign raised awareness about the importance of data quality and lifecycle management. Employees learned to assess what data is needed, for how long, and under what conditions.

Data Deletion Competency: Participants developed confidence in using digital systems, applying retention rules, and deleting responsibly.

Ecological Impact: The 2024 edition of the campaign led to the deletion of over 120 terabytes of data—translating into measurable resource savings and reduced energy consumption.

Information Security: Removing unnecessary data decreased digital attack surfaces and improved internal compliance with data minimization principles.

As part of the national CDR-Initiative, the project is also embedded in a broader effort across more than 50 organizations each year (CDR-Initiative, 2024b). "More than 6000 BARMER employees participated in the first 'Data Cleanup Day,' making BARMER the most active contributor in terms of deleted data volume per employee in 2022. It was a huge success in the last two rounds," says Maria Hinz, Project Lead and CDR Teamlead of BARMER, and continues: "Beyond numbers, the initiative has contributed to a change in digital culture: it normalized conversations around digital waste, sustainability, and the value of mindful deletion. The recurring nature of the campaign, now institutionalized as an annual event, ensures lasting momentum. It also demonstrates how a simple but well-communicated measure can deliver on multiple CDR goals simultaneously: ecological responsibility, cybersecurity, digital literacy, and cross-functional engagement."

The campaign's visibility, supported by video documentation and public reporting, also strengthened internal recognition. Thus, the Digital Data Cleanup is a CDR best practice: practical, participatory, and powerful in its long-term effects.

7 Learnings from Practice

Over the course of implementing CDR, BARMER has identified several key insights that may serve as guidance for other organizations seeking to start or further develop their own CDR journey. These learnings are not abstract recommendations but rather emerge directly from practical experiences and concrete implementation examples described in the previous sections: (Hinz & Rydzewski, 2023)

1. **Top-level support is indispensable.** Without consistent and visible backing from the executive board and top management, digital responsibility will not yield its full potential. Ethical transformation needs legitimization, prioritization, and resourcing at the highest level. As described in the governance section, the successful anchoring of BARMER's ethical compass and the endorsement of the CDR Codex were only possible due to this leadership support.
2. **You need passionate leadership.** At least one person must be willing to drive the topic with conviction and perseverance. This personal commitment often acts as the spark that brings cross-functional momentum. The operationalization of CDR at BARMER was significantly driven by roles such as the Digital Coordinator, whose commitment helped to activate broad engagement across departments.
3. **Cross-sectoral exchange is invaluable.** Collaborating with other organizations, particularly in platforms such as the CDR-Initiative, enables mutual learning and shared problem-solving. Many challenges are not unique, and the best solutions are often collective ones. For example, BARMER's active participation in joint initiatives like the whitepaper on disinformation and its leading role in the CDR-Initiative contributed directly to actionable insights.
4. **It is a marathon, not a sprint.** Embedding values into digital transformation takes time. Cultural change, iterative implementation, and ethical reflection are slow, continuous processes that require patience and perseverance. The development and ongoing refinement of BARMER's eight ethical values, including their application in project decisions, reflect this long-term, iterative process.
5. **External visibility reinforces internal credibility.** Communicating progress externally via reports, awards, or conferences enhances the internal perception of importance. Sometimes, internal stakeholders only take CDR seriously when it gains external recognition. "Do good and talk about" helps in this case. BARMER's public recognitions, such as the CDR Award, invitations to national conferences, and media visibility, have increased internal legitimacy and motivated broader organizational engagement.
6. **Start small, and then grow.** CDR does not require an elaborate master plan right at the beginning. Initial steps, such as implementing a CDR-Check, defining values, or simply starting with a data clean-up or some awareness workshops, can grow into a broader, strategic program over time. This was evident in BARMER's early actions, like awareness workshops and a small group of DigiCoaches, which laid the groundwork for structured projects and a more strategic view.

7. **Focus on what matters for the company.** It is entirely legitimate to prioritize CDR measures that solve the most pressing challenges for the organization. This relevance-driven approach enhances acceptance and practical impact. BARMER's emphasis on transparency and human centricity (for example, regarding product development but also digital literacy for employees) – two values crucial to the healthcare context – demonstrates how contextual relevance strengthens the effectiveness and resonance of CDR initiatives.

These learnings reaffirm that CDR is not about perfection, but about progress. It can be adapted to any organizational context as long as it is anchored in sincerity, participation, and learning.

8 Future Outlook: Ethical AI and Organizational Transformation

Looking ahead, BARMER is sharpening its focus on ethical artificial intelligence (AI) and long-term digital sustainability. A major organizational development is the integration of BARMER.i, the internal innovation unit, into the core organizational structure. This structural shift reinforces the strategic importance of innovation and ensures that digital responsibility is embedded in all transformation initiatives.

In 2024, BARMER also launched a dedicated AI unit called "BARMER.K"." This newly formed department will be responsible for developing and operationalizing AI governance strategies and driving AI implementation at BARMER.

BARMER is committed to developing AI guidelines that are based on both the internal ethical value system and the principles outlined in the CDR-Code. These guidelines will be co-created through a multi-stakeholder process supported by academic expertise. In line with its understanding of CDR, BARMER acknowledges that artificial intelligence is not merely a technological matter, but fundamentally an ethical and cultural issue that requires inclusive and value-based governance.

Currently, BARMER.KI is actively preparing for the operational implementation of the EU AI Act. This includes not only the technical and legal compliance aspects, but also the development of internal training programs aimed at fostering data and AI literacy across all employee levels.In addition to technical governance, BARMER is investing in organizational readiness by designing AI and data learning journeys for its staff. These journeys will be supported by platforms like DigiTal and the internal DigiCoach network, ensuring continuity with previous digital transformation strategies.

Beyond internal development, BARMER also sees its role in addressing sector-wide ethical challenges posed by algorithmic complexity and data asymmetries in healthcare. BARMER aims to proactively shape public discourse and regulatory interpretation through its engagement in cross-sector initiatives, for example, in the ethically charged domain of women's health, where data quality, AI-driven diagnostics, and equitable care access converge.

As part of this future agenda, several questions guide BARMER's ethical reflections:

- How can data-driven systems strengthen, rather than undermine, patient sovereignty?
- In what ways can we ensure transparency without overwhelming or confusing users?
- How can algorithmic decision-making be inclusive and fair, especially for vulnerable populations?
- What role should statutory health insurances play in setting standards for responsible AI in healthcare?
- How can we use AI in a more sustainable way?

These questions will continue to shape the design and evaluation of digital services. With the institutionalization of BARMER.KI and the implementation of AI guidelines, the organization sends a strong signal: Responsible digitalization is not an afterthought. It is a matter of principle and a pillar of its transformation strategy.

Competing Interests The author has no conflicts of interest to declare that are relevant to the content of this chapter.

References

BARMER. (2020). *Unsere Werte, wenn es um Digitales geht*. Retrieved August 07, 2025, from https://www.barmer.de/verantwortung/digitale-verantwortung/cdr-news#anchor-1078414

BARMER. (2021). *Digitale Ethik bei der BARMER*. Retrieved August 07, 2025, from https://www.barmer.de/resource/blob/1026284/e6cae9d0dbe5a08fdf9441dab91d4b9e/digitale-ethik-bei-der-barmer-barrierefrei-1700501nl-data.pdf

BARMER. (2022a). *CDR-Bericht*. Retrieved August 07, 2025, from https://www.barmer.de/cdr-bericht

BARMER. (2022b). *Digitale Ethik: Verantwortung und Wertesystem*. Retrieved August 07, 2025, from https://www.barmer.de/verantwortung/digitale-verantwortung/cdr-news/digitale-ethik-barmer-1056692

BARMER. (2025a). *Fünftes Handlungsfeld: Einbindung von Mitarbeitenden*. Retrieved August 07, 2025, from https://www.barmer.de/verantwortung/digitale-verantwortung/cdr-bericht1/mitarbeitendenbindung-1138558

BARMER. (2025b). *Viertes Handlungsfeld: Inklusion und Teilhabe*. Retrieved August 07, 2025, from https://www.barmer.de/verantwortung/digitale-verantwortung/cdr-bericht2/inklusion-und-teilhabe-1241452

BARMER. (2025c). *Ihre digitale Identität. Der universelle und sichere Zugang zur digitalen Gesundheitswelt*. Retrieved August 07, 2025, from https://www.barmer.de/digitalegesundheit/digitale-identitaet

BARMER. (2025d). *Pflegealltag meistern mit dem BARMER Pflegecoach*. Retrieved August 07, 2025, from https://www.barmer.de/unsere-leistungen/pflege/pflegecoach

BARMER & SINUS-Institut. (2024). *SINUS-Jugendstudie 2023/2024*. Retrieved August 07, 2025, from https://www.barmer.de/verantwortung/digitale-verantwortung/cdr-bericht2/gesundheit-und-bildung-1241454

CDR-Initiative. (2021). *CDR-Code.* Retrieved June 12, 2025, from https://www.cdr-initiative.de/kodex

CDR-Initiative. (2024a). *Diversity Impact Assessment.* Retrieved August 07, 2025, from https://cdr-initiative.de/uploads/files/Broschuere-Diversity-Folgenabschaetzung.pdf

CDR-Initiative. (2024b). *Digitaler Datenputz: Nachhaltigkeit durch Datenlöschung.* Retrieved August 07, 2025, from https://cdr-initiative.de/news/digitaler-datenputz-2024

CDR-Initiative. (2025). *BARMER Mitgliedsseite der CDR-Initiative und CDR-Berichte.* Retrieved August 07, 2025, from https://cdr-initiative.de/unternehmen/barmer

Hinz, M., & Rydzewski, M. (2023). Digitale Ethik in der Krankenkasse. Manuskript BARMER – Ethik & Transparenz. In C. Straub (Ed.), *Transparenz im Gesundheitswesen.* MWV Medizinisch Wissenschaftliche Verlagsgesellschaft.

Maria Hinz is Team Lead of Corporate Health, Diversity, Sustainability, and Corporate Digital Responsibility (CDR) and former Digital Coordinator at BARMER, one of Germany's largest statutory health insurance providers. In this role, she is responsible for the strategic direction and implementation of initiatives that promote healthy working environments, advance diversity and inclusion, and strengthen sustainability and digital responsibility within the organization. Beyond BARMER, she contributes her extensive expertise in digital transformation and CDR to various committees and initiatives, including the CDR Initiative of the German Federal Ministry for the Environment (BMUV). Maria is a communications and digital expert and has held various (leadership) positions in politics, associations, and the private sector.

Responsibility in the Digital World: From Corporate Social Responsibility to Corporate Social and Digital Responsibility at KPMG Austria in the Context of Sustainability Management

Alexandra Prinz and Katharina Mosor

Abstract

This article outlines KPMG Austria's strategic shift from Corporate Responsibility (CR) to a more comprehensive Corporate Social and Digital Responsibility (CDR) framework. It highlights the importance of aligning CDR with core values and emphasizes the integration of digital responsibility into the company's sustainability management practices. Drawing upon the "CDR Building Bloxx," the authors demonstrate how CDR has been embedded into both client-facing consulting services and internal operations, including corporate governance structures. The article offers practical guidance for large organizations seeking to implement CDR by encouraging them to assess existing initiatives and focus on areas where they can generate real impact. It highlights KPMG Austria's commitment to fostering a culture of digital responsibility and innovation, guiding the reader from the definition of CDR at KPMG to concrete measures such as user-centered digital transformation, trustworthy AI, the KITE training program, and KPMG's strong focus on cybersecurity.

1 From CSR to CDR at KPMG Austria

In addition to our role as a social actor ("Corporate Social Responsibility") we also took a closer look at the concept of "Corporate Digital Responsibility" (CDR) for the first time when preparing for last year's sustainability reporting. We have made a conscious decision to link our sustainability efforts to the concept of CDR. In

A. Prinz (✉) · K. Mosor
KPMG Austria, Vienna, Austria
e-mail: aprinz@kpmg.at; kmosor@kpmg.at

A.-S. Christ (ed.), *Corporate Digital Responsibility*, Future of Business and Finance, https://doi.org/10.1007/978-3-032-14793-6_11

doing so, we are guided by our core values – **Integrity**, **Excellence**, **Courage**, **Together**, and **For Better** (KPMG Austria, 2025b) – which have always shaped our actions and now also form the basis for responsible action in a modern digital information environment and other technology-driven contexts (Fig. 1).

CDR at KPMG means taking responsibility where digital technologies are specifically used – for example, in data analysis, automated decision-making, or the development of new digital solutions for ourselves or our customers. It is important to us that CDR is not understood as the fulfillment of a collection of self-evident or purely legally binding measures. We start where we have room for action – and thus can also have an impact.

Ethical behavior in the digital context is particularly evident in the question of how technologies are designed, used, and monitored. In doing so, we are primarily guided by our value of **Courage** – the courage to ask critical questions, to address risks openly, and to take responsibility before problems arise. After all, technological decisions can have far-reaching consequences – for individual employees, for society, and for trust in our company.

With CDR, we are adopting a stance that aligns with our established corporate practices: Through the necessary structures, processes, and standards, we can responsibly guide the use of technological developments. Although we have not yet formulated any targeted metrics or goals, it was important to us to align our existing measures and initiatives with an acknowledged CDR framework as a first step. In doing so, we took our cue from the CDR Building Bloxx of the German Association for the Digital Economy (BVDW, 2025c), as they offer an established and practical framework with a clear distinction between general principles and concrete fields of action. For this reason, we refer specifically to the respective CDR Building Bloxx in the individual sections and supplement the short description provided by the BVDW for better classification (Fig. 2).

Be it our commitment to Global Cyber Day, our internal program KITE (KPMG Information Technology Education Program), our human-centered consulting approach in digital transformation projects, or our own internal digitalization measures and our AI use case innovation management approach: we have found that certain initiatives can already be classified from the point of view of "digital responsibility of companies."

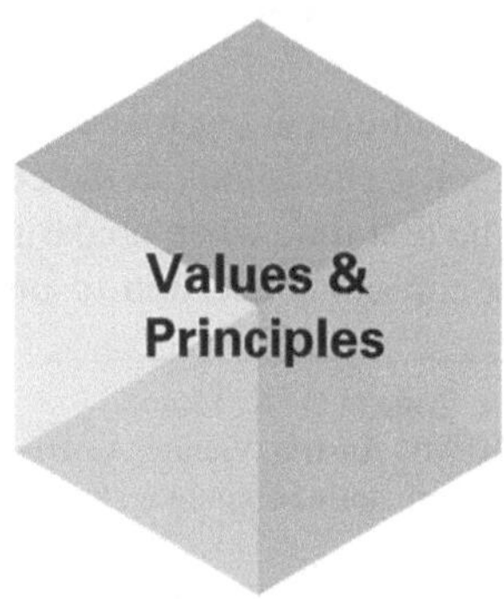

Fig. 1 General CDR Building Bloxx "Values & Principles". *"Responsible digitization is value-based. It follows the basic principle of treating individuals, society, and the environment respectfully"* (BVDW, 2025i)

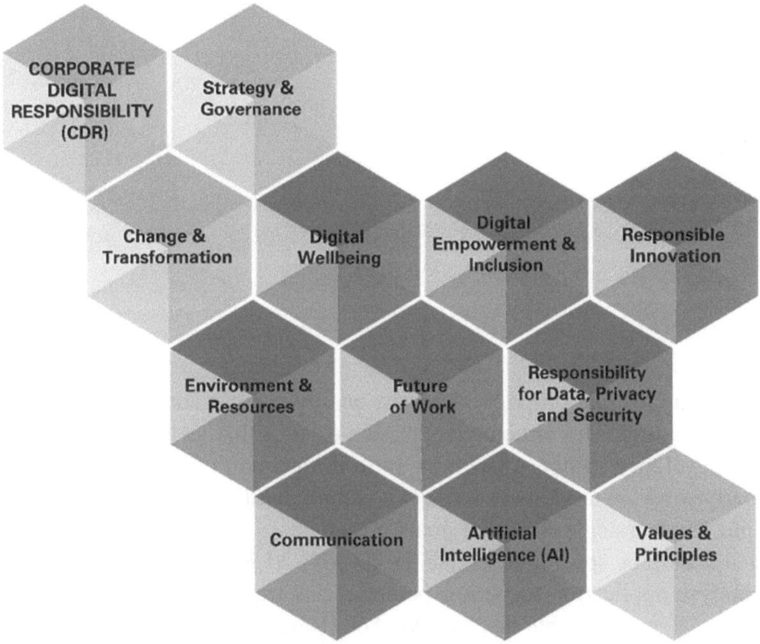

Fig. 2 The CDR Building Bloxx of BVDW (2025)

At the same time, there is a shared understanding within the company that meaningful KPIs (Key Performance Indicators) must first be defined in order to meet the self-imposed requirement to agree on objectives beyond the expected minimum.

2 Embedding CDR into Company-Wide Governance Structures in a Targeted Manner

At KPMG, we view **responsible technology as an integral part** of our commitment to quality. We do not treat technological innovations as standalone entities; instead, we integrate them into our existing compliance and governance frameworks (Fig. 3). For instance, risk and independence assessments, which are standard in all our services, have been adapted for technological solutions as well. New tools and systems undergo a thorough evaluation to address both functional risks and regulatory requirements, guided by the quality assurance principles in **KPMG International's Global Quality and Risk Management Manual**. Our goal is to identify quality risks early, implement effective controls, and regularly assess their effectiveness, particularly for technology-based solutions.

Technology compliance at KPMG is embedded within our governance and quality processes. New or significantly altered technology products must go through mandatory testing and approval processes. These include systematic business and risk analyses, independence assessments, information security requirements, data

Fig. 3 General CDR Building Bloxx "Strategy & Governance". *"Digital responsibility has a significant influence in determining the corporate culture, structure, and strategy"* (BVDW, 2025h)

protection, intellectual propriety analysis, quality assessment, and detailed technical documentation. This structured approach ensures that technological solutions – whether developed in-house (such as those in data and analytics, AI, or ESG) or third-party software used in our services – comply with regulatory standards, ethical principles, and strategic corporate goals.

We also employ specific tools like the **KPMG AI Risk Catalogue** to systematically analyze application scenarios, potential risk triggers, and suitable mitigation strategies, as required by the EU AI Act (Regulation [EU] 2024/1689). This approach helps us identify risks early, ensure technology compliance, and take preventive measures. The AI Compliance Partner plays a crucial role in managing technology-related risks and ensuring compliance with relevant standards. These processes address ethical, legal, and security concerns early on, especially for AI-supported solutions, in line with the EU AI Act requirements. By closely integrating quality and technology management, we ensure our clients benefit from our proactive approach to technological innovations and trends, translating them into reliable, safe solutions. Our clients gain from our active role in shaping technological developments, guided by clear standards, thorough risk analysis, and a deep understanding of regulatory dynamics.

At the same time, we recognize our responsibility towards our employees. Accordingly, we continuously invest in digital learning and enablement of our employees to ensure they have the necessary skills and knowledge to successfully navigate a rapidly changing digital landscape. For instance, we offer specialized AI use case enablement training and collaboration tools training, each adapted to employees' corporate functions and operational fields. By promoting the safe and ethical use of digital technologies, we create a work environment that both supports the professional development, innovation mindset of our employees and helps us meet our standards of digital responsibility.

Although an in-depth mapping of our existing fields of action with all the principles of the CDR framework is still pending, we feel it is essential to deal with this dimension of responsible action to a greater extent. Therefore, it was also very important to us **to be actively involved in the CDR Austria** (2024a) **network** to responsibly help shape the digital transformation in companies. KPMG was represented at the **CDR Congress 2024** (CDR Austria, 2024b) as a Premium and Location

Partner and continued this commitment at the **CDR Network Meeting 2025 in Innsbruck** – including workshops on audit of AI and with AI, the strategic operationalization of CDR from the perspective of the internal audit department, and digital accessibility. The aim of this cooperation is to work together with partners in business, science, and administration to develop concrete solutions for a value-oriented digital future.

3 From Principles to Practice: Selected Examples of Concrete CDR Measures by KPMG Austria

3.1 Human-Centered Approach to Digital Transformation

Our human-centered consulting approach takes a holistic view of digitization, digitalization, digital transformation, and process design. Our goal is to make technological innovation not only efficient, but also sustainable and responsible (Fig. 4). Through the application of **human-centered design**, we develop products, services, and systems that are specifically oriented towards the needs, skills, and preferences of the users. In doing so, we place particular emphasis on understanding human behaviors, emotions, and usage contexts – the result is user-friendly, competitive, and ethically sound solutions.

Together with users, we design **end-to-end processes** that are geared towards clearly defined objectives – so-called happy cases. Only those user stories that contribute to these goals are prioritized and implemented. With a high degree of standardization and a holistic mapping of the **customer journey** in tools such as **KPMG Discovery**, we create efficiency, transparency, and traceability. Our individualized approach combines technological feasibility with the active involvement of employees and customers. In this way, needs and challenges can be identified at an early stage, and structural changes can be accompanied in a targeted manner.

At the same time, we pay attention to the **long-term integration of new solutions into existing organizational structures**. We ensure that technological feasibility and necessary structural changes are taken into account to ensure long-term acceptance and integration into existing organizational structures. Through targeted

Fig. 4 CDR Building Bloxx "Responsible Innovation". *"The introduction of new technologies and innovations should be value-based, meaningful and vigilant"* (BVDW, 2025f)

measures in change management, we promote a sustainable transformation that supports both **acceptance and long-term integration into the corporate culture.** Our approach guarantees that only solutions that have potential are implemented. In doing so, we rely on proven methods such as **design thinking**, structured idea development, and innovation training to enable employees with an open mindset to develop creative and value-oriented solutions themselves.

Our concrete CDR-oriented measures in the field of innovation and innovation management include:

- **Product and service development**: Customer-oriented, ethically responsible and sustainable solutions
- **Process innovation**: Efficiency gains and resource savings, enabled by streamlined digital processes, co-designed with end users
- **Business model innovation**: Development of new business models in areas such as ESG and Risk Management with a focus on social and environmental impact
- **Innovation training**: Empowering employees to develop sustainable innovations by equipping them with creative thinking skills and a strong ethical foundation

These approaches are particularly suitable for AI use case generation using the "idea funnel" method: identifying effective AI use cases requires more than just creativity – it requires structure, user focus, and a culture that promotes innovation. The so-called idea funnel (Fig. 5) supports this process by combining four central advantages:

- **Focus on ideas with potential**: All ideas are welcome – but only those that promise both real user-added value and strategic benefits for the company will be further developed.

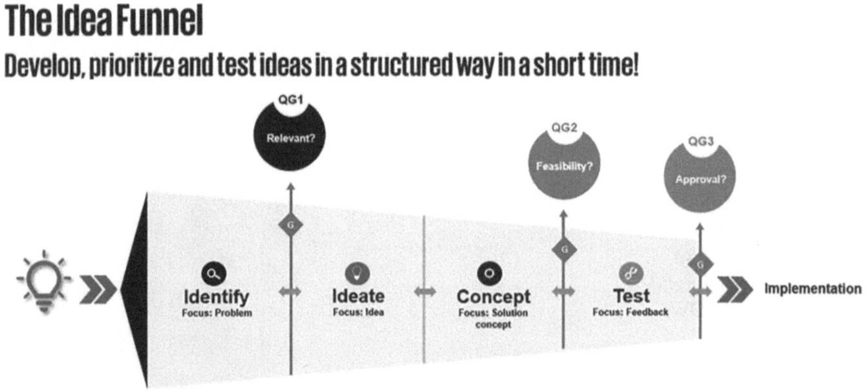

Fig. 5 KPMG Austria's idea/innovation funnel (© KPMG Austria)

- **Structured creativity**: A clear methodological framework provides orientation in the development of ideas and ensures transparency throughout the entire company in the selection and decision process.
- **User centricity**: Ideas are consistently thought through, tested, and further developed from the perspective of the user – in order to address real needs.
- **Innovation mindset**: Employees are actively involved in the development of ideas and thus become part of the innovation process – a central building block for sustainable implementation and acceptance.

3.2 Internal Digital Transformation

This **human-centered, structured approach to innovation** not only shapes our customer projects – it also forms the **basis for our internal digital transformation.** As a central unit for technological development and digitalization, our internal innovation team Lighthouse works with the business departments to develop customized solutions that optimize our internal processes while continuously increasing KPMG's digital maturity (Figs. 6 and 7).

Internally, we therefore also consistently rely on human-centered, participatory innovation methods (such as the idea funnel). User-centered innovation workshops serve as a lever for identifying challenges and suitable technical solutions. The results of these workshops range from use cases such as the automated comparison of due diligence reports to the digital end-to-end monitoring of audit review processes. Close cooperation with our IT demand management and active co-responsibility by those who generate ideas ensures sustainable implementation. This is flanked by an open feedback culture; an internal innovation hub that offers **low-threshold, practical, and everyday** access to methods, trends, and new tools **via MS Teams**; and continuous support from the Lighthouse team – which, as a central interface between departments and IT, ensures that digital solutions meet professional, organizational, and technological requirements in equal measure.

A central element of this internal innovation landscape is the **GenAI platform Maple Waltz** (Ginner et al., 2025), which is made accessible to all employees. Providing access to this platform to all employees not only promotes **Data**

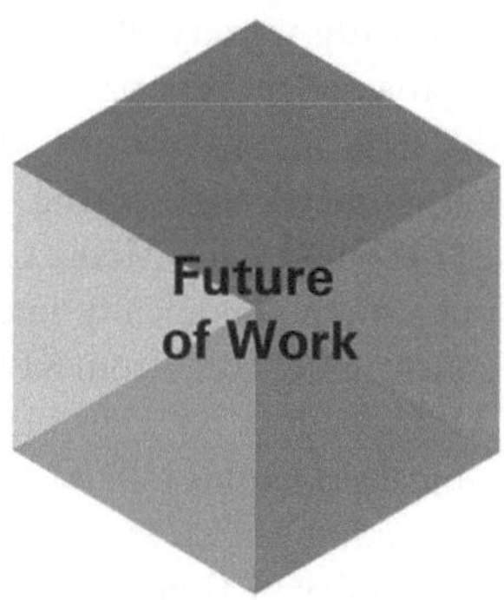

Fig. 6 CDR Building Bloxx "Future of Work". *"Businesses create framework conditions allowing people to mature in an increasingly digitized world"* (BVDW, 2025e)

Fig. 7 General CDR Building Bloxx "Change & Transformation". "*Digital change focuses on the action by people – The transformation of processes, products, and technologies requires deliberate and adaptive management*" (BVDW, 2025b)

Protection in the company (our platform being hosted on our Azure tenant with high data protection and security standards) but is also an essential component of our **internal IT transformation and fosters AI literacy**. The solution developed by our own engineers is also available to our customers to be operated in their own cloud instance. This dual use creates valuable synergies: It facilitates the joint identification of new use cases for **process improvement**, **resource conservation,** and **social sustainability** and at the same time strengthens our market-oriented development of competencies. Maple Waltz was also developed **in accordance with the Web Content Accessibility Guidelines (WCAG)** (World Wide Web Consortium, 2025) and is therefore also accessible to people with impaired vision – another expression of our human-centered, inclusive understanding of innovation.

3.3 Trustworthy AI

Trustworthy AI is often reduced to **technical security** or **regulatory compliance** – i.e., to what is immediately visible, comparable to the tip of an iceberg (Fig. 8). However, beneath the surface lies a multilayered system of requirements that goes far beyond compliance with minimum legal standards. It encompasses ethical, social, legal, and organizational dimensions that are equally crucial for responsible AI development (Fig. 9).

In order to address this complexity in a targeted and practical way, KPMG relies on a **wide variety of methods**. The following applies: Not every methodology or approach fits every project or customer's need – the decisive factor is the choice of the right method for the respective use case and customer context. For example**, value-based engineering**, according to the international standard **ISO/IEC/IEEE 24748-7000** (DIN Media GmbH, 2022), can be used where ethical system design is to be methodologically integrated at an early stage. As part of an internal training course, employees from KPMG Austria were certified as "**Value-Based Engineering Ambassadors**" – a visible sign of our commitment to systematically integrating ethical principles into AI systems.

In addition, we are currently investigating the use of the **Ethics Compass by the University of Graz** (n.d.) for specific use cases (e.g., in the implementation of our

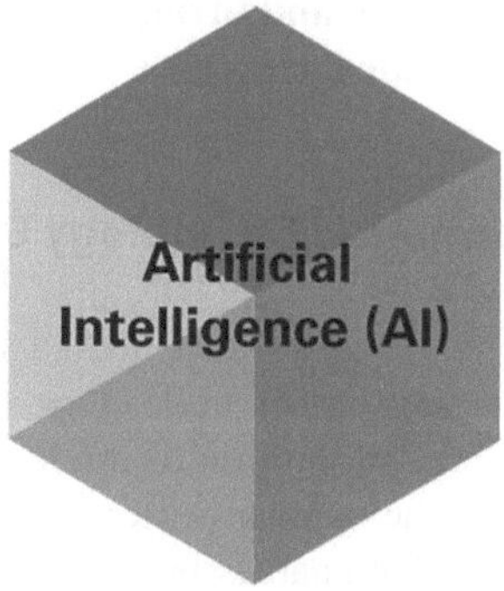

Fig. 8 CDR Building Bloxx "Artificial Intelligence (AI)". *"Businesses deploy and use Artificial Intelligence (AI) responsively and transparently. Legal, social, and environmental implications must be considered when expanding the application of AI systems. The implementation of AI systems should increase people's scope of action in a value-based manner. Principles of fundamental rights, autonomy, and self-determination must be respected consistently"* (BVDW, 2025a)

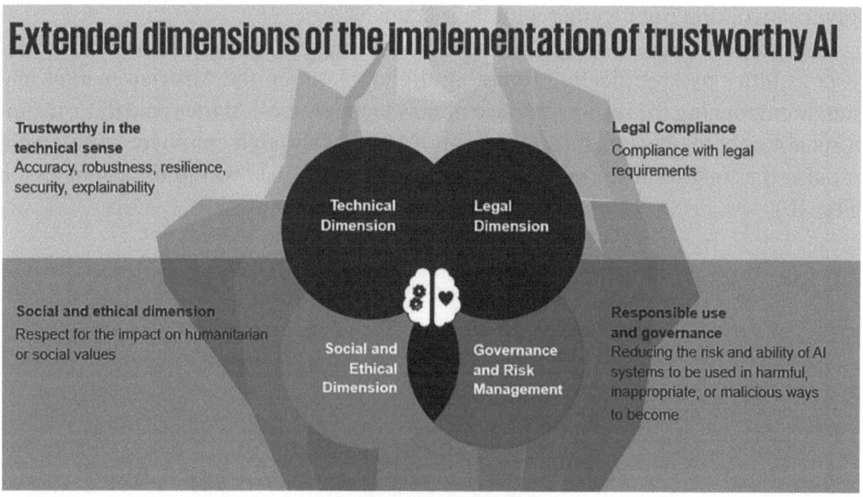

Fig. 9 KPMG Austria's extended dimensions of the implementation of trustworthy AI (© KPMG Austria)

web-based GenAI platform "Maple Waltz" for company-specific AI use cases). It helps to introduce central values such as fairness, transparency, or autonomy into development and decision-making processes at an early stage and to evaluate individual use cases with structured reflection.

This approach is flanked by KPMG methodologies such as the **Trusted AI Risk and Control Framework** (KPMG International, 2025), the **AI Readiness Survey**, the **AI Model Risk Assessment Tool,** and principles from **DevSecOps** (Development, Security, Operations) and **Human-Centered Design**. Together, these tools result in a flexible, scalable toolkit that can be used to implement AI projects in a **practical, responsible, and fitting** manner – tailored to the maturity, risk, and objectives of each individual customer.

3.4 KITE (KPMG Information Technology Education Program)

Our KITE program has been in existence since 2020 and has established itself as an in-house talent factory, providing our IT colleagues with new talent and closing training gaps. Every year, a large proportion of trainees are taken on as permanent employees in different areas of the company after completing their training.

KITE is a training program that enables business college, higher technical college, and bachelor graduates, as well as career changers, to gain experience and new insights in the tech world. The program lasts a total of 9 months and consists of three different phases. In the first 3 months, there is theoretical input to bring all trainees up to the same level of knowledge. The second part is a combination of customer projects and department-specific learning content. The participants spend the last third of their training exclusively on projects and can thus immerse themselves in working life together with their teams.

The program makes a significant contribution to corporate digital and social responsibility by specifically promoting digital skills on the Austrian market and thus strengthening the responsible use of new technologies. At the same time, it supports not only the personal development of trainees through employee enablement but also the long-term strengthening of digital competence within the organization (Fig. 10).

Fig. 10 CDR Building Bloxx "Digital Empowerment & Inclusion". *"The active empowerment of employees towards the achievement of new competencies must be the primary goal and prospect of a company. Employees must be supported regarding the maximization of their individual potential"* (BVDW, 2025d)

Fig. 11 CDR Building Bloxx "Responsibility for Data, Privacy and Security". *"Compliance with information security standards is explicitly demanded by national and international regulation. However, the creation of a trustworthy processing environment requires further voluntary commitment. The secure processing of data and protection of data spaces from external interference must have priority"* (BVDW, 2025g)

3.5 KPMG's Cyber Security Focus

For many years, KPMG Austria has been supporting companies in strengthening their **cyber resilience holistically** – far beyond technical protective measures. As the current **KPMG Cybersecurity Study 2025** (KPMG Austria, 2025a) shows, cyber threats continue to increase in intensity and complexity. Many companies are facing growing challenges, but do not have sufficiently anchored strategies to mitigate risk. KPMG therefore offers a comprehensive portfolio of services: from **risk assessments and vulnerability assessments** to the implementation of legal requirements (GDPR, NIS2, DORA, PCI DSS) and the development of robust **IT governance structures**, **business continuity**, and **disaster recovery plans** (Fig. 11).

We are also particularly concerned with **social education in** the field of cybersecurity. With **KPMG Cyber Day** (KPMG Austria, 2025c), a citizenship program for schools, we specifically promote the **cyber literacy of young people**. Our goal is to sensitize students to Internet dangers, data protection, and digital responsibility at an early stage – low-threshold, practical, and interactive. This initiative is a living expression of our digital responsibility, which shows that CDR does not start in the company, but in school.

4 Where and How to Get Started and Next Steps

In implementing CDR, KPMG Austria – like many other companies – is faced with the challenge of **credibly and effectively integrating digital responsibility into existing structures** without misunderstanding it as a pure compliance mechanism. Our experience shows that CDR is effective when measures are taken where competence is available and there is a concrete need. In our case, this means a strong

focus on internal **digital transformation**, which we consciously shape in a human-centered way and in line with our established values.

We strongly recommend that other companies follow the **CDR Building Bloxx** or other structured models for CDR implementation that help set priorities sensibly. It is essential not to confuse CDR with the mere **implementation of regulatory requirements**. Anyone who simply declares legally required standards as CDR measures risks losing credibility and misses the opportunity to generate real cultural change.

Another key success factor is the **linking of CDR with existing governance structures** and the company's lived foundation of values. This is the only way to anchor digital responsibility as a component of corporate integrity – and not as a detached individual project.

We are at the beginning of a continuous learning process. Next, we will focus more on the topic **of mental health and well-being in the digital work context** – an area where digitization can increasingly become a burden and requires new answers. This is also CDR in action: **responsibly shaping what is technologically possible** – and **never losing sight of the human factor.**

Competing Interests The authors have no conflicts of interest to declare that are relevant to the content of this chapter.

References

BVDW. (2025). *CDR Building Bloxx*. Retrieved July 3, 2025, from https://www.cdr-building-bloxx.com.

BVDW. (2025a). *CDR Building Bloxx: Artificial Intelligence*. Retrieved July 3, 2025, from https://www.cdr-building-bloxx.com/artificial-intelligence/?lang=en

BVDW. (2025b). *CDR Building Bloxx: Change & Transformation*. Retrieved July 3, 2025, from https://www.cdr-building-bloxx.com/change-transformation/?lang=en

BVDW. (2025c). *CDR Building Bloxx: Corporate Digital Responsibility – Strategie und Umsetzung*. Retrieved July 3, 2025, from https://www.cdr-building-bloxx.com/cdr-building-bloxx-framework/

BVDW. (2025d). *CDR Building Bloxx: Digital Empowerment & Inclusion*. Retrieved July 3, 2025, from https://www.cdrbuilding-bloxx.com/digital-empowerment-inclusion/?lang=en

BVDW. (2025e). *CDR Building Bloxx: Future of Work*. Retrieved July 3, 2025, from https://www.cdr-building-bloxx.com/future-of-work/?lang=en

BVDW. (2025f). *CDR Building Bloxx: Responsible Innovation*. Retrieved July 3, 2025, from https://www.cdr-building-bloxx.com/responsibleinnovation/?lang=en

BVDW. (2025g). *CDR Building Bloxx: Responsibility for Data, Privacy and Security*. Retrieved July 3, 2025, from https://www.cdr-buildingbloxx.com/responsibility-data-privacy/?lang=en

BVDW. (2025h). *CDR Building Bloxx: Strategy & Governance*. Retrieved July 3, 2025, from https://www.cdr-building-bloxx.com/strategy-governance/?lang=en

BVDW. (2025i). *CDR Building Bloxx: Values & Principles*. Retrieved July 3, 2025, from https://www.cdr-building-bloxx.com/values-principles/?lang=en

CDR Austria. (2024a). *Digital responsibility. Ethics and technology*. CDR Austria. Retrieved July 3, 2025, from https://www.cdr-austria.com/

CDR Austria. (2024b). *CDR Austria Kongress*. Retrieved July 3, 2025, from https://www.cdr-austria.com/cdr-kongress-2024/

DIN Media GmbH. (2022). *ISO/IEC/IEEE 24748-7000: Systems and software engineering – Life cycle management – Part 7000: Standard model process for addressing ethical concerns during system design*. https://www.dinmedia.de/en/standard/iso-iec-ieee-24748-7000/361765782

Ginner, M., Niederwimmer, K., & Hiebl, M. (2025). *Implementierung eines internen Chaptbot in einer Wirtschaftsprüfungsgesellschaft*. Johannes Kepler Universität Linz.

KPMG Austria. (2025a). *Cybersecurity in Austria 2025 – A new reality*. Retrieved July 3, 2025, from https://kpmg.com/at/de/home/insights/2025/05/cybersecurity-studie-2025.html

KPMG Austria. (2025b). *Our values: Integrity, excellence, courage, together and for better*. Retrieved July 3, 2025, from https://kpmg.com/at/de/home/about/kpmg-kompakt/unsere-verantwortung/unsere-werte.html

KPMG Austria. (2025c). *Safe surfing – Our IT expert teams in action at Cyber Day*. Retrieved July 3, 2025, from https://kpmg.com/at/de/home/careers/karriereblog/cyber-day.html

KPMG International. (2025). *KPMG trusted AI framework*. Retrieved July 3, 2025, from https://kpmg.com/xx/en/what-we-do/services/ai/trusted-ai-framework.html

Regulation (EU) 2024/1689 of the European Parliament and of the Council of 13 June 2024 laying down harmonised rules on artificial intelligence (Artificial Intelligence Act). European Union. https://eur-lex.europa.eu/eli/reg/2024/1689/oj/eng

University of Graz. (n.d.). *Ethik Kompass*. Retrieved July 3, 2025, from https://ethikkompass.uni-graz.at/de/

World Wide Web Consortium. (2025). *WCAG 2 overview*. Web Accessibility Initiative. Retrieved July 3, 2025, from https://www.w3.org/WAI/standards-guidelines/wcag/#intro

Alexandra Prinz is a Senior Manager at KPMG Austria, leading the internal innovation team "Lighthouse." She focuses on human-centered digital transformation, innovative business models, and digital ethics and spearheads the internal CDR initiative. She brings deep public–private sector experience and advocates for value-based engineering and digital humanism.

Katharina Mosor is a sustainability manager at KPMG and is responsible for implementing sustainable business practices and enhancing social responsibility. In this role, she is often involved in cross-functional initiatives, as is the case with CDR.

[illegible]

Tradition Drives Innovation: CDR at Weleda AG

Romana Pflieger and Jakob Wößner

Abstract

The digital transformation compels companies to integrate ethical responsibility into their technological advancements. This article examines how Weleda AG, a pioneer in Corporate Digital Responsibility (CDR), successfully bridges tradition and innovation to foster sustainable digital practices. Weleda's CDR framework is built on 12 digital ethical principles, structured into 3 pillars: responsible data and algorithm management, human-centered digital workplaces, and sustainable innovations. These principles ensure alignment with the company's core values while addressing privacy, transparency, and ecological sustainability. A standout example is the AI-powered chatbot WeAsk, which enhances employee learning and innovation while prioritizing data security and ethical AI usage. The article also delves into Weleda's governance structure, particularly the Digital Responsibility Council, which ensures adherence to ethical standards through transparent decision-making processes. Despite challenges such as aligning digital innovations with sustainability goals and balancing ethical standards with corporate objectives, Weleda's proactive approach demonstrates how ethical principles can drive sustainable innovation. By showcasing Weleda's journey, this article provides actionable insights for organizations aiming to navigate the complexities of digital transformation responsibly while preserving their core values.

R. Pflieger · J. Wößner (✉)
Weleda AG, Schwäbisch Gmünd, Germany
e-mail: cdr@weleda.de

A.-S. Christ (ed.), *Corporate Digital Responsibility*, Future of Business and Finance, https://doi.org/10.1007/978-3-032-14793-6_12

1 The CDR Understanding of Weleda and Its Principles

The digital transformation presents companies with new challenges, particularly regarding ethical responsibility. This article highlights how Weleda AG, as a pioneer in Corporate Digital Responsibility (CDR), builds a bridge between tradition and innovation to promote sustainable digital practices.

Weleda, a company with over a century of experience, has always been at the forefront of natural cosmetics and holistic health care. Founded in 1921, Weleda has consistently pursued a mission to work in harmony with humans and nature. This commitment is reflected in its approach to CDR, which integrates ethical digital practices into its established values of quality, sustainability, and social responsibility (Fig. 1).

The strategic objectives of Weleda in the realm of CDR are driven by the need to navigate the digital transformation responsibly, ensuring that technological advancements are aligned with the company's core values. Central motivations for engaging in CDR activities include the protection of privacy, transparency in data usage, and the promotion of sustainable digital innovations. Weleda's commitment to CDR extends beyond legal standards, aiming to establish a benchmark for ethical digital practices in the industry.

Weleda has taken a leading role in the development of CDR practices since 2018, establishing a comprehensive framework of 12 digital ethical principles that guide its projects and decision-making processes (Fig. 1).

These principles are structured into three fundamental pillars, which serve as the foundation for a sustainable and responsible digital transformation. The pillars encompass the handling of data and algorithms, human-centered digital working, and the promotion of sustainable innovations. Each pillar defines specific guidelines rooted in scientific and ethical principles.

Fig. 1 Weleda's digital ethical principles (own creation)

1.1 Good Handling of Data and Algorithms

The first pillar emphasizes the responsible use of data and algorithms. Data is regarded as a valuable resource that must be handled with care and in alignment with ethical standards.

- **Protection and Respect for Privacy**: Safeguarding personal data is a core principle to ensure the privacy of individuals.
- **Transparency of Data and Algorithms**: Ensuring the traceability and openness of data processing and algorithmic decision-making fosters trust.
- **High Data Security**: Robust security measures are essential to protect data from misuse and unauthorized access.
- **Data as a Valuable Resource**: Data is treated as a raw material that must be utilized responsibly and sustainably.

1.2 Human-Centered Digital Working

The second pillar highlights the central role of humans in the digital workplace. Technology is seen as a tool to support, not replace, human decision-making and responsibility.

- **Fair and Healthy Working Conditions**: Creating work environments that promote well-being and fairness is of utmost importance.
- **Employee Participation**: Actively involving employees in digital transformation processes strengthens engagement and fosters a participatory organizational culture.
- **Promotion of Digital Competence**: Continuous training and development in digital skills are critical to ensuring employees' digital sovereignty.
- **Human Responsibility and Decision-Making**: Despite automation, humans remain the central authority for ethical and strategic decisions.
- **Leadership as a Key Factor**: Leadership plays a pivotal role in implementing and promoting digital ethics.

1.3 Sustainable Innovations

The third pillar focuses on the development and promotion of innovations that align with ecological and social sustainability goals.

- **Mindful Use of Resources**: The use of digital technologies should be resource-efficient to promote harmony between humans and nature.
- **Supporting Sustainability Goals**: Digital projects and innovations should actively contribute to achieving global sustainability objectives.

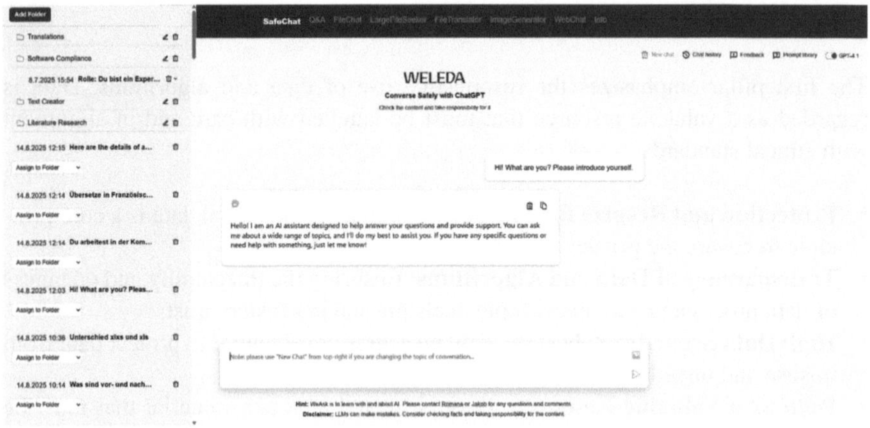

Fig. 2 WeAsk: Weleda's generative AI Chatbot (own creation)

– **Responsible Shaping of Digital Innovation**: Innovations should be designed to have long-term positive impacts on society and the environment.

These principles are actively integrated into the corporate governance, ensuring that every digital endeavor is assessed for its ethical implications. This progress is evident in initiatives like the generative AI Chatbot WeAsk, which embodies responsible AI usage by prioritizing data security and user privacy (Fig. 2).

Weleda's engagement with CDR is also reflected in its participation in the Digital Responsibility Resort of the Federal Association of the Digital Industry (BVDW, 2025), which promotes corporate responsibility in the digital transformation. Weleda's CDR report showcases the commitment to going beyond legal requirements, actively shaping the digital world for the benefit of society. This initiative aligns with Weleda's values, emphasizing the importance of ethical digital practices and sustainable development.

2 CDR Best Practice: AI Chatbot WeAsk

The WeAsk Chatbot is a prime example of how Weleda combines tradition with innovation. By leveraging over 140 years of knowledge of the company and the conducted research, WeAsk empowers employees to learn and innovate using AI. This tool is not just about technological advancement; it represents a commitment to preserving heritage while embracing modern capabilities. The Chatbot is trained with Weleda's extensive knowledge base, ensuring that it supports the creation of products with the highest quality, efficacy, and purity.

WeAsk serves as a central ecosystem that enables employees to interact with the entire body of corporate knowledge through an intuitive user interface, enhanced by powerful AI functionalities. The solution includes specialized features such as a secure LLM chat with up-to-date information, the processing of large documents, the File Translator for automatic translations of entire documents and texts, as well as the Image Generator for AI-powered visual content creation. All of this operates within a secure environment to ensure data protection, security, and transparency.

Another significant aspect is the commitment to human-centered digital working. Employees are actively involved in decision-making processes, fostering a culture of participation and empowerment. Through the promotion of digital competence and the provision of training programs, the workforce is prepared to address the challenges of digitalization, enabling them to make informed decisions and contribute to the organization's digital transformation.

The WeAsk Chatbot, developed in collaboration with a diverse group of employees, exemplifies the commitment to human-centered digital working. This interdisciplinary approach ensures that the Chatbot meets the varied needs of Weleda employees, enhancing their ability to innovate and learn.

Another notable example of best practice in the context of human-centered digital working at Weleda is the company's comprehensive AI training program. This initiative is designed to equip all employees with foundational knowledge regarding the responsible use of artificial intelligence. The program begins with an introductory module that familiarizes participants with the basic principles of interacting with AI systems. In this initial phase, potential risks associated with AI are discussed, alongside recommendations for responsible data handling when using AI technologies.

The training is structured as a four-stage program. Building on the introductory knowledge, the next stage consists of prompt engineering workshops. The first of these workshops introduces the fundamental principles of effective interaction with AI, focusing on how to communicate efficiently with AI systems. The subsequent workshop delves deeper into the formulation of queries, enabling participants to obtain precise and relevant responses tailored to their specific professional needs.

In the final stage of the program, participants develop specific use cases relevant to their respective departments. Through design thinking workshops, teams systematically analyze existing processes.

This structured approach not only enhances digital competence across the organization but also fosters a culture of responsible AI adoption, supporting Weleda's broader commitment to ethical digital transformation.

The implementation of WeAsk has led to remarkable results: administrative efficiency has been increased fourfold. The solution has been rolled out across all countries where the Weleda Group operates and includes 15 department-specific chatbots tailored to the needs of areas such as marketing, finance, and research.

3 Practice Development: Governance and Processes

Weleda's core principles (Fig. 1) are seamlessly woven into the corporate governance structures, influencing decision-making, risk management, and stakeholder engagement. The Digital Responsibility Council functions as a central governance body to ensure alignment with the organization's digital ethical principles. It provides binding recommendations and serves as a point of contact for all digital-ethical questions. Additionally, the council is designed to provide strategic direction and oversight for digital initiatives, to ensure compliance with ethical standards, and to promote sustainable and responsible innovation. (Fig. 3).

The council is organized by the Group Data and AI ##team and includes permanent members from various key departments. Depending on the specific topic under discussion, additional experts, such as members of the Executive Board, may be involved. The council's structure reflects a multidisciplinary approach, integrating diverse perspectives.

One exemplary practice involves the organization's approach to data handling and algorithm transparency. Data is regarded as a valuable resource, akin to raw materials, and its quality and security are ensured through systematic assessments. The systems are designed to respect privacy and promote transparency, allowing users to understand how their data is processed. This approach aims to protect user interests and foster trust within the community (Fig. 4).

The process outlines the approach to ensuring alignment of projects and activities with the organization's digital ethical principles. It consists of several steps:

1. **Assessment of projects and activities:** Projects and activities are initially reviewed for potential digital-ethical dilemmas. This preliminary evaluation helps identify issues that may require further consideration. Employees can contact the Digital Responsibility Council (DR Council) at any time to seek support.
2. **Consultation and involvement of experts:** The DR Council consults and advises on identified dilemmas.
3. **Transparent deliberations:** Discussions and consultations within the DR Council take place on a collaboration platform, ensuring transparency throughout the decision-making process.

Fig. 3 CDR council (own creation)

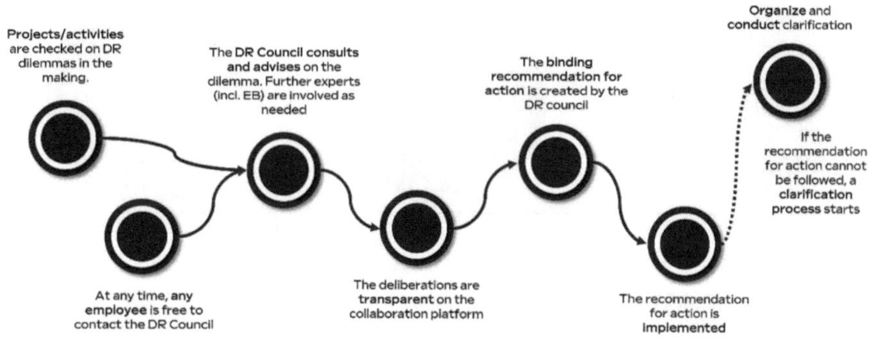

Fig. 4 CDR decision-making process (own creation)

4. **Creation of binding recommendations**: Based on the deliberations, the DR Council formulates binding recommendations for action to address the identified dilemmas.
5. **Implementation of recommendations:** The recommendations are implemented unless further clarification is required.
6. **Clarification process**: If the recommendations cannot be implemented, a clarification process is organized and conducted to explore alternative solutions.

This process ensures a structured and transparent approach to addressing digital-ethical challenges while promoting adherence to the organization's ethical principles.

4 Implementation Challenges and the Way Forward

Weleda faces several challenges in implementing CDR practices, despite notable achievements. Balancing digital responsibility with broader corporate objectives requires careful navigation of competing priorities. One unresolved challenge is ensuring that digital innovations align with sustainability goals. As new technologies are developed, it is essential to continuously assess their environmental impact and resource consumption.

To address these challenges, Weleda employs a strategic approach that involves continuous evaluation and adaptation of CDR practices. A framework for technology impact assessment has been established to identify potential conflicts and develop solutions that align with ethical standards. This proactive approach ensures that digital initiatives contribute positively to corporate objectives while upholding organizational values.

For companies beginning their CDR journey, it is recommended to establish a clear set of ethical principles that guide digital practices. It is crucial to integrate these principles into corporate governance structures, ensuring that they influence decision-making and risk management processes. Additionally, fostering

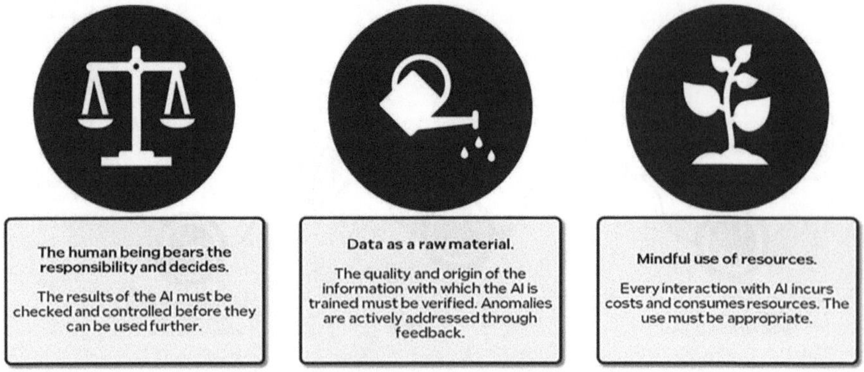

Fig. 5 Guiding ethical principles for AI Chatbot WeAsk (own creation)

transparency and stakeholder participation can enhance engagement and support responsible digital transformation.

Weleda's experience with the WeAsk Chatbot provides valuable insights into managing implementation challenges and highlights the importance of prioritizing human responsibility in AI applications. By ensuring that AI serves as a supportive tool rather than an autonomous decision-maker, employee autonomy is preserved while productivity and efficiency are enhanced (Fig. 5).

Furthermore, Weleda's commitment to sustainability is evident in initiatives such as the Digital Spring Cleaning and the flexible room and seating concept. These projects underscore the organization's focus on resource conservation and environmental protection, aligning with its broader sustainability goals.

In conclusion, Weleda's transition from tradition to innovation illustrates the integration of digital practices into corporate values in a responsible manner. By prioritizing ethical standards and adopting a digital responsibility framework, the organization aims to contribute to a sustainable and balanced future. Weleda's experience serves as a valuable guide for other companies seeking to navigate the complexities of digital transformation while preserving their core values.

5 Detailed Insights and Recommendations

This article highlights the importance of CDR as an integral part of digital transformation. Using Weleda as an example, it demonstrates how ethical principles can be embedded into corporate practice to promote sustainable innovation, transparency, and responsible decision-making. The following recommendations provide practical approaches for successfully implementing CDR in organizations.

5.1 Understanding CDR

CDR is a concept that extends beyond legal requirements, focusing on ethical digital practices that benefit society. At Weleda, CDR is a self-commitment that guides the digital transformation, ensuring alignment with Weleda's values. This commitment involves addressing dilemmas, which are tension fields triggered by technology, such as purpose, economic efficiency, nature, market, and social acceptance.

Weleda's CDR framework is built on 12 digital ethical principles (Fig. 1), which are documented in a guideline and are binding company-wide. These principles include sustainable innovations, human-centered digital working, and good handling of data and algorithms. They serve as a foundation for assessing and aligning IT topics and projects with our ethical standards.

The Weleda CDR Council plays a crucial role in implementing CDR practices. This council, composed of representatives from various departments, provides binding recommendations and serves as a point of contact for all digital-ethical questions. The council's decisions are supervised by the executive board, ensuring that the digital initiatives align with ethical principles.

5.2 Recommendations for Companies

Companies that proactively integrate CDR into their organizational strategies not only contribute to societal and environmental well-being but also position themselves for long-term competitive advantages. The following recommendations are based on insights from the CDR Building Bloxx framework developed by the BVDW and the practical implementation experience of Weleda (BVDW, 2022). This framework aims to support companies in structured embedding CDR effectively and credibly within their operations.

1. **Establish Clear Ethical Principles**: Develop a set of digital ethical principles that guide your company's digital practices. These principles should be integrated into corporate governance structures to influence decision-making and risk management processes.
2. **Foster a Culture of Transparency and Participation**: Encourage transparency and participation in digital initiatives to enhance stakeholder engagement and drive responsible digital transformation.
3. **Prioritize Human Responsibility and Decision-Making**: Ensure that AI serves as a supportive tool rather than an autonomous decision-maker, preserving employee autonomy while enhancing productivity and efficiency.
4. **Commit to Sustainability**: Align digital innovations with sustainability goals, assessing their environmental impact and resource consumption.
5. **Continuous Evaluation and Adaptation**: Implement a framework for technology impact assessment to identify potential conflicts and devise solutions that align with ethical standards.

6. **Leverage Interdisciplinary Collaboration**: Involve diverse groups of employees in digital projects to ensure that initiatives meet varied needs and enhance innovation.
7. **Promote Digital Competence**: Provide training programs to prepare employees for the challenges of digitalization, ensuring they are equipped to make informed decisions and contribute to digital transformation.
8. **Engage with Industry Initiatives**: Participate in industry initiatives like the CDR Initiative to promote corporate responsibility in the digital transformation and share best practices.

Values-driven and responsible digital practices are expected to become standard consumer expectations and competitive differentiators in the near future. Companies that embrace CDR now will be better positioned to navigate the complexities of digital transformation while contributing to societal and environmental goals. By fostering collaboration among businesses, policymakers, and consumers, CDR can help shape a digital economy that aligns with human and ecological values. The CDR Building Bloxx framework provides a practical tool for companies at all stages of their CDR journey, from newcomers seeking entry points to advanced practitioners refining their strategies.

Competing Interests The authors have no conflicts of interest to declare that are relevant to the content of this chapter.

References

BVDW. (2025). Gremien: Digital responsibility—is the contact for responsible digitalization. Retrieved August 9, 2025, from https://www.bvdw.org/en/committees/digital-responsibility/.

BVDW. (2022). CDR Building Bloxx @ Weleda. https://www.bvdw.org/news-und-publikationen/whitepaper-cdr-building-bloxx-weleda-veroeffentlicht-1/?highlight=bloxx.

Romana Pflieger, Generative AI & Knowledge Engineer at Weleda AG, drives the development of generative AI technologies, particularly the self-developed internal chatbot, and ensures compliance with ethical and legal standards. She monitors AI performance and emerging innovations, integrates new functionalities and models, and advises teams in integrating AI into business processes.

Jakob Wößner is a passionate advocate for digital-ethical transformation, currently leading Group Data & AI at Weleda AG. With a focus on digital ethics, empowerment, and innovation, he drives innovations in areas such as data lakes, analytics, generative AI, and machine learning.

Tools and Experiences from Facilitators

AI for AI: Leveraging AI to Enable AI Opportunities in Germany's Public Sector

Moritz Schirmer

Abstract

Artificial intelligence (AI) could transform the public sector by boosting efficiency, cutting costs, and improving services. Yet current efforts remain fragmented, small-scale, and risk-focused. This paper identifies three blind spots that limit progress and uses Theory U to frame solutions, considering the AI Act, KIVO draft, trustworthy AI, and ethics. First, AI is judged mainly by its outputs or processes, while the "place of origin"—the conditions shaping adoption—is overlooked. Second, AI is often treated only as a risk, without comparing it to human-based alternatives that also contain biases and inefficiencies. Third, AI is excluded as an active part of decision-making, despite its potential to add value through data, connectivity, and probabilistic reasoning. The central claim is that AI must be integrated into the very point where decisions about its use are made. Recognizing AI as both relational and intrinsic to governance design is essential to move beyond current dysfunctions. Doing so will unlock its transformative potential, ensure compliance and ethics, and support the development of trustworthy AI in the public sector.

1 Introduction

The riskiest decision regarding AI is the decision to negotiate AI deployment without using AI.

Previous initiatives for artificial intelligence (AI) in the public sector have largely told a story of failure: big announcements, limited impact (McKinsey & Company,

M. Schirmer (✉)
IHK Digital, Berlin, Germany
e-mail: schirmer.moritz@ihkdigital.de

A.-S. Christ (ed.), *Corporate Digital Responsibility*, Future of Business and Finance, https://doi.org/10.1007/978-3-032-14793-6_13

2025; Capgemini Research Institute, 2024; OECD, 2024; Bundesrechnungshof, 2023). Accordingly, the focus of this paper is a proposal for how AI initiatives in the public sector can fundamentally adopt a more successful approach: big announcements, big impact.

Public Sector vs. Private Sector The distinction between the private and the public sector is fundamental when it comes to understanding the context for the successful adaptation of artificial intelligence (AI). The private sector is typically characterized by market-oriented objectives, direct profit and competition incentives, more flexible personnel and remuneration mechanisms, as well as comparatively centralized decision-making and governance structures. By contrast, public organizations exhibit different institutional characteristics: public accountability, fragmented distributions of authority, legal constraints, and heightened requirements of legitimacy and fairness. These are central features that shape how innovation processes differ between sectors (Demircioglu & Audretsch, 2024).

From this sectoral difference, several concrete factors can be derived that make the adaptation of AI more difficult in the public sphere. Among these are restrictive legal frameworks, obligations of transparency, low tolerance for risk, outdated legacy IT systems, fragmented and limited human capacities, and the absence of competitive incentive systems to attract and retain AI expertise (Selten & Klievink, 2024). All of these differences are well known, extensively described, and thoroughly analyzed in their interrelations. The persistent problem, however, is that many AI initiatives in the public sector are announced but rarely scaled or sustainably integrated. In other words, they fail to deliver. The central question, therefore, is how a mode of engagement might be developed that proves more effective than the existing patterns of failure, without abandoning the defining features of the public sector, as described above.

This is where the design of an alternative mode of engagement with AI in the public sector positions itself in relation to the opportunity-driven approach. Instead of focusing predominantly on risks (ethical risks, data protection, data biases, accountability issues, legal uncertainties, reputational losses), the emphasis shifts to opportunities (Neumann et al., 2024).

The guiding premise should not be a repeated lament that less state and more private-sector characteristics are required. Rather, the guiding question is how to establish a mode of engagement within the existing state-specific characteristics that can realize the opportunities of AI initiatives despite the unfavorable contextual conditions. The aim is not to abolish the defining features of the public sector, but to enable success in spite of them.

To pursue this guiding question, this paper examines three blind spots and outlines conditions for an approach that systematically incorporates the potential success of AI initiatives in the public sector.

This is achieved by shifting the focus of observation from the outcome (output) to the *place of origin* (first blind spot). The question is no longer how the anticipated effect should be evaluated from today's perspective, but rather which materials are made available as a reference for assessing potential impacts. Attention is directed to the location where the materials for negotiating possible AI effects are considered.

This is further achieved by including innovative and digital materials as reference points within the negotiation materials at the place of origin (second blind spot). Currently, proven and analog materials serve as the reference for evaluating potential AI effects and determining associated risks. What is missing, however, is a comparative reference: what is the risk assessment if innovative and digital materials (i.e., AI) are not utilized? The question is not whether AI exists as an absolute factor, but how AI compares to non-AI alternatives. This perspective transforms the place of origin from an absolute assessment of AI risk to a relational evaluation, considering AI relative to non-AI as a measure of comparative risk.

Finally, this is achieved by recognizing innovative and digital materials (i.e., AI) as intrinsic elements within the negotiation at the place of origin (third blind spot). Currently, the discourse on AI initiatives is based solely on the proven and analog status quo, while AI itself is not represented as an independent contributor with functional surplus. By expanding the subset of materials to include both proven and analog with innovative and digital (i.e., AI) elements, the analog materials become one part of the negotiation at the place of origin, alongside the digital elements. This expansion enables negotiators to account for AI's functional surplus within the available materials, thereby embedding AI as an active and evaluable component of the decision-making context itself.

Against this background, conditions are consolidated that highlight and make the three blind spots visible. At the same time, a design imperative emerges: any approach to AI in the public sector should incorporate these conditions to significantly increase the likelihood of success, while ensuring the qualities of the public sector. In practical terms, the proposed suggestions enable public sector decision-makers to leverage and safeguard the functional surplus of AI at the place of origin during their deliberations. In short, successful AI outcomes require AI to be present at the point of origin, where its deployment is negotiated. Or even more concisely, AI needs AI.

2 Fundamental Observations on the Status Quo of AI Initiatives in the Public Sector

To design an approach for AI initiatives in the public sector that at least addresses their blind spots and ensures the specific qualities of the public sector, it is first necessary to establish the context in which these initiatives take place. Accordingly, foundational observations are presented that motivate attention to these blind spots and raise the question of how a more successful approach could be achieved.

Artificial Intelligence (AI) Has Impact The deployment of AI technologies has the potential to fundamentally transform the public sector in Germany. Current studies indicate that AI not only delivers efficiency gains and cost savings but also significantly enhances service quality (e.g., McKinsey & Company, 2025). While initial pilot projects in digital administration and e-government demonstrate concrete applications, systematic forecasts suggest that scaling these technologies could yield substantial productivity and quality improvements in public service delivery (BMWE, 2025). It also opens new opportunities for strategic planning and management: AI-supported predictive models can simulate urban and traffic flows (Bahamazava, 2025), calculate energy demands, or anticipate environmental impacts (Ugbehe et al., 2025). In social policy, patterns can be detected early to enable targeted interventions, creating a proactive state that anticipates risks and allocates resources more precisely (Sansone & Zhu, 2023). In summary, AI has the potential to provide a measurable performance differential compared to the current status quo in the public sector. Systematically and at scale, AI, therefore, would produce tangible effects beyond the existing capabilities of the public sector.

AI as Reality AI is reality. Once AI produces effects, these effects are just as real as those generated by the proven and analog public sector: a notice, a decision, or a service is legally binding and socially effective, regardless of whether a human or a machine executes it. AI is therefore not merely an abstract or virtual simulation but constitutes an independent form of effect, which should be recognized as its own reality. This means that AI does not create a subordinate or ontologically reducible practice that is "less real" than analog services. The difference in medium does not justify any difference in the quality of its reality. Even if this may appear disconcerting to long-standing public sector practitioners and decision-makers in Germany, the reality of AI should be acknowledged just as we acknowledge the reality of traditional processes (proven and analog). Accordingly, AI should be understood not merely as a tool but as an independent bearer of state authority, whose effects are as valid as those of proven and analog processes. Artificial intelligence is thus a tangible, socially and legally effective entity within the public sector. When it exists. When applied in administrative contexts—for instance, issuing a notice, deciding on funding, or providing a service—AI generates effects that are formally and functionally equivalent to those produced by humans. The critical factor is not whether a human or an AI system makes the decision, but that the operation is binding, verifiable, and socially recognized. Legal obligations, citizen rights, and administrative responsibilities apply equally, independent of the medium. A notice generated by AI is therefore no less real than one produced manually. This non-reducibility of AI's effects justifies recognizing AI as an independent agent of state action. In summary, AI is not merely a tool but an integral part of administrative reality and must be acknowledged as a distinct bearer of state authority. Assuming AI were to be implemented in the public sector in Germany.

AI Impact Fails Artificial intelligence has the potential to be transformative, yet its deployment in the German public sector has largely been marked by failure. Despite the existence of hundreds of projects across federal ministries, analyses reveal a pattern characterized by announcements, isolated pilot projects, and project terminations (McKinsey & Company, 2025; Capgemini Research Institute, 2024; OECD, 2024; Bundesrechnungshof, 2023). The central observation is clear:

although AI could generate tangible effects, its implementation has systematically fallen short, resulting in minimal measurable transformation or efficiency gains. Key challenges include technical and organizational fragmentation, as many projects were developed in isolation without integration into existing administrative processes; a lack of standardized data and interfaces, which hinders effective AI application; and the absence of strategic frameworks, as projects were often implemented in a project-based manner without overarching roadmaps, limiting sustainability and scalability. International comparisons indicate that, relative to other OECD countries, Germany lags in practical AI deployment within the public sector (OECD, 2024). Despite substantial investment in pilot projects, genuine, scalable transformation remains elusive.

The overarching conclusion is that AI represents a real and distinct potential that has yet to be successfully realized. Its capabilities cannot be reduced to the proven and analog practices of public administration. Against this backdrop, critical questions arise: why has AI not achieved greater success in the public sector, and how could its deployment be made more effective? These questions point to the need for a fundamentally improved approach, which the following analysis seeks to address by identifying key blind spots in current practices.

3 Key Points of Reference for Engaging with AI in the Public Sector

Building on these fundamental considerations, the focus here is on the elements that offer reference points in the debate on AI in the public sector and thereby shape the current status quo of its approach. On the regulatory side, these elements include the EU AI Act and its German derivation (KIVO). As a normative framework, situated between governance and ethics, the concept of trustworthy AI is addressed. And, as the ethical and societal dimension, the broader set of ethical claims is presented briefly. The relevance of these elements lies in the fact that the debate would take a fundamentally different shape in their absence. They are therefore essential for analysis and must be included as reference points.

Regulation We inevitably arrive at regulatory practice as a core part of the negotiation material, on how to engage with AI in the public sector. In reference to the regulatory framework, the regulation (EU) 2024/1689 of the European Parliament and of the Council of 13 June 2024 lays down harmonized rules on artificial intelligence (Artificial Intelligence Act). Its objectives are to ensure safety, protect fundamental rights, and promote innovation. The Act follows a risk-based classification approach, categorizing AI systems according to their use and associated hazards, ranging from unacceptable risk to high, limited, or minimal risk. Article 2 defines the scope, covering AI systems placed on the market, put into service, or used within the EU. This approach is continued relatively consistently in the draft bill for the KIVO Implementation Act (Bundesministerium für Digitales und Staatsmodernisierung, 2025). The draft concerns the regulation of the practical implementation of the EU

AI Act in Germany. It defines responsibilities such as market surveillance authorities, innovation support bodies, and accreditation procedures. Instruments include market surveillance, fines, and regulatory sandboxes (§ 14), and the Act applies to AI systems within the meaning of Article 2 of the EU AI Act.

Trustworthy AI The debate on trustworthy AI is largely framed by the European High-Level Expert Group on AI (EU, 2019). This component of the debate on AI in the public sector emerged relatively early and serves as a normative frame of reference, shaping the discourse between governance and ethical premises. Trustworthy AI is defined through the following three foundational principles:

1. Lawfulness—AI systems must comply with applicable laws and regulations, including data protection, safety standards, and labor or consumer rights.
2. Ethical alignment—AI must adhere to ethical values such as human dignity, autonomy, fairness, and nondiscrimination. Ethical compliance ensures that AI respects societal norms and moral expectations.
3. Robustness—AI must be technically reliable, resilient, and safe, with mechanisms for risk management, transparency, and accountability to maintain trust.

Ethics The ethical imperative focuses primarily on the potential impact of AI and then asks how principles such as fairness, transparency, accountability, and the avoidance of discrimination can be safeguarded (Floridi et al., 2018). The ethical debate on AI in the public sector extends beyond regulatory compliance and technical robustness, addressing fundamental questions of democratic legitimacy. Central issues include transparency and explainability of automated decisions (Bullock, 2019), fairness and nondiscrimination in serving vulnerable populations, and accountability and human oversight in decision-making processes (Alshahrani, et al., 2024). Beyond identifying these challenges, the debate also involves normative claims about how public institutions ought to act, claims which are not fixed but subject to ongoing societal negotiation and contestation.

These briefly outlined components of the debate on AI must be taken into account in order to ask how a more effective approach to AI in the public sector can be envisioned.

4 Framework for Identifying Critical Blind Spots: Level of Observations

To explore how AI deployment in the public sector could become more successful, Otto Scharmer's *Theory U* (2016) provides a useful conceptual framework. Theory U distinguishes three levels of observation through which any phenomenon can be examined:

1. **Output level**—This refers to the result itself. In the case of AI, it means focusing on the deployed system and the tangible outcomes it produces. For example, a municipality may evaluate whether an AI chatbot for citizen inquiries successfully answers questions, reduces call center traffic, or speeds up service delivery. Or to what extent the AI chatbot complies with regulatory requirements and ethical standards, avoids generating risks, and ensures compatibility.
2. **Process level**—This concerns the mechanisms that generate the outcome. In AI adoption, this could include data quality, interoperability between administrative databases, the presence of data silos, outdated IT infrastructures, unclear lines of responsibility, and decision-making procedures. Dysfunction emerges when these factors interact negatively, such as when incompatible legacy systems prevent the integration of predictive models into welfare or tax administration.
3. **Source or Place-of-Origin Level**—This refers to the moment or place that precedes the process, the underlying conditions that make processes possible in the first place. Scharmer illustrates this with the analogy of painting: the place of origin is what happens before the first brushstroke. Applied to AI, it means examining the underlying materials, from which the AI process unfolds. This includes the foundational elements (materials) that constitute the way AI is approachable.

Taken together, these three levels suggest that understanding AI initiatives in public administration requires going beyond visible outputs and processes to include the *constitutive place of origin.* Without this level, the analysis remains partial and reactive.

5 First Blind Spot: Output Fixation in Public Sector AI

Despite the importance of all three levels, most current public sector AI initiatives focus almost exclusively on the output (what the AI delivers and how the impact is categorized in terms of risk and ethics) and, to a lesser extent, on the process (how results are produced). The place of origin—examine the materials upon which AI decisions are negotiated—is often neglected. This neglect constitutes the *first blind spot.* A critical perspective must be considered if the dysfunctional patterns in AI initiatives in the public sector are to be overcome. The concrete takeaway from the first blind spot is focus on the material that constitutes the place of origin of AI decision-making in the public sector. This refers to the question of which references are actually available for negotiating AI. In practical terms, many AI initiatives continue to be framed solely through the lens of proven and analog materials, without allowing innovative and digital resources to enter the constitutive process that shapes their very foundation. For instance, if decision-making frameworks for AI are grounded only in analog practices or risk-driven categories, they constrain what AI can contribute before deployment of AI even begins. The main question to ask here is: are they exclusively proven and analog references, representing the status quo from which AI is negotiated? Or are innovative and digital materials also available at the place of origin, allowing for relational assessment and providing alternative capacities that make it possible to negotiate AI in the first place?

The consequence of this first blind spot, if not taken into account, is, that governments relate failure of AI initiatives to *bad AI impacts* (in terms of regulatory risks, trustworthiness and ethics) or *fragmented processes,* but the deeper constitutive conditions are ignored. This systematically narrows the space of possibilities and reproduces the same options without taking into account the conditions of their emergence. In doing so, we perpetuate dysfunctional and low-impact modes of engagement, without reconceptualizing them at a fundamental level. For example: Is a potential use of AI reduced to the requirements of the proven and analog, thereby becoming the sole negotiation material available at the place of origin of the AI decision? Or is the innovative and digital already inscribed as material at the place of origin itself? And does this, in turn, make the relation between the two negotiable, thus enabling an AI initiative to emerge? Depending on which negotiation materials are embedded at the place of origin, the possibilities for AI deployment are systematically shaped.

6 Second Blind Spot: Negotiating AI as a Relational Reference at the Place of Origin

Following the insight of the first blind spot, we arrive at the second blind spot. Is AI negotiated at its place of origin as an absolute entity, or is it negotiated in relation to alternatives?

Regulatory The regulatory logic focuses primarily on output: what the AI system does and the risks it produces, rather than its place of origin. This aligns with the view that the AI system's output is the material of interest within the place of origin of negotiation, while other elements remain excluded. Accordingly, the German KIVO Implementation Act adopts the output perspective of the AI Act one-to-one: what matters is what the AI system delivers, how it is used, and what risks it creates for security and fundamental rights. These are determined by the context of deployment and potential consequences, not by the place of development. The draft mentions placing on the market, putting into operation, and using terms all aimed at the level of output. No provision can be found that regulates, for example, that the very decision to deploy an AI system itself constitutes a risk and would therefore have to be part of the classification system.

Both regulatory frameworks explicitly avoid addressing the question of whether the mode of decision-making regarding deployment (e.g., human, automated, organizationally centralized, or decentralized) could itself constitute a risk factor. Output (i.e., the effects of results) remains the sole benchmark. This produces a blind spot: AI is constituted as an absolute risk at the place of origin. What is regulated are the risks generated by AI systems once deployed. What is not regulated are the modalities and conditions under which deployment decisions are made, nor the risks that may arise when AI is not used at all. Consequently, the current constitutive material of the place of origin does not acknowledge that AI represents a relative risk in relation to an already existing alternative: the proven and analog practices in the public sector that rely on no AI. As an alternative to the innovative and digital (AI-based) approach, public sector functions can continue to be carried out in proven and analog forms. What, then, is the associated risk, and how is it to be assessed in relation to one another? The blind spot is precisely this relation to the proven and analog status quo that operates without AI. And this is certainly not free of risk.

What is missing is a risk classification that differentiates, both in terms of decision-making and effects, between human (proven and analog) and AI-supported (innovative and digital) procedures, and that integrates both as part of the constitutive place of origin in relational terms. What emerges in this blind spot of the place of origin is the following: (1) the innovative and digital (i.e., AI) is not the same as the proven and analog (the performance differential is taken as justification for regulation) and (2) the innovative and digital (i.e., AI) is, in principle, always associated with greater risk than the proven and analog (an asymmetrical assessment). This becomes particularly striking when it is evident that proven and analog practices are neither perfect nor free from error. Humans are prone to bias (e.g., discrimination on the basis of age, gender, or origin, or the overvaluation of available as opposed to missing information, etc.). Proven and analog processes are also susceptible to fatigue and inconsistency. By contrast, AI can enable more objective and consistent decisions. Without AI, the structural risks of human error persist and could represent a higher level of risk. Human errors also scale: in large-scale administrative processes (e.g., 100,000 social welfare decisions per year), small individual errors accumulate into substantial harm. AI has the potential to reduce such risks by conducting systematic checks or providing support. A further issue is the lack of transparency in human decision-making. Humans often document the grounds of their decisions only in rudimentary form, whereas AI systems can provide greater traceability and record-keeping. Without AI, the risk of opaque decision-making remains. If public authorities refrain from using AI, they operate less efficiently, more slowly, and under greater strain. This in itself constitutes a risk. Given these arguments, this is not captured by the AI Act or its derivative, the KIVO Implementation Act.

What is missing is a comparative category that asks: "How risky is the same decision without the relative reference to AI?" The result is a regulatory asymmetry: AI is subject to strict regulation, even where it may objectively be safer, while human decision-making remains unregulated, even where it may be riskier.

Trustworthy AI The central factors of the normative formulation are lawfulness, ethical alignment, and robustness (EU, 2019). Here, the same blind spot emerges: the expectation is imposed that AI in the public sector must meet these normative requirements, and it must be demonstrated that it does so. Meanwhile, the alternative—the status quo of proven and analog practices—is not considered as a relational benchmark. What should be shown, then, is how exactly proven and analog practices in the public sector are trustworthy. Are the decisions being made legally beyond doubt? As two examples illustrate, one can recall that former transport minister Scheuer ensured that €243 millions of taxpayers' money was spent without any service in return (Magoley, 2023). More recently, the issue of masks and minister Spahn involved billions of euros of public funds spent without direct benefit to taxpayers (Tagesschau, 2025). Even if these cases ultimately do not result in personal liability, and I do not claim to make a legal judgment, it is clear that perfect legal alignment cannot be assumed.

To what extent the public sector's status quo consistently upholds ethical values, human dignity, and fairness without flaw is equally questionable. Regarding robustness in terms of effectiveness and efficiency, there is no need for discussion: it is evident that the current public sector performs significantly worse than AI could potentially achieve. Once again, the same pattern emerges: the innovative and digital (i.e., AI) is held to the standard of trustworthiness, assessed as an isolated entity, without any comparative evaluation of whether the proven and analog practices already fulfill these standards.

Ethics The central argument in the ethical realm follows that the innovative and digital (i.e., AI) is deficient in securing these claims (fairness, transparency, accountability, and nondiscrimination) and must therefore be regulated and subordinated to the proven and analog status quo. Once again, AI is posited as the absolute: AI is biased and cannot be trusted. This is, in itself, true. Yet the same applies to the proven and analog. Human actors, current processes, and decision-making practices in the public sector are likewise biased and do not provide a perfect solution to the ethical demands of fairness, transparency, accountability, and nondiscrimination. Put succinctly, the following occurs: something that is manifestly biased (the proven and analog) excludes something else (the innovative and digital) on the grounds of being biased. The truly pressing question only arises in the relational perspective: what precisely is biased, to what degree, and how does the interplay between the proven and analog and the innovative and digital in the public sector shape the pursuit of fairness, transparency, accountability, and nondiscrimination? And the exclusion of the innovative and digital as reference material—precisely because it is not part of the constitutive place of origin from which AI initiatives in the public sector are conceived—creates a further distortion. The mode of engagement reduces what is excluded to the material of what is included: *you are different, but you must become like me.* At the same time, the proven and analog system fails to recognize itself as flawed, being too preoccupied with excluding the other on account of its flaws.

Taken together, the sketched regulatory framework, trustworthiness of AI, and the ethical imperative lead to the following conclusion: within the constitutive material of the place of origin for AI in the public sector, both subsets must be inscribed and considered in relation to one another. Each must serve as the comparative reference for the other. This must be embedded as material at the constitutive place of origin for AI in the public sector, from which both processes and outcomes are derived.

Accordingly, the demand arising from this blind spot is the following: integrate the digital and innovative (i.e., AI) into relation with the proven and analog as a reference within the constitutive place of origin from which processes are designed and outcomes negotiated. The task is not to conceptualize AI in isolation and in absolute terms, but in relation to its alternative, with regard to both regulatory risk, trustworthiness and ethical claims. In this way, the space for successful decision-making is systematically opened—rather than being reduced to the overly simplistic baseline logic: *AI = risk; without AI = no risk; relational comparison = unnecessary.* This is simply false and not helpful.

7 Third Blind Spot: Negotiating AI with AI

The first blind spot concerns the fact that AI in the public sector is primarily viewed in terms of outcomes, while attention to the constitutive material of the place of origin is lacking. The second blind spot follows from this, showing that AI is not conceived as a reference in relation to non-AI but is instead treated as an absolute entity, without relational evaluation, within the material of negotiation at the point of origin. The third blind spot takes this one step further. The core thesis is that AI must not only be introduced as a reference in relation to non-AI but must also be established as an equivalent entity in its own right within the material of the place of origin. Specifically, the third blind spot highlights the need for public sector actors to ground their negotiations in the functional surplus that AI provides at the place of origin. Put briefly, successful AI in outcomes requires AI at the place of origin of negotiation. Or more concisely still, AI needs AI.

AI as an Irreducible Reality The blind spot here lies in the fact that AI is not introduced as an entity in its own right within the constitution of the place of origin of AI negotiation. Yet the digital is nothing other than the duplication of the world in the form of data (Nassehi, 2019). The resulting material (data) constitutes a transformation of analogue units into digital form (measurement), which is characterized by the fact that the analogue form is no longer available within the digital. Its origin is forgotten. The central difference lies in the capacity of digitally standardized units to be networked, thereby overcoming analogue separations (which are not networkable). Analogue distinctions are unified in the structuring of digital information (data) and thereby rendered relatable. Specifically, it concerns the ways in which they would not relate to one another in analogue form.

AI is therefore grounded in (1) digital form (measurement) and (2) the capacity for networking across analogue boundaries. Artificial intelligence extends this foundation by employing such digital operations as values within (partially) autonomous probabilistic procedures. It is not an end in itself, but a mode of effectuation (cf. Nassehi, 2019). What is specific to AI is that repeatability and determinability cannot, in fact, be externally imposed (cf. Nassehi, 2019). AI generates degrees of freedom that we would otherwise ascribe only to human agents. From this arises the central performance promise that characterizes the efficacy of AI: it employs data-based duplications as the self-reference of the digital, interconnects these across domains, and thereby makes available something that analogue modalities (proven and analog material) cannot provide. Thus, a fundamental difference emerges between the capacities that can be produced through analog means and those that can be generated by AI. In summary, this means that AI, as a potential mode of effectuation, cannot be reduced to proven and analogue forms of effectuation, because, in comparison, it introduces a functional surplus. The innovative and digital (i.e., AI) can achieve more than the proven and analog. The third blind spot lies in the fact that this functional surplus is not itself incorporated as material of negotiation at the place of origin. Neither current risk classifications, trustworthiness, nor ethical imperatives account for this. The EU AI Act and the KIVO Implementation Act both proceed from the assumption: AI deployment = risk. They do not take into account the risk of *non*-deployment (second blind spot: relational evaluation). Nor do they consider that AI, as an autonomous entity, could contribute a functional surplus to decision-making about AI itself. What is the risk of making deployment decisions about AI without AI? Conversely, what is the risk of making such decisions *with* AI, and how do these compare? How can the ethical requirements of fairness, transparency, accountability, and the avoidance of discrimination be met if they are negotiated with AI? Especially, when compared to negotiating them without AI, how can trustworthiness in the public sector be enhanced in this way?

To make this concrete: when public sector units decide whether and how to deploy AI without using AI themselves, their decisions are grounded solely in proven and analog material. In other words, the constitutive place of origin is often shaped by subjective assessments, political preferences, fears, or a lack of expertise. Yet this itself constitutes a risk: human decision-makers are frequently unable to fully capture the regulatory, technical, and ethical complexities to the extent that AI could (functional surplus). AI-supported analyses could assess risks more systematically, comprehensively, and on a data-driven basis. Decisions made without AI are therefore more heavily influenced by individual biases, vested interests, or political opportunism than they would be with AI (functional surplus). Regulatory or organizational implementation is delayed when negotiations occur without digital decision support, whereas AI could ensure both effectiveness and efficiency (functional surplus).

All of this can be clearly observed in the ubiquitous record of AI failures in the public sector in Germany. When the third blind spot is considered, it becomes apparent that a significant risk arises when AI itself is not introduced as material at the place of origin for AI deployment decisions. Designers can thereby anchor decisions about AI deployment in the functional surplus that AI itself provides.

8 Place of Origin First, Output Second

The Paradoxical Consequence Efforts to implement AI in the public sector in Germany have produced a mode of engagement that (1) is systematically unsuccessful, (2) potentially generates higher risk, and (3) fails to adequately meet ethical requirements. This creates a paradoxical situation: the intention to achieve successful state modernization, uphold ethical imperatives, enhance trustworthiness, and comply with regulations may, due to the blind spots, lead to the opposite of the intended outcome.

A More Successful Mode of Engagement The three blind spots outlined above provide points of departure for moving away from dysfunctional patterns and point toward an alternative mode of engagement. Specifically, this approach yields guidance that identifies characteristics of a more successful mode of engaging with AI in the public sector:

1. **Focus on the place of origin:** Take stock of the material at the place of origin, which is what produces the negotiation of processes and outcomes in the first place.
2. **No absolute entity:** Do not treat AI in isolation as an absolute unit; rather, incorporate both the proven and analogue and the innovative and digital as material at the place of origin.
3. **Relational evaluation:** Evaluate AI not in isolation, but in comparison to alternatives, considering how ethical requirements and risks are negotiated.
4. **Non-reducibility:** The functional capacity of the innovative and digital is not reducible to that of the proven and analogue and should be taken into account.
5. **Functional surplus:** Decisions regarding AI in the public sector must be able to anchor themselves in the capacities of both the proven and analogue and the innovative and digital, in order to leverage the functional surplus.

By adopting the guidelines outlined above, the public sector does not merely improve the management of AI initiatives—it fundamentally creates the conditions under which trustworthy AI, regulatory compliance, and sovereign control can exist successfully. Currently, decisions about AI deployment are made almost exclusively through analog and proven materials, meaning that the potential contributions of AI itself are systematically excluded from the constitutive negotiation of these initiatives. As a result, ethical, regulatory, and strategic considerations cannot fully leverage AI's capabilities to implement AI successful.

The five conditions—focusing on the place of origin, treating AI relationally rather than as an absolute entity, enabling relational evaluation, acknowledging non-reducibility, and leveraging functional surplus—invert this logic. By embedding AI directly into the place of origin of decision-making, AI itself becomes part of the constitutive material. Decisions about AI are no longer purely human-driven analog assessments (proven and analog) but are co-negotiated with AI, allowing its capabilities for systematic, data-driven, and networked analysis to shape both risk evaluation, trustworthiness, and ethical deliberation.

Implications If these five central conditions are taken as the foundation for engaging with AI in the public sector, this has fundamental implications. I argue that trustworthy AI, legally compliant AI, and ethically anchored AI are most effective when it is generated in connection with AI itself. Human oversight is not replaced but strengthened, as AI informs and structures the negotiation with functional surplus, allowing fairness, accountability, and transparency, compliance, and robustness to be actively deliberated. Through this co-creative process, the biases of both domains—the established and analog, on the one hand, and the innovative and digital, on the other—can be mutually reduced. As a result, AI initiatives in the public sector can become not only more trustworthy but also more capable of achieving success. The functional surplus of AI (digital form, capacity for networking and autonomous probabilistic) provides tangible value when AI itself is included in the negotiation of its deployment. For lawfulness, AI can systematically analyze regulatory frameworks, identify compliance gaps, and simulate outcomes under different legal constraints, ensuring that deployment decisions are aligned with applicable laws from the outset. For ethical alignment, AI can highlight potential biases in human and procedural decision-making, quantify fairness implications, and propose options that balance competing ethical priorities, enabling informed deliberation rather than post-hoc corrections. For robustness, AI supports risk assessment, monitors system reliability, and models failure scenarios, thereby embedding technical resilience into the decision-making process.

Importantly, trustworthiness is reinforced simply because AI is more likely to succeed when guided by these five conditions. Alternatively, it will not be any less successful, since the reference point is already at zero. When AI demonstrates functional effectiveness in deployment, it creates a factual basis for trust: stakeholders can meaningfully discuss lawfulness, ethics, and robustness only because the AI system is operational and capable, rather than speculative.

One Step Further "The riskiest decision regarding AI is the decision to negotiate AI deployment without using AI." In light of the sections presented in this paper, the cited statement aptly captures the core idea: AI needs AI. If this approach is followed consistently, the central thesis emerges: AI initiatives that do not include AI in their own negotiation are less likely to succeed and less likely to comply with ethical and legal frameworks (paradoxical consequence, see above). From this follows a key requirement for AI initiatives in the public sector if they are to be considered trustworthy. That is, to be successful, compliant, and ethically aligned, they must demonstrate (1) that AI has been used and (2) how AI has been used in the negotiation of the AI initiative itself. If this cannot be shown, there is no reason to assume that the mode of negotiating AI would be helpful for the development of AI initiatives and should therefore not be pursued further.

Moreover, by addressing and overcoming the three blind spots, the functional surplus of AI can be fully leveraged for its own adaptation within the public sector. This represents the core opportunity-driven perspective: not merely the opportunities that AI itself offers, but the opportunity of AI to enable AI. It is this reflexive potential, the ability of AI to participate in shaping its own deployment, that lies at the heart of a genuinely transformative and innovation oriented approach in public administration.

Competing Interests The author has no conflicts of interest to declare that are relevant to the content of this chapter.

References

Alshahrani, A., Griva, A., Dennehy, D., & Mäntymäki, M. (2024). Artificial intelligence and decision-making in government functions: Opportunities, challenges and future research. *Transforming Government: People, Process and Policy, 18*(4), 678–698.

Bahamazava, K. (2025). AI-driven scenarios for urban mobility: Quantifying the role of ODE models and scenario planning in reducing traffic congestion. *Transport Economics and Management, 3*, 92–103.

BMWE. (2025). Digitale Stratgie 2025. Retrieved September 21, 2025, from https://www.bundeswirtschaftsministerium.de/Redaktion/DE/Publikationen/Digitale-Welt/digitale-strategie-2025.html.

Bullock, J. B. (2019). Artificial intelligence, discretion, and bureaucracy. *The American Review of Public Administration, 49*(7), 751–761.

Bundesministerium für Digitales und Staatsmodernisierung. (2025). *Entwurf eines Gesetzes zur Durchführung der Verordnung (EU) 2024/1689. Retrieved September 21, 2025, from* https://bmds.bund.de/service/gesetzgebungsverfahren/gesetz-zur-durchfuehrung-der-ki-verordnung.

Bundesrechnungshof. (2023). *Verfahren der Datenanalyse und der künstlichen Intelligenz in der Bundesverwaltung*. Bericht nach § 99 BHO. Retrieved September 21, 2025, from https://www.bundesrechnungshof.de/SharedDocs/Downloads/DE/Berichte/2023/ki-da-volltext.pdf?__blob=publicationFile&v=5&utm.

Capgemini Research Institute. (2024). *State of AI in the Public Sector 2024 [Report]*. Capgemini.

Demircioglu, M. A., & Audretsch, D. B. (2024). Public vs. Privat. In *Public sector innovation* (pp. 23–39). Cambridge University Press.

European Commission. (2019). High-level expert group on artificial intelligence. *Ethics guidelines for trustworthy AI*. Retrieved September, 21, from https://www.europarl.europa.eu/cmsdata/196377/AI%20HLEG_Ethics%20Guidelines%20for%20Trustworthy%20AI.pdf.

Floridi, L., Cowls, J., Beltrametti, M., Chatila, R., Chazerand, P., Dignum, V., et al. (2018). AI4People—an ethical framework for a good AI society: Opportunities, risks, principles, and recommendations. *Minds and Machines, 28*(4), 689–707.

McKinsey & Company. (2025). A pivot for Germany: All for growth and growth for all. McKinsey Global Institute. Retrieved September 21, 2025, from https://www.mckinsey.com/de/~/media/mckinsey/locations/europe%20and%20middle%20east/deutschland/news/presse/2024/2024-09-30%20wachstumswende%20deutschland/a%20pivot%20for%20germany_final%20version.pdf.

Magoley, N. (2023). Maut-Skandal: Warum Ex-Verkehrsminister Scheuer nicht zahlen muss. Universität zu Köln. Retrieved September 21, 2025, from https://verwaltungslehre.uni-koeln.de/aktuell/artikel/maut-skandal-warum-ex-verkehrsminister-scheuer-nicht-zahlen-muss.

Nassehi, A. (2019). *Muster: Theorie der digitalen Gesellschaft*. CH Beck.

Neumann, O., Guirguis, K., & Steiner, R. (2024). Exploring artificial intelligence adoption in public organizations: A comparative case study. *Public Management Review, 26*(1), 114–141.

Organisation for Economic Co-operation and Development (OECD). (2024). *OECD artificial intelligence review of Germany*. OECD Publishing. Retrieved September 21, 2025, from https://www.oecd.org/en/publications/oecd-artificial-intelligence-review-of-germany_609808d6-en.html

Regulation (EU) 2024/1689 OF THE EUROPEAN PARLIAMENT AND OF THE COUNCIL. Retrieved September 21, 2025, from Regulation (EU) 2024/1689 of the European Parliament and of the Council of 13 June 2024 laying down harmonised rules on artificial intelligence and amending Regulations (EC) No 300/2008, (EU) No 167/2013, (EU) No 168/2013, (EU) 2018/858, (EU) 2018/1139 and (EU) 2019/2144 and Directives 2014/90/EU, (EU) 2016/797 and (EU) 2020/1828 (Artificial Intelligence Act)Text with EEA relevance.

Sansone, D., & Zhu, A. (2023). Using machine learning to create an early warning system for welfare recipients. *Oxford Bulletin of Economics and Statistics, 85*(5), 959–992.

Scharmer, C. O. (2016). *Theory U: Leading from the future as it emerges*. Berrett-Koehler Publishers.

Selten, F., & Klievink, B. (2024). Organizing public sector AI adoption: Navigating between separation and integration. *Government Information Quarterly, 41*(1), 101885.

Tagesschau. (2025). *Masken-Kosten: Bundesrechnungshof rügt Spahn.* Retrieved September 21, 2025 from https://www.tagesschau.de/inland/innenpolitik/masken-kosten-spahn-bundesrechnungshof-100.html.

Ugbehe, P. O., Diemuodeke, O. E., & Aikhuele, D. O. (2025). Electricity demand forecasting methodologies and applications: A review. *Sustainable Energy Research, 12*(1), 19.

Dr. Moritz Schirmer is a postdoctoral researcher specializing in Organizational Development and AI Adoption, combining academic expertise with practical innovation. As a startup founder funded by the German Federal Ministry for Economic Affairs and Climate Action and AI Manager at IHK Digital, he actively shapes the public sector's approach to AI. His unique profile bridges the worlds of research and entrepreneurship, bringing both scientific rigor and hands-on experience to the evolving field of artificial intelligence.

Making CDR Work: Generative AI as a Catalyst for Responsible Innovation in SMEs

Saskia Dörr

Abstract

Small and medium-sized enterprises (SMEs) increasingly commit to corporate digital responsibility (CDR) principles such as fairness, transparency, and sustainability, yet face persistent gaps in translating these ambitions into everyday practice due to limited resources and expertise. This chapter examines how domain-specific generative AI (GenAI) can address this challenge through the case of GreenGate AG, a German software company. The *Ethos Advisor*—a GenAI-based prototype developed by WiseWay—was designed to support sustainability and responsibility leads in ethical communication, guideline drafting, and capability building. Integrating large language model capabilities with curated CDR knowledge, the system operates within a guided, human-in-the-loop framework. A mixed-methods evaluation revealed that the tool enhanced efficiency, content quality, and user confidence, while fostering inclusive engagement and informal learning. Key enablers were speed, structure, and empowerment; trust depended on transparency, source traceability, and optional expert validation. The chapter argues for a shift from abstract AI ethics frameworks to embedded, socio-technical practices and offers concrete design principles for integrating responsible GenAI agents into lean organizational structures. Ultimately, the Ethos Advisor case illustrates that with thoughtful design, generative AI can become not just a tool of automation but a catalyst for embedding responsibility more consistently and effectively into digitally transforming organizations.

S. Dörr (✉)
WiseWay, Bonn, Germany
e-mail: saskia.doerr@wiseway.de

A.-S. Christ (ed.), *Corporate Digital Responsibility*, Future of Business and Finance, https://doi.org/10.1007/978-3-032-14793-6_14

1 The CDR Implementation Gap: From Good Intentions to Daily Practice

Imagine you are the managing director or sustainability officer of a small or medium-sized enterprise. During a recent strategy workshop, you and your team developed guiding principles for a responsible digital transformation. The discussion was lively and constructive—touching on fairness, transparency, and the ethical use of emerging technologies. Everyone agreed: these matters.

Then Monday morning comes. Operations must continue, customers are waiting, supply chains are under pressure, and new questions arise: A colleague asks whether she can use ChatGPT for sales outreach. A trainee is looking for guidance on how to handle sensitive customer data. The next sustainability report is due, but how can the company credibly reflect its responsibilities in dealing with algorithms?

The vision of digital responsibility that once felt so clear now seems abstract. Resources are limited, there is no dedicated CDR officer, and many employees are already wearing multiple hats. A gap opens between strategic ambition and day-to-day reality—not because of a lack of interest, but because of a lack of orientation, time, and practical tools.

This is the CDR implementation gap.

Corporate digital responsibility (CDR) has gained traction across sectors. Companies increasingly acknowledge their duty to not only innovate digitally but to do so ethically, sustainably, and transparently (cf. Dörr, 2025a; Lobschat et al., 2021). Yet especially in small and medium-sized enterprises (SMEs), the path from principle to practice remains unclear. Limited resources, lack of internal expertise, and the complexity of ethical digitalization pose significant barriers (cf. Kunz & Wirtz, 2023).

1.1 The Case for Practical, Scalable Tools

The challenge is not commitment, but capacity. SMEs are often willing to act responsibly but lack the time, templates, or trusted guidance to do so systematically (cf. Hrgović & Mak, 2024). What is missing are tools that:

- Translate ethical ambitions into operational workflows.
- Support non-experts in navigating complex CR topics.
- Do so with speed, relevance, and contextual sensitivity.

At the same time, the rise of generative AI offers new opportunities (cf. Noy & Zhang, 2023). If designed responsibly, GenAI agents can assist in precisely those areas where CDR work gets stuck—documentation, reflection, communication, and capacity-building—effectively bridging some of the resource and knowledge gaps. However, these technologies also raise new questions of trust, governance, and control that cannot be ignored (cf. Elliott et al., 2021; Dörr, 2023). Balancing innovation with responsibility thus requires practical support mechanisms that are themselves ethically sound.

1.2 Exploring the Role of GenAI in CDR Implementation

This chapter explores how a domain-specific GenAI agent—the Ethos Advisor—was used in a real SME setting to support responsible digital transformation. It presents a case study conducted at GreenGate AG, a German software company, where the Advisor was deployed to assist with sustainability communication, ethical reflection, and internal CR development.

The central question: Can generative AI serve not just as a technical tool but as a meaningful partner in embedding responsibility into digital practice? We argue that it can—if designed thoughtfully, embedded wisely, and used collaboratively. In the following sections, we outline the design and application of the Ethos Advisor, discuss its impact in the field, and reflect on what this means for the future of CDR in practice. This is not a story of automation. It is a story of augmentation, co-creation, and what it takes to make responsibility real—even on a Monday morning.

2 The Ethos Advisor Case Study: Context and Objectives

To illustrate these principles in a real-world setting, the following case study presents the Ethos Advisor, outlining its design, objectives, and application within GreenGate AG.

2.1 Introducing the Ethos Advisor: A Concept Prototype for Responsible AI Use

The Ethos Advisor is a domain-specific GenAI agent developed by WiseWay and based on a custom GPT model tailored to the needs of corporate responsibility (CR) professionals. As a concept prototype, it integrates curated CR knowledge and ethical framing into a generative AI environment to support sustainability managers and CR experts in their daily responsibilities (cf. Dörr, 2025b; cf. Fig. 1).

Conceptual UI mockup illustrating core functions (starter prompts, chat window/history, "Expert Check"). *Note: This mockup served for conceptual illustration only and was not used in the project.*

Designed as a guided conversational agent, the Ethos Advisor offers assistance in formulating sustainability goals, drafting ethical guidelines for AI usage, generating content for CSR reports, and supporting internal capability building. It combines the generative capacity of large language models (LLMs) with structured knowledge from CR practice, using curated prompts and context-sensitive framing (Fig. 2).

Fig. 1 Ethos-Advisor: Concept prototype (Mockup) (Author's illustration)

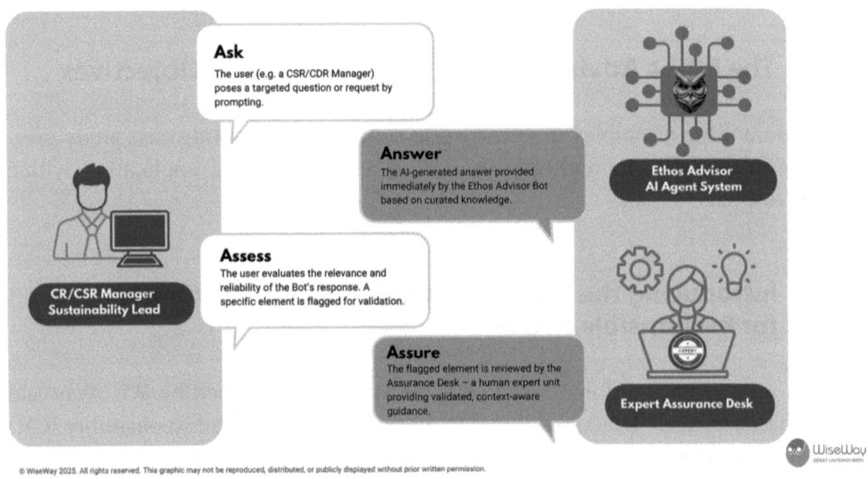

Fig. 2 Ethos Advisor interaction loop (Author's illustration)

The Ethos Advisor is not intended as a general-purpose chatbot but as a purpose-driven companion operating within clear responsibility boundaries. It embodies a hybrid model of human–AI collaboration, which includes an optional Human Assessment Service (HAS) for validating AI-generated outputs through expert review.

2.2 Case Context: GreenGate AG

The case study was conducted with GreenGate AG, a mid-sized German software company with approximately 50 employees. GreenGate specializes in digital solutions for infrastructure and environmental management and has been actively expanding its sustainability initiatives.

According to the managing director, the company had long been engaged in sustainable projects, yet struggled to communicate these efforts effectively and to position them as added value for clients. The team aimed to feature sustainability achievements more prominently on the website, in other corporate media, and in the sustainability report. However, resources for such communication were limited. Drafting and refining content required considerable time and expertise—an area where targeted AI support could potentially reduce effort and improve output quality.

As a B2B company with limited internal resources for specialized sustainability roles, GreenGate provided an ideal context to explore the use of GenAI to augment CR capacities. The management team was interested in embedding digital responsibility into operational workflows while maintaining lean organizational structures. In practice, this meant that staff— none of whom were full-time CR or sustainability experts—would interact with the Ethos Advisor to support their work on sustainability and business ethics topics. This real-world setting allowed observation of how a responsible AI tool could fit into the routines of an SME without significant additional hiring or budget (cf. Dörr, 2025b).

Before the Ethos Advisor was introduced, sustainability and ESG-related communication tasks were handled by employees alongside their primary responsibilities. Generative AI tools had not been used in this context, and there was little awareness of how such systems might assist or what risks and limitations might apply to their outputs. Preparing texts for the sustainability report or other communication materials required considerable time and effort.

Within the project, the Ethos Advisor was tested as a potential support tool. It provided structured suggestions and examples relevant to sustainability topics, while also highlighting where human review was essential. This enabled participants to explore the capabilities and boundaries of GenAI in a practical setting, without altering existing workflows.

2.3 Objectives of the Case Study

The Ethos Advisor case study aimed to explore the practical applicability, benefits, and limitations of GenAI-assisted CR work in an SME environment. Specifically, the case focused on three main objectives:

1. **Support Sustainability Communication**:
   - Use the Advisor to improve the clarity, consistency, and efficiency of sustainability reporting and stakeholder communication.

2. **Build Internal Digital and Ethical Competencies**:
   - Enable team members to interact with and learn from the system in ways that enhance their understanding of ethical issues in digitalization.
3. **Explore Integration into Lean Organizational Structures**:
   - Test how a GenAI agent can be embedded in CR processes without requiring large-scale investments or dedicated capacities.

In this sense, the case study functioned both as a practical implementation trial and as an exploratory design research intervention. It generated insights into user behavior and tool performance, as well as the systemic conditions under which responsible AI agents can add value in real-world settings. Collaboration with academic partners (University of Frankfurt) provided methodological guidance in the research design and evaluation framework, helping to ensure robustness and transferability.

3 Methodology and Evaluation Framework

This section outlines the methodological approach used to evaluate the Ethos Advisor, detailing the case design, data collection, and analytical framework applied in the study.

3.1 Case Design and Scope

The case study at GreenGate spanned 5 months (January–May 2025) and applied the GenAI-based Advisor to real-world tasks in corporate digital responsibility and sustainability management. Primary application domains were sustainability reporting and the communication of sustainability measures. A hybrid evaluation logic combined practical use in teams with structured observation and guided reflection. Participants received onboarding materials and access to a dedicated AI companion; the Human Assessment Service was available for optional expert validation of generated outputs. This setup simulated a realistic SME deployment while safeguarding against potential AI errors through human oversight.

3.2 Data Collection

The evaluation combined quantitative and qualitative instruments to capture both measurable outcomes and deeper insights into user experience. Quantitative data were gathered via a structured online survey (Typeform) covering usability, trust, perceived value, and recommendation likelihood. Likert-scale items assessed satisfaction with AI-generated results, the importance of human validation, and expectation fulfilment. Qualitative data came from in-depth semi-structured interviews with key users, complemented by observations during onboarding and follow-up sessions and optional free-text feedback. This mixed-methods design enabled a triangulated understanding of how the Ethos Advisor was received, used, and evaluated within the organizational context.

3.3 Evaluation Dimensions

Four central evaluation dimensions guided the analysis:

1. **Usability**: How intuitive and effective was the use of the Ethos Advisor in practice?
2. **Trust**: To what extent did users trust the quality, origin, and reliability of AI-generated content?
3. **Perceived Impact**: What tangible benefits (e.g., time saved, quality of output, empowerment) were observed?
4. **Implementation Potential**: How well did the system fit into existing processes, and what enablers and barriers to broader adoption were identified?

These dimensions align with core criteria for the responsible deployment of generative AI in professional contexts, especially within SMEs; trust and usability are critical for acceptance, while impact and integration speak to business value and feasibility over time (cf. Söllner et al., 2025).

3.4 Academic Collaboration

The case study was conducted in collaboration with the University of Frankfurt (Prof. Dr. Oliver Hinz and Dr. Kim Valerie Carl, cf. Carl et al., 2024) as part of a joint research project on the effectiveness of corporate digital responsibility (CDR) measures in SME contexts. The study also examined how GenAI-supported sustainability communication influences stakeholder perceptions, using pre-/post-customer surveys as an evaluation method. A scientific publication highlighting the empirical effects of CDR in practice is planned.

4 Key Findings: Experience and Effects in the Field

This section presents the key results of the GreenGate case study, focusing on how the Ethos Advisor performed in a real SME environment. The findings are structured around three core aspects: the enablers that facilitated its use, the observed impacts on communication and learning, and the trust-related factors that shaped adoption. Particular attention is given to the role of human-in-the-loop practices, which proved to be a central condition for both the quality and credibility of outputs.

4.1 Enablers: Speed, Structure, and Empowerment

The Ethos Advisor demonstrably improved the efficiency and structure of sustainability-related workflows at GreenGate. Users reported significant reductions in the time required to complete complex tasks. In one instance, a participant reported using the Advisor to complete a previously postponed sustainability communication task, highlighting its structured support and referring to a highly relevant time-saving for that specific activity. Another participant emphasized how the Advisor transformed bullet points into publishable content, describing it as a helpful text generator that enhanced both structure and formulation.

The Advisor enabled a "Time Saved – Quality Gained" effect by turning unstructured ideas into publishable content in a co-creative manner. These observations align with broader evidence that generative AI can substantially raise productivity in writing tasks (cf. Noy & Zhang, 2023).

The AI assistant functioned as a co-creative partner, offering structure, phrasing support, and relevant terminology (especially for sustainability topics), which not only improved content quality but also increased users' confidence. Nonexpert team members felt more empowered to engage in complex topics, knowing they had a knowledgeable assistant to kick-start their work. In this way, the Ethos Advisor acted as an enabler for participation in responsibility-related communication. What might have been intimidating or time-consuming tasks were now more approachable, allowing staff from various departments to contribute to CR efforts with guided AI support.

4.2 Observed Impacts: Individual Learning and Clarity in Communication

Beyond efficiency, participants reported that the Advisor's suggestions helped them express sustainability topics more clearly and consistently. One user, for example, used the tool to improve the structure and tone of a policy draft based on an outline of bullet points. The iterative interaction—prompting the AI, reviewing its output, and refining the prompt—fostered critical reflection on the subject matter. In effect, the AI served as a sounding board, highlighting where explanations were needed or where jargon could be clarified. This process contributed to individual learning: by seeing how the AI framed certain issues (like the sustainability advantages of software solutions) in plain language, the users gained insight into effective communication strategies for these topics.

Although we did not systematically measure changes in team-wide terminology usage, users acknowledged the potential for shared use of the Advisor to harmonize language across sustainability workstreams. In short, the tool doubled as a micro training platform—each use not only produced content but also reinforced good practices in CDR communication. This kind of informal learning-by-doing is particularly valuable in SMEs, where formal training programs on digital ethics may be scarce.

4.3 Trust and Its Limits: Transparency as a Prerequisite

A critical finding concerns the perceived trustworthiness of the AI-generated outputs. The users rated their trust in the Ethos Advisor at slightly above medium (6.5 out of 10), reflecting a cautious but constructive stance. The main limiting factor was the lack of visible sources and provenance information. Participants reported that they withheld Advisor-generated content from official documents—especially when quantitative data or normative claims were involved—because they could not assess the reliability or origin of the underlying information.

This confirms the principle that "Trust needs Transparency": trust is not built by performance alone, but by visible origins, citation traceability, and contextual understanding. Even if the content quality is high, users require signals that allow them to verify where information comes from and how it should be interpreted.

In this context, the Human Assessment Service (HAS) provided by WiseWay was rated very positively (9/10) for its validating effect. Users appreciated the availability of a second opinion, even when they did not always make active use of it. The mere option of expert validation created a sense of psychological safety and professional credibility.

Human oversight not only ensures correctness but also enhances user trust and comfort when experimenting with AI. A recent study by Zarifis and Cheng (2024) found that for vague or complex queries—common in sustainability communication—having a human-in-the-loop is one of the four key factors contributing to trust in generative AI, alongside transparency, accuracy, and usability.

This illustrates a "Dual Use, Dual Value" logic: GenAI contributes speed and structure, while human validation adds trust and contextual judgment. The interplay of both generates outcomes that are both efficient and credible.

To move from prototype to trusted tool, future versions should implement "Transparency-by-Design" mechanisms, including source traceability, linkable references, and explainability features. These additions will be critical for expanding the Advisor's use in legally or reputationally sensitive contexts and for embedding GenAI tools more deeply into professional responsibility workflows.

4.4 Human-in-the-Loop: The Value of Hybrid Collaboration

The case study confirmed the necessity of a human-in-the-loop approach for the responsible use of GenAI in sustainability and CDR work. While the Ethos Advisor provided structured, often high-quality output, users consistently took on the role of critical reviewers. This dynamic aligns with emerging best practices for hybrid AI systems, where the AI acts as a collaborator rather than an autonomous decision-maker (cf. Shneiderman, 2020). Users consistently emphasized that co-creation—rather than full automation—was the real value: "Co-creation Beats Automation" emerged as a design principle for trust and engagement.

What users missed most were onboarding aids and prompt literacy training. One participant explicitly requested community calls, prompt libraries, and learning sessions to support a more creative and effective use of the tool. This points to the need for socio-technical embedding of such tools, especially in knowledge-intensive or ethically sensitive application fields.

The case study demonstrates that generative AI, when coupled with expert validation and clear usage framing, can significantly enhance the operationalization of CDR measures in SMEs. However, trust barriers must be addressed through transparency features, onboarding support, and active co-creation formats. The Ethos Advisor case study illustrates how AI can empower responsible innovation when embedded in a thoughtful human-machine collaboration model.

4.5 Results in Overview

In summary, the Ethos Advisor case demonstrates that generative AI—when coupled with expert validation and clear usage framing—can significantly enhance the operationalization of CR measures in SMEs. The key enablers were speed and structure (which saved time and improved outputs) and user empowerment (which broadened participation in CR tasks). We also observed positive impacts on individual learning and communication clarity, suggesting that AI assistance can have educational side benefits in addition to efficiency gains. However, we identified important limitations around trust: without transparency, users are reluctant to fully rely on AI content in formal documents.

The human-in-the-loop model proved valuable, both for catching errors and for maintaining a sense of human agency and accountability. Finally, successful integration of such a tool requires more than just technical deployment—it calls for user engagement strategies, training, and perhaps an internal community of practice to realize the full potential. These findings illustrate both the promise and the pitfalls of bringing GenAI into the realm of CDR.

5 CDR Goes Operational: Insights from Hybrid AI Practice

Building on the findings from the GreenGate case study, this section distills what the practical use of the Ethos Advisor reveals about translating CDR from principle into practice. It examines how hybrid human–AI collaboration shaped outcomes, where GenAI acted as an enabler rather than a replacement, and what governance considerations emerged for SMEs. The discussion is structured to reflect the interplay between speed, trust, and human oversight—themes that proved decisive for the system's acceptance and effectiveness in the field.

5.1 Translating Principles into Action: The Role of Hybrid Systems

The case study demonstrates that GenAI-based tools like the Ethos Advisor can act as effective bridges between the normative principles of corporate digital responsibility and practical, everyday actions. CDR is often discussed in high-level ethical terms or codes of conduct (cf. CDR Initiative, 2021), but operationalizing these values within SME workflows has remained a challenge (cf. Esselmann et al., 2020).

Our findings suggest that a well-designed hybrid system can make abstract concepts tangible. For example, when the Advisor helped draft a text passage for a sustainability report, it was essentially translating broad principles into context-specific language and steps for the company. This points to a broader lesson: hybrid human–AI systems offer a promising path for embedding ethics into business processes. The integration of the Human Assessment Service in our case was essential to establishing trust and ensuring quality. In hindsight, the dual approach (AI + human validator) mitigated the risks of over-automation and reinforced human agency in ethical deliberation. Rather than replacing ethical decision-making, the AI expanded the users' capacity to apply their principles under real constraints. This echoes the concept that responsibility in AI systems must be *shared*—designers can encode certain values, but humans in the loop ultimately guide and approve the outcomes (cf. Shneiderman, 2020).

5.2 GenAI as an Enabler, Not a Silver Bullet

The case study also tempers overly optimistic narratives surrounding GenAI. While the Ethos Advisor clearly improved efficiency and access to CR-relevant content, it did not replace the need for critical thinking, contextual judgment, or strategic decision-making. Rather, its main value lay in its ability to scaffold these processes: by accelerating first drafts, generating alternative perspectives, or offering structure where none existed.

This confirms a broader insight from responsible AI practice: the role of AI is to augment human expertise, not to obviate it (cf. Söllner et al., 2025). Particularly in an ethically sensitive domain like CR, AI augmentation must be done in a transparent, explainable, and value-aligned manner. The Ethos Advisor's success was contingent on users' understanding its suggestions and being willing to adapt or reject them as needed. If someone had treated the AI output as infallible, problems would surely have arisen. Thus, GenAI should be seen as an enabler or catalyst for CR efforts—a means to lower the barriers (time, knowledge, phrasing) that often slow down good initiatives—but not a "silver bullet." Organizations still need to invest in human capacity and a culture that values ethical reflection in order to effectively leverage what AI can offer.

5.3 Lessons for SMEs: Tailored, Accessible CR Support

The findings are especially relevant for small and medium-sized enterprises, which often lack dedicated resources for sustainability and CR. The Ethos Advisor case study illustrates how tailored, accessible AI tools can democratize access to CR know-how and reduce barriers to action (cf. Dörr, 2025a). Participants appreciated the ability to work independently, test ideas, and improve outputs without extensive prior expertise.

However, adoption hinges on more than technical availability. Participants explicitly requested support formats such as onboarding materials, prompt libraries, and community calls to foster creative and confident use.

The findings underscore that "Guidance is key for adoption": onboarding, prompt literacy, and embedded learning formats are essential enablers of sustained use. These socio-technical elements should be considered integral components of any responsible AI deployment strategy in SMEs.

Beyond their immediate function, these formats contribute to capability-building. Prompt literacy is emerging as a new capability dimension within digital sustainability roles—akin to reporting literacy or regulatory awareness. Developing this skillset will be crucial for embedding responsible GenAI usage into day-to-day CR practice.

5.4 Early Governance Insights: Embedding Responsibility in Lean Structures

One of the most valuable insights from the case study concerns the governance of GenAI in lean or decentralized organizations. Unlike large corporations with formal ethics boards or compliance teams, SMEs must integrate digital responsibility into existing roles and processes (cf. Handley & Molloy, 2022). The Ethos Advisor's lightweight, modular nature aligns well with this need—but only when embedded in a governance framework that clarifies accountability, validation, and escalation paths. It did not require the company to overhaul its org chart or create new departments; instead, it *augmented* the capabilities of people already wearing multiple hats.

However, this works only if a basic governance framework is in place to clarify accountability. From our experience, even a simple policy can help, e.g., a one-page guideline stating when to use the AI, when to seek human validation, and how to document AI-assisted work. Our users also needed clarity on the division of labor: which parts of a task should the AI handle versus the human? Over time, they developed an intuition (for example, "I use the AI for initial research and drafting, but I (the human) do the final edit and fact-checking"). Codifying such expectations can prevent misunderstandings and ensure the technology is used consistently and responsibly. We also recommend transparency in process—if AI helped write a report, the organization should be open about that in internal discussions or even externally, if appropriate, to build stakeholder trust.

In essence, we saw the beginnings of an *AI governance model for SMEs*: one that embeds human oversight by default, provides flexible usage guidelines suited to smaller teams, and clarifies how outputs are validated and presented. It moves the conversation from abstract "ethical AI" principles to pragmatic, context-fitting practices that evolve with the organization's needs.

Table 1 Innovation themes from the Ethos Advisor case study

Innovation theme	Description	Strategic relevance
Trusted validation as a service	Expert review is not just a safety net—it becomes a co-responsibility model, supporting trust formation	High relevance for managing directors and governance design
Trust is UX, not just AI	Trust arises not only from system accuracy but from how clearly origin, context, and limits are communicated	Important for innovation managers and UX strategists
Agentic collaboration beats automation	Users perceive the advisor as a cognitive sparring partner, not a replacement—enhancing engagement and agency	Relevant for team development and digital empowerment
Prompt literacy as a new sustainability skill	The ability to steer GenAI meaningfully is becoming a core competence in sustainability and responsibility work	Transformative for capability building and workforce design

5.5 From Experiment to Practice

The Ethos Advisor case study marks a promising step from experimental GenAI usage toward embedded, responsible practice. It shows that with the right framing, tools, and support, even resource-constrained organizations can leverage GenAI to advance their CDR ambitions.

More importantly, the case surfaces several innovation themes that redefine how GenAI can be used responsibly in real-world contexts. These insights are summarized in Table 1 below and highlight four novel usage and design principles that emerged during the pilot phase.

These patterns offer a new vocabulary and orientation for responsible innovation. At the same time, they underscore the importance of ongoing evaluation, user-centered development, and governance innovation to ensure that GenAI technologies not only align with organizational goals and societal values but also become embedded in day-to-day practice through collaborative human–AI teaming. This sets the stage for our concluding reflection on how such systems can make responsibility work—even on a Monday morning.

6 Making Responsibility Work, Even on a Monday Morning

We began with a common dilemma in SMEs: the gap between ethical intent and operational capacity. The Ethos Advisor case study has shown that domain-specific GenAI agents can serve as practical, low-threshold tools to bridge that gap. Crucially, they do so *not by replacing human expertise but by enabling it.*

The results from GreenGate suggest that with careful design, framing, and support, even a concept prototype can make ethical principles more actionable. From improving sustainability texts to stimulating reflection and learning, the Ethos

Advisor proved to be more than a writing assistant: it became a conversational partner in responsible digital transformation.

As the managing director of GreenGate, Frank Lagemann put it:

> With limited time and resources, we needed a tool that fits seamlessly into our workflow. The Ethos Advisor delivered exactly that—while also enabling strategic reflection on sustainability and responsibility.
>
> Mit begrenzter Zeit und knappen Ressourcen brauchten wir ein Tool, das sich nahtlos in unsere Arbeitsabläufe einfügt. Der Ethos Advisor hat genau das geliefert – und zugleich strategische Reflexion über Nachhaltigkeit und Verantwortung angestoßen.

At GreenGate, an AI "colleague" helped a busy team turn lofty principles into concrete outputs—from improved sustainability report texts to more reflective conversations about AI use. With careful design, framing, and support, even a concept prototype can make ethical principles more actionable. The Advisor became more than a writing assistant; it served as a conversational partner in responsible digital transformation.

This illustrates the broader potential of human–AI teaming: AI not as a substitute but as a trusted collaborator that amplifies human capability in complex, value-driven work. It brought speed and relevant knowledge to tasks that would otherwise have strained the team's limited bandwidth.

Most importantly, it offered proof of concept that ethical digitalization can be scaled to SME size—and made practical for the Monday morning rush. At the same time, the pilot surfaced clear needs for further development. Trust and transparency remain essential before such a tool can be relied upon for official use (users still want "sources and footnotes"). Onboarding, transparency, and education also proved critical: technology alone is not enough if users do not know how to make the most of it. These insights are invaluable as we move from prototype to a more robust system.

7 Next Steps: From Prototype to Scalable Practice

The current version of the Ethos Advisor has proven the feasibility and user value of a domain-specific GenAI assistant for corporate responsibility. Moving from concept to a scalable system, our next phase will focus on strengthening trust, usability, and integration capabilities. This includes enhancing transparency, enabling more intuitive interaction, and offering supportive onboarding formats aligned with SME workflows. We also aim to create flexible integration paths to embed the Advisor into existing digital environments.

Throughout this evolution, governance and validation mechanisms tailored to SME realities will remain core design principles. This trajectory—from pilot to product—lays the groundwork for a scalable, responsible GenAI solution that empowers organizations to embed digital responsibility into everyday practice.

8 Join Us in Shaping the Future of Responsible GenAI

The Ethos Advisor is still evolving—and its future depends on collaboration. We invite the following:

- **Corporate responsibility and sustainability teams** who want to pilot the system in their organizations. Your real-world challenges will help shape the tool's features and ensure it delivers value where it matters most.
- **Institutions and associations** interested in co-creating support formats, training pathways, or sector-specific adaptations. For example, industry bodies could help develop guidelines for AI-assisted reporting in their sector, using Ethos Advisor as a platform.
- **Researchers** committed to exploring the socio-technical dynamics of hybrid GenAI use. There are rich research questions around user interaction, trust calibration, and impact measurement that we are only beginning to understand.

If your organization is exploring how to translate digital ethics into daily action, let us build this future together.

To learn more or become a pilot partner, please contact: saskia.doerr@wiseway.de.

This is not just a tool; it is an invitation to rethink how we practice responsibility in the age of intelligent systems. By working together, we can ensure that technologies like generative AI become forces for good in corporate practice—helping even the smallest company make *responsibility* work, every day of the week.

Acknowledgment The author used ChatGPT 4 as an assistant for preparation, structuring, and text passages, but all final texts were verified by the author.

Competing Interests The author has no conflicts of interest to declare that are relevant to the content of this chapter.

References

Carl, K. V., Mihale-Wilson, C., Zibuschka, J., & Hinz, O. (2024). A consumer perspective on corporate digital responsibility: An empirical evaluation of consumer preferences. *Journal of Business Economics, 94*, 979–1024. https://doi.org/10.1007/s11573-023-01142-y

CDR Initiative. (2021). *Our objectives: The CDR code*. Corporate digital responsibility Initiative, Germany. Retrieved July 2, 2025, from https://cdr-initiative.de/kodex.

Dörr, S. (2023). Artificial intelligence demands corporate digital responsibility (CDR): Aligning the moral compass for employees in AI-enabled workplaces. In I. Knappertsbusch & K. Gondlach (Eds.), *Work and AI 2030. Challenges and strategies for tomorrow's work*. Springer. https://doi.org/10.1007/978-3-658-40232-7

Dörr, S. (2025a). *Corporate digital responsibility: Managing corporate responsibility and sustainability in the digital age*. Springer. https://doi.org/10.1007/978-3-662-63853-8

Dörr, S. (2025b). Welcome to ethos advisor. WiseWay. Retrieve July 2, 2025, from https://wiseway.de/ethos-advisor/.

Elliott, K., Price, R., Shaw, P., Spiliotopoulos, T., Ng, M., Coopamootoo, K., & van Moorsel, A. (2021). Towards an equitable digital society: Ethics and fairness in algorithmic systems. *Society, 58*(3), 179–188. https://doi.org/10.1007/s12115-021-00594-8

Esselmann, F., Golle, D., Thiel, D. & Brink, A. (2020). Corporate digital responsibility: Unternehmerische Verantwortung als Chance für die deutsche Wirtschaft. Positionspapier, Zentrum Digitalisierung Bayern. Retrieved July 2, 2025, from https://www.bayern-innovativ.de/seite/corporate-digital-responsibility

Handley, K., & Molloy, C. (2022). SME corporate governance: A literature review of informal mechanisms for governance. *Meditari Accountancy Journal.* https://doi.org/10.1108/MEDAR-06-2021-1321

Hrgović, J. & Mak, M. (2024). Corporate digital responsibility in small and medium-sized enterprises. The COEUS Project. Interreg Central Europe.

Kunz, W., & Wirtz, J. (2023). Corporate digital responsibility (CDR) in the age of AI—implications for interactive marketing. *Journal of Research in Interactive Marketing, 18.* https://doi.org/10.1108/JRIM-06-2023-0176

Lobschat, L., Mueller, B., Eggers, F., Brandimarte, L., Diefenbach, S., Kroschke, M., & Wirtz, J. (2021). Corporate digital responsibility. *Journal of Business Research, 122*, 875–888. https://doi.org/10.1016/j.jbusres.2019.10.006

Noy, S., & Zhang, W. (2023). Experimental evidence on the productivity effects of generative artificial intelligence. *Science, 381*(6654), 187–192. https://doi.org/10.1126/science.adh2586

Shneiderman, B. (2020). Design lessons from AI'S two grand goals: Human emulation and useful applications. *IEEE Transactions on Technology and Society, 1*(2), 73–82. https://doi.org/10.1109/TTS.2020.2992635

Söllner, M., Arnold, T., Benlian, A., Bretschneider, U., Knight, C., Ohly, S., Rudkowski, L., Schreiber, D., & Wendt, D. (2025). ChatGPT and beyond: Exploring the responsible use of generative AI in the workplace. *Business & Information Systems Engineering, 67*, 289–303. https://doi.org/10.1007/s12599-025-00932-8

Zarifis, A., & Cheng, X. (2024). How to build trust in answers given by generative AI for specific and vague financial questions. *Journal of Electronic Business & Digital Economics.* https://doi.org/10.1108/JEBDE-11-2023-0028

Saskia Dörr is an expert in Corporate Digital Responsibility (CDR) and responsible digital transformation. As the founder of WiseWay, she supports leaders in translating ethical and sustainable principles into digital and AI-driven practice. With over 25 years of experience, she bridges management strategy, emerging technologies, and sustainability. Her work focuses on making digital responsibility human-centered, concrete, and actionable for organizations.

The CDR Maturity Model: Guiding Digital Responsibility in Turbulent Times

Alexander Brink, Frank Esselmann, and Leonhard Henke

Abstract

In the context of accelerating digitalisation and rising sustainability expectations, companies are facing the strategic and ethical challenge of the so-called "twin transformation". Corporate digital responsibility (CDR) offers a normative and practical framework to guide organisations in aligning digital innovation with social, environmental, and economic values. This chapter introduces the CDR Maturity Model developed by the German CDR Initiative as a central tool for implementing and advancing CDR in practice. Based on ethical principles and structured around five key fields of action—data handling, education, climate and resource protection, employee involvement, and inclusion—the model supports organisations in systematically developing their digital responsibility across five maturity levels. It is grounded in the logic of Capability Maturity Models and operationalised through tools like the CDR Quick Check and flexible partnership formats. The chapter situates the model within the broader architecture of CDR governance and explores its philosophical underpinnings, practical applications, and strategic relevance. By combining ethical orientation with organisational usability, the maturity model provides actionable guidance for navigating digital responsibility in turbulent times.

A. Brink (✉) · F. Esselmann · L. Henke
CONCERN GmbH, Cologne, Germany
e-mail: alexander.brink@uni-bayreuth.de; frank.esselmann@concern.de; leonhard.henke@concern.de

A.-S. Christ (ed.), *Corporate Digital Responsibility*, Future of Business and Finance, https://doi.org/10.1007/978-3-032-14793-6_15

1 The Twin Transformation Challenge

The term "twin transformation" describes the simultaneous implementation of digital progress and sustainable development. The term was coined in 2021 by the management consultancy Accenture (cf. Accenture, 2021). According to studies, companies that are leaders in both areas—so-called twin transformers—are considered to be particularly fit for the future.

There are several reasons for this: Firstly, twin transformers are characterised by the fact that they specifically combine sustainable business models with digital technologies. Secondly, they strategically pool resources in order to effectively scale sustainable innovations. Thirdly, they assume holistic responsibility, which is also reflected in the consideration and measurement of nonfinancial key figures. Fourthly, they work closely with partners to create sustainable lifecycles. And fifthly, they actively empower and integrate their employees in this process of dual transformation (cf. ibid).

Data from Accenture research shows that companies that consistently combine digitalisation and sustainability have significantly higher chances of success than companies that only serve one of the two fields (cf. ibid)—especially if they pursue a combined strategy. However, the debate remains largely superficial: although sustainability is often described as an economic opportunity or a social mandate, there is usually a lack of concrete ethical guidelines or links to the UN Sustainable Development Goals (SDGs), for example. Climate policy aspects are also often overemphasised, while social goals such as poverty reduction, health, or food security remain underexposed.

It should also be noted that digital innovations can also have adverse consequences—for example, through rebound effects, where efficiency gains are neutralised by increasing consumption. Truly sustainable transformation, therefore, requires more than technological efficiency: it needs normative orientation, critical reflection, and the willingness to make conflicting goals transparent. It must be recognised that the twin transformation is a continuous learning and development process. No company is perfect—organisations are vulnerable, operate under changing conditions, and have to keep pace with rapid technological progress.

In short, the twin transformation is not just a management strategy but an ethical and social challenge. Anyone who takes it seriously must think beyond climate protection—and must not reduce sustainability to communication or individual measures. Otherwise, there is a high risk of greenwashing—especially if the learning character in a changing world is ignored and the impression of a kind of final solution is created.

2 The Corporate Digital Responsibility Journey

The digital transformation is profoundly changing the economy and society. New technologies are opening up enormous potential—from automation and data analysis to networked systems. However, this progress also raises fundamental questions:

How can technology be designed in such a way that it serves people, not just economic interests? How can data be used responsibly and digital autonomy protected? And how can digitalisation be made sustainable, fair, and inclusive?

2.1 CDR as the Key to Human-Centred Digitalisation

This is precisely where Corporate Digital Responsibility (CDR) comes in. CDR describes the responsibility of companies to use digital technologies and data in an economically, socially, and ecologically responsible way. The aim is not only to fulfil regulatory requirements but also to actively contribute to the common good and a resilient, just society. CDR thus forms the foundation of human-centric digitalisation—digitalisation that is geared towards people's needs, rights, and values (cf. Brink, 2025).

CDR covers key areas such as the responsible data handling, the promotion of digital education, climate and resource protection, the involvement of employees, and ensuring digital participation (cf. CDR Initiative, 2021). These five fields of action of the CDR Code provide companies with concrete guidance on how they can shape digital innovations based on values and in the interests of the common good. All fields of action aim to promote trust in digital innovations and safeguard core values such as justice, nondiscrimination, and self-determination. For example, Principle 5 "Autonomy" of the CDR Initiative states that consumers should be able to make self-determined decisions about their data. In addition, Principle 1 ("Fundamental social values") requires technical systems to be used in accordance with democracy, freedom, and equal treatment (cf. ibid). Scientifically, CDR is described as a *set of shared values and norms guiding an organisation's operations* (Lobschat et al., 2021). CDR is closely linked to digital ethics, which deals with fundamental moral issues in the use of digital technologies (cf. Brink, 2022).

At the same time, digitalisation is highly ambivalent—in other words, it can have both positive and negative effects. For example, artificial intelligence can help to make medical diagnoses faster and more accurately—and thus save lives. However, the same technology can lead to discrimination if it is nontransparent or biased, for example, in automated application procedures or credit scoring. This ambivalence makes it clear that digitalisation is not a sure-fire success—it has to be shaped in a human-centric way (cf. Brink, 2025). Corporate digital responsibility provides the necessary ethical and strategic framework for this and supports companies in exploiting the opportunities of digitalisation without losing sight of the risks. In these highly transformative times of uncertainty and inexplicability, this is perhaps more important than ever before in human history.

2.2 The Role of the CDR Initiative and the Forms of Cooperation

The CDR Initiative, founded in 2018 by the Federal Ministry of Justice and Consumer Protection, defines CDR as:

> (…) voluntary entrepreneurial activities that go beyond legal requirements, particularly in the interests of consumers, and play an active role in shaping the digital world for the benefit of society. (CDR Initiative, 2021)

The CDR Initiative pursues the goal of strategically anchoring digital responsibility in companies. It supports organisations in further developing their processes, products, and systems in terms of value-based digitalisation. The initiative supports companies not only in terms of content but also methodically: through workshops, dialogue formats, feedback processes, and practical guidelines. It is considered one of the most advanced and strongest initiatives for shaping the twin transformation, in Europe and beyond.

> The launch of the German CDR-code in June 2021 is a milestone in capturing the threats from digital transformation through voluntary commitments from signatories (…). (Merbecks, 2023, p. 1027)

In order to enable companies and organisations at different stages of development and with different objectives to participate, the CDR Initiative offers three clearly differentiated forms of cooperation:

1. **Membership:** Membership is aimed at companies that wish to make a long-term and strategic contribution to the further development of CDR. Members are actively involved in the CDR Initiative network, contribute their own experience, and at the same time benefit from the exchange with other organisations, academia, politics, and civil society. They contribute to key topics, help shape the content of the initiative, and support the dissemination of CDR Principles in business and society.
2. **Thematic partnership:** Thematic partnerships offer the opportunity for targeted collaboration on specific issues or projects. This form of cooperation is particularly suitable for organisations that wish to contribute their expertise or interests in specific areas such as data ethics, diversity, algorithmic fairness, or disinformation. Thematic partners participate selectively, for example, in working groups, studies, pilot projects, or dialogue formats, and thus make an important contribution to the thematic deepening and practical implementation of CDR.
3. **Development partnership:** The development partnership is aimed at organisations that want to systematically integrate CDR into their structures and processes. They receive methodological and content-related support from the CDR Initiative, for example, through workshops, coaching, maturity analyses, and action planning. The aim is to embed CDR in a company-specific way, promote internal anchoring, and achieve sustainable development goals in a digital

context. Development partners benefit from tried-and-tested tools and access to empirical values from the CDR network.

These models enable flexible access to the initiative—whether as a driving force, learning partner, or implementation driver.

2.3 New Requirements for the CDR Initiative: Flexible, Focused, Impact-Oriented

The relevance of corporate digital responsibility is growing—and with it, the demands on the initiative itself. Over the past few years, the team behind the CDR Initiative has worked diligently and with persistence to advance its mission. While significant progress has been made, they continue to learn and evolve, refining their approach as the landscape develops. This is because CDR cannot be viewed in isolation, but is directly linked to current social, political, and economic developments—the most current and urgent of which are:

1. **Technological change:** The pace of innovation is enormous: artificial intelligence, quantum computing, neurotechnologies, and cloud infrastructures are changing business models, working methods, and realities of life. At the same time, the influence of these technologies on people is becoming ever stronger—digital and real are merging.
2. **Social pressure:** The digital divide is deepening: tech-savvy groups are increasingly integrating digital tools into their everyday lives, while other sections of the population are sceptical or overwhelmed. Trust and participation are becoming imbalanced.
3. **Geopolitical dependencies:** Europe is often dependent on monopolised providers for key digital infrastructures. Digital sovereignty is becoming a strategic issue—also in the context of data protection, security, and ethics.
4. **Economic transformation:** Traditional market mechanisms are coming under pressure due to monopolisation and a lack of transparency. At the same time, sustainability is becoming a cross-cutting issue. Companies must think about ecological responsibility and digital innovation together.

The dynamic development in the digital and social environment also presents the CDR Initiative with new challenges. Its relevance and visibility are growing continuously—especially at a time when questions of digital responsibility, ethics, and social impact are increasingly coming to the fore. At the same time, however, it is clear that the CDR Initiative cannot cover all topics at the same time. The digital transformation is complex and fast-moving and encompasses a broad spectrum of technological, regulatory, and social issues. Complete coverage of this diversity by a centralised initiative is neither realistic nor strategically expedient.

Furthermore, CDR should not be seen as a mere subtopic within the sustainability debate. Although there are close links in terms of content—for example, with regard to ecological responsibility, social participation, or the design of sustainable supply chains—CDR brings its own perspectives, special issues, and specific technical expertise, particularly in the areas of data ethics, algorithmic transparency, digital autonomy, and corporate responsibility in the digital space. The CDR Initiative is therefore faced with the need to adapt more quickly and flexibly to new developments without losing its depth and substance. This means that it must prioritise in a focused manner but at the same time remain open to new impulses and future challenges.

The experiences of recent years provide important insights for this further development. They are particularly clear: Firstly, joint learning across industry boundaries is a decisive success factor. The exchange of perspectives, experiences, and solutions not only promotes the quality of the dialogue but also contributes to innovation and practicality. Secondly, it is clear that a holistic perspective is necessary—a perspective that links the economic, social, and ecological aspects of digitalisation and considers them in their interaction. Isolated measures fall short; integrated approaches are needed that keep an eye on the big picture. Thirdly, there is a clear need for action in the area of digital responsibility in many companies, but there is often no clear starting point. The issues are complex, responsibilities are not clearly defined, and existing resources are often focused on short-term digital projects.

What is more, CDR-relevant activities are already taking place in many organisations, but are not explicitly recognised as part of corporate digital responsibility. They therefore remain invisible, disorganised, and without strategic impact—even though they certainly contribute to digital responsibility in terms of content. This is where the CDR Initiative comes in: through methodological support, networking, orientation, and structured development paths, it aims to enable organisations to make digital responsibility visible, systematise it, and integrate it into their own strategy.

With this in mind, the CDR Initiative has formulated a central methodological goal:to create a flexible, adaptive framework that offers companies orientation and concrete development opportunities—regardless of industry, size, or previous experience. At the heart of this approach is a maturity model that visualises a company's level of digital responsibility and, at the same time, derives recommendations for action. It serves as a structured basis for self-assessments, workshops, action plans, and continuous improvement. This model makes it clear where a company stands, what it is already doing, and what the next sensible step could be. It promotes targeted learning, strengthens internal acceptance, and systematically links CDR with existing sustainability and digital strategies, for example, in the context of ESG reporting.

2.4 The Architecture of CDR

CDR, as understood by the CDR Initiative, is based on a clear and structured architecture that provides companies with guidance for responsible digitalisation and whose "masterpiece" is the maturity model. It consists of a total of seven elements that complement each other and together create a practical framework for digital responsibility. In addition to this technical architecture of the seven elements, there is an equally central, albeit often implicit, dimension: the governance of the CDR. It encompasses the management, coordination, and further development of the elements as a coherent overall system—in other words, the "choreography" of the maturity process. In this sense, governance forms the organisational framework for responsible digital transformation.

1. The nine ethical **CDR Principles** form the normative foundation. They define fundamental values such as basic social values, fairness, transparency, and sustainability and serve as guidelines for digital corporate strategies.
2. The **CDR Code** is a voluntary commitment for companies that goes beyond legal requirements. It ensures that digital responsibility does not just remain theoretical but becomes visible through corporate action.
3. In order to put the principles into practice, the code defines five central **CDR Fields of Action**: (1) data handling, (2) education, (3) climate and resource protection, (4) employee involvement, and (5) inclusion. Each of these fields addresses specific challenges of the digital transformation.
4. The fields of action contain concrete **CDR Goals** that companies can use as a guide for their measures. They range from data protection and algorithmic fairness to the promotion of digital participation and sustainable IT structures.
5. These goals are realised through specific **CDR Measures** that companies can take to assume digital responsibility. These include training on digital ethics, strategies for sustainable IT use, and the transparent design of algorithms.
6. To assess and develop their digital responsibility, companies can use the **CDR Quick Check**, which provides an initial assessment of where they stand.
7. Finally, the **CDR Maturity Model** helps companies to systematically record and further develop their progress.

The seven elements are sensibly coordinated with each other and result in a coherent overall concept that has been developed over several years, in close dialogue between politics and business. The individual elements are now explained in detail.

Element 1: CDR Principles

The nine principles form the ethical foundation for decisions and actions. They set the direction for responsible digitalisation. The CDR Initiative of the BMUV has defined the following nine principles in a multi-stakeholder process (cf. CDR Initiative, 2021).

1. **Fundamental social values**: Technology must support democracy, freedom, the social market economy, and equal treatment.
2. **Human-centricity**: People are at the heart of digital innovation.
3. **Creating benefits**: Technologies must offer tangible added value and be ethically justifiable.
4. **Avoid harm**: Digital systems should be secure, calculable, and free of risks for consumers.

5. **Autonomy**: Consumers should have self-determination over their data and digital decisions.
6. **Fairness**: Access to the digital world must be open and nondiscriminatory for everyone.
7. **Transparency**: Companies must provide clear information about how their technologies work.
8. **Accountability**: Clearly defined human decision-makers bear responsibility for digital processes.
9. **Sustainability**: Digitalisation should conserve resources and be in line with the UN Sustainable Development Goals.

The member companies undertake to follow these principles, which serve as guidelines for the CDR Code.

Element 2: CDR Code

The CDR Code of the CDR Initiative is a voluntary commitment by companies that go beyond legal requirements and represents a clear commitment to digital responsibility. Companies that sign up to this code voluntarily commit to actively shaping the digital world for the benefit of society (cf. ibid).

The CDR Code is more than a collection of good intentions—it is a clear framework for action for a digital future based on responsibility, sustainability, and fairness. The public commitment of the signatory companies not only creates transparency but also sends a strong signal for a digital world that puts people at the centre. The digital transformation can only become a success story for everyone if it is shaped with ethical principles and social responsibility. The CDR Code provides a valuable basis for this—a promise for a sustainable, fair, and responsible digital future. These member companies commit to complying with the CDR Code and publish a CDR report in which they outline their measures and progress in the area of digital responsibility (e.g., DKB, 2023; ING-DiBa AG, 2023; Otto GmbH & Co KG, 2023; Telefónica Deutschland Holding AG, 2023). The code is concretised in the CDR Fields of Action.

Element 3: CDR Fields of Action

Fields of action are thematic areas in which specific measures and strategies are implemented in order to achieve overarching goals. They serve as operational guidelines that help companies or organisations to put their principles and commitments into practice. The CDR Initiative has defined five fields of action (cf. CDR Initiative, 2021):

1. **Data handling**: Data protection, ethical data use, and protection against algorithmic bias.
2. **Education**: Strengthening digital skills, raising awareness of risks, and promoting responsible behaviour.
3. **Climate and resource protection**: Developing environmentally friendly IT solutions and reducing the energy consumption of digital systems.

4. **Employee involvement**: Prepare employees for the digital transformation and actively involve them in decision-making processes.
5. **Inclusion**: Ensure that no one is excluded by digitalisation and that everyone benefits from technological advances.

Data is the core component of digital responsibility and forms the basis for all other areas of CDR. It is the raw material that drives digital change, and its responsible use determines the quality and impact of all further CDR endeavours. Only if data is processed responsibly can the digital responsibility of companies be realised in a sustainable and socially effective way. Each field of action has specific CDR Goals that the member companies are guided by.

Element 4: CDR Goals
In the respective fields of action, specific goals were defined together with the member companies of the CDR Initiative in an elaborate coordination process. Most of the goals were adopted for data handling, as this is the central field of action in the code (cf. ibid).

Goals in Field of Action 1: Data Handling

- Working actively to counter bias in data analysis
- Responsible, fair, and transparent profiling
- Ensuring consumer sovereignty and autonomy
- Promoting responsible design of technology in data handling
- Ensuring responsible data handling in the company
- Taking responsibility for data handling beyond our own company
- Systematically enhancing data and cybersecurity

Goals in Field of Action 2: Education

- Informing about opportunities and risks and empowering consumers and employees to take autonomous action
- Informing about ethical issues of digitalisation

Goals in Field of Action 3: Climate and Resource Protection

- Strengthening digital solutions to protect our environment
- Designing and using information and communication technologies that protect the environment and resources

Goals in Field of Action 4: Employee Involvement

- Involving employees in design and decision-making in the digital transformation
- Preparing employees for change and supporting them during the transformation

Goals in Field of Action 5: Inclusion

- Working to counter access barriers to products and services
- Promoting solutions to support participation
- The goals are implemented through measures reported on by the member companies. These measures are considered best practice.

Element 5: CDR Measures

CDR Measures are concrete corporate activities that serve to realise the CDR Goals in the defined fields of action. While the CDR Goals provide the strategic framework, the CDR Measures are the operational steps with which companies actually put digital responsibility into practice. The following is an example of one goal per field of action with a company example (e.g., DKB, 2023; ING-DiBa AG, 2023; Otto GmbH & Co KG, 2023; Telefónica Deutschland Holding AG, 2023; Zalando SE, 2023) (Table 1).

The examples illustrate how diverse the approaches of the member companies of the CDR Initiative are when it comes to promoting responsible and sustainable digitalisation. The CDR Quick Check and the CDR Maturity Model are intended to ensure that companies can continue to develop. This also explicitly addresses companies that are not yet as advanced in CDR development but are willing to become more involved in this area. In this sense, the CDR Initiative of the BMUV sees itself as a teaching and learning platform.

Element 6: The CDR Quick Check

The CDR Quick Check is a self-assessment tool that helps companies analyse their current status in the area of corporate digital responsibility (CDR). Companies can quickly and in a structured manner determine how well they are already implementing digital responsibility. The quick check enables an initial assessment of the

Table 1 Exemplary interaction of CDR Field of Action, CDR Goal, and CDR Measure of the member companies (Own Illustration)

CDR field of action	CDR goal	CDR measure of a company
Data handling	Systematically enhancing data and cybersecurity	DKB: Introduction of an information security campaign on data and cybersecurity
Education	Informing about ethical issues of digitalisation	ING: Contact point for employees for ethical issues relating to data collection and use
Climate and resource protection	Designing and using information and communication technologies that protect the environment and resources	Otto Group: Environmentally conscious software development through sustainable programming
Employee involvement	Preparing employees for change and supporting them during the transformation	Telefónica: "Digital Basics Learning Journey" learning program to teach digital skills
Inclusion	Promoting solutions to support participation	Zalando: Adapting the online platform for people with disabilities

current situation and identifies the need for action in the five CDR Fields of Action. The results help to derive targeted measures to systematically further develop digital responsibility.

The CDR Quick Check is based on the fields of action and objectives of the CDR Code. The CDR Quick Check is a low-threshold entry point for systematically recording digital responsibility and developing it further in a targeted manner. Companies receive a clear overview of strengths and areas for development. This means that the original idea of viewing the CDR Code merely as a reporting tool is increasingly becoming the basis for actively assuming digital responsibility. The CDR Quick Check puts the code into practice and helps companies to orient themselves.

Element 7: The CDR Maturity Model

Building on this, the maturity model is a systematic assessment framework that companies can use to record and further develop their current status in the implementation of CDR. Based on the CDR Quick Check, it helps and motivates companies to anchor digital responsibility in the organisation in a structured and gradual manner. Companies can analyse how far they have come with the implementation of their CDR strategy. They can also document the current status of the transformation process and facilitate internal communication and increase acceptance within the organisation.

The model also shows which steps are necessary to expand digital responsibility in a targeted manner. Companies can set their individual priorities without having to bring every topic to the highest level of maturity. Governance is not understood here as a separate function, but as an integrative control mechanism that enables the strategic embedding and continuous improvement of CDR processes. It combines normative principles with organisational implementation and translates values into operational reality.

- The maturity model is based on the Capability Maturity Model Integration (CMMI) and consists of five maturity levels. This is a globally recognised model that helps organisations to improve their processes and make them more efficient. (CMMI, 2025) (Table 2):

Table 2 The maturity model (Authors' illustration)

Maturity level	Maturity level description
Initial	CDR topics are addressed sporadically, but not yet systematically
Projected	Initial structures are created, and the organisation experiments with CDR approaches. Temporary contradictions with other company goals are still acceptable
Defined	CDR Goals are clearly formulated, tasks are assigned and communicated throughout the organisation
Controlled	Progress is regularly reviewed, and key performance indicators are in place to measure success
Optimised	The CDR Measures are continuously improved and have a high priority in the corporate strategy

3 The Philosophy of Maturity Models and Their Technical Concretisation

The philosophical background to maturity models can be found in Aristotle's idea of the development of human potential and the capability approach of Amartya Sen and Martha Nussbaum. Aristotle understands maturity as a process in which a being approaches its inner goal ("telos")—through practice, virtue, and rational action, a person achieves a successful life ("eudaimonia") (Aristotle, 1999). Sen and Nussbaum take up this idea and develop it further into the question: What does a person need in order to be able to live a truly free and self-determined life? Their focus is not on mere results but on real capabilities, i.e., on what opportunities and possibilities a person actually has to realise their potential (cf. Sen, 1999; Nussbaum, 2011). Applied to organisations and technical systems, this means that maturity is not only reflected in performance or structure but also in the growing ability to pursue meaningful goals, take responsibility, and empower people. In this sense, maturity models are more than just tools for increasing efficiency—they are oriented towards the quality of development in terms of realising potential and ethical responsibility.

This idea of maturity as the development of potential and empowerment can not only be applied to individuals but also offers a viable analogy for the development of organisations and technical systems. Just as people develop according to their abilities and values, organisations can also mature by becoming capable of learning, taking responsibility, and networking ethically with their environment. Even technical systems, for example, in the context of digitalisation, do not merely follow functional progress, but go through complex development phases in which their maturity is measured by their ability to support human needs in a meaningful way (cf. Brink, 2025).

The maturity model is to be understood precisely in this sense: It is a technical system development based on a human-centred understanding of maturity. It not only measures the state of technology or processes but also reveals the extent to which an organisation is prepared to shape digital innovation in harmony with human development, social values, and ecological responsibility. It thus combines technological structure with ethical depth. Maturity models offer organisations a structured approach for the systematic classification and further development of complex topics. The CDR Initiative deliberately chose this tool in order to address key challenges in the field of CDR—including technological dynamics, social polarisation, and regulatory complexity—in a methodologically sound manner.

The origins of maturity models lie in quality and process management. Philip B. Crosby's "Quality Management Maturity Grid" is regarded as the first structured stage model that offered companies five development phases for assessing and improving their quality processes (cf. Crosby, 1979). It paved the way for later standardised frameworks such as the Capability Maturity Model (CMM), which was initially introduced in the 1990s for the assessment of software development processes. In its further development into the CMMI (Capability Maturity Model Integration), the model was widely used in various organisational areas (cf. CMMI, 2025).

Maturity models divide complex transformation processes into comprehensible development stages, for example, the Industry 4.0 Maturity Index organises the process towards digitally networked industrial production in the context of Industry 4.0 (cf. acatech 2020). They fulfil three central functions (cf. Pöppelbuß/Röglinger, 2011):

1. **Descriptive:** They enable a structured determination of the current status.
2. **Prescriptive:** They offer recommendations for further development.
3. **Compensatory:** They create comparability between organisations (benchmarking).

In this way, they not only provide a development logic but also an orientation framework for the internal management and external communication of progress, especially in multilayered areas such as CDR (cf. Pöppelbuß/Röglinger, 2011; Lasrado, 2018; Bititci et al., 2015; Dijkman et al., 2016).

Despite their standardised structure, maturity models have an inherent flexibility that allows them to be adapted to specific industry requirements and different organisational sizes. This adaptability is particularly crucial in the diverse context of CDR, which encompasses numerous fields of action such as data handling, climate and resource protection, and inclusion, on the one hand, and addresses a wide variety of organisational forms, on the other hand. Companies can therefore set individual priorities and effectively integrate the models into their existing management systems.

A key feature of successful maturity models is their ability to systematically combine different fields of action. By taking a holistic view of different subject areas, they create synergies and promote an integrated approach within the organisation. At the same time, maturity models are explicitly geared towards continuous organisational learning. They enable regular self-reflection and systematic further development on the basis of defined criteria, which leads to a sustainable improvement in organisational performance in the long term.

Particularly, in the context of network organisations such as the CDR Initiative, maturity models also serve as common reference points that support cross-organisational exchange and knowledge building. Particularly, in the membership concept of development partnerships, they offer a common language and clear orientation for the practice-oriented further development of CDR Measures, including concrete challenges and solution approaches.

4 A CDR Maturity Model and Its Applications

The maturity model developed in the CDR Initiative has proven to be stable and viable in various application contexts. At its centre are the principles, fields of action, and objectives of the CDR Initiative, which offer consistent orientation despite their flexibility. The conceptual strength of the model lies in its ability to understand CDR not as an isolated topic but as an integrative component of corporate behaviour. CDR is not a separate function—rather, it forms the basis for responsible, sustainable organisational action as a whole.

A central development principle was: No development without a benefit perspective. Specific added value was therefore formulated for each maturity level, which can be directly realised in practice, for example, through increased process reliability, better decision-making ability, regulatory protection, or improved impact on stakeholders. This focus on benefits has proven to be particularly suitable for organisations that pursue CDR not for compliance reasons but out of strategic conviction. Based on previous experience with development partners, three typical stages can be distinguished:

1. **Creating Orientation Through the CDR Quick Check:** The CDR Quick Check is the low-threshold introduction. In around 10–20 min, organisations receive an initial assessment of their digital responsibility practices along key areas of action. The tool is deliberately kept lean and provides an initial assessment of strengths, weaknesses, and development potential. It is particularly suitable for internal self-reflection and awareness-raising as well as for preparing a workshop, for example, for the strategic positioning or prioritisation of measures.
2. **Establishment of Lean Governance Without Bureaucracy:** If CDR is pursued further, a lightweight governance set-up is recommended. Four pragmatic steps have proven successful in several development partnerships:
   - **Anchoring:** Explicit inclusion of digital responsibility in the vision and strategy, for example, through digital guidelines
   - **Focusing:** Prioritising the key fields of action
   - **Stocktaking:** Detailed analysis of the status quo and development of a perspective plan
   - **Change support:** Planning of communication and participation formats to support the cultural change
     These steps can be realised with manageable effort. The establishment of a lightweight governance structure marks a key development step in this process: it creates organisational commitment and the necessary coordination between the elements of the CDR architecture. Governance here does not mean bureaucracy, but rather meaningful anchoring, reflection, and assignment of responsibility.
3. **Integration From Project to Practice:** After the initial implementation and first measures, CDR is increasingly establishing itself as part of regular structures. Organisations such as Deutsche Telekom show how the topic can be integrated into existing processes, roles, and routines after a project phase. This is not only just about rules and regulations but also about cultural work: CDR is becoming part of the common orientation, for example, in product development, personnel development, or stakeholder dialogue.

5 Conclusion and Outlook

A key success factor of the CDR Maturity Model lies in its consistent orientation towards corporate practice. In recent years, the CDR Initiative has built up a broad portfolio of case studies—from small and medium-sized enterprises to large corporations—which not only provides orientation but also facilitates exchange between organisations. These practical references promote peer learning, encourage reflection, and create spaces for constructive dialogue on corporate responsibility in the digital age.

The CDR Maturity Model combines ambition with suitability for everyday use: it makes digital responsibility tangible without overburdening organisations. The three development stages provide a low-threshold but structured introduction to the implementation of CDR. They promote systematic learning, create a common frame of reference, and strengthen cross-organisational connectivity—particularly relevant in times of twin transformation, in which ecological and digital requirements are increasingly intertwined.

At the same time, it is important to reflect self-critically: Maturity models are not patent solutions. They can help to provide orientation and make progress visible, but they run the risk of oversimplifying complex developments or becoming rigid in checklists. The real added value lies not in the model itself but in its lively application—in dialogue, in adapting it to the respective context, and in continuously questioning one's own positions.

The coming years will show whether and how the CDR Maturity Model establishes itself as a permanent management tool. One thing is clear: the requirements for corporate responsibility in the digital transformation continue to increase—but the tools are also evolving. The CDR Initiative model offers a practical, adaptive framework that is open to further development and new application scenarios. In the future, it will be crucial to further develop the governance of the CDR Initiative as well as its substantive architecture. Only if control processes, learning cycles, and normative guidelines are given equal consideration can corporate digital responsibility unfold its full effect.

Competing Interests A condensed and translated version of this chapter was previously published in an open-access publication: Brink, A., Esselman, F., & Henke, L. (2025). Das CDR-Reifegradmodell. Leitfaden für digitale Verantwortung in turbulenten Zeiten. In A. Brink (Eds.). Fairness im Zeitalter von KI. (pp. 67–84). Nomos. This reuse was made with the permission of the publisher of that edition.

References

Accenture. (2021). *The European double up: A twin strategy that will strengthen competitiveness*. Retrieved July 29, 2025, from https://www.accenture.com/content/dam/accenture/final/a-com-migration/r3-3/pdf/pdf-144/accenture-the-european-double-up.pdf.

Aristotle. (1999). *Nicomachean ethics* (T. Irwin, Trans.). Hackett Publishing.

Bititci, U. S., Bourne, M., Cross, J. A., Farris, J. A., Nudurupati, S. S., & Sang, K. (2015). Towards a theoretical foundation for performance measurement and management. *International Journal of Management Reviews, 17*(4), 534–536. https://doi.org/10.1111/ijmr.12086

Brink, A. (2022). Digital ethics. In M. S. Aßländer (Ed.), *Handbook of business ethics* (2nd ed., pp. 615–624). Metzler.

Brink, A. (2025). *Corporate digital responsibility: Human-centred digitalisation*. NOMOS.

CDR Initiative. (2021). *Corporate digital responsibility code: Voluntary self-commitment with report*. Retrieved July 29, 2025, from https://cdr-initiative.de/uploads/files/2024-01_Kodex_CDR-Initiative.pdf.

CMMI. (2025). Retrieved July 29, 2025, from https://cmmiinstitute.com/.

Crosby, P. B. (1979). *Quality is free: The art of making quality certain*. McGraw-Hill.
Dijkman, R., Lammers, S. V., & de Jong, A. (2016). Properties that influence business process management maturity and its effect on organisational performance. *Information Systems Frontiers, 18*(4), 717–734. https://doi.org/10.1007/s10796-015-9554-5
DKB. (2023). *CDR code of action report*. Retrieved July 29, 2025, from https://cdr-initiative.de/uploads/files/Berichte/DKB-Report-2023.pdf.
ING-DiBa AG. (2023). *CDR code of conduct action report*. Retrieved July 29, 2025, from https://cdr-initiative.de/uploads/files/Berichte/ING-Report-2023.pdf.
Lasrado, L. A. (2018). Set theoretic approach to maturity models (PhD thesis, Copenhagen Business School). Copenhagen Business School.
Lobschat, L., Mueller, B., Eggers, F., Brandimarte, L., Diefenbach, S., Kroschke, M., & Wirtz, J. (2021). Corporate digital responsibility. *Journal of Business Research, 122*, 875–888. https://doi.org/10.1016/j.jbusres.2019.10.006
Merbecks, U. (2023). Corporate digital responsibility (CDR) in Germany: Background and first empirical evidence from DAX 30 companies in 2020. *Journal of Business Economics, 94*(7–8), 1025–1049. https://doi.org/10.1007/s11573-023-01148-6
Nussbaum, M. C. (2011). *Creating capabilities: The human development approach*. Belknap Press of Harvard University Press.
Otto GmbH & Co KG. (2023). *CDR code of conduct action report*. Retrieved July 29, 2025, from https://cdr-initiative.de/uploads/files/Berichte/Otto-Group-Report-2023.pdf.
Pöppelbuß, J., & Röglinger, M. (2011). What makes a useful maturity model? A framework for general design principles for maturity models and its demonstration in business process management. In V. Tuunainen (Ed.), *Proceedings of the 19th European conference on information systems (ECIS 2011)*, Helsinki, Finland, June 9–11, 2011. ISBN 978-952-60-3574-1.
Sen, A. (1999). *Development as freedom*. Alfred A. Knopf.
Telefónica Deutschland Holding AG. (2023). *CDR code of conduct action report*. Retrieved July 29, 2025, from https://cdr-initiative.de/uploads/files/Berichte/Telefonica-Report-2023.pdf.
Zalando, S. E.. (2023). *CDR code of conduct action report*. Retrieved July 29, 2025, from https://cdr-initiative.de/uploads/files/Berichte/Zalando-Report-2022.pdf.

Prof. Dr. Alexander Brink, Professor of Business Ethics, Partner at CONCERN GmbH and Scientific Advisor to the CDR Initiative at Federal Ministry of Justice and Consumer Protection.

Dr. Frank Esselmann, Partner at CONCERN GmbH and Market Advisor to the CDR Initiative at Federal Ministry of Justice and Consumer Protection.

Leonhard Henke, Project Manager at CONCERN GmbH and Governance Advisor to the CDR Initiative at Federal Ministry of Justice and Consumer Protection.

Corporate Digital Responsibility (CDR) and Its Role in AI Governance

Sergio Genovesi and Ismael El-Hadj

Abstract

This chapter examines the application of Corporate Digital Responsibility (CDR) principle to the implementation of AI governance frameworks. With the introduction of the EU AI Act, organizations face new regulatory demands that classic IT governance cannot fully address, especially regarding AI-specific risks and ethical considerations. The chapter argues that effective AI governance must go beyond compliance, embedding principles such as transparency, fairness, privacy, accountability, sustainability, and stakeholder engagement into organizational processes. It highlights the challenges of translating high-level ethical values into actionable requirements, particularly in fast-paced, resource-constrained environments. The authors emphasize the importance of cross-functional collaboration, continuous AI literacy training, and the allocation of clear responsibilities to ensure responsible AI development and deployment. By leveraging existing governance structures and fostering a culture of ethical reflection, organizations can better manage the risks and societal impacts of AI. Ultimately, the chapter demonstrates that CDR provides a comprehensive foundation for responsible AI governance, enabling organizations to align innovation with ethical standards and societal expectations in an evolving regulatory landscape.

S. Genovesi (✉) · I. El-Hadj
SKAD, Frankfurt am Main, Germany
e-mail: s.genovesi@sk-advisory.com; i.el-hadj@sk-advisory.com

A.-S. Christ (ed.), *Corporate Digital Responsibility*, Future of Business and Finance, https://doi.org/10.1007/978-3-032-14793-6_16

1 AI Governance Beyond Regulatory Compliance

Since 2023, the Frankfurt-based management consulting company SKAD AG has pioneered the implementation of AI governance frameworks in several companies and groups in the financial, insurance, and other sectors. This chapter draws from our project experience and provides practical insights about establishing best practices, corporate values, and policies for the responsible development and use of AI within companies.

In August 2024, the European Artificial Intelligence Act (EU AI Act) (Regulation (EU), 2024/1689) entered into force, introducing new regulatory requirements for AI systems and duties for the actors involved in their value chain. To prepare for EU AI Act compliance, companies have increasingly become interested in establishing AI governance frameworks to ensure their alignment with the new rules. Indeed, during the last decade, AI systems were usually managed within classic IT governance frameworks, missing AI-specific risk management measures. Because of the lack of focus on AI risks, these frameworks are now proving unfit to address the higher quality standards for AI systems set by the EU AI Act. Therefore, one of the most important requirements for our AI Governance projects is to guarantee legal compliance with the EU AI Act. However, in our understanding, the goals of a functioning AI Governance are not limited to guaranteeing legal compliance and include many other aspects—ranging from facilitating processes inside the organization and ensuring functional knowledge transfer and communication to analyzing AI-specific risks and establishing ethical principles and best practices in developing responsible AI.

The fundamental principles of responsible AI governance are best understood through the lens of Corporate Digital Responsibility (CDR). CDR focuses on a company's ethical, sustainable, and accountable management of digital technologies and data throughout their life cycle, considering the impact on customers, employees, society, and the environment (Lobschat et al., 2021). It also emphasizes the importance of embedding moral obligations related to digital transformation, such as responsible data governance, transparency, and explainability, into an organization's culture and processes (Carl & Hinz, 2024). Furthermore, CDR encourages organizations to look beyond mere compliance, promoting the active alignment of digital strategies and practices with the long-term goal of building trust and digital sustainability among all stakeholders (Knopf & Pick, 2023). Applied to AI governance, this approach means not only meeting regulatory requirements but also proactively addressing ethical risks, fostering openness and stakeholder engagement within the organization, and ensuring continuous monitoring of the societal effects of AI systems. In this way, CDR serves as a comprehensive and value-driven foundation for a responsible governance of AI technologies.

2 Corporate Digital Responsibility as Framework for AI Governance

Corporate Social Responsibility (CSR) has long been the main concept guiding organizations in fulfilling their social and environmental obligations. However, over the last years, the rapid advancement of digital technologies has generated novel ethical, societal, and environmental issues that traditional CSR frameworks are not fully equipped to address. As a response, the concept of CDR has emerged, focusing specifically on the opportunities and risks associated with digitalization. The introduction of this new area of action has sparked considerable debate among scholars regarding its precise relationship to CSR. Some see CDR as a subdomain within the broader field of digital CSR, while others insist that the scale and complexity of ethical challenges posed by digital technologies justify framing CDR as a distinct and independent discipline (Knopf & Pick, 2023; Lobschat et al., 2021). Regardless of which position is adopted, there is general agreement that companies could benefit from developing a CDR concept to guide their own digital development and transformation processes (Knopf & Pick, 2023).

Applying CDR to AI governance, it is possible to identify several dimensions that are recurring both in CDR literature (Trier et al., 2023) and in ethical guidelines for the responsible development and use of AI (High-Level Expert Group on AI, 2019). These dimensions are as follows:

- **Transparency**: Organizations must ensure system traceability, intelligibility, and explainability, as well as communication of relevant information to different stakeholders according to their skills and responsibilities (Trier et al., 2023; High-Level Expert Group on AI, 2019; Genovesi et al., 2025).
- **Fairness**: Companies are required to identify and address possible sources of discrimination, as well as proactively design software and its application environment in an inclusive way (Trier et al., 2023; High-Level Expert Group on AI, 2019; Genovesi et al., 2024).
- **Privacy and data governance**: Organizations need to treat data in a privacy-aware and purpose-bound manner and establish mechanisms for quality and integrity assurance as well as information access management (Trier et al., 2023; High-Level Expert Group on AI, 2019).
- **Accountability and human oversight**: It is necessary to identify roles and responsibilities for the design and deployment of AI systems and to establish audit, reporting, and management processes for new risks and incidents (Trier et al., 2023; High-Level Expert Group on AI, 2019).
- **Sustainability**: Companies should focus on the environmental and social impacts of digital technologies, including energy consumption of data centers, resource-intensive hardware production, and long-term societal consequences of digitization (Trier et al., 2023; High-Level Expert Group on AI, 2019; van Wynsberghe, 2021).
- **Security, technical robustness, and safety**: Organizations must protect digital assets and infrastructure against malicious attacks, data breaches, and system

failures and test system performance to ensure general safety, accuracy, reliability, and reproducibility (Trier et al., 2023; High-Level Expert Group on AI, 2019).
- **Stakeholder engagement**: Companies should include internal and external stakeholders in processes related to AI design, implementation, and oversight, thereby enhancing procedural legitimacy and ensuring that multiple perspectives inform the deployment of digital technologies (Wirtz et al., 2022; Trittin-Ulbrich & Böckel, 2022; Trier et al., 2023).

Taken together, these dimensions constitute a CDR framework adaptable to many specific contexts and provide guidance for organizations in the enactment of ethical principles while implementing AI solutions. This is especially important in domains where traditional compliance frameworks reach their limits, as is the case for AI governance today. AI technologies not only operate in ways that are difficult to monitor but also disrupt established ideas about accountability and ethical responsibility. As a result, while we do not have standardized solutions for many ethical problems yet, the speed and unpredictability of technological change continue to challenge existing regulatory and organizational structures. In this context, CDR serves a dual purpose: to provide ethical orientation in an uncertain landscape and to provide an institutional structure for embedding ethical responsibility in organizations. It adds value in helping determine practical organizational solutions under conditions of technological acceleration and social ambivalence.

3 Implementation Challenges and Actionable Insights for a Responsible AI Governance

Translating CDR principles into concrete organizational practice presents several challenges. The transition from setting aspirational corporate values to integrating them meaningfully in day-to-day processes often reveals persistent gaps between ethical intent and operational reality. These gaps are due in part to technical and regulatory factors, but are affected as well by deeper organizational and cultural aspects (Rugeviciute & Courboulay, 2024; Wallraff et al., 2024). Moving to actionable requirements demands a deep understanding of the IT development and deployment processes within the organization.

The difficulties are both technical and economic in nature. On the technical side, it is not always clear what is feasible: how, for instance, can fairness or transparency be meaningfully defined, measured, and incorporated into diverse AI systems? Determining appropriate metrics, data sources, or thresholds is a complex and often contested task. On the economic side, organizations must manage to implement responsible AI measures in a way that is compatible with their business processes and that preserves or even enhances the business value brought by AI technologies.

A major tension lies in balancing the drive for rapid AI-powered innovation with the need for responsible, accountable development. Organizations often find themselves in fast-paced and competitive situations, where the use of AI is now regarded as critical to efficiency and competitive advantage (Wirtz et al., 2022). Especially start-ups and small and medium enterprises can face considerable resource constraints in this race to AI since they might not have planned dedicated budgets for governance projects and often lack access to appropriate expertise in the field (European Commission, 2024). Further complicating these factors is that many systems have complex, often opaque underlying algorithmic and data structures that make it difficult to foresee and manage their risks, especially if the system has a general purpose (Stahl, 2024).

To better understand how CDR can move from ambition to effective practice, we will examine some common obstacles organizations encounter, as well as the factors that contribute to successful implementation. One of the main challenges that corporations willing to enact responsible AI principles face is ascribing responsibility for their digital ecosystems (Stahl, 2024) and, ultimately, locating ownership for AI governance. This is a management decision that highly depends on the internal structure of the organization. Our best practice is to leverage existing governance frameworks to foster a resource-efficient implementation (Genovesi, 2025). This way, departments usually having key responsibilities in IT governance, such as information security or data governance, are actively participating in framework design and implementation. While the involvement of some departments is limited to consultation, those prospectively carrying more responsibility might take a coordinating role, promote the creation of an AI office, or even host the position of AI officer.

In the process of deciding about the allocation of responsibilities, stakeholders are faced with the challenge of transforming high-level principles and requirements into an actual implementation plan. To address this challenge, our consulting process (see Fig. 1) follows a structured, collaborative approach. After aligning with the client on project scope, ambition, and stakeholder roles, we assess the AI

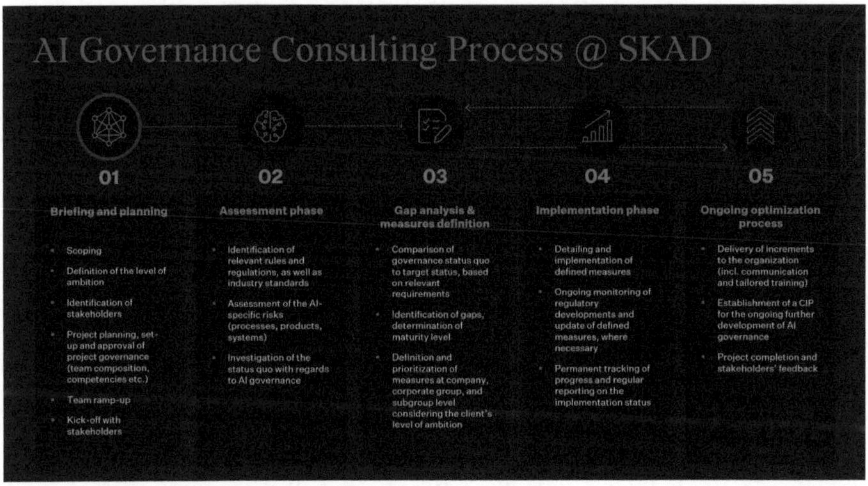

Fig. 1 SKAD's AI governance consulting process (SKAD)

governance goals in light of relevant regulations, industry standards, and internal policies. We then conduct a comprehensive gap analysis of the client's current policies, IT development procedures, and governance structures, benchmarking them against both ethical considerations and the current regulatory landscape. Involving key stakeholders across business, technical, and compliance teams, we define and prioritize actionable measures that are tailored to the company's structure and strategic objectives. These measures are then integrated into core business processes—such as software development, procurement, and risk management—ensuring that responsible AI principles are embedded in day-to-day operations. Implementation is supported by ongoing monitoring, regular progress reporting, and targeted training to build internal capacity. Finally, a continuous improvement process ensures that AI governance remains adaptive and aligned with evolving ethical and regulatory standards.

Since the development of comprehensive EU guidelines and international standards to facilitate the responsible development and monitoring of AI systems is still underway, it may still take several years before detailed technical specifications become available. In the interim, companies that have the internal resources and commitment are advised to proactively gather best practices and define clear, measurable benchmarks. This allows them to track the degree to which core values and principles for responsible AI are achieved in practice. For example, a company might develop fairness metrics that monitor the distribution of prediction errors among different user demographics for a specific AI use case, or adopt standardized model cards to document decisions around critical models, thereby enhancing transparency. Harmonizing standards across decentralized organizations and setting common methods to measure the impact of specific AI governance initiatives is a practice that can help corporations deal with regulatory uncertainty and reduce bureaucratic overhead (Mökander et al., 2022).

While defining benchmarks to achieve responsible AI, it is important to recognize that simply introducing checklists, metrics, or periodic assessments is not enough. At its core, CDR requires organizations to critically reflect not only on how AI is developed and deployed within their own structures but also on the broader impact of AI on its application environment. This means considering the ethical implications of introducing AI into specific real-world contexts and assessing the potential consequences for customers, stakeholders, and society as a whole. Ensuring that employees can question, challenge, and improve both AI-driven decisions and the ways in which AI is integrated into business operations helps foster this wider perspective. Such an approach drives a genuine cultural shift—embedding ethical reflection into everyday practices (Horn et al., 2025), encouraging cross-functional dialogue, and empowering staff at all levels to engage with the societal as well as the corporate impact of AI. Without this broader, value-driven transformation, AI governance risks becoming a mere box-ticking exercise rather than a meaningful part of organizational purpose and societal contribution.

In this regard, a key strength of our approach is the in-depth AI literacy and training program we design for each client. Based on a holistic competence framework developed by us, we systematically map the AI-related competencies relevant to various roles in the organization, taking into account different levels of responsibility and technical proficiency (see Fig. 2). This skill mapping is then cross-checked with existing training offerings within the company, allowing us to identify exactly where new or enhanced training is needed. As a result, we deliver actionable suggestions for closing knowledge gaps, supporting employees from operational staff to senior management in developing the skills necessary for the responsible use, oversight, and management of AI. This approach addresses the AI literacy requirements set out in the EU AI Act (Regulation, 2024/1689, Art. 4), but goes far beyond minimum compliance by laying the groundwork for a culture of digital responsibility and informed engagement with AI at every level of the organization.

An instructive analogy from the broader field of corporate responsibility helps illuminate the challenge of anchoring responsible AI in organizational culture: the distinction between conduct-based and integrity-based approaches to business ethics (Roth et al., 2022). Just as with environmental or social responsibility, both perspectives play a role in digital and AI responsibility. The conduct-based approach—anchored in rules, codes of conduct, and compliance procedures—is essential for setting clear expectations, assigning responsibility, and ensuring that minimum standards are consistently met. This is usually a response to regulatory obligations and drives adherence through external controls and the fear of consequences for noncompliance. However, the limitations of relying solely on conduct-based systems become evident when organizations face novel ethical issues that codes of conduct cannot anticipate or when employees are asked to navigate complex, rapidly evolving digital environments. Here, the integrity-based approach plays a crucial role: ethical behavior is grounded in principles that guide individual judgment even in the absence of explicit rules. Internalization of core values encourages employees to adopt an ethical mindset and make responsible choices out of personal conviction, rather than mere obligation.

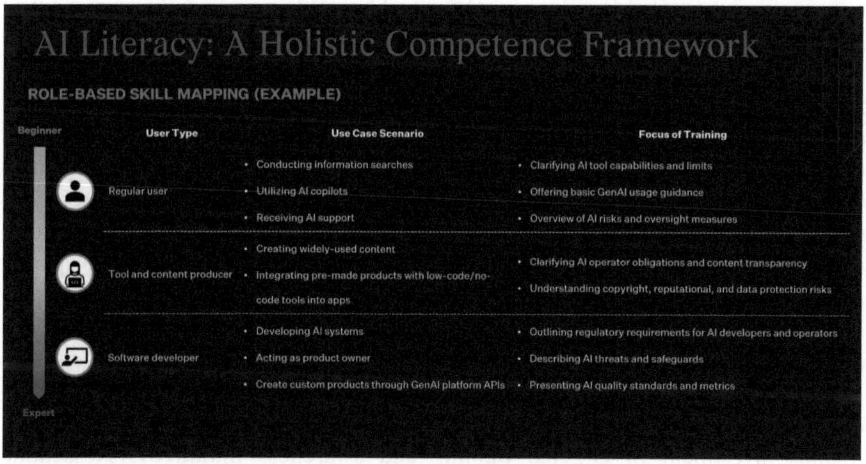

Fig. 2 AI Literacy: A holistic competence framework (SKAD)

Fostering such an integrity-based culture requires more than just policy documents; it involves dialogue, the empowerment of employees, practical training, and ongoing reflection on the wider impact of AI. Through a dual approach focused on both integrity and conduct, organizations not only ensure compliance with legal requirements and codes of practice but also cultivate the ethical maturity needed to address emerging risks and societal expectations. Responsible AI thus becomes embedded not just in the organization's structures but in the attitudes, decisions, and daily actions of its people.

4 Future Trends and Best Practices

The future of AI governance is strongly influenced by several interrelated trends, each of which will shape both regulatory and organizational practice in the coming years. At the forefront is the implementation of the EU AI Act, which shifts the focus of AI governance towards the protection of fundamental rights, health, and safety of users and other affected stakeholders. This regulatory development puts ethical considerations at the center of governance frameworks, requiring organizations to integrate CDR principles into their strategies and daily operations. The EU AI Act's focus on fundamental rights will increasingly demand that organizations systematically assess and address ethical risks, data governance, fairness, transparency, and accountability. To prepare for and demonstrate compliance in this legal framework, companies are advised to accurately document all phases of the AI lifecycle. Recording development decisions, data provenance, risk assessments, and model limitations enables organizations to ensure traceability, facilitate explainability, and support both internal reviews and external audits, forming a solid foundation for responsible AI deployment.

Alongside regulatory change, the demand for transparency from AI systems and model providers is rapidly growing. Many software solutions still function as closed boxes, offering limited insight into where and how AI is applied. As awareness of AI-related risks rises, clients and business partners increasingly expect to know more about the functioning and limitations of these systems. This shift is not just regulatory but market-driven: organizations now recognize that transparency is crucial for identifying and mitigating risks, establishing trust, and meeting customer expectations. Addressing this trend necessitates early and structured engagement with vendors and technology suppliers. Defining clear expectations around transparency, compliance, and risk management helps ensure that third-party AI solutions meet organizational and regulatory requirements, while transparent partnerships reduce uncertainty and enable more effective risk controls.

A third trend is the rising importance of AI literacy, especially as AI tools and advanced analytics become widely accessible across all organizational levels. The growing phenomenon of "shadow AI"—the unsupervised use of AI tools by employees—brings new challenges for compliance, security, and ethical use. Here, continuous investment in targeted training and awareness initiatives is essential. Establishing clear guidelines and empowering employees to act responsibly helps build a culture of digital competence and shared responsibility and will determine whether organizations can harness the opportunities of AI while maintaining accountability and public trust.

5 Conclusion

In this chapter, we have outlined how the evolving regulatory landscape, especially with the advent of the EU AI Act, calls for approaches that address the ethical and operational risks of AI. We explored key CDR dimensions that apply to AI governance, such as fairness, transparency, and stakeholder engagement. We highlighted major challenges to the translation of CDR principles into actionable organizational measures and pointed to established governance best practices to overcome recurring common obstacles. Through practical insights, we demonstrated the value of integrating CDR into AI governance frameworks, fostering AI literacy, and promoting a culture that unites rule-based compliance with the internalization of ethical values. Ultimately, we showed that responsible AI governance is not simply a matter of adhering to new regulations but also of embedding ethical reflection and digital responsibility into the core of organizational strategy.

Acknowledgments We would like to thank Felix Broßman and Dennis Kautz for their valuable feedback, their trust, and their support.

Competing Interests The authors have no conflicts of interest to declare that are relevant to the content of this chapter.

References

Carl, K. V., & Hinz, O. (2024). What we already know about corporate digital responsibility in IS research: A review and conceptualization of potential CDR activities. *Electron Markets, 34*(27). https://doi.org/10.1007/s12525-024-00708-0

European Commission. (2024). Impact assessment accompanying the proposal for a regulation of the European Parliament and of the Council Laying Down Harmonised Rules on Artificial Intelligence (Artificial Intelligence Act) and Amending Certain Union Legislative Acts. Retrieved June 27, 2025, from https://digital-strategy.ec.europa.eu/en/library/impact-assessment-regulation-artificial-intelligence.

Genovesi, S., Mönig, J. M., Schmitz, A., Poretschkin, M., Akila, M., Kahdan, M., Kleiner, R., Krieger, L., & Zimmermann, A. (2024). Standardizing fairness-evaluation procedures: Interdisciplinary insights on machine learning algorithms in creditworthiness assessments for small personal loans. *AI and Ethics, 4*, 537–553. https://doi.org/10.1007/s43681-023-00291-8

Genovesi, S. (2025). Introducing an AI governance framework in financial organizations. Best practices in implementing the EU AI Act. In *Symposium on scaling AI assessments (SAIA 2024)*. Open access series in informatics (OASIcs), (Vol. 126, pp. 1–9:7), Schloss Dagstuhl—Leibniz-Zentrum für Informatik.

Genovesi, S., Haimerl, M., Merget, I., Prange, S. M., Obert, O., Wolf, S., & Ziehn, J. (2025). Evaluating dimensions of AI transparency: A comparative study of standards, guidelines, and the EU AI Act. In *Symposium on scaling AI assessments (SAIA 2024)*. Open access series in informatics (OASIcs), (vol. 126, 10, pp. 1–10:17), Schloss Dagstuhl—Leibniz-Zentrum für Informatik.

High-Level Expert Group on Artificial Intelligence. (2019). Ethics guidelines for trustworthy AI. European Commission. https://digital-strategy.ec.europa.eu/en/library/ethics-guidelines-trustworthy-ai.

Horn, N., Genovesi, S., Lorenz, A., & Scheiber, P. (2025). Von der Theorie zur Praxis: Digitalethische Reflexion von KI-Systemen. Denkimpuls der AG Ethik der Initiative D21. Retrieved June 27, 2025, from https://initiatived21.de/uploads/03_Studien-Publikationen/Denkimpulse-Ethik/18-Von-der-Theorie-zur-Praxis/D21_Denkimpuls_2025_Theorie_Praxis.pdf.

Knopf, T. & Pick, D. (2023). Corporate responsibility for digital innovation: A systematic review of the literature. Proceedings of the 18th European conference on innovation and entrepreneurship, European Conference on Innovation and Entrepreneurship.

Lobschat, L., Mueller, B., Eggers, F., Brandimarte, L., Diefenbach, S., Kroschke, M., & Wirtz, J. (2021). Corporate digital responsibility. *Journal of Business Research, 122*. https://doi.org/10.1016/j.jbusres.2019.10.006

Mökander, J., Sheth, M., Gersbro-Sundler, M., Blomgren, P., & Floridi, L. (2022). Challenges and best practices in corporate AI governance: Lessons from the biopharmaceutical industry. *Frontiers in Computer Science, 4*. https://doi.org/10.3389/fcomp.2022.1068361

Regulation (EU). (2024/1689). Of the European Parliament and of the Council of 13 June 2024 laying down harmonised rules on artificial intelligence (Artificial Intelligence Act). European Union. https://eur-lex.europa.eu/eli/reg/2024/1689/oj/eng.

Rugeviciute, A. & Courboulay, V. (2024). Empowering organizations for sustainable digitalization: A corporate digital responsibility maturity model approach. *2024* 10th international conference on ICT for sustainability (ICT4S), (pp. 87–98).

Roth, B., Faber, E., Gebhardt, J., & Hefter, K. (2022). Core elements of conduct and ethics in *the context of non-financial risk*. In N. Gittfried, G. Lienke, F. Seiferlein, J. Leiendecker, & B. Gehra (Eds.), *Non-financial risk management in the financial industry* (pp. 241–269). Frankfurt School Verlag.

Stahl, B. C. (2024). From corporate digital responsibility to responsible digital ecosystems. *Sustainability, 16*(12). https://doi.org/10.3390/su16124972

Trier, M., Kundisch, D., Beverungen, D., et al. (2023). Digital responsibility. *Business & Information Systems Engineering, 65*, 463–474. https://doi.org/10.1007/s12599-023-00822-x

Trittin-Ulbrich, H., & Böckel, A. (2022). Institutional entrepreneurship for responsible digital innovation: The case of corporate digital responsibility. *Creativity and Innovation Management, 31*(3), 447–459. https://doi.org/10.1111/caim.12513

van Wynsberghe, A. (2021). Sustainable AI: AI for sustainability and the sustainability of AI. *AI and Ethics, 1*, 213–218. https://doi.org/10.1007/s43681-021-00043-6

Wallraff, B., Brossmann, F., Hasselbach, A., Klapdar, H., Schlieker, N., Lombardo, S., & Kautz, D. (2024). *Skalierung von Künstlicher Intelligenz—Ein empirisches Reifegradmodell und Handlungsempfehlungen für Unternehmen*. cbs International Business School.

Wirtz, J., Kunz, W. H., Hartley, N., & Tarbit, J. (2022). Corporate digital responsibility in service firms and their ecosystems. *Journal of Service Research, 26*(2), 173–190. https://doi.org/10.1177/10946705221130467

Dr. Sergio Genovesi is a Senior Consultant at SKAD AG in the field of AI Governance and Ethics. Dr. Genovesi is actively involved in standardization activities concerning AI and cooperates with major standardization organizations. He was a postdoctoral researcher at the University of Bonn and was actively involved in the KI.NRW flagship project "Certified AI." Dr. Genovesi holds a PhD in epistemology from the universities of Bonn, Paris I, and Chicago, and is actively engaged in research on AI ethics and governance.

Ismael El-Hadj is a Senior Consultant at SKAD AG specializing in AI governance, IT compliance, and risk management. He advises enterprises on designing and implementing AI governance frameworks, aligning with regulatory requirements such as the EU AI Act. With extensive project experience, Ismael El-Hadj has managed regulatory implementation initiatives and facilitated risk management concepts in highly regulated environments. Currently, he is a PhD candidate at HHL Leipzig Graduate School of Management, with research focusing on corporate responsibility.

CDR Implementation in SMEs: Overcoming Typical Challenges

Bartosz Przybylek and Felix von Roesgen

Abstract

Accelerating digitalization and increasing regulatory requirements, such as the European Accessibility Act and the EU AI Act, have placed Corporate Digital Responsibility (CDR) at the center of attention for small and medium-sized enterprises (SMEs). While legal frameworks mandate digital inclusion, transparency, and risk management, the rise of generative AI introduces both opportunities for innovation and new ethical, legal, and operational risks. For SMEs, CDR is therefore not merely a matter of compliance but a strategic imperative. Proactive engagement can strengthen resilience against cyber risks and geopolitical uncertainties, build trust among customers and partners, and enhance competitiveness and employer attractiveness. Yet, implementation in SMEs often remains fragmented due to limited resources and a lack of practical guidance. To address this gap, a four-stage framework is proposed, enabling a step-by-step approach: (1) orientation and definition, (2) collection and assessment of existing measures, (3) goal setting and planning, and (4) implementation and anchoring. Complemented by practical examples and solutions, the framework helps SMEs overcome typical barriers and embed CDR sustainably into organizational structures. In doing so, CDR evolves from a regulatory obligation into a lever for sustainable value creation and responsible digital transformation.

B. Przybylek (✉) · F. von Roesgen
ifok GmbH, Hamburg, Germany
e-mail: bartosz.przybylek@ifok.de; felix@vroesgen.de

A.-S. Christ (ed.), *Corporate Digital Responsibility*, Future of Business and Finance, https://doi.org/10.1007/978-3-032-14793-6_17

1 Introduction

In the context of accelerating digitalization and growing societal expectations for ethically sound and sustainable business practices, Corporate Digital Responsibility (CDR) has evolved into a relevant framework for guiding the responsible use of digital technologies within organizations.

Recent regulatory developments have served as critical catalysts for a more serious engagement with CDR. Notably, the European Accessibility Act, implemented in Germany through the Barrierefreiheitsstärkungsgesetz (Bundesrepublik Deutschland, 2021), places new obligations on businesses to ensure that digital products and services are accessible to all users, including those with disabilities. This legal framework underscores the growing expectation that digital inclusion is not merely a best practice but a binding requirement. At the same time, the EU's AI Act introduces comprehensive rules for the development and deployment of artificial intelligence systems, emphasizing transparency, risk management, and human oversight—principles that lie at the heart of CDR. For SMEs (small and medium-sized companies), these shifts in the regulatory landscape demand a critical reassessment of their digital offerings and processes. Yet many lack the legal expertise, structural capacity, or strategic foresight that larger corporations may already have in place, making the implementation of CDR not only a legal necessity but also an organizational challenge.

In parallel, the emergence and rapid diffusion of generative AI (GenAI) technologies, such as large language models, have introduced new layers of complexity and urgency. These tools challenge existing digital processes by enabling novel forms of data creation, automation, and personalization, while simultaneously raising questions, for example, around data provenance, algorithmic bias, intellectual property, and human oversight. For SMEs, the integration of GenAI presents both opportunities for innovation and significant ethical, legal, and operational risks that demand careful consideration.

Over the past years, we have increasingly observed a growing practical relevance and translation of CDR into action. Sector-specific approaches, such as CDR Building Bloxx (BVDW, 2025) in the digital economy, the Service Firms CDR Calculus by Wirtz et al. (2023), or publications in the construction sector (Weber-Lewerenz, 2024), illustrate how CDR principles are becoming operationalized. Cross-sectoral developments, such as the establishment of a unified CDR definition (Carl et al., 2025) and the recent efforts by the German DIN-NIA (Normenausschuss Informationstechnik und Anwendungen) to form a CDR working committee, further contribute to orientation and standardization.

Despite these developments, a comprehensive and systematic implementation of CDR in organizations remains the exception. Most companies address individual aspects of digital responsibility, such as data protection, ethical AI, or digital inclusion, without framing them explicitly under the CDR label. This is also reflected in the diverse initiatives recognized by the CDR Award (BVDW & Bayern Innovativ, 2024), where many organizations present innovative solutions, even in the absence of a holistic CDR strategy.

Our consulting work confirms this: many companies already act responsibly in specific areas of digital practice but do not yet reflect this systematically under the CDR concept. While awareness of the terminology remains limited, the underlying themes, from algorithmic fairness to IT security and sustainable digitalization, are often already well developed.

However, CDR is neither the sum of single actions nor merely a matter of regulatory compliance but a strategic imperative. It requires SMEs to critically reassess and, where necessary, redesign their digital infrastructures and workflows, embedding principles of fairness, transparency, security, and sustainability at every stage of the digital value chain. This article explores the key challenges SMEs face in the implementation of CDR, analyzing how legal pressures, technological disruptions, and resource constraints intersect to shape their capacity for responsible digital transformation.

2 Why SMEs Benefit from CDR Engagement

Engaging proactively with CDR offers strategic advantages for SMEs that go far beyond regulatory compliance. By integrating responsible digital practices, SMEs can strengthen their resilience amid growing cyber threats, supply chain disruptions, and shifting data governance frameworks. A well-defined CDR strategy supports risk mitigation and organizational adaptability, especially for SMEs operating internationally or in sectors where regulation does not provide sufficient guidance.

Geopolitical developments such as trade disputes, regulatory shifts, and supply chain instability are shaping the direction of CDR. While some discussions, like those around the CSRD or EU Omnibus regulations, advocate for regulatory flexibility, global competition simultaneously increases the pressure to secure digital infrastructures and build resilient ecosystems. As organizations reevaluate their dependencies, particularly on non-European providers, there is growing momentum to integrate privacy, sustainability, and security into procurement and vendor management.

This shift is echoed in changing consumer expectations. With increased sensitivity to data sovereignty and transparency, trust in digital services has become a decisive factor in purchasing and investment decisions—offering SMEs that prioritize CDR a competitive edge in evolving markets.

Moreover, a visible commitment to digital responsibility can serve as a powerful driver of reputational capital. In an environment where consumers, clients, and business partners are becoming increasingly conscious of how companies handle data, privacy, and algorithmic decision-making, CDR functions as a trust-building mechanism. Our experience with SMEs shows that transparent, fair, and secure digital practices are essential for building long-term customer loyalty, as digital ethics and accountability increasingly serve as key differentiators in competitive markets. The financial advantages of CDR are also becoming more tangible. Responsible digital behavior can lead to improved customer retention, reduce the risk of data breaches and associated penalties, and open access to new market segments that prioritize ethical business conduct. Furthermore, in the ongoing struggle for qualified personnel, especially in digital and technical fields, SMEs that visibly prioritize ethical digital governance and values-driven innovation are better positioned to attract and retain talent. Younger generations of employees increasingly seek purposeful work environments aligned with their personal values, and CDR can play a central role in shaping such an organizational culture (Deloitte, 2025).

In sum, the integration of CDR principles is not only a response to external pressures but also a lever for competitive advantage, operational stability, and sustainable growth in an increasingly digital economy.

3 Challenges for SMEs in Engaging with CDR

Despite the strategic and operational advantages of engaging with CDR, we observe in our consulting work that many SMEs continue to struggle with initiating this transformation. One key barrier lies in the lack of accessible, practical guidance tailored to the specific realities of smaller enterprises. While large corporations increasingly publish CDR reports and develop dedicated governance structures, SMEs often lack comparable reference cases or best-practice models that reflect their limited financial, technical, and human resources. Our experience shows that this absence of relatable examples makes it difficult for SMEs to assess where and how to begin and contributes to the perception that CDR is either too abstract or too complex to implement meaningfully within their own organizational context.

Compounding this challenge is the fact that digital responsibility is typically cross-functional, requiring coordination between data management, legal compliance, IT security, customer relations, and employee engagement. For SMEs without dedicated departments in these areas, the perceived effort of aligning digital practices with ethical and regulatory expectations can be overwhelming. As a result, CDR risks being deprioritized or addressed only reactively—if at all.

To address this gap, there is a growing need for structured, scalable frameworks that can support SMEs in systematically approaching the topic of CDR. Such frameworks offer a pragmatic entry point by breaking down the broad and often diffuse concept of CDR into manageable components, making it easier to identify relevant fields of action, define priorities, and measure progress.

To provide SMEs with a structured entry point into CDR, we have developed the following four-stage framework. This model offers a scalable and systematic approach that enables organizations to build internal competence, assess their current standing, define meaningful goals, and embed CDR measures sustainably. Each stage is designed to be accessible even to organizations with limited prior engagement in the field.

1. **Orientation and Definition**
   The first stage focuses on building internal awareness and understanding. Before responsible digital practices can be effectively implemented, it is essential that employees involved in CDR are familiarized with the multifaceted

nature of CDR—including data ethics, privacy, digital sustainability, algorithmic fairness, and corporate transparency. This phase aims to create a shared knowledge base and a common vocabulary, enabling a more informed and cohesive approach across teams and departments. Methods such as workshops, guided readings, and interactive training can be used to introduce relevant concepts and facilitate reflection on their relevance to the organization.

2. **Collecting and Assessing**

   In the second stage, SMEs conduct a systematic inventory of existing CDR-related measures and processes. This includes identifying formal policies (e.g., data protection guidelines), technical safeguards (e.g., encryption standards), cultural initiatives (e.g., digital literacy programs), and informal practices already contributing to digital responsibility. By mapping the current state, organizations gain clarity on their status quo, uncover potential overlaps, and, crucially, identify gaps where further action is possible. This step lays the foundation for evidence-based planning and avoids redundant efforts.

3. **Goalsetting and Planning**

   Based on the insights gained in the previous stage, the third phase focuses on setting clear goals and defining targeted measures to address identified gaps. Goal setting is essential for translating abstract CDR principles into actionable priorities. It provides orientation, enables progress tracking, and creates accountability. These goals should be realistic, value-driven, and aligned with both legal obligations and operational capacities. From there, measures can be derived that range from technical improvements (e.g., updating IT security protocols) to organizational changes (e.g., introducing ethical review processes for new digital tools) or communicative strategies (e.g., transparent reporting on data usage). Cross-functional collaboration and stakeholder involvement remain key success factors in this phase.

4. **Implementing and Anchoring**

   The final stage is concerned with the long-term integration and communication of CDR measures. Implementation involves not only the rollout of concrete initiatives but also their anchoring in organizational routines and structures to ensure durability. This includes defining responsibilities, embedding practices in workflows, and providing ongoing training. Equally important is the internal and external communication of CDR efforts. By transparently reporting on goals, processes, and outcomes, SMEs can strengthen trust among employees, customers, and partners—consolidating both legitimacy and impact.

Taken together, this four-stage framework offers SMEs a practical roadmap for entering the field of Corporate Digital Responsibility. It allows for a gradual, yet comprehensive, engagement with the topic, tailored to the specific conditions of smaller organizations. In doing so, it transforms CDR from a perceived burden into a source of strategic orientation and organizational development.

4 Challenges of Using the Framework and How to Overcome Them

While the four-phase framework provides a clear and structured approach to implementing CDR, each phase presents its own set of challenges that can hinder progress if not addressed with appropriate strategies. SMEs often encounter obstacles such as limited internal expertise, fragmented digital infrastructures, and uncertainty regarding legal and ethical expectations. These difficulties can vary significantly depending on the organization's size, sector, and digital maturity.

However, insights gained from collaboration with a range of SMEs show that pragmatic, context-sensitive solutions can effectively support each phase of the process. By leveraging internal strengths, promoting cross-functional cooperation, and adopting low-threshold tools and methods, SMEs can overcome typical barriers and build momentum in their CDR initiatives.

The following sections examine each phase of the framework in greater detail, highlighting common pain points and presenting proven practices that have emerged from real-world implementations in small and medium-sized enterprises. These examples aim to offer not only theoretical orientation but also practical guidance for SMEs seeking to take their first or next step toward responsible digital transformation.

The first phase, ***Orientation and Definition,*** aims to establish a foundational understanding of CDR among those involved in the project. For SMEs, however, this initial step often proves particularly challenging. A frequently cited barrier is a lack of time and capacity: In smaller organizations where employees frequently assume multiple roles, dedicating focused time to the exploration of a new and broad topic like CDR can be difficult. This is compounded by a scarcity of tailored best practices. While large corporations may serve as abstract inspiration, their resources and organizational structures often make their approaches inapplicable to SMEs. As a result, many smaller firms are left without practical models or reference points that resonate with their specific realities.

One solution that has proven effective in overcoming these hurdles is the implementation of asynchronous learning formats. These allow employees to engage with CDR-related content at their own pace, adapting the learning process to individual schedules and responsibilities. Such formats reduce the pressure of synchronous training sessions and enable gradual, sustainable knowledge building. A notable example of this approach is an initiative by the Bavarian Ministry of Consumer Protection (n.d.), which has launched an online learning platform specifically designed for SMEs. This portal offers structured educational content on data ethics, privacy, and digital responsibility in a format that is both accessible and flexible, thereby lowering the threshold for initial engagement.

In addition to individual learning formats, peer exchange has proven to be a valuable driver in building CDR understanding—regardless of an organization's current level of maturity. Engaging directly with peers allows SMEs to derive practical insights and context-relevant learnings from others' CDR experiences, even across differences in sector, structure, or size. Within the growing CDR community, platforms such as the CDR Conference and the CDR Lab offer structured spaces for dialogue and mutual learning. Functioning much like a Community of Practice, these forums allow for open exchange of challenges and best practices, helping SMEs identify approaches that align with their own context and capabilities.

In the second phase, ***Collecting and Assessing***, the goal is to gain a clear picture of existing CDR-related activities within the organization. At first glance, this may seem straightforward. However, in practice, SMEs often find this phase unexpectedly challenging. A common obstacle lies in the fact that numerous relevant measures already exist, but are not explicitly recognized as part of CDR. This disconnect stems, in part, from the terminological diversity surrounding the topic: terms such as *digital ethics*, *sustainable IT*, or *data responsibility* are frequently used interchangeably or in isolation, making it difficult to recognize their collective relevance under the broader umbrella of CDR.

Moreover, many employees are unfamiliar with the thematic breadth of CDR, which spans topics as varied as ecological impacts of digital infrastructure, algorithmic transparency, digital accessibility, and employee data protection. As a result, existing efforts—such as energy-efficient server use, privacy training, or inclusive web design—are often viewed as isolated initiatives rather than as interconnected components of a responsible digital strategy.

To address this challenge, a structured classification tool can help make existing activities visible and connect them to the CDR framework. Based on work with several SMEs, we developed a 2x2 matrix that organizes CDR measures along two key dimensions:

- On the X-axis, we distinguish between
  1. *Digitalization for sustainability*—how digital tools contribute to broader sustainability goals
  2. *Sustainable digitalization*—how digital processes themselves are designed to be sustainable
- On the Y-axis, we differentiate between the following:
  1. *Ecological sustainability*
  2. *Social sustainability*

This matrix (Fig. 1) enables SMEs to systematically map existing practices and identify white spots. By providing concrete examples in each quadrant, the matrix also serves as a cognitive aid, helping staff recognize familiar activities as meaningful components of their CDR engagement.

In the third phase, *Goalsetting and Planning*, a central challenge lies in the differing expectations and assumptions among employees regarding how far-reaching the company's CDR engagement should be. The multidimensional nature of CDR often leads to varying interpretations of what constitutes sufficient action, creating ambiguity and slowing down decision-making.

	Sustainability for Digitalization	Sustainability in Digitalization
ecological	**Tech for Environment** • Smart energy management • Sustainable logistics solutions • Data based agricultural optimazation	**Green Digitalization** • Green coding • Circular IT hardware • Green IT infrastructure
social	**Tech for Society** • Technical solutions for inclusion • Digital plattforms for citizen participation • Blockchain for transparent distribution of donations	**Social Digitalization** • Digital inclusion • AI bias mitigation • Digital wellbeing

Fig. 1 2x2 Matrix (ifok)

To address this, it is essential to establish a common understanding of the company's desired level of ambition across the four categories of the CDR matrix. Developing and discussing scenarios for different ambition levels, ranging from minimal compliance to strategic leadership, has proven to be a helpful tool in creating transparency around the implications of each approach. This process enables project teams to reflect on feasibility, organizational priorities, and potential impact. Ideally, teams jointly agree on a target ambition level before proceeding, thereby creating alignment and a clear foundation for the subsequent design of concrete measures.

A central challenge in the final phase, ***Implementing and Anchoring***, is that embedding CDR often necessitates new roles, routines, or committees—each requiring resources for both setup and sustained operation. Moreover, establishing CDR as a standalone structure can unintentionally reinforce its isolation, rather than highlighting its cross-functional relevance. Since CDR inherently intersects with existing domains such as IT, compliance, HR, sustainability, and communications, siloed implementation risks undermine its integrative potential.

A promising approach lies in leveraging existing anchoring instruments within the organizational structures and routines that employees already know and use. This not only conserves resources but also emphasizes the interdependencies between CDR and existing business functions. For instance, if a company uses Objectives and Key Results (OKRs) as an objective-setting and performance management tool, it is advisable to formulate CDR objectives and measurable key results within that system. Embedding CDR into the OKR logic makes its relevance for day-to-day operations tangible, fosters shared responsibility, and provides a basis for structured internal communication.

A similar logic applies to external communication. Instead of developing a separate CDR report—which may appear disconnected from existing sustainability efforts—CDR topics should be integrated into established reporting formats, such as Corporate Social Responsibility (CSR) reports. By including a dedicated chapter on CDR within the CSR framework, organizations can highlight the contributions of digital responsibility to social and environmental goals, thereby reinforcing CDR's cross-cutting nature and increasing its visibility among stakeholders. This approach also aligns with growing expectations from investors and the public for coherent, holistic sustainability communication.

5 Conclusion

In the face of accelerating digital transformation, growing regulatory demands, and evolving societal expectations, CDR has become a strategic imperative—especially for small and medium-sized enterprises (SMEs). Legal frameworks such as the European Accessibility Act and the EU AI Act have shifted digital responsibility from voluntary best practice to binding obligation, while technological advances like generative AI introduce new risks and ethical considerations. These developments create both pressure and opportunity for SMEs to engage more systematically with CDR.

Importantly, CDR is more than compliance; it can be a source of competitive advantage. Proactive engagement fosters digital resilience, strengthens stakeholder trust, and enhances attractiveness in both markets and labor pools. When embedded across functions and aligned with existing structures, CDR supports long-term adaptability and sustainable value creation.

Although CDR is increasingly operationalized across sectors, its comprehensive adoption remains rare. SMEs already implement responsible digital practices, but do so without a cohesive framework or clear strategic direction. As a result, efforts often remain fragmented and disconnected from broader goals. The four-stage model presented offers SMEs a pragmatic roadmap to structure their CDR engagement in line with their specific capacities and constraints.

To realize its full potential, CDR must evolve from isolated measures into an integrated organizational strategy—one that reflects ethical values while preparing SMEs for the demands of a rapidly changing digital environment. The proposed four-stage model, along with the discussion of key challenges and practical solutions, is intended to contribute to building such a strategy in a tangible and accessible way.

Competing Interests The authors have no conflicts of interest to declare that are relevant to the content of this chapter.

References

Bavarian State Ministry of the Environment and Consumer Protection. (n.d.). CDR Bayern. Retrieved September 27, 2025, from https://www.cdr.bayern.de/cdr_praxis/verantwortungswerkstatt/1-schritt/index.html

Bundesrepublik Deutschland. (2021). Gesetz zur Stärkung der Barrierefreiheit (Barrierefreiheit sstärkungsgesetz – BFSG) [Act to strengthen accessibility]. *Bundesgesetzblatt, Teil I, Nr. 40*, 22. Juli 2021, 2970–2993. https://www.bgbl.de/xaver/bgbl/start.xav?startbk=Bundesanzeiger_BGBl&start=//*%5B@attr_id=%27bgbl121s2970.pdf%27%5D

BVDW. (2025). *CDR Building Bolxx*. Retrieved September 27, 2025, from https://www.cdr-building-bloxx.com/

BVDW & Bayern Innovativ. (2024). *Corporate Digital Responsibility Award 2024*. Retrieved September 27, 2025, from https://www.cdr-award.digital/

Carl, K. V., Blachetta, M., Bilfinger, B., Brink, A., Cerulli-Harms, A. K., Christ, A.-S., Dietl, K., Dörr, S., Hauer, M. P., Hinz, M., Jänig, J.-R., Keilhofer, K., Kurtz, C., Mihale-Wilson, C.,

Mueller, B., Przybylek, B. A., Schaufler, N., Schlegel, I. K., Scholz, M., von Roesgen, F., & Wößner, J. (2025). Establishing common ground in corporate digital responsibility: Integrating understandings, definitions, and expert perspectives. In *INFORMATIK 2025, Potsdam, Germany*.

Deloitte. (2025). *2025 Gen Z and millennial survey: Growth, the pursuit of money, meaning, and well-being* (14. Jahr der Global-Studie). Deloitte Global. Retrieved June 30, 2025, from https://www.deloitte.com/global/en/issues/work/genz-millennial-survey.html

Weber-Lewerenz, B. (2024). *Die Bewertbarkeit von Corporate Digital Responsibility (CDR) im Bauwesen 5.0 – Teil 1: Eine Einschätzung. Risk, Fraud & Compliance*, (6/2024), 255–264. Erich Schmidt Verlag.

Wirtz, J., Kunz, W. H., Hartley, N., & Tarbit, J. (2023). Corporate digital responsibility in service firms and their ecosystems. *Journal of Service Research, 26*(2), 1–18. https://doi.org/10.1177/10946705221130467

Bartosz Przybylek specializes in digitalization and sustainability as a strategy consultant with over ten years of experience. At ifok, he advises institutions on Corporate Digital Responsibility, supporting strategic development, practical implementation, and organizational change. He is also a recognized speaker and initiator of dialogue formats on digital responsibility.

Felix von Roesgen specializes in the interplay between digitalization and sustainability, with a particular focus on the societal impacts of artificial intelligence. At ifok, he designs projects, workshops, and dialogue formats on Corporate Digital Responsibility and contributes to the development of an innovation network on AI for the common good. He is also active as a speaker and moderator in various formats, addressing the opportunities and risks of digitalization for society and the environment, as well as strategies for organizations to responsibly navigate them.

Shaping the Next Phase of Digital Transformation: CDR and the Digital Society

Marie Blachetta and Lena-Sophie Müller

Abstract

The future of digital transformation is shaped by decisions made today, rather than being technologically predetermined. This chapter explores corporate digital responsibility (CDR) as a societal imperative and organizational strategy to align innovation with ethical principles, democratic participation, and economic resilience. As digital technologies increasingly influence social life, ethical and regulatory frameworks must evolve to keep pace. CDR bridges this gap by embedding responsibility into digital business strategies and governance structures. Initiative D21 e.V., Germany's largest nonprofit organization to represent the digital society, traces the origins of CDR in digital ethics, emphasizes Europe's role as a regulatory pioneer, and argues for an expanded understanding of responsibility that includes not just corporations but also public institutions, civil society, and individuals. The digital society is not a passive recipient but an active co-creator of digital futures. Shared responsibility and inclusive engagement are prerequisites for legitimate, trustworthy innovation. CDR thus becomes a vehicle for connecting economic and societal goals, fostering resilience, inclusion, and trust. The chapter concludes by advocating for a broadened ecosystem of Organizational Digital Responsibility (ODR), where diverse actors collaborate to shape responsible digital transformation. In times of rapid technological change, CDR must not only manage risks but also imagine, design, and implement futures worth building.

M. Blachetta (✉) · L.-S. Müller
Initiative D21, Berlin, Germany
e-mail: kontakt@initiatived21.de

A.-S. Christ (ed.), *Corporate Digital Responsibility*, Future of Business and Finance, https://doi.org/10.1007/978-3-032-14793-6_18

1 CDR as a Societal Imperative: Why we Act

The future of digital transformation is not predetermined—it is actively shaped by the choices we make today. As technologies advance faster than our societal frameworks can adapt, the need for a shared digital responsibility based on values becomes more urgent. Corporate digital responsibility (CDR) provides a structure to align innovation with ethical foresight, economic resilience, and democratic participation. In this chapter, we reflect on the interdependencies of CDR and the digital society.

As digital technologies rapidly reshape our societies, their ethical, social, and political implications demand proactive engagement. In this chapter, we explore the drivers behind the engagement of CDR—from ethical concerns to public expectations and geopolitical developments. Understanding *why we act* is the first step toward shaping a digital transformation grounded in shared values and collective responsibility. As shown in Fig. 1, this chapter is divided into four parts. Together, the sections build a multilevel logic: from normative grounding to societal interaction and ecosystem expansion. The figure illustrates these conceptual layers to enhance comprehension and highlight the interdependence of ethical intent, societal engagement, and practical implementation.

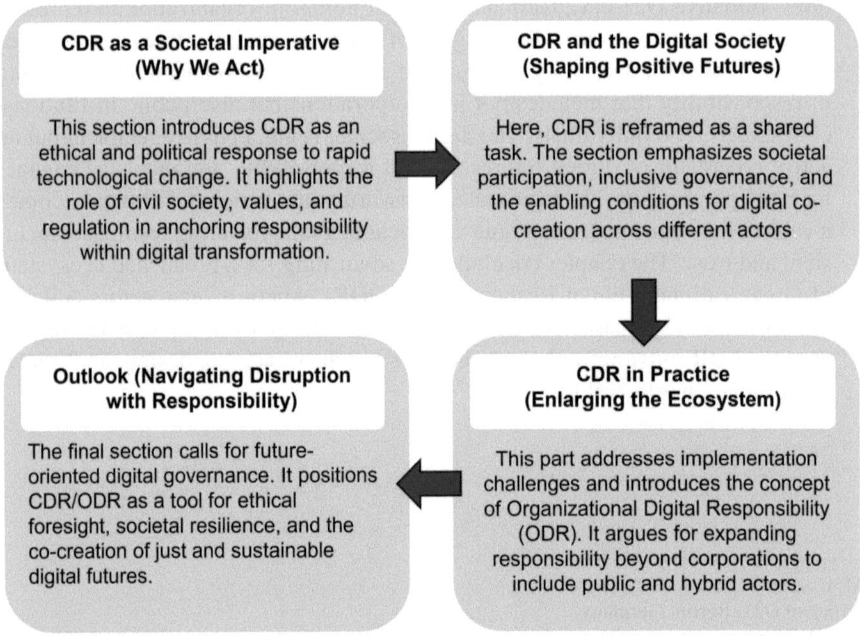

Fig. 1 Structural overview of the chapter: From ethical foundations to future-oriented governance (Authors' illustration)

1.1 Ethical Challenges in an Accelerated Digital Environment

Digital technologies deployed by organizations and institutions are transforming societies at a pace that outstrips traditional governance frameworks. Decision-making systems powered by artificial intelligence (AI), facial recognition technologies, and autonomous digital agents are no longer abstract possibilities; they are being implemented in ways that create economic, societal, and ethical challenges. These technologies raise essential questions about fairness, accountability, and transparency in machine-based decision-making processes (Deutscher Ethikrat, 2023), as seen in algorithmic credit scoring or automated hiring systems that have faced criticism for biased outcomes.

However, it is important to recognize that these developments are not occurring in a vacuum. In order to address the demands of innovation cycles and competitive imperatives, organizations frequently implement new digital tools. At the same time, economic pressures and dynamics are intense. However, they also create fertile ground for rethinking business models and embedding responsibility at the core of digital strategy. Indeed, it has become evident that both political institutions and economic actors must proactively shape the digital transformation. Governments define the normative and legal boundaries, while companies translate these boundaries into innovations, products, and services that influence everyday life.

As demonstrated in the study D21-Digital-Index (2024/25) and shown in Fig. 2, public attitudes towards digital transformation remain polarized, with certain parts of the population either disengaging from or being overwhelmed by the perceived complexity and pace of change (Initiative D21, 2025, pp. 6–7).

To our mind, bringing these technological, corporate, economic, and societal developments together within a chance-oriented perspective is one of the substantial challenges in the digital age. Grimm et al. (2023) argue that addressing the ethical and moral questions that arise with digital technology is a prerequisite for fostering an enlightened relationship between humans, machines, and systems.

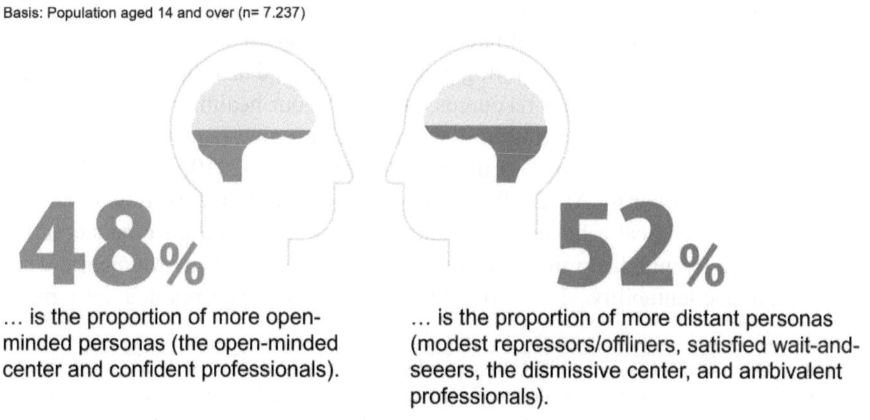

Fig. 2 Attitude towards digital transformation (Initiative D21, 2025)

1.2 From Digital Ethics to CDR: A Civil Society Perspective

Our engagement with CDR[1] emerged from our long-standing involvement in digital ethics. In 2017, we established the Working Group on Digital Ethics with the objective of translating ethical principles into the digital domain, fostering interdisciplinary discourse, and providing orientation amidst rapid technological shifts. We recognized early on that ethical reflection needed a counterpart in the digital corporate domain—especially as companies increasingly became not just adopters but developers and diffusers of digital technologies (Müller & Andersen, 2017).

This has led us to raise awareness of CDR within our network and beyond. CDR focuses on "holistic responsible corporate action with regard to the impact of digital technologies and data" (Carl et al., 2025). It addresses the fact that companies are not only subject to digital transformation but also drivers of its shape, pace, and societal impact (Müller, 2020). In this context, CDR has the potential to act as a driver of innovation and differentiation. It encourages companies to embed responsibility in strategic decision-making; to align digital innovation and data handling with human rights, sustainability goals, and democratic values; and to take active measures to mitigate social harm.

As Floridi et al. (2021, p. 26) highlight, the role of society is also pivotal in terms of the acceptance and adoption of technological developments, particularly in the domain of AI:

> Public acceptance and adoption of AI technologies will occur only if the benefits are seen as meaningful and risks as potential, yet preventable, minimisable, or at least something against which one can be protected, through risk management (e.g., insurance) or redressing.

1.3 Europe as an Enabler of Value-Based Innovation

Europe plays a crucial role in anchoring CDR within a broader ecosystem of value-based digital governance. A comprehensive examination of AI systems by the European Commission (EC) points out their significant role for the society, for example, they can "help to facilitate the achievement of the UN's Sustainable Development Goals, such as promoting gender balance and tackling climate change, rationalising our use of natural resources, enhancing our health, mobility and production processes, and supporting how we monitor progress against sustainability and social cohesion indicators" (European Commission, 2019, p. 4). The EC's guidelines on trustworthy AI (2019) cover seven key requirements: human agency and oversight, technical robustness and safety, privacy and data governance, transparency, diversity, nondiscrimination and fairness, societal and environmental well-being, and accountability. These principles have been incorporated into many

[1] Initiative D21 contributes to the CDR discourse by introducing the topic early and supporting it through different projects, e.g., the Digital Future Challenge and a dedicated online magazine. Its focus lies in fostering responsible digital transformation and encouraging companies to take an active role in shaping it for societal benefit.

organizational frameworks. In addition, with the recent enactment of the AI Act (Regulation (EU) 2024/1689), the EU has established itself as a normative power in the digital age—providing a model for responsible innovation aiming to harmonize fundamental rights with economic competitiveness (Odelberg, 2024; OECD, 2024). The AI Act, with its risk-based approach and mandatory safeguards for high-risk AI systems, tackles many principles central to CDR—such as transparency, fairness, and human oversight.

In addition to the AI Act, the regulatory landscape is undergoing further evolution. Legislative instruments such as the General Data Protection Regulation (GDPR) (Regulation (EU) 2016/679), the Digital Services Act (DSA) (Regulation (EU) 2022/2065), and the Digital Markets Act (DMA) (Regulation (EU) 2022/1925) are setting clear boundaries and expectations for responsible digital behavior. The regulatory basis establishes obligations of accountability, protects fundamental rights, and creates incentives for the development of digital systems that are more transparent and fairer (European Commission, 2019).

At the same time, CDR must go beyond mere regulation—it must be actively shaped and aligned with the organization's values, stakeholder dialogue, and long-term societal impact. Digital technologies cannot be viewed without considering the global context. The European culture of values and regulatory directives thus provide an umbrella for value-based digital innovation as well as data handling and, in turn, the setting for digital responsibility.

2 CDR and the Digital Society: Shaping Positive Visions of Futures

As technologies increasingly influence everyday life, it becomes essential to consider how collective responsibility can guide digital futures. CDR must therefore be understood in relation to the digital society: not as an external environment but as a central actor in shaping technological pathways. In this chapter, we examine how different societal actors—from individuals to institutions—contribute to, influence, and are affected by digital innovation. Shaping positive visions of the future requires that responsibility is shared, distributed, and grounded in inclusive participation.

2.1 A Shared Responsibility: Beyond the "C"

While the term "Corporate" in CDR underscores the importance of companies as responsible actors (given their role as the primary drivers of digital transformation), the responsibility for shaping desirable digital futures for society does not rest solely on their shoulders. In addition to, for example, the concepts of political digital responsibility and corporate digital responsibility, there is also social and individual digital responsibility. This reinforces the necessity for multi-actor collaboration involving policymakers, civil society, academia, and the broader public.

Political digital responsibility is ultimately about defining the boundaries and rules of the digital playing field, as von Broock describes it (CDR-Magazin, 2020). This approach is not about restricting digital progress; rather, it is an effort to enable it based on shared expectations and enforceable norms. As is the case in any functioning game, a reliable playing field requires clarity: Who is responsible for what? What are the rules of fair conduct? And what happens when responsibilities are ignored? Political frameworks create such a field.

The Hamburg Declaration on Responsible AI for the Sustainable Development Goals (DSGs) (United Nations, 2015) offers a pertinent example. The German Federal Ministry for Economic Cooperation and Development (BMZ), in collaboration with the United Nations Development Programme (UNDP), has issued a call to governments, regional and international organizations, companies, academia, and civil society to collaborate in promoting the responsible, just, and sustainable use of AI worldwide (BMZ, 2025). Public trust, civic literacy, and institutional coordination are critical enablers of meaningful digital responsibility.

In the contemporary business landscape, companies increasingly hold large repositories of data that are relevant beyond their immediate business context. These data sets possess the potential to support responses to societal challenges such as the energy transition, mobility planning, agricultural sustainability, and demographic change. This opens the possibility for businesses to contribute to the common good, for instance, by making selected data or insights available for public use. This approach has the potential to enhance transparency, foster collaboration with public actors, and support evidence-based decision-making in areas of shared societal concern (Lautermann & Frick, 2023, p. 103).

In this context, shared responsibility is closely linked to digital resilience: only when public and private actors coordinate their efforts can society as a whole develop the capacity to adapt to—and benefit from—digital change. The recent D21-Digital-Index (2024/25) survey conducted in Germany shows that digital resilience is distributed unequally, with factors such as education, income, and access to infrastructure playing a significant role in this disparity (Initiative D21, 2025).

However, there are two different levels in the interaction between society and digital responsibility, as illustrated in Fig. 3. On the one hand, there is the level of the impact of (ir)responsible digital actions, such as environmental pollution or discrimination through bias[2] (OECD, 2024). On the other hand, there is also a societal digital responsibility.

2.2 Digital Society as Stakeholder and Co-creator

Digital technologies and artificial intelligence (AI) have now found their way into almost all areas of public and private life. For the ethical evaluation of such developments and their

[2] This is sometimes referred to as corporate digital citizenship. However, this term refers to purely voluntary social engagement (Lautermann & Frick, 2023). In our understanding, CDR is not limited to this.

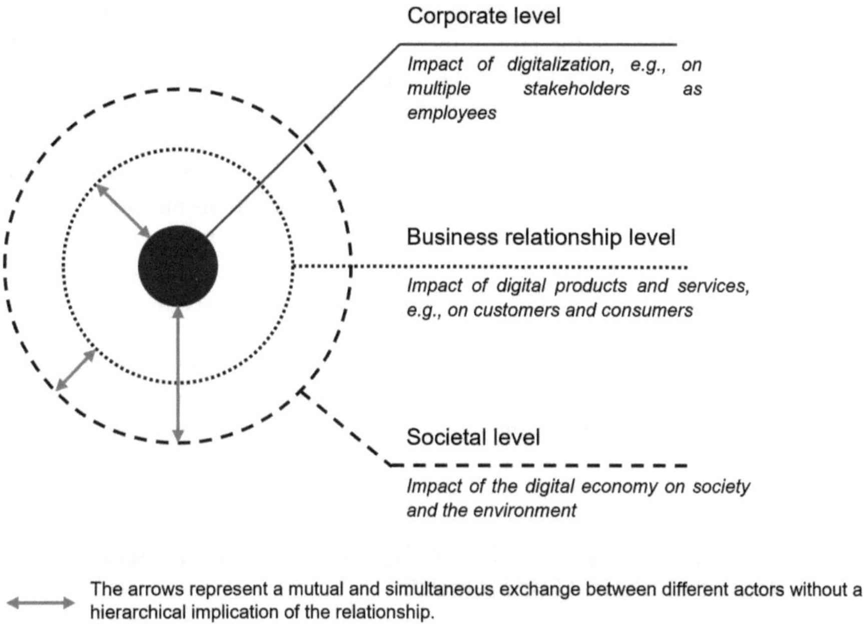

Fig. 3 Different interaction layers of CDR (Based on Deloitte, 2022)

> use in various areas, it is necessary to understand not only the technologies themselves, but also their interactions with the people who use them or are affected by their application. The central question here is what impact this will have when activities that were previously reserved for humans are delegated to machines. (Deutscher Ethikrat, 2023, p. 11)

Digital transformation is not solely driven by technological factors; it is also influenced by the interplay of social forces, behaviors, and expectations. The digital society does not merely passively receive innovation—rather, it is a co-creator. Through its choices, resistance, and engagement, it shapes how technology evolves, which norms emerge, and which futures have the potential to become reality.

Rather, a digitally empowered society—equipped with the rights, skills, and spaces to engage—can become a meaningful counterpart in the governance of digital transformation (Lautermann & Frick, 2023). These considerations include questions of inclusion, data sovereignty, and the fair distribution of benefits and burdens. However, civic participation requires certain enabling conditions. A society overwhelmed by technical complexity or burdened by systemic exclusion is unable to fulfill its role as co-creator. Therefore, digital responsibility also means strengthening digital literacy, fostering critical awareness, and safeguarding democratic agency. Digital literacy is not only a matter of individual competence; rather, it is a structural prerequisite for inclusive governance.

Yet, this potential for participation is not equally distributed. According to the D21-Digital-Index (2025), digital competence and resilience vary significantly across age, income, and education levels in Germany. While 63 percent of people have expressed confidence in handling digital change, large parts of society feel left behind or overwhelmed in the face of these changes (Initiative D21, 2025). CDR must account for this reality and expand its horizon from this viewpoint. It is imperative that CDR addresses not only the responsibilities of companies but also their role in supporting societal resilience and agency. This includes investments in accessible technologies, support for open data initiatives, and collaboration with civil society to co-create governance frameworks. Organizations also have considerable leverage to reach certain segments of society—such as people who are not (or no longer) participating in school or further formal education or professional development—with continuing education opportunities related to the digital transformation.

In essence, the digital society is no external audience; rather, it is a co-creator of digital futures. Recognizing this interdependence is key to designing and engineering systems that are not only technologically advanced but also socially grounded and legitimate.

2.3 Individual Responsibility in the Digital Society: Between Expectation and Enablement

The digital transformation gives rise to a fundamental question: How much individual digital responsibility can reasonably be demanded? While citizens and users increasingly engage in algorithmic decision-making, digital platforms, and AI-based services, the ability to fully understand, challenge, or meaningfully influence these systems is limited. To what extent can individuals operating within highly technical digital environments (in a heterogeneous digital society) be expected to act responsibly—for example, through digital literacy, informed consent, or privacy management? Digital responsibility must therefore be reframed as a collective and distributed task. While individual action matters, it depends heavily on the enabling structures provided by companies, regulators, and civil society.

CDR plays a pivotal role in negotiating this balance. On the one hand, companies are obligated to design technologies that are transparent, fair, and accessible. This includes the integration of usability and clarity into user interfaces, the minimization of cognitive and legal complexity, and the proactive avoidance of manipulative design ("dark patterns"). On the other hand, individuals must be empowered with a sense of responsibility. That requires meaningful digital education, public awareness campaigns, and mechanisms for democratic engagement.

2.4 Connecting Narratives and Designing Futures Worth Building

A central tenet of our work is the notion that economic and societal goals do not have to be in tension. CDR offers an approach to dissolve such dichotomies and to show how economic and societal objectives can be aligned.

Organizations that proactively engage with digital responsibility can position themselves as leaders in innovation and legitimacy. According to the World Economic Forum (2024), trust, inclusion, and sustainability are becoming central criteria for long-term competitiveness in a "blended reality"—a world in which digital and physical systems are deeply interconnected. When technologies are developed with an eye toward ethical integrity and user empowerment, they are not only more just—but they are also more resilient, scalable, and accepted.

A similar phenomenon occurs on a societal level. A digitally literate and resilient public is better able to engage in civic processes, navigate digital services, and shape innovative trajectories through informed participation. Public institutions and civil society actors benefit when companies offer accessible technologies, transparent practices, and responsive platforms. To illustrate this point, consider the field of education:

- From a societal perspective, digital education has been demonstrated to foster equity, lifelong learning, and democratic agency.
- From a corporate perspective, it builds the foundation for an adaptable, innovation-ready workforce.

Or the field of ethical AI:

- Societally, it serves to reduce discrimination, to promote inclusion, and to safeguard fundamental rights.
- Economically, it contributes to a reduction in reputational risks, facilitates compliance, and enhances market trust.

This dual narrative can be extended to many domains, including sustainable IT and human-centered platforms. Organizations that embrace the dual narrative not only reduce risk but also gain reputation, loyalty, and innovation capacity (Lee et al., 2021).

CDR is not only a governance approach—it is a cultural commitment to shaping desirable futures. This requires imagination, dialogue, and experimentation. Futures thinking and ethical foresight can help companies move from compliance to contribution. By explicitly connecting these narratives, organizations can build shared value, whereby the advancement of one goal serves to reinforce the other. Consequently, designing futures worth building means designing systems, strategies, and services that embody this dual value logic.

This narrative connection must be co-developed and co-owned by political and economic institutions. Public actors have the ability to define long-term visions, create incentives, and safeguard public interest, while the private sector has the capacity to embed these values into real-world applications. Together, they can turn responsibility into a strategic resource for societal resilience.

While the promise of shared value is compelling, the operational reality of CDR remains complex. The following section will explore where the concept meets its limits in practice and what is necessary to broaden its reach and systemic relevance.

3 CDR in Practice: Why We Need to Enlarge the Ecosystem

CDR has become an established concept in the discourse on ethical digital transformation, and an increasing number of organizations are beginning to engage with it. However, its potential to broaden its adoption across organizations and sectors remains high. At the same time, many impactful initiatives originate not only in companies but also in public institutions, NGOs, and hybrid actors. This calls for an expanded understanding of responsibility as a shared task across sectors, better captured by the broader notion of Organizational Digital Responsibility (ODR).

3.1 Responsibility With(out) ROI?

Despite the growing conceptual maturity of CDR (Carl et al., 2025), there is still considerable potential in terms of comprehensive implementation. While many companies acknowledge the ethical relevance of digital responsibility, the concept of CDR often struggles to align with traditional corporate logics like the return on investment. Key Performance Indicators (KPIs) or budget structures could be helpful in gaining more legitimacy for broader implementation. For example, the CDR study by the Institute for Ecological Economic Research (Lautermann & Frick, 2023) highlights different ideas on how to integrate CDR into core reporting processes or strategies. In addition, the CDR Initiative has published the CDR Code, which contains specific proposals for measures that are suitable for reporting purposes (CDR Initiative, 2021).

Especially in times of economic hardship, responsible digital behavior must be understood as value-creating, not just value-protecting. The "CDR Calculus" (Wirtz et al., 2023) posits a foundation for quantifying this value by integrating ethical intent with measurable outcomes. Nevertheless, further evidence and practical tools are needed to overcome the perception that CDR lacks economic relevance.

3.2 Beyond the "C": Toward Organizational Digital Responsibility

Many of the most compelling examples of responsible digital practice do not come from corporations alone. Public institutions, nongovernmental organizations (NGOs), and foundations are increasingly engaging in digital responsibility—whether through inclusive AI projects, ethical data governance, or community-oriented digital education. In this regard, some have argued that the term "corporate" may be too narrow and that an expanded concept of Organizational Digital Responsibility (ODR) is necessary. This expanded concept would include public institutions, NGOs, and hybrid actors.

This raises a conceptual question: Should the "C" in CDR be as central as it is? The term ODR may better capture the distributed nature of digital ethics and accountability in today's ecosystem. In initiatives such as the CDR Award

(Bundesverband Digitale Wirtschaft, Bayern Innovativ, 2024) and the Digital Future Challenge (Deloitte-Stiftung, Initiative D21), we observe that actors from public administration, hybrid institutions, and civil society play a significant role among the awarded projects—demonstrating that digital responsibility cannot be limited to the private sector.

Expanding from CDR to ODR could also contribute to a depolarization of the discourse surrounding digital responsibility. Currently, there is often a perceived divide: large corporations are expected to lead but are also subject to skepticism, while smaller actors such as public institutions or civil society organizations are engaged but underrecognized. ODR offers an approach in which diverse actors—regardless of their size or sector—can contribute meaningfully to a shared agenda. It values not only scale but also contextual relevance, stakeholder proximity, and ethical ambition. By incorporating a variety of perspectives into the responsibility ecosystem, ODR fosters mutual learning, legitimacy, and a broader sense of collective digital responsibility.

4 Outlook: Navigating Disruption with Responsibility

Digital transformation is no longer a linear process—it is exponential, volatile, and deeply intertwined with global sociopolitical shifts, and it is far from complete. On the contrary, we are witnessing technological accelerations—driven by physical AI, generative AI, increased automation, and data-centric infrastructures—that are reshaping how societies function, how organizations act, and how values are contested. The task lies now in proactively shaping desirable digital futures: ethically, inclusively, and in alignment with societal goals.

The challenge for CDR, as explored throughout this chapter, is not only to meet current expectations but also to co-create future norms, desirable futures, governance structures, and modes of engagement. In line with Grimm et al.'s (2023) understanding of digital ethics, we also see the potential for CDR to enlighten the relationship between humans, machines, and systems. CDR can help to identify ethical trade-offs, to navigate competing expectations, and to translate normative goals into concrete action. This commitment encompasses a wide range of initiatives, including the design of nondiscriminatory AI systems, the management of algorithmic transparency, and the development of inclusive digital education platforms.

The D21-Digital-Index (2025) highlights that digital competence and resilience are pivotal to future employability and innovation capacity. However, competence gaps and unequal access persist—leaving significant parts of the workforce excluded from the benefits of the digital transformation (Initiative D21, 2025). In this context, CDR functions as a lens for anticipating internal transformation: How do we lead ethically in times of technological upheaval? How do we redistribute the gains of automation fairly? How do we design meaningful human-AI collaboration?

Successful digital responsibility depends on collective responsibility and collective gain. In Fig. 4, the three main points of this chapter are visually summarized,

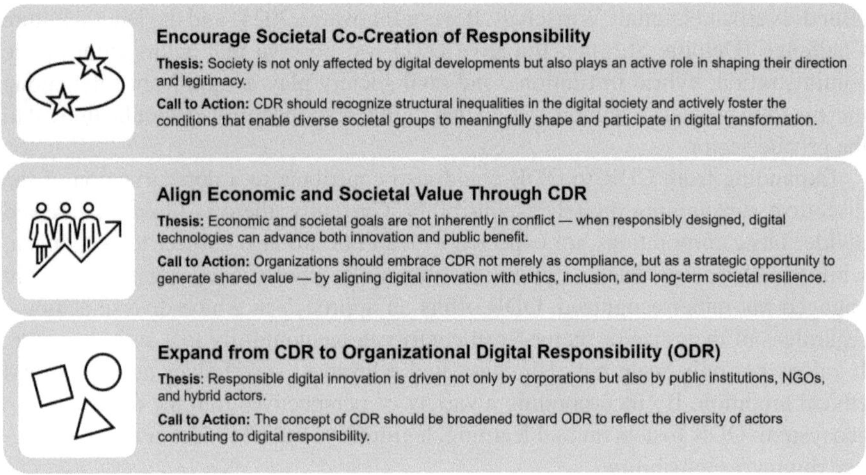

Fig. 4 Illustration of three key points with calls to action (Authors' illustration)

each highlighting a key proposition for advancing corporate digital responsibility (CDR) in relation to societal needs. The figure emphasizes the importance of enabling inclusive participation, aligning ethical and economic objectives, and broadening responsibility from corporations to a wider ecosystem of public and civil society actors.

Competing Interests The authors have no conflicts of interest to declare that are relevant to the content of this chapter.

References

Bundesverband Digitale Wirtschaft & Bayern Innovativ. (2024). *Corporate Digital Responsibility Award 2024*. Retrieved May 24, 2025, from https://www.cdr-award.digital/

Carl, K. V., Blachetta, M., Bilfinger, B., Brink, A., Cerulli-Harms, A. K., Christ, A.-S., Dietl, K., Dörr, S., Hauer, M. P., Hinz, M., Jänig, J.-R., Keilhofer, K., Kurtz, C., Mihale-Wilson, C., Mueller, B., Przybylek, B. A., Schaufler, N., Schlegel, I. K., Scholz, M., von Roesgen, F., & Wößner, J. (2025). Establishing common ground in corporate digital responsibility: Integrating understandings, definitions, and expert perspectives. In *INFORMATIK 2025, Potsdam, Germany*.

CDR-Initiative. (2021). *Corporate digital responsibility-Kodex: Freiwillige Selbstverpflichtung mit Bericht*. Retrieved May 24, 2025, from https://cdr-initiative.de/uploads/files/2024-01_Kodex_CDR-Initiative.pdf

CDR-Magazin. (2020). *Dilemmata, Purpose Washing und globale Perspektiven: Ein Interview mit Martin von Broock über CDR und Ethik*. Retrieved May 24, 2025, from https://corporate-digital-responsibility.de/wissenschaft/dilemmata-purpose-washing-und-globale-perspektiven-ein-interview-mit-martin-von-broock-uber-cdr-und-ethik/

Deloitte. (2022). *Corporate digital responsibility survey 2022*. Retrieved May 24, 2025, from https://www2.deloitte.com/content/dam/Deloitte/de/Documents/Corporate%20Responsibility/Corporate%20Digital%20Responsibility%20Survey%202022.pdf

Deutscher Ethikrat. (2023). *Mensch und Maschine—Herausforderungen durch Künstliche Intelligenz: Stellungnahme*. Retrieved May 24, 2025, from https://www.ethikrat.org/publikationen/stellungnahmen/mensch-und-maschine

European Commission. (2019). *Ethics guidelines for trustworthy AI*. Publications Office. Retrieved May 24, 2025, from https://data.europa.eu/doi/10.2759/346720

Floridi, L., Cowls, J., Beltrametti, M., Chatila, R., Chazerand, P., Dignum, V., & Luetge, C. (2021). An ethical framework for a good AI society: Opportunities, risks, principles, and recommendations. In L. Floridi (Ed.), *Ethics, governance and policies in Artificial Intelligence* (pp. 19–41). Oxford University Press. https://doi.org/10.1007/s11023-018-9482-5

German Federal Ministry for Economic Cooperation and Development (BMZ). (2025). *Call to sign the Hamburg Declaration on responsible AI for the SDGs*. Retrieved May 24, 2025, from https://www.bmz.de/en/news/press-releases/hsc-call-to-sign-declaration-on-responsible-ai-for-the-sdgs-253194

Grimm, P., Keber, T. O., & Zöllner, O. (2023). *Digitale Ethik: Leben in vernetzten Welten* (p. 252). Reclam. https://doi.org/10.21240/merz/2020.1.29

Initiative D21. (2025). *D21-Digital-Index 2024/25: Jährliches Lagebild zur Digitalen Gesellschaft*. Retrieved May 24, 2025, from https://initiatived21.de/download/248068/D21_Digital_Index_2024_2025_final.pdf

Lautermann, C., & Frick, V. (2023). *Corporate Digital Responsibility. Wie Unternehmen im digitalen Wandel Verantwortung übernehmen*. Schriftreihe des IÖW. https://www.ioew.de/fileadmin/user_upload/BILDER_und_Downloaddateien/Publikationen/2023/IOEW_SR_227_Corporate-Digital-Responsibility.pdf

Lee, M. S. A., Floridi, L., & Denev, A. (2021). Innovating with confidence: Embedding AI governance and fairness in a financial services risk management framework. In L. Floridi (Ed.), *Ethics, governance and policies in artificial intelligence* (pp. 353–372). Oxford University Press. https://doi.org/10.1007/978-3-030-81907-1_20

Müller, L.-S. (2020). Corporate Digital Responsibility: Wie Unternehmen jetzt die digitale Verantwortung mitdenken müssen. *Handelsblatt Journal KI*, 6–8.

Müller, L.-S., & Andersen, N. (2017). *Denkimpuls Digitale Ethik: Warum wir uns mit Digitaler Ethik beschäftigen sollten. Ein Denkmuster*. Initiative D21 Denkimpulse. Retrieved May 24, 2025, from https://initiatived21.de/download/51290/d21-denkimpuls-ethik02-warum-digitale-ethik.pdf

Odelberg, T. (2024). *Understanding the future of AI governance: Comparing the EU AI Act and the U.S. Executive Order on Safe AI*. Research Report: Science, Technology and Public Policy, University of Michigan. https://doi.org/10.7302/24392

OECD. (2024). *Assessing potential future artificial intelligence risks, benefits and policy imperatives*. OECD AI Papers. Retrieved May 24, 2025, from https://www.oecd.org/en/publications/assessing-potential-future-artificial-intelligence-risks-benefits-and-policy-imperatives_3f4e3dfb-en.html

Regulation (EU) 2016/679 of the European Parliament and of the Council of 27 April 2016 on the protection of natural persons with regard to the processing of personal data and on the free movement of such data, and repealing Directive 95/46/EC (General Data Protection Regulation). European Union. https://eur-lex.europa.eu/eli/reg/2016/679/oj/eng

Regulation (EU) 2022/1925 of the European Parliament and of the Council of 14 September 2022 on contestable and fair markets in the digital sector and amending Directives (EU) 2019/1937 and (EU) 2020/1828 (Digital Markets Act). European Union. https://eur-lex.europa.eu/eli/reg/2022/1925/oj/eng

Regulation (EU) 2022/2065 of the European Parliament and of the Council of 19 October 2022 on a Single Market for Digital Services and amending Directive 2000/31/EC (Digital Services Act). European Union. https://eur-lex.europa.eu/eli/reg/2022/2065/oj/eng

Regulation (EU) 2024/1689 of the European Parliament and of the Council of 13 June 2024 laying down harmonised rules on artificial intelligence (Artificial Intelligence Act). European Union. https://eur-lex.europa.eu/eli/reg/2024/1689/oj/eng

United Nations. (2015). *Transforming our world: The 2030 agenda for sustainable development (A/RES/70/1)*. United Nations. https://sdgs.un.org/2030agenda

Wirtz, J., Kunz, W., Hartley, N., & Tarbit, J. (2023). Corporate digital responsibility in service firms and their ecosystems. *Journal of Service Research, 26*(2), 173–190. https://doi.org/10.1177/10946705221130467

World Economic Forum. (2024). *Shared commitments in a blended reality: Advancing governance in the future internet*. WEF Report Series. Retrieved May 24, 2025, from https://www.weforum.org/publications/shared-commitments-in-a-blended-reality/

Dr. Marie Blachetta is an expert in digital responsibility. In her work, she focuses on the question of how we can shape digital futures in a technologically responsible manner and which aspects of social and ecological sustainability play a role in this. Initiative D21 is the largest non-profit network for the digital society in Germany.

Lena-Sophie Müller leads Initiative D21 e.V. as CEO and is recognized as an expert in digital transformation. Her work centers on developing new technologies to benefit people while examining their societal impact. Initiative D21 represents Germany's largest network connecting politics, business, science, and civil society for the digital society.

Digital Ethics, Resilience, and Strategic Corporate Management

Daniela Hanauer, Saskia Becke, and Lars Distelrath

Abstract

Organizations today face unprecedented complexity driven by technological disruption, sustainability imperatives, and expanding regulation. Resilience emerges as a strategic competence when these domains are integrated rather than addressed in isolation. The chapter introduces the strategic triad of technology, sustainability, and digital ethics, emphasizing their role in strengthening corporate governance, enabling ecosystem collaboration, and shaping long-term competitiveness. By embedding regulatory compliance into strategic planning, fostering ethical technology adoption, and empowering people across organizations, companies can transform compliance burdens into innovation levers. Practitioners are encouraged to view resilience as a proactive capability—anchored, interconnected, responsible, and future-oriented business models.

1 Interconnected: Technologies, Ethics, and Regulations

In recent years, the corporate landscape has undergone changes of such magnitude that even experienced executives are facing unprecedented challenges. Global crises, volatile markets, geopolitical tensions, fragile supply chains, and an ever-expanding web of regulatory requirements define the operating environment of modern organizations. In this context, one concept has been gaining increasing importance: resilience (PwC, 2025a). This refers not only to the ability to withstand external shocks but also to the capacity to leverage them as catalysts for adaptation, further development, and long-term stability (Roth et al., 2021, p. 7).

D. Hanauer · S. Becke (✉) · L. Distelrath
PwC Germany, Munich, Germany
e-mail: daniela.hanauer@pwc.com; saskia.becke@pwc.com; lars.distelrath@pwc.com

A.-S. Christ (ed.), *Corporate Digital Responsibility*, Future of Business and Finance, https://doi.org/10.1007/978-3-032-14793-6_19

Additionally, the transition of industries into interconnected ecosystems has become a new narrative, highlighting how businesses can thrive through collaboration and integration across traditional sector boundaries. This concept underscores the interconnectedness of today's global economy, where resilience is built not just within the confines of individual companies but across entire ecosystems that include suppliers, partners, and stakeholders (PwC, 2025a).

At the same time, there is a growing impression that a significant portion of corporate resources is currently devoted to meeting regulatory obligations. This is particularly true in the areas of sustainability reporting, digital regulation, data protection, and artificial intelligence, where European institutions have adopted a multitude of directives and regulations in recent years (e.g., European Declaration 2023/C 23/01; Regulation (EU) 2016/679; Regulation (EU) 2024/1689). Implementing these requirements is unquestionably necessary: it ensures legal compliance, minimizes liability risks, and provides transparency to investors, customers, and the public. Yet, all too often, this engagement is reduced to a reactive fulfillment of compliance demands. What is often lacking—or underdeveloped—is the strategic integration of these topics into the long-term orientation of the company (PwC, 2025b, p. 8).

Especially in an environment defined by uncertainty, it is crucial to regard regulatory developments not merely as an operational necessity but as strategic levers. From this perspective, technology deployment, sustainability regulation, and digital ethics are not isolated disciplines but interconnected areas of action that, when properly integrated, directly strengthen an organization's resilience. This requires consciously reintegrating these issues into the strategic planning process. While the immediate fulfillment of reporting obligations may demand attention, it becomes even more impactful to embed these activities into a strategic framework (PwC, 2023, p. 2, 5). Such an approach demonstrates how investments in technology, sustainability initiatives, and ethical frameworks can not only support long-term competitiveness but also feedback into an expanded and forward-looking reporting approach.

This chapter, therefore, aims to encourage viewing resilience as the beginning of a new phase—one in which companies take a proactive role in shaping their and our future.

2 Technology, Sustainability, and Digital Ethics as a Strategic Triad

The idea of considering technology, sustainability, and digital ethics as a unified framework underscores the intentional interaction of these three crucial dimensions in modern corporate management. While not officially recognized in theory as a specific concept, these areas can be considered collectively as a strategic triad.

The concept of the *strategic triad* describes the deliberate interaction of technology, sustainability, and digital ethics as three key dimensions of modern corporate management. Technology and sustainability rank among the central transformation fields currently shaping economic development (It et al., 2024). Both are subject to intense regulatory evolution and therefore remain at the forefront of corporate attention (Directive (EU) 2022/2464; Regulation (EU) 2024/1689).

Digital ethics, by contrast, serves as the connecting element between these two domains (PwC, 2023, p. 5). Unlike technology and sustainability, it is still less driven by external regulation and instead primarily forms part of a company's internal self-governance. This positioning gives it particular strategic significance: it enables technological innovation and sustainability initiatives to be linked in a coherent, responsible, and future-oriented manner (PwC, 2023, p. 5).

In this context, technology is more than an efficiency driver. It is a transformational instrument that permeates business models, value chains, and customer interactions. Automation, data-driven decision-making, digital platforms, and artificial intelligence are reshaping not only processes but also the expectations of markets and society. Yet these potentials come with highly relevant ethical questions: How are algorithmic decisions made and monitored? How can data protection be ensured without hindering innovation? How can technological solutions avoid reinforcing existing inequalities? (PwC, 2023, p. 2).

This is where digital ethics emerges as a guiding principle. It not only defines what is technically possible but also what is deemed right and responsible in a societal and corporate context (PwC, 2023, S. 5). When combined with sustainability regulation and transformation, a dual strategic effect is created: on the one hand, technology is deployed in a targeted manner to achieve sustainability goals, such as through digital systems for CO_2 measurement, improving resource efficiency, or optimizing supply chains. On the other hand, it ensures that the use of such technologies is itself defensible from both sustainability and ethical perspectives (PwC, 2023, p. 5).

For such initiatives to be effective, they must be supported by a receptive organizational environment. This requires consistent *people enablement*, the systematic development of skills, the creation of awareness (Kirchmer, 2017, p. 67) for the far-reaching impact of digital and sustainability-related decisions, and the promotion of interdisciplinary collaboration. Changes in processes and technologies only translate into lasting competitive advantages if they are embraced by the people within the organization. This demands not only qualification but also the ability to convey the strategic relevance of these changes and to build acceptance. In the context of digital ethics, this means that values, principles, and ethical guidelines must not only be defined but actively embedded in training, decision-making processes, and leadership culture (PwC, 2023, p. 16). *People enablement* thus becomes a key instrument for ensuring that the standards defined in digital ethics are effectively applied in daily practice.

From a governance perspective, these requirements can be operationalized through a structured model such as the Target Operating Model (TOM). It creates a clear link between a company's value-based objective, its organizational anchoring, and its implementation in day-to-day operations (PwC, 2023, p. 7). The TOM effectively aligns industry ecosystems with organizational goals, ensuring that resilience and innovation stem from both internal and external collaborations. The combination of strategic vision, defined responsibilities, and implemented processes ensures that digital ethics embeds sustainability principles and technology not as isolated projects but as a permanent element of corporate governance.

3 Resilience as a Strategic Competence

In this understanding, resilience is the result of a consistent, long-term integration of technological expertise, sustainable value creation, and ethically grounded decision-making, and ecosystem interconnectivity (PwC, 2023). Companies that view digitalization merely as a tool for short-term efficiency gains overlook the risks of an unbalanced, purely technology-driven transformation. Equally insufficient is an approach to sustainability that limits itself to meeting formal reporting requirements without embedding substantive changes into the business model. Only by integrating these dimensions into a coherent strategy can organizations develop the ability not merely to respond to external shocks but to translate them into progress (Capgemini Consulting, 2011, p. 5).

In an economic environment defined by uncertainty and disruptive developments, the corporate agenda should not be reduced to short-term compliance. Digital ethics, the application of technology, and sustainability regulation must be understood as strategic investments in future viability. This requires the courage to set clear priorities, the willingness to embrace profound organizational change, and the consistent empowerment of those who will drive that change. Companies that master this integration will secure a competitive advantage—making resilience a core competency of their operations.

We see our strategic advantage, both for ourselves and our clients, in developing positive narratives, embedding them sustainably, and continuing to shape them over time. With the concept of industry ecosystems, we are poised to chart a course where collaboration and mutual growth define our strategic trajectories. This is a task that, like many others, is best accomplished together and through dialogue, allowing us to tap into shared expertise, accelerate innovation, and amplify our impact. We invite you to reach out and become part of our network—learning from one another and creating value together.

Competing Interests The authors have no conflicts of interest to declare that are relevant to the content of this chapter.

References

Capgemini Consulting. (2011). *Digital transformation: A roadmap for billion-dollar organizations*. MIT Sloan Management. https://www.consultancy.nl/media/Capgemini%20-%20Digital%20Transformation%20Study%202011-2588.pdf

Directive (EU) 2022/2464 of the European Parliament and of the Council of 14 December 2022 amending Regulation (EU) No 537/2014, Directive 2004/109/EC, Directive 2006/43/EC and Directive 2013/34/EU, as regards corporate sustainability reporting (OJ L 322, pp. 15–80). https://eur-lex.europa.eu/legal-content/EN/TXT/?uri=CELEX:32022L2464 2025q

European Declaration on Digital Rights and Principles for the Digital Decade (2023/C 23/01). Official Journal of the European Union, C 23/1. https://eur-lex.europa.eu/legal-content/EN/TXT/?uri=OJ:JOC_2023_023_R_0001

It, N., Khuong, N. G., & Tuan, N. T. (2024). Path to sustainability: Technological innovation and digital economy as main drivers of green economic development. In L. T. Tung, N. H. Sinh, & P. Ha (Eds.), *Disruptive technology and business continuity*. Springer. https://doi.org/10.1007/978-981-97-5452-6_1

Kirchmer, M. (2017). *High performance through business process management*. https://doi.org/10.1007/978-3-319-51259-4_4

PwC. (2023). *Digital ethics & responsibility – Embedding responsible digital transformation in your company for the long term*. PwC. https://www.pwc.de/en/sustainability/embedding-digital-ethics-and-responsibility-in-your-company-for-the-long-term.html

PwC. (2025a). *Business decisions must be considered in an ecosystem context*. Retrieved August 9, 2025, from https://www.pwc.de/en/corporate-innovation/successful-in-the-business-ecosystem.html

PwC. (2025b). *Mastering ESG reporting and steering*, 8. https://www.pwc.de/en/data-and-ai/data-day-2025/mastering-esg-reporting-and-steering.pdf

Regulation (EU) 2016/679 of the European Parliament and of the Council of 27 April 2016 on the protection of natural persons with regard to the processing of personal data and on the free movement of such data (General Data Protection Regulation), Official Journal of the European Union, L 119, 1–88. https://eur-lex.europa.eu/legal-content/EN/TXT/?uri=CELEX%3A02016R0679-20160504

Regulation (EU) 2024/1689 of the European Parliament and of the Council of 13 June 2024 laying down harmonised rules on artificial intelligence and amending Regulations (EC) No 300/2008, (EU) No 167/2013, (EU) No 168/2013, (EU) 2018/858, (EU) 2018/1139 and (EU) 2019/2144 and Directives 2014/90/EU, (EU) 2016/797 and (EU) 2020/1828 (Artificial Intelligence Act), Official Journal of the European Union L 2024/1689. https://eur-lex.europa.eu/eli/reg/2024/1689/oj/eng

Roth, F., Warnke, P., Niessen, P., & Edler, J. (2021). *Insights into systematic resilience from innovation research [Policy brief]* (p. 7). Fraunhofer ISI. https://www.isi.fraunhofer.de/content/dam/isi/dokumente/policy-briefs/policy_brief_resilience_en_web.pdf

Daniela Hanauer is a Partner in the Sustainability Services division at PwC Germany, orchestrating a strong European and global network with experts from relevant disciplines, including sustainability, compliance, risk management, operations, and legal for transformational sustainability programs. She has over 20 years of experience specializing in governance, risk, and compliance, with a strong focus on sustainability, business values and ethics, digital ethics, and environmental and human rights. She has led numerous sustainability and compliance-related transformational projects, guiding organizations through the complexities of regulatory requirements. Daniela Hanauer's work is deeply rooted in value orientation across various sectors, including automotive, healthcare, technology and telecommunications, and industrial services. In addition to her consulting endeavors, Daniela is a speaker at multiple events and hosts several initiatives for PwC and its clients: the LkSG Center of Excellence, the Human Rights Officer & Allies Network, and the Women Driving Integrity Network. She is also an active member of the Deutsches Netzwerk Wirtschaftsethik.

Saskia Becke is a Manager in the Sustainability Services division at PwC Germany, based in Munich. She has over eight years of experience in consulting and assurance, with a particular focus on the intersection of digitalization and sustainability. Her core expertise lies in strategically embedding Digital Ethics and Corporate Digital Responsibility (CDR) within companies. With great passion, she drives the development of PwC's service offerings. She supports companies in designing digital transformation processes that are values-based, human-centric, and sustainable—including aspects such as stakeholder communication, process optimization, and training. In addition, she supports clients in creating and managing sustainable value chains in accordance with regulations such as LkSG, CSDDD, and EUDR.

Lars Distelrath is a Senior Associate at PwC Germany with several years of experience in sustainability consulting. His work focuses on the analysis and implementation of regulatory requirements at the intersection of law, finance, sustainability, and risk management. With his interdisciplinary expertise, he supports companies in systematically identifying ESG risks, developing sustainable business strategies, and ensuring regulatory compliance.

Epilogue by Prof. Dr. Georg Müller-Christ

Georg Müller-Christ

Here, the arc of this volume concludes with an observation from sustainability-focused management thinking: companies never make decisions that are entirely "value-free"; they operate within conflicting decision premises. Traditionally, efficiency and functionality predominate—they set the pace, define the rhythm, and often serve as the benchmarks for success. Responsibility and ethics, on the other hand, are relatively new decision premises. They only truly become valid when efficiency and functionality are willing to step aside—not as an act of renunciation, but as a conscious choice in situations where digital possibilities might otherwise surpass social and ecological limits. This book begins precisely at that tipping point: it demonstrates that in the digital economy, a company's "license to operate" increasingly depends on how we shape the digital landscape, not just on how quickly we move.

The book's intention marks this paradigm shift: digital transformation and corporate responsibility are no longer separate spheres but a twin transformation whose synergies create value—and whose externalities must be actively shaped. This explains why Corporate Digital Responsibility (CDR) grows out of the Corporate Social Responsibility (CSR) tradition while extending it into new domains: data and algorithm governance, fairness, accessibility, security, and transparency. The volume names a stubborn implementation gap: many ethical aspirations remain abstract if they are not translated into decision logics, processes, and metrics.

In this situation, a values perspective helps explain why the real issue is the ordering of premises: values may stem from within the organization (purpose, leadership, culture) or from external sources (regulation, stakeholders, public discourse)—and in digitally shaped contexts, they often relate to one another in new ways. Whether CDR is more a continuation of CSR or an independent domain is decided in practice, where companies translate these value conflicts into governance: guidelines, roles, checkpoints, and escalation paths. The volume shows that many successful practitioners craft hybrid answers here: they recalibrate some

G. Müller-Christ
University of Bremen, Bremen, Germany

A.-S. Christ (ed.), *Corporate Digital Responsibility*, Future of Business and Finance, https://doi.org/10.1007/978-3-032-14793-6

traditional values while strongly weighting distinctly digital ones, such as transparency of data provenance or algorithmic traceability.

The case and practice chapters accordingly demonstrate how responsibility can become a guiding decision premise: not as a moral appendix, but as decision design. Where an organization formulates data-ethics directives and translates them into accountabilities, indicators, and processes, the hierarchy of premises shifts in concrete ways—efficiency remains important but no longer solely determinative. Examples range from company-wide data-ethics guardrails to maturity models that bring CDR into everyday work step by step.

To me, particularly instructive is the look at an Ethos Advisor as a domain-specific GenAI companion: here, the supposed opposition between efficiency/functionality and responsibility is productively resolved. The system delivers speed and structure, yet human-in-the-loop and transparency-by-design anchor trust and accountability. Users prefer co-creation over full automation; "trust needs transparency" becomes a user experience (UX) rule—sources, traceability, and optional expert validation are not ornamentation but what makes responsible use broadly acceptable. In this way, efficiency is conditioned by responsibility, and responsibility is enabled by usable tools.

For decision-makers, this distills into a simple Monday-morning pragmatics: lightweight governance (a one-page policy, clear roles, defined checkpoints), embedded learning formats (onboarding, prompt literacy, community of practice), and a toolchain that exposes sources and builds in human review. The young premise of "responsibility" thus takes hold not despite but because of intelligent tools—because the organization chooses to tie speed to conditions: explainable, reviewable, documented. This shifts the ranking in the jostle: efficiency and functionality remain means, but what gains standing is what secures long-term legitimacy, resilience, and societal fit. That is the essence of this volume: responsibility becomes strong where we operationalize it—as a deliberately designed decision premise embedded in digital routines.

September 2025

MIX
Papier aus verantwortungsvollen Quellen
Paper from responsible sources
FSC® C105338

If you have any concerns about our products,
you can contact us on
ProductSafety@springernature.com

In case Publisher is established outside the EU,
the EU authorized representative is:
Springer Nature Customer Service Center GmbH
Europaplatz 3, 69115 Heidelberg, Germany

Printed by Libri Plureos GmbH
in Hamburg, Germany